Institute of Social and Religious Research

THE CHURCH IN THE CHANGING CITY

H. PAUL DOUGLASS

THE CHURCH IN THE CHANGING CITY

CASE STUDIES
ILLUSTRATING ADAPTATION

BY

H. PAUL DOUGLASS

NEW YORK
GEORGE H. DORAN COMPANY

THE CHURCH IN THE CHANGING CITY
— B —
PRINTED IN THE UNITED STATES OF AMERICA

PREFACE

The demand for case studies, particularly of the so-called "down-town" church, was earnestly expressed as early as 1922 by experts in the city church field who had been consulted in connection with previous projects of the Institute of Social and Religious Research. The case studies presented herein are offered in partial response to that demand.

They constitute the fourth of a series of studies in urban religious institutions. The first two were general religious surveys of cities: namely, St. Louis, Mo., and Springfield, Mass., the latter involving rather detailed investigation of individual churches.[1] At the completion of the Springfield survey, the request for case studies was again considered, but the project was postponed in favor of an extensive description and classification of more than 1000 city churches.[2] This book included about thirty brief case studies; and all along the case study method has been recognized as affording one of the promising approaches to the urban church problem. Accordingly, in planning a 1925 project in this field, the present study was suggested by the staff of the Institute. Such a study, it was believed, would help to meet the expectations of the Institute's public, and, at the same time, would serve to test and illuminate some of the generalizations tentatively emerging from its more extensive studies.

As at first projected, it was hoped that the studies might cover 250 cases and result in somewhat important theoretical discoveries filling gaps in previous knowledge of the city church. But when the plan was submitted to counselors (including influential pastors and administrators in the city church field) an almost unanimous opinion was expressed that it would be more profitable to study a few cases somewhat inten-

---

[1] Douglass, *The St. Louis Church Survey* (New York; Doran, 1924) and *The Springfield Church Survey* (New York; Doran, 1926).
[2] Douglass, *1000 City Churches* (New York; Doran, 1926).

sively. Finally, as a result of a formal conference with these counselors, it was decided to focus investigation on such churches as exhibited conscious urban adaptations, thus limiting the study to a few related types. It was also decided not to attempt evaluations of results by consensus of judgment nor to attempt to devise objective criteria; but, instead, to allow each church to be judged in the light of its own acknowledged objectives. The project as thus modified was formally approved by the directors of the Institute in October, 1924, and got under way during the spring of the following year. Field work began in July, 1925, and continued, overlapping the period of statistical work and interpretation, until June, 1926.

From October, 1925, to February, 1926, the Director had the assistance of the Rev. Wilbur C. Hallenbeck, now Secretary of the Oakland Council of Churches, in the field work of Cases I, III, V, VII, IX, XI, XII, and XVI, and from December, 1925, to March, 1926, that of Mr. John J. Hader, in the field work of Cases XIII and XIV. Mrs. William A. Leech, Jr., assisted in the field work of Case VIII. The secretary of the project from the beginning was Mrs. Emorene Allen Steiger.

Each case study was submitted to the church concerned for criticism and correction of factual statement. Appreciative acknowledgment is made of the coöperative spirit exhibited throughout the project by pastors and others. It is recognized as evidence of exceedingly good sportsmanship, as well as of Christian fair-mindedness, that they should have been willing to have the intimate issues of church life and administration so thoroughly overhauled and exposed, even by objective processes and in the mood of friendly scientific detachment.

Besides such values as may be found directly in the case studies, it is felt that the project has measurably served the needs of the Institute as a further development of its methods of research and as throwing certain light on basic problems that have not yet been fully solved.

INTRODUCTION

This book seeks to illuminate part of the field of the Protestant city church through semi-intensive case studies of twenty-six city churches, sixteen of which it presents through individual studies.[1]

The part of the field from which these instances were drawn is in general that in which the church is under the greatest pressure from adverse external circumstances. Circumstances may either favor a church, as when large numbers of well-to-do church-members predisposed to it are moving into its vicinity; or they may bear heavily against it, as when its best supporters are rapidly moving away. But one knows in advance that the lot of the majority of churches falls between these extremes and that their fortunes shade almost imperceptibly from the most advantageous to the worst.

In looking, therefore, to the side of the field where the most adverse fortunes lie, one must start at the neutral point and look along the line of increasing difficulty till it ends in conditions which no church can withstand. It is in this direction that the present project has found its cases, selecting them from among churches that were felt to have met their special problems with a certain originality and distinction. The degree of their actually representative character within the loosely defined group of churches under more than average environmental pressure was not known. It is not asserted that they constitute a complete series of demonstrably typical cases.

The Churches Studied

The denomination, location and pastoral leadership of the churches studied are shown in the following list. It will be noted that the distribution among thirteen cities and seven of the larger denominations makes the cases about as representative in these respects as their limited number permits.

---

[1] One case consisted of six churches combined under a single administration, so that an actual total of thirty-one ecclesiastical units was covered.

City	Church	Pastor at Time of Field Study
Chicago	* Fourth Presbyterian	Rev. John Timothy Stone, D.D.
	* Olivet Institute Presbyterian	Rev. Norman B. Barr, D.D.
	St. Chrysostom's Protestant Episcopal	Rev. Norman Hutton, S.T.D.
Cleveland	* Broadway Methodist Episcopal	Rev. M. M. Brown, D.D.
	* Pilgrim Congregational	Rev. Dan F. Bradley, D.D.
Denver	* Grace Community Methodist Episcopal	Rev. G. S. Lackland, D.D.
Detroit	* Central Methodist Episcopal	Rev. Lynn Harold Hough, D.D.
	First Congregational	Rev. Gaius Glenn Atkins, D.D.
	* First Presbyterian	Rev. Joseph A. Vance, D.D.
	* St. John's Protestant Episcopal	Rev. R. W. Woodroofe
Kansas City	First Christian	Rev. Roy Rutherford
Los Angeles	* City Parish Methodist Episcopal	Rev. G. Bromley Oxnam, D.D.
	Church of All Nations	
	Grace	
	East 38th Street	
	Elysian Gardens	
	Epworth	
	Brooklyn Heights	
Minneapolis	Hennepin Ave. Methodist Episcopal	Rev. Lucius Hatfield Bugbee, D.D.
Newark	* Roseville Methodist Episcopal	Rev. Karl K. Quimby
	* South Park Presbyterian	(Vacant)
New York	Central Park Baptist	Rev. Milton W. Pullen
	Intercession Protestant Episcopal	Rev. Milo H. Gates, D.D.
	Park Avenue Presbyterian	Rev. Tertius Van Dyke
	* Hanson Place Methodist Episcopal (Brooklyn)	Rev. J. Lane Miller, D.D.
Oakland	* First Baptist	Rev. John Snape, D.D.
St. Louis	Kingshighway Presbyterian	Rev. Henry H. Forsyth, D.D.
	Pilgrim Congregational	Rev. Russell H. Stafford, D.D.
	Second Baptist	(Vacant)
	Union Methodist Episcopal	Rev. Thomas Oliver Grieves, D.D.
San Francisco	* Trinity Center Presbyterian	Rev. Homer K. Pitman
Washington	* Mt. Vernon Place Methodist Episcopal, South	Rev. William A. Lambeth, D.D.

* Churches of which case studies are published in the following pages are starred, except Case I which asked to be presented anonymously.

These churches, as a group, are standing where many churches have fallen or are all but prostrate. This, as already indicated, does not mean that each and every one is under extremely adverse environmental pressure nor that the pressure is at all equal. Rather, in order to secure examples of a variety of reactions, a series of situations was sought, beginning with that of a church enjoying a positively favorable environmental setting, following with several in which the environment was essentially neutral or only moderately unfavorable and ending with a number suffering from extremely adverse circumstances. But the most favored case presented was that of a church that had only escaped an excessively bad situation by removal and the only moderately unfavorable situations were clearly growing worse.

Consequently not only the group as a whole but every individual church in it, at the hour of the study, had recently been beset, was beset at the time, or was in danger of being beset by such changes of fortunes as often destroy city churches. They were or had recently been either down-town churches outright, or near-down-town churches situated in areas of acute deterioration; or they were under special handicaps because of foreign antecedents or of location in foreign communities or in areas now threatened, if not in process of being over-run, by movements of foreign (or Negro) populations.

Their story—a recent one if not actually contemporaneous —is essentially simple, though varied in detail: "This vicinity used to be a good neighborhood for our church, but has now become unfavorable. It is difficult to get either people to attend or money to run the church along old lines."

The validity of this representation is verified in every case by objective social data which appear in the section on Environment in the several studies. Corroborative evidence was generally available in church statistics showing sharp institutional decline over a period of years, often succeeded by improvement following a radical change in the church's policy. Finally, concrete illustrations of the church's consciousness of and deliberate attempt to meet the adverse change were almost always present.[2] How successful these attempts were, institutionally speaking, and what ways they took, the individual case histories reveal. It was not presumed to apply moral judgments or to imply that one attempt was more courageous or Christian than another.

INSTITUTIONAL CHARACTERISTICS

The cases studied represent churches in the upper ranges of urban church development. The evidence of this is definite. While not all of them are vast institutions, their programs are much broader on the average, their parish relationships more complicated, their staffs of paid workers larger and more specialized, their plants and equipment more extensive and complete, and the cost of their operations greater than the average.

The degree to which the cases studied exceed the average church in breadth of program was measured in terms of thirty-three items of current program whose frequency was established by means of a well-distributed sample of 357 churches, selected without bias, in large cities. Comparison on the basis of these thirty-three items showed that the most frequent ones occurred about 10 per cent. more often in the twenty-six cases; those of average frequency about 40 per cent. more often; the infrequent ones four times as often, and the very infrequent ones five times as often as they occurred in the 357 cases. In other words, while not generally super-churches, the twenty-six cases very distinctly represent the upper ranges of the development of program in city churches.

Again, the cases studied have much more widely scattered constituencies than those of average city churches. They are forced to do church work over greater distances at greater cost of time and expense of transportation. They deal largely with people not closely associated with the neighborhood of the church building. They have to depend to an unusual extent

---

2 Since the present studies depended upon existing social data pertaining to many different cities, no method was available for measuring exactly the degrees of a church's environmental advantage or adversity, such as might have been found if they had all been in a single city, or such as was used in previous studies of individual cities, for example, the St. Louis and Springfield Church Surveys.

upon publicity, impersonal relations, administration and indirect means of communications.

As compared with 220 cases in which the parish distribution of constituencies had previously been studied,[3] the twenty-six cases are found to have only half as many compact parishes. Parishes of medium dispersal are about equally frequent. But scattered and very scattered parishes are twice as frequent. Five of the seven churches within the twenty-six cases that have compact parishes are the small and peculiarly circumstanced ones included in the Los Angeles Methodist Episcopal City Parish. None of these would have been admitted into the list of cases had they stood independently. If these are omitted, only two of the twenty-six cases have the compact parish characteristic of the neighborhood church.

The contrast between the staff, plant and cost of the twenty-six churches, and those of the average city church, could have been similarly measured. Not only is the staff of the former known to be larger, but it includes many more kinds of workers, many of them highly specialized. Not only is the plant larger, but it includes rooms for many more purposes and a much greater range of working equipment. Not only is the cost greater, but the particular operations for which the money goes frequently reach beyond anything that is found in the average church.

If, then, it is asked what kind of churches were included in the present case studies, the answer is: Such churches as illustrate, partially at least, the higher ranges of urban church development.[4] Roughly speaking, they represent the churches ranking in upper third or fourth. Within this range as many degrees of difference as possible were included.

BASIS OF SELECTION

How were the twenty-six cases chosen? A number of them, included in 1,044 cases studied during the immediately

---

[3] *1000 City Churches.*

[4] The four smaller churches of the City Parish, Los Angeles, independently considered, stand in interesting contrast as illustrating the lower ranges of urban church development.

preceding project in the city church field, were already super-ficially known and had been technically classified; so that their qualifications for the present study were assured. Data concerning numerous additional cases had been added in connection with parallel studies. From these sources a long list of possibilities was compiled consisting of churches showing more than average development, along with special pressure of environment. The list was further supplemented by cases recommended by secretaries of church federations in the major cities, more than twenty of which sent in lists of the more important churches in their respective communities. Still again, as the study proceeded certain churches of importance, which seemed to qualify, asked to be included.

A long process of elimination followed, amounting in the end to a virtually accidental choice within a list of admitted possibilities. It was the Institute's to propose; the churches' to dispose. Some flatly said: "We don't want you"; others, with varying degrees of frankness: "You don't want us." Sometimes it was simply intimated that the church's internal situation was not so happy as it seemed. In other cases, the church cheerfully gave its confidence and revealed unsuspected problems and difficulties which made it naturally unwilling to subject itself to a searching investigation the results of which it was proposed to publish. Still other cases simply found it inconvenient or untimely to have the study made when suggested. Finally the field work stopped in its tracks when the financial resources available for that phase of the project were exhausted. This outcome left the most intensively urban territory of the United States inadequately represented by five completed case studies in Greater New York and one in Washington. Except for these, no church was studied in any city east of Cleveland. Thus, all told, the study was a sort of fishing expedition in waters where the more highly developed city church was supposed to be. It caught such fish as it could and stopped when its bait gave out. So far as deliberate selection pertained, even in the limited sense, variety rather than individual distinction was the thing directly sought. There was no predetermined schedule of characterizing situations, exam-

ples of which were to be discovered; and the particular significance of a given case was not and could not have been known
in advance of the detailed study.

A still further process of selection grew out of the necessity
of confining the published presentation to a moderate-sized and
relatively inexpensive volume. The sixteen cases that make
up the body of this book were chosen for the sake of revealing many different ways of meeting urban situations. They
are not the better cases in the sense of being more successful
or worthy of imitation, and it is not determined whether they
are actually the more typical.

METHOD

No statement of the technical methodology used in the study
is presented, but a fairly complete series of methodological
notes is introduced topic by topic in the Appendix. They serve
to define the categories and to indicate the more general character of the processes by which the results embodied in the
studies were obtained.

In presentation, all the case studies follow essentially the
same order of topics. Each falls into two main divisions:
(1) The major aspects of the church, and (2) agencies, resources and methods. These are followed by a concluding
section setting forth the urban adaptations which the case
presents. The numerous comparisons introduced are not limited to the sixteen published cases, but involve all twenty-six
studied.

The Uses of the Study

VALUE TO THE CHURCHES STUDIED

In consenting to act as "cases" in the studies under consideration, the several churches concerned generally indicated
points on which they felt the need of light or projects concerning which they were seeking evidence. During the field work
opportunity was taken to discuss tentative findings on these

and other points with the respective pastors, who often found immediate suggestions in them. The complete studies, as previously stated, were sent back to the churches for criticism and correction as to factual statement. Frequently some of the facts disclosed were accepted as challenging in detail and as searching in their cumulative impression. In most cases the statement was cordially volunteered that the investigation had brought new comprehension of their problems to those most concerned. Occasionally it was added that specific recommendations had been successfully adopted.

Even larger values to the churches studied may be expected as they reëxamine their own cases comparatively in the published volume. Some of them may even find grounds for passing moral verdicts upon their previous policies and behavior— verdicts which it is not the business of the studies themselves to make.

USE BY OTHER CHURCHES

In asking for case studies of city churches, the ecclesiastical leaders and officials who advised and assisted in formulating the project said in effect: "Show us what the other man is doing in cases possibly analogous to ours and let us draw our own conclusions." In the light of this attitude, the main duty of the present studies has been regarded as completed when they have furnished objective data and the means of comparison and interpretation. The best excuse for being that the project can offer is just this possibility of independent use by responsible churchmen. And to one inclined to stop with this, any formal comparisons or interpretations that have crept into the studies may properly be regarded as mere by-products.

Understanding the City Church

The makers of the study, however, are not quite prepared to regard their product as delivered when it is dumped in a heap for the passer-by to pick up and use as he will. As already indicated, the case studies were chosen with reference to and are consequently arranged for presentation in a significant sequence; and this arrangement inevitably implies a hypothesis as to the relation between environmental pressure and institutional development in the group of churches concerned.

This hypothesis is now to be stated and its more direct consequences formulated; after which the reader is left pretty much to make what he can of the sixteen cases.

THE CHURCH'S BEHAVIOR UNDER UNUSUAL PRESSURE

Briefly stated, the hypothesis is that, except when other fairly recognizable influences intervene, exceptional environmental pressure may be expected to result in institutional evolution on the part of the Protestant church. The more important and consistent of these intervening influences are: (1) a less than average degree of numerical and economic strength; (2) exceptional fixity of religious and theological tenets; and (3) especial tenacity of a racial or social group in maintaining its customary behavior.[5]

These inhibitions affect the response of most churches under pressure, with the consequence that there is only a rough correlation between the degree of pressure and the degree of institutional change. One can, however, see the determinative force of these influences in extreme situations like the following:

(1) A church of very poor people, generally new and strange in the city, living near the border line of economic subsistence, will be institutionally unmodified by environmental pressure. Such a church comes into being as a child of adversity, already adapted to the most adverse conditions on a level of bare existence. It may die, but it has no strength to change. Such are numerous little churches of rural immigrants and Negroes or of the sporadic and emotional sects.

---

[5] Such exceptions, together with lack of adverse environmental pressure in great areas of the city, explain the fact that types of churches do not decisively reflect the environmental characteristics of their immediate vicinities. All kinds of churches are found in all kinds of environments. See *1000 City Churches*.

(2) When, as is usually the case, these churches hold beliefs having an extremely other-worldly cast, they are doubly inured to adversity and at the same time withheld from change. The fixing of attention exclusively upon subjective experience, the entirely secondary value assigned to the church as an institution, and the frequent conviction that the world is soon to end, enable such institutional forms as they have to survive unchanged, if they survive at all. This is merely another example of the use of the classic human device for escaping from objective misery: namely, by ignoring it. Churches that are too feeble institutionally to respond to pressure and that contrive subjectively to rise above it thus constitute exceptions to the Protestant rule.

(3) These two conditions often coincide in churches of certain racial groups, or in those marked by an unusually definite social tradition. Clannishness alone, but especially clannishness reënforced by economic weakness and extreme theology, renders a church tenacious of its institutional character even under stern environmental pressure. Consequently foreign-speaking churches, or churches of denominations that are exceptional in a given region, often survive little changed in areas where other Protestant churches have been driven out, extinguished or greatly modified.

When, however, such exceptional situations are not present, the likelihood is strong that a Protestant church will attempt to meet adverse environmental conditions by some change in its institutional scope and functioning. It will try new ways. In spite of them it may die. If it succeeds, however, one can trace the marks of its institutional adaptation.

In the light of this hypothesis, the cases studied are viewed as a series illustrating the range of institutional reactions that city churches are likely to make to exceptional environmental pressure when none of the exceptional conditions above enumerated is present.

Of the many different reactions possible, it is not assumed that all the churches combined have yet made all that will be made before the adjustment of Protestant institutions and the city is complete. It is believed, however, that the most typical ways in which contemporary churches actually do react are illustrated by the cases presented.

Ways of Meeting Urban Change

The control of an institution by its environment, either immediate or remote, is, of course, not absolute. Between successful devices for avoiding the natural consequences of adverse environmental change and the complete acceptance of the changed situation as furnishing the clew to what the church ought to be and do institutionally, there intervenes a considerable series of compromises and transitional stages. Some of the typical patterns of behavior in which these principal ways of meeting the situation work out are the following:

AVOIDANCE METHODS

(1) The most radical means of avoiding the consequence of adverse environmental changes is for a church to break away from them and remove to another location where the environment is favorable. This method is illustrated by Case I.

(2) Short of the radical solution of removal, the most common means of escape from adverse environmental pressure is through the selective operation of the church in the original vicinity; that is to say, by its appeal to a limited number of people of a given sort. Under conditions of average density of population in large cities, the constituency of a church, even the largest, is scarcely more than a drop in the bucket. Cities in their most characteristic areas present extreme contrasts in social fortunes on the part of people living within a short distance of one another. Very wealthy people, for example, may inhabit little patches of territory, like islands in a sea of less favored society. Mixed areas do not go entirely bad, nor do bad areas go bad all at once. Hence, in many cases, at least for a time, a church can get along fairly well in its original location in spite of extreme environmental change, if it confines itself to its own kind of people and avoids the particular areas of extremest disadvantage where its own kind is not

present. Cases II, III and IV illustrate various versions of this solution.

(3) Another method of avoiding the consequences of environmental change is to retain the church site but to substitute a new and distinctly urban basis of human association for that of the original church group based on proximity. The church plant continues to stand where it was, but the church as identified by the residences of its members almost entirely removes itself from the locality of the church building. It then proceeds to draw a new following from a distance. This means that the mobility of urban population and the accessibility of central institutions have been adopted as the principles of religious fellowship. The dominance of this principle in cities is such that, in the most extreme cases, a church with almost no constituents living anywhere near it becomes so related to the city as a whole that its site continues to be as good as or even better than before, from the standpoint of prestige and general institutional advantage. The centralizing forces of the city, the habitual use of its down-town focus by all its inhabitants, irrespective of their place of residence, and a certain down-town-mindedness in city populations, all find religious expression in the vogue and popularity of the great central church. Such churches have become virtually independent of environment as defined by the character of population and by the social conditions prevailing in the immediate vicinity of its plant. Case V is an extreme illustration of this method of meeting the situation.

METHODS OF COMPROMISE

Very often a city affords no room for a church to move and still retain its former prestige and advantage. Yet changed local conditions may be too acute for the selective cultivation of its old field to be fully successful. A church may cherish a strong conviction of its mission on its historic site or possess a particularly sensitive conscience as to its duty to the people of its locality—yet without seeing how to make either the main clew to policy or to connect them with practical resources of church support. Such a church naturally seeks some method of compromise.

(4) The most obvious method is to go a step or two in the direction of adaptation, continuing to work selectively along old lines and developing distant constituencies which urban mobility and the prestige of central locations make available. Such churches also add to the old program distinct though generally limited ministries designed expressly to meet the needs of the dominant populations now living in the vicinity. The methods through which compromising churches seek to serve such populations are varied. But almost always they are obviously in the nature of appendages to their established activities and they not infrequently appear somewhat foreign and incongruous. Churches thus develop separate programs for dual and even for triple constituencies. This mixed method of meeting the situation is illustrated with variations by Cases VII, VIII and IX. The ratio of the new elements of the program to the total program may be relatively small, as in Case VII, or relatively great, as in Case VIII, which latter case consequently tends to show some of the unstability of an overextended institution.[6]

TRANSITIONAL CASES

(5) At any given moment churches whose circumstances are not unduly exigent and whose tentative adaptations are taking several directions at once will be hard to characterize. They retain a selective hold on the locality, while, at the same time, they are building up a city-wide prestige and drawing on widely scattered constituents which they hope to continue to hold as the local supply diminishes. They may also maintain limited ministries to distinct populations. Such transitional situations are naturally more numerous than "pure" cases. Case VI is of this sort.

---

[6] For discussion of institutional ill-balance as the result of attempted adaptations, see *1000 City Churches*, pp. 118 ff.

RE-ADAPTATION

Coming down now to that stratum of churches whose institutional characters unmistakably bear the marks of the effort to fit themselves consciously to environment and which proclaim the purpose of their ministries in terms of adaptation, one still finds striking variation of method.

(6) New activities and elements of program, which begin as few and loosely attached additions to the old institution, may become so numerous, well-established and successful that they end in characterizing the church in the public mind and ultimately in dominating its own thought and purposes. Thus, without intending to be changed, the church gets profoundly changed. This fact being accomplished, it ultimately makes a conscious policy of what had already become a habit. Such seems to have been essentially the history and experience of Case X. Re-adaptation after this fashion is a most vital and characterizing process.

(7) Again, there may be a revolutionary shift in the emphasis of the church's life, but one that is not primarily localized in expression, that does not completely register itself in the reshaping of method, and that does not reflect the special needs of any particular neighborhood. This is to say that a church's adaptation may be to certain broad aspects of urban life as a whole.

The typical situations that reveal the urban spirit in its most characteristic experiences are often non-localized. Thus, industrial struggle as it goes on continuously for the control of public opinion, the generalized issues between organized labor and organized employers; or, equally, the struggle for racial equities shown in the multiform issues of assimilation and adjustment, find organized expression on a city-wide and nation-wide scale and virtually divide civilization into opposing camps. Highly developed group interests create their central forums for generalized utterance. This identifies them quite as definitely as they are revealed in specific controversies. They evolve general movements, appoint official leaders, maintain organs of agitation and follow recognized voices.

A church may adapt itself to urban civilization by concerning itself with such aspects of organized group interests centering in cities and without concerning itself exclusively with the social needs of any territorial neighborhood.

Obviously it is rarely open to the church wholly to control or directly to operate such far-reaching movements. But it may express its concern in them by entering upon definite working alliances.

The church studied as Case XI, while doing distinctive community work as defined by the needs of the local neighborhood, is characterized by the fact that, on the one hand, it is making a city-wide appeal to a somewhat select supporting constituency, while, on the other, it is advocating, facilitating and fostering the objectives and self-expression of organized labor groups. It is by these alliances that its work gets peculiar flavor, outreach and interest.

The successful use of the foregoing methods of avoidance, of compromise or of re-adaptation is virtually reserved for the centrally located church. To the church in the deteriorating residential district it is generally not open to escape the consequences of adverse environmental change by any of these means.

(8) What, then, can the residential church do in similar circumstances? Unless it moves, it can die or become negligible (continuing for a time to live but at a "poor dying" rate); or it can adapt itself radically to the immediate environment. This acceptance of the situation involves, on the whole, the complete inner transformation and modification of program and method. It is illustrated by Cases XII, XIII and XV which show the characteristic widening of program in the community-serving church to meet the needs of a changed and often handicapped population.

Such churches obviously must generally solve their financial problems by getting support from outside their own fields and constituencies; and they rarely escape a serious warping and unbalance of institutional structure.

(9) Finally, a church may have successfully grown up with,

or it may deliberately from its foundation have chosen to enter upon and be identified with a hard situation. These situations also almost inevitably imply that from the first and continuously thereafter the church will be more or less dependent upon outside financial support. But the fact that its adaptation was complete from the beginning frequently saves it from the one-sidedness of the hastily re-adapted types. Cases XIV and XVI illustrate these ultimate situations.

The more highly developed of these latter types of institution have so little the character of churches and are so much those of something besides churches that the name "church" ceases to fit them. They consequently supplement it with a secondary name like that of "Institute" in the example presented. This case marks the limits of adaptation within the ecclesiastical form.[7]

The present series of cases thus illustrates a wide range of distinct logical possibilities and probably covers most of the major directions of actual adaptation to environment exhibited by churches in large city communities. Future environmental change may make the situation of some of the cases studied still more exigent. Multitudes of other churches are still to be caught in the currents which unmake as well as remake cities. The church at least has "not here an abiding city." Its hands ought to be strengthened against adverse change by the somewhat systematic knowledge of some of the successful ways in which similar experiences have been met and by glimpses of the principles underlying them. Such knowledge the following studies in some measure afford.

Summary

It is in order, finally, to summarize some of the character-

---

[7] The next logical step passes outside of the church field altogether. Why continue to call this a church, one finally says, when it is nine-tenths or nineteen-twentieths something else? So the Christian center or settlement house comes into being. It carries on definitely religious work and may aspire to create church material ultimately—but it is not now a church and never has been. It consequently falls beyond the scope of the present study.

istics of the completed study that throw light upon both its method and its limitations.

(1) It is an objective study of aspects of the church that are comparable by means of measurement. On a few points systematically recorded impressions were admitted, as in the section concerned with public services and worship, because no valid method of strictly comparable investigation was discovered. But in the main the data are such as measure objective likenesses and differences.

That much of value escapes a method thus limited, no one can be more conscious than those who use it frequently.

(2) The study is institutional rather than psychological. It deals with churches rather than with the persons who make or unmake churches. The reader will be disappointed if he expects a setting forth of the traits and capacities of the pastors and their colleagues. Names are only occasionally mentioned in the text, and, unless clearly determinative, the rôle of the pastor in influencing the adaptive behavior of the church has been ignored. Nothing short of competent psychoanalysis could have put this aspect of investigation on the same level of objectivity with that of most of the other phenomena concerned; and the pastors did not sit for any such revealing picture.[8]

(3) The study attempts to describe rather than to explain (except as to the single hypothesis already developed in this Introduction) or directly to evaluate. In ordinary scientific method, comparison has to follow description before it is possible to get very far with explanation. The present studies do not involve enough cases to make generalizations valid except as the data can be integrated with the total results of previous studies with which they are not strictly comparable in form. Hence an intermediate stage of translation is necessarily in-

---

[8] It may be guessed that the pastor of a church under adverse pressure usually will not find such opportunity to make an impression distinct from that of his institution as the pastor of the church on Easy Street sometimes enjoys. Not infrequently the latter church comes to be a sort of platform for a dominating personality. Greater men, measured against sterner difficulties, may make less of an independent show, while sharing greatly in the high significance of the situation with which they are identified.

volved which is not yet complete or formally summarized, and which consequently does not yield conclusions ripe for publication. As to the causes that enter into the particular results portrayed, a large measure of ignorance remains. Especially lacking is any adequate ground of discrimination between the influences of general ecclesiastical tradition and those of local circumstances and experiences in the making of the individual church what it is.

(4) The study is incomplete in the special sense that its practical limitations of time and money did not permit it to carry on to the point of formally summarizing the comparisons between churches already introduced into the text of the individual studies. These comparisons are presented and then left dangling. For students who may use the case studies it would afford a valuable exercise to arrange and rank the cases on point after point of the data, to note in individual cases departures from or agreements with the group tendency and to set up tentative explanations of behavior illustrative both of the rule and of the exception. Maturer readers will find their own range of comparisons widened and their conclusions checked by the data even as they stand.

(5) The study is essentially contemporaneous. Only to a slight degree is historical material used for creating the necessary background for understanding. This limitation of studies of religious institutions to the present will have to continue until resources can be secured to support scientific observation over a period of time. Until then, social investigation in this field will be using only one of its two eyes.

(6) The study is semi-intensive. For example, no technical study of religious education has been attempted commensurate with those frequently made of that subject in city churches. The study of the plant was made by the same methods that were used in the well-known Malden Survey, and the results might easily have been expanded into a small volume. Indeed, as much time might profitably have been spent upon any of the major topics as was available for the entire study. What is presented in each case study is what could be done by one

person in the time specified (ten days to two weeks), with local assistance in the assembling of material.

(7) The study was only semi-critical with respect to its raw materials. It is based upon already existing original data of many sorts. No new records were created. Old ones originating in very diverse processes were simply brought together and used without much opportunity for checking the validity of the original methods of securing them. The inaccuracies and infelicities of church record-keeping and accounting have often been exposed. Limitations growing out of the inaccurate data (which in general are all there are relating to the church) will continue until the exact keeping of records by means of standard forms over a period of time can be secured.

CONTENTS

LIST OF TABLES

CENTRAL METHODIST EPISCOPAL CHURCH, DETROIT, MICH.

MOUNT VERNON PLACE METHODIST EPISCOPAL CHURCH, SOUTH, WASHINGTON, D. C.

CHARTS

THE CHURCH IN THE CHANGING CITY

CASE I

ANONYMOUS—CHURCH Z

This church presents one of the simplest of the twenty-six cases studied. On a list of sixty current organizations, activities and practices of city churches, its program ranks third from the smallest. In total annual attendance upon all regular organizations and continuous activities it ranks fifth from the smallest. Its marks of specific environmental adaptation are, to say the least, not very striking.

In what sense then is Church Z a significant example of a city church?

(1) It illustrates one of the genuine solutions of the church's problem of urban adaptation so far as the local church is concerned. When its environment became uncongenial, it removed to one that it liked better. Having found the right location in an essentially homogeneous area, it has not been under the necessity of further specific adaptation.

(2) Specifically it shows what a church of notable influence, recognized as one of the leading ones of its city, and blessed with considerably more than average resources, may do in an extra-advantageous environment if it has forward-looking general ideas but is under no great and directive external pressure.

History

Church Z belongs to a distinguished group of churches in its city which have solved their immediate environmental problems within the last quarter of a century by moving to the West End. The advantageous results of such removal, institutionally speaking, are in this case very clear.

The church was organized ecclesiastically in 1866. Its location at that time was about a mile and a half west of the center

41

of the city. Its subsequent history, as related to the growth of the city and to its own growth, measured statistically, is summarized in Table I.

TABLE I—PERIODS OF DEVELOPMENT IN HISTORY OF CHURCH Z*

Period	Characteristics	Pop. of City (Approx.)	Membership at End of Period	
			Church	Sunday School
1853-1866	Mission Sunday school preceding church	100,000	45	Not known
1866-1872	Organization of church; erection of building	160,000	112	225
1872-1901	Growth, culmination and decline of development	575,000	842	266
1901-1907	Agitation of removal; erection of present church	650,000	748	267
1907-1926	Development in present location	825,000	1,264	575

* Data from the Church Z *Year Book,* 1926.

When the courses of annual church and Sunday-school growth are charted, three trends are clear: (1) the church's rapid development for the first eighteen years following the completion of its original building; (2) its subsequent checking and decline; and (3) new growth, at a rate almost paralleling that of the first period, following the church's relocation.

The curve of Sunday-school growth went up with that of the church, but went down sooner and faster. The Sunday school, also, recovered much less completely after the change of location and did not grow so fast as the church after the post-war period.

The utterly untenable character of the area surrounding the former location to support the kind of church that Z was and always has been was scientifically demonstrated in a subsequent survey of the city. The church could not have remained without extremely radical transformation of program and relationships. Removal was thus the decisive breaking of an institutional deadlock by an institution which did not desire to change its essential character.

I. MAJOR ASPECTS OF THE CHURCH

In turning from history to the study of Church Z as it exists to-day, it should be noted that the plan of investigation distinguishes between what may be termed the major aspects of the church as a social entity and certain subordinate aspects of the church in action.

In classifying the topics immediately following; viz., "members and constituents," "parish and geographical distribution of constituency," and "environmental relations" under the head, "Major Aspects of the Church," two assumptions are implied: namely, (1) that these factors lie behind and condition all the rest; (2) that they are themselves products of large forces, chiefly instinctive in origin and operating according to long-time trends; so that to alter them is beyond the immediate control of the church's purpose or of such relatively short-time policies as the planning of pastors and the votes of church meetings usually have to do with.

The truth of these assumptions need not be argued here. They are simply confessed as the working hypotheses of this series of studies, hypotheses which the reader may accept or reject as he will. If they are accepted, the most immediately pertinent consequence will be this: that praise and blame will not be ascribed to a church for what appear as the basic factors of its existence in the same sense that they may be ascribed to conditions immediately resulting from contemporary decisions and alterable by a mere change in method or policy.

Members and Constituents

First of the basic factors of the church to be studied is its human components commonly identified as members and constituents.

The determinate or definitely connected constituency of Church Z, consisting of 1,469 persons, is mainly drawn from constituent families, though about one-third are individuals whose families are not attached to the church. Compared with the total population of the city, this constituency contains

relatively fewer adolescents and adults, but more children.
These characteristics are shown in Table II.

TABLE II—CONSTITUENTS BY AGE AND SEX

AGE-GROUP	TOTAL			NUMBER FAMILY GROUP			INDIVIDUALS			PER CENT. DISTRIBUTION	
	Total	*Male*	*Female*	*Total*	*Male*	*Female*	*Total*	*Male*	*Female*	*Church Z*	*The City*
Total	1,469	609	860	947	416	531	522	193	329	100	100
Adults (21 and over)	1,017	393	624	700	301	399	317	92	225	69	72
Adolescents (15-20)	121	52	69	67	33	34	54	19	35	8	11
Children (5-14)..	308	150	158	161	69	92	147	81	66	21	17
Minors (age unknown)	23	14	9	19	13	6	4	1	3	2	0

Church Z is a compactly organized body centering upon a
large core of close adherents who stand in many and overlapping relationships with the church. Adolescents constitute the
most highly organized single element. The church, however,
has not succeeded in gathering around it the average number
of remotely connected adherents whom it can gradually assimilate into full membership. It has, so to speak, a smaller reservoir from which to draw close adherents than many churches
have.

Behind these specific data one discerns the characteristics of
the particular population with which the church is dealing. It
is a population normally distributed according to age and sex;
not, as in so many urban areas, one distorted by the preponderance or the lack of one or another element. The church,
accordingly, is not one-sided in composition, but is essentially
a cross section of its fairly homogeneous community. The
slight preponderance of children perhaps registers the effect of
its assiduous cultivation of young families.

The Present Environment

The "West End," to which the migrating churches have
almost uniformly moved, is the distinctively American sector

of Church Z's city; the most desirable section in social esteem; the earthly paradise of successful people, and hence the immediate heaven of the Protestant churches.

Its size and exact boundaries may be variously defined. For the purposes of this study, they are identified by the continuous area, lying west of "Grand Avenue," in which people pay high and very high rents. More than half of it lies beyond the political boundaries of the city. The area includes roughly a population of 110,000, and, with its remoter suburbs, about 130,000—the fortunate tenth of the population of the metropolitan community.[1]

But the West End itself is not strictly of one piece. Calculations have been made for areas within a mile radius of thirteen churches so located (Chart I) as to constitute a cross section of this part of the city. The results tell approximately how many families are living within a mile of each church, what kind of dwellings they live in, and what average rent they pay; also how much poverty there is in their vicinity. These are very accurate indices of differences in wealth and social status and consequently of differences in the prospects and possible responsibilities of the churches dependent upon each given area.[2]   Table III summarizes the facts.

Among the more significant aspects of the following data is their evidence of decreased density of population from east to west. This is expressed in terms of housing by the fact that, where the West End begins at Grand Avenue, only 16 per cent. of all families enjoy the spaciousness of single-family residences. From a point about a mile west of Grand Avenue to the western limits of the city, this per cent. of single-family

---

[1] The reputation of the West End was objectively justified in detail by means of a long series of carefully determined criteria through an extensive survey made in 1921-22. The survey district within which Church Z is located ranked next to the best in the city on the basis of these data; and also on eleven separate religious criteria.

[2] These calculations are based primarily on the important housing and rent studies made by a well-known local newspaper in 1925. These studies covered the entire metropolitan area and were intended to show standards of living and purchasing power of the different areas of the city, with a view to the sale of goods through advertising. It is obvious that they throw equal light upon the environments and parishes of churches. In securing the data, the newspaper made a house-to-house canvass, employing thirty people for a period of five months. Data concerning charity cases were furnished by the Community Council of the city from its district studies.

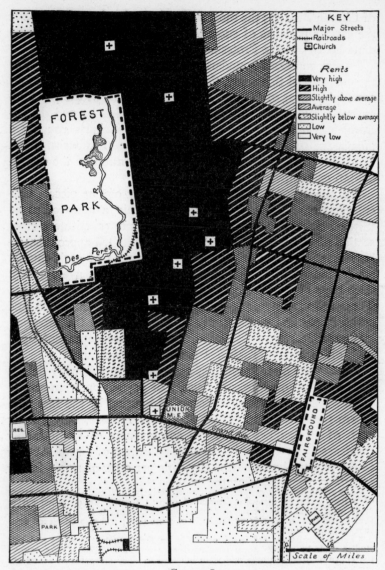

KEY
— Major Streets
⊞ Railroads
⊞ Church

Rents
Very high
High
Slightly above average
Average
Slightly below average
Low
Very low

FOREST

PARK

Des Peres R.

RES.

UNION M.E.

FAIRGROUND

PARK

Scale of Miles

CHART I
Economic Environment of Church Z

TABLE III—FAMILIES, TYPES OF DWELLINGS, RENTS AND CHARITY CASES WITHIN A MILE RADIUS OF SPECIFIED WEST-END CHURCHES

CHURCHES IN ORDER OF LOCATION FROM EAST TO WEST*

	1 & 2	3	4	5 & 6	7 & 8	9, 10, 11†	12	13
Number of families	21,749	19,023	12,767	13,844	17,683	15,984	12,431	3,320
Per cent. living in—								
Residences	16	23	29	28	31	30	29	48
Flats	58	51	44	42	45	43	21	22
Apartments	4	9	17	27	22	25	50	30
Lodging houses ...	7	5	3	1	1	1	0	0
Light housekeeping rooms	15	12	7	2	1	1	0	0
Per cent. paying—								
Very high rents...	7	19	61	57	42	55	79	78
High rents	12	15	19	23	38	32	12	22
Slightly above average rents	36	41	20	18	18	10	5	0
Average rents	19	25	0	2	2	3	4	0
Slightly below average rents	0	0	0	0	0	0	0	0
Low rents........	26	0	0	0	0	0	0	0
Very low rents....	0	0	0	0	0	0	0	0
Number of charity cases	343	160	110	71	73	43	19	6

* Churches are so clustered on adjoining sites that the eight columns of this table afford data for thirteen churches.
† Church Z.

homes increases to about thirty, while in the nearer suburbs it reaches nearly fifty. Flats steadily decrease, and apartment houses increase from east to west as far as the city limits; then the latter yield to the single-family house of the suburbs. Lodging-houses and light housekeeping rooms mark the area on the eastern edge of the West End and now penetrate far into it. These are distinctly less desirable forms of housing, and are symptomatic of a number of social changes for the worse.

Where the West End begins less than one-third of the population pays high or very high rents (Chart I). About one-half a mile farther out, the proportion rises to about one-third. In the heart of the West End, 80 per cent. pay high and very high rents, while on the western border and nearer suburbs, nearly 80 per cent. pay the very highest rents.

Again, within equal areas, poverty correspondingly decreases from east to west.

With two other churches, Church Z occupies the central area of the West End, a district strikingly homogeneous as to housing. In the vicinity of these three churches, the distribution of dwellings of all types is essentially identical. With respect to the average level of rents and the degree of poverty, the environment of Church Z is better than that of the other churches which have similar housing conditions, though it is less favorable than that of the churches on the western border and in the suburbs. All told, the social quality of Church Z's immediate environment is distinctly better than the average of the West End.

It is not so clear that these present advantages are to be permanent. A study of the geography of families occupying lodging-houses and light housekeeping rooms is perhaps the best single index of the movement of transient and socially undependable population. Chart II shows the block of contiguous territory in which housing of these types provides for more than 10 per cent. of the families, and also locates the further movement of deterioration along two axial streets where as yet the proportion of families in lodging houses and light housekeeping rooms is only from 5 to 10 per cent. Here obviously a second zone of transient residence is forming. The frontiers of this secondary area reach almost to the doors of the church, which stands in an exact line with the major movements of deterioration as thus measured.[3]

To have avoided the consequences of adverse changes in a former environment by change of location thus appears in this case rather a temporary solution. While, however, the present relatively homogeneous environment lasts no special necessity

---

[3] In addition to the menace of an ever-increasing congestion and transiency of population, the West End faces the loss of its chief protective and stabilizing force: namely, the city's zoning ordinance which the Supreme Court of the state declared invalid in 1924. The location of seventy-two structures erected in the

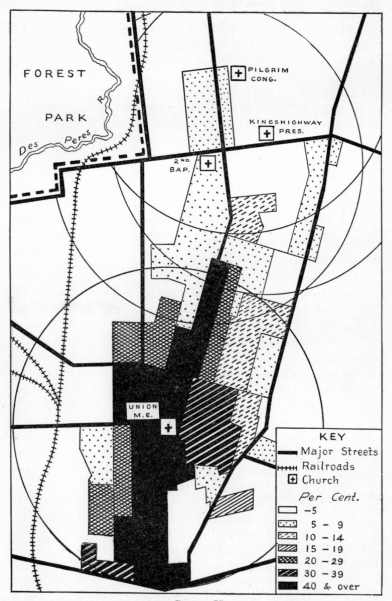

FOREST

PARK

Des Peres R.

PILGRIM
CONG.

KINGSHIGHWAY
PRES.

2ND.
BAP.

UNION
M.E.

KEY
— Major Streets
┼┼┼┼ Railroads
✚ Church
Per Cent.
☐ —5
⋯ 5 − 9
▨ 10 − 14
▤ 15 − 19
▦ 20 − 29
▧ 30 − 39
■ 40 & over

CHART II
Rooming-house Area in Church Z's City

is laid upon the church to adapt its program or methods to a particular local situation. That it does not do so is shown in detail in the following sections.

The Parish

In general Church Z has a fairly compact parish, somewhat asymmetrical in shape in that it tends to avoid lower-rent territory to the northeast of the building, while it is correspondingly elongated in the direction of the higher-rent territory to the southwest, which is also the direction of the city's greater growth. Sixty-six per cent. of all adherents live within one mile, and 44 per cent. within one-half mile of the church. In few of the churches studied are the adherents massed so closely about the building in which their corporate life centers.

DENSITY OF OCCUPANCY

The relative density of the constituency with reference to the church building is shown for distance zones and directional sectors on Chart III, from which it will be seen that the heaviest adherent population lies within half a mile to the northwest of the church. Within this distance little difference in density is found between the other three sectors. It is in the second half mile that the lack of adherents toward the northwest becomes sharply evident. To the southwest the same relative density is maintained in the second half mile and in the second mile, although Forest Park occupies much of the area in these directions. The probable explanation of the parish's avoidance of the northeast and its tendency toward the southwest has already been suggested. The correctness of the explanation becomes obvious when one superimposes the parish map (Chart III) upon a map showing average rents by small districts (Chart I). Judged by these basic social data, Church Z registers, in considerable detail, a weakness in all areas except those paying the highest rents. Thus, its parish shows no prejudice against

West End within fourteen months following the lapse of the ordinance, which would have been illegal and prohibited if the law had held, have been mapped as part of this study. An inspection of the map reveals that the entire West End section has been badly riddled and the character of many of its areas permanently changed.

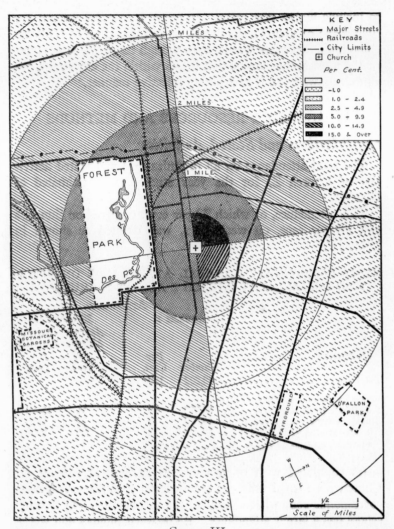

CHART III
Parish of Church Z

expanding to the southeast so long as this direction continues to include higher rent areas. In general, in equal sectors, the percentage of constituents comes up in proportion as rents become high. In other words, even though its parish area is one of the most homogeneous that exists within the city limits, the church draws upon it in a highly selective manner.[4]

II. AGENCIES, RESOURCES AND METHODS

Organizations and Stated Activities

The total attendance on all organizations and stated activities of Church Z, for the year studied, was estimated at 48,202.[5]

This attendance, of which 72 per cent. occurred on Sundays and 28 per cent. on week days, was divided as shown in Table IV.

TABLE IV—ESTIMATED ANNUAL ATTENDANCE ON SPECIFIED OCCASIONS AT CHURCH Z AND AT 26 CHURCHES

	ATTENDANCE			
	CHURCH Z		26 CHURCHES	
			Approx. Median	Range of Variation
OCCASION	Number	Per Cent.	Per Cent.	Per Cent.
Total	48,202	100		
Formal religious services (Sunday and week day)..........	24,072	50	51	15–75
Sunday school	13,528	28	24	9–38
All other stated activities.......	10,602 *	22	22	9–51

* Includes meetings of church officers and committees.

As compared with other churches studied, attendance on Church Z's formal religious services and subsidiary programs corresponds somewhat closely to the median; but the Sunday school has a larger attendance. As between Sunday and week-day activities, the latter take more than average proportions

---

[4] The term "selective" is used in this connection in its sociological significance, which does not imply deliberate choice. The church is not conscious of avoiding the low-rent districts. As indicated in the introduction to this section, the parish distribution of churches is not ordinarily the result of their conscious policies.

[5] For definition and method of calculation, see page 449.

on account of the church's well organized though rather conventional social life.

The estimated attendance of 9,974 upon activities other than church services, Sunday-school sessions and officers' meetings is divided between age-groups and sex-groups as follows:

TABLE V—ESTIMATED ANNUAL ATTENDANCE ON SUBSIDIARY ORGANIZATIONS AND STATED ACTIVITIES

ORGANIZATIONS		ATTENDANCE	
No.	Type	Number	Per Cent.
10	Total	9,974	100
0	Mixed adults.............................	0	0
1	Adult men..............................	504	5
2	Adult women............................	3,472	35
2	Mixed young people *....................	2,043	20
1	Young men	200	2
1	Young women............................	480	5
2	Mixed boys and girls....................	2,085	21
1	Boys	1,190	12
0	Girls	0	0
0	Mixed children..........................	0	0

* Between 15 and 23 years of age.

Attendance on organizations of the Women's Association accounts for more than one-third of the subsidiary program, while attendance upon the Young People's Society, and upon the mixed organizations for boys and girls each constitute about one-fifth. Most of the churches studied have more organizations, have carried sex segregation further in their parish organization, and have developed distinctive programs for young men and young women more highly (though not necessarily more effectively) than Church Z.[6]

Staff

The paid staff of Church Z consists of four workers: pastor, Director of Religious Education, secretary, and secretary to the Director of Religious Education, whose education, experience, tenure and salaries are shown in Table VI.[7]

A classified account of the work of the staff for one week was kept according to a generalized form, and the summary

[6] For evidence that this concentration upon few organizations is deliberate, see page 64.

[7] The data summarized below were secured through personal interviews with staff members and entered on schedules covering the points indicated in the text.

TABLE VI—ANALYSIS OF PAID STAFF

	Pastor	Director of Religious Education	Church Secretary	Secretary to Director of Religious Education *
Sex	Male	Male	Female	Female
Degree of education				
Academic	College	College	High school	High school
Professional or special.	Theological Seminary Post-graduate	Theological Seminary Post-graduate	...	...
Years of employment				
Prior to this position				
Secular work ....!....	...	6	19	4½
Religious work	15	13	...	...
In this position........	3	1½	3	1
Present salary				
Cash	$8,000	$4,200	$1,680	$600
Perquisites				
Nature	Parsonage	...	...	...
Value	$1,500	...	...	...
Entitled to ecclesiastical				
pension	Yes	Yes	No	No
Length of vacation	2 months	6 weeks	1 month	1 month

* Part time.

of results revealed numerous blanks. The latter indicated types of work characteristically performed by staffs of churches carrying on broader or more specialized types of program, but absent, at least from this particular week, in Church Z. In a distribution of the 191 hours, the total paid work of the week, clerical duties were found to occupy more time than any other. Pastoral work came second, administrative duties third, and homiletical preparation, with its closely allied general cultural pursuits, fourth. The male members of the staff worked respectively eight and one-half and nine hours per day on a seven-day basis.[8]

The noteworthy aspects of these data are: (1) that the only

---

[8] Large fluctuations in the distribution of functions would doubtless occur from week to week, but the showing is probably fairly representative of the more active season of the year.

distinct staff specialization is that upon religious education; (2) that the amount of time spent in administration is small —indicating probably the direct and informal relation of the workers; (3) that the provision of clerical assistance is very ample; (4) that pastoral work is very actively pursued; and (5) that the pastor gives an exceptional amount of time to general cultural pursuits. These characteristics of staff work clearly mark a church of unusual resources, one stressing its pulpit ministry, but also one that is unusually successful in recruiting new members.

In relation to the size of the church's enterprise, the provision of four paid workers is unusually generous. For every hundred attendants during the year the staff does twenty-one hours of work. Only eight of the twenty-six churches studied exceed Church Z in this respect.

Plant

The church building occupies a corner fronting on a prominent boulevard. The relation of its location to the structure of the city has had earlier comment.[9] The building is a substantial structure, erected in 1907, its exterior of Italian Gothic design. The Sunday-school and parish rooms are located at the rear of the auditorium. The entire structure is set well back from the lot lines on two sides behind a well-kept lawn.

Among the twenty-five plants studied, that of Church Z ranks tenth on the Interchurch thousand-point scale, scoring a total of 624 points. The median rank of the twenty-five churches is about 600 points.[10]

The strong and weak points of the plant are summarized in Table VII.

---

[9] Page 45.

[10] For explanation of the Interchurch scale, see *Standards for City Church Plants*, and for its application to a group of churches, Athearn, *The Malden Survey* (both Interchurch World Movement, 1920). The scale rates a church plant on 121 separate items, each of which is given a numerical value—the total equaling, 1,000.

TABLE VII—SUMMARY OF SCORE OF PLANT

Items	Standard Score	Points Scored		Rank in 25 Cases
		Number	Per Cent.	
Total	1,000	624	62	10
Site	130	104	80	7
Building or buildings.........	150	117	78	12
Service systems..............	160	99	62	8
Church rooms	170	135	79	5
Religious school rooms........	200	112	56	18
Community service rooms.....	190	57	30	20

In spite of its spaciousness, the church does not have an up-to-date Sunday-school plant, and its service systems are not fully modern. Judged by the standard fixed by the score-card, its provision for community service is also quite deficient.

Many improvements in ventilation and service systems have, of course, been imported into the accepted standards of first-class public buildings since the erection of the plant, and facilities for community service need not be expected of a church unless it wishes to attempt work of that character. But, in view of the church's stress on religious education, the lack of suitable rooms for fully departmentalized Sunday-school work is administratively and educationally serious.

Unfortunately the shape of the church site has left little space for any additions. The serious deficiencies in plant can thus hardly be remedied without additional land and the erection of a secondary structure in harmony with the rather exacting architectural lines of the original.

Finances

The receipts of the church during 1925 for its current expenses (including those of the Sunday school and the Women's Association) were about $42,000. Of this amount $4,582 consisted of receipts on account of the year 1924. Well toward one-half ($19,398) came from individual pledges and gifts and nearly one-third came from pew rentals. Only about 5 per cent. was received in loose collections.

The benevolence total of about $25,000 includes individual gifts reported to the church for credit. Of the total, nearly three-fifths came through the Women's Association. The grand total of current and benevolent receipts was about $67,000.

EXPENDITURES

Current expenditures for 1925 were $42,964 (including an approximation of the expenses of the Women's Association). They were divided as shown in Table VIII.

TABLE VIII—FINANCIAL EXPENDITURES OF THE CHURCH

Item	Amount	Per Cent.
Grand Total	$42,964	
Total Current Account	39,824	100
Salaries (religious work staff)	14,280	36
General administrative expenses	2,559	6
Music (including salaries)	5,037	13
General operation and upkeep of property	9,372	24
Expenses of departments specially budgeted	1,666	4
Sunday school and Daily Vacation Bible School	$866	
Women's Association (approximate)	800	
Publicity	2,710	7
Miscellaneous (including payments on account of 1924)	4,200	10
Investment Account		
Payments on parsonage loan	3,140	

A debt of about $20,000 still rests on the church parsonage.

The percentage of total expenditures that goes to the operation and upkeep of the plant is relatively large and indicates its intensive use by the constituency according to a rather opulent standard.

Of benevolent expenditures of approximately $25,000, less than 2 per cent. went to family and individual relief and to courtesies within the parish; while 84 per cent. was contributed to denominational objects.

Public Services and Worship

Measured by the total annual attendance, public services and worship (including the mid-week service) constitute just about half of the total operations of the church. Attendance is carefully counted. For the thirty-six Sundays of the year, when the church is felt to be in normal operation, there was, in 1925, an average congregation on Sunday mornings of 513, and for the sixteen Sundays on which a musical vesper service was held there was an average afternoon congregation of 164.

About one-third of the average audience appears to be composed of men and two-thirds of women. The morning service, occupying an hour and a half, is moderately liturgical in character, with gowned ministers and vested choir, and with choir responses after the prayers. The prayers are habitually read. The children of the congregation withdraw after the general service of worship for their own separate service of instruction.

The mid-week service, maintained for twenty-eight weeks of the year, with an average attendance of 150, follows a six o'clock church sociable and dinner. Devotions begin immediately after the clearing of the tables. The pastor, rising in the manner of an after-dinner speaker, delivers a brief but fully prepared sermon. This religious service, an hour in length, is conducted on schedule and closes early enough to enable the participants to meet other evening engagements.

An examination of the sermon topics of a year reveals the consistent treatment of religious and ethical topics interestingly and aptly announced without sensationalism.

The entire scheme of pulpit ministry is carefully prepared for a year in advance with reference to seasons and celebrations, communion services, etc., so as to secure a balanced treatment of Christian concerns. Serial sermons as such are not common; and "causes" as such are not directly presented, though their claims are habitually enforced by pulpit discussions of basic ethical principles.

Religious Education

Measured by attendance on the Sunday school, as well as by specialization in the paid staff, Church Z puts somewhat more than average emphasis on religious education. In theory, it is intended to gather up all church activities of children and young people in the idea of religious education and to give an organized and rounded expression to their interests, so far as possible under their own plans and initiative. The Children's Church League is composed of Sunday-school pupils, but its session, though in charge of the Director of Religious Education, is not recorded as strictly part of the Sunday school.

No traditional Young People's Society of the Christian Endeavor type is maintained. The young people's service on Sunday evening is regarded, however, as a meeting of the young people's department of the Sunday school. This department maintains a social hour with refreshments as a feature of its Sunday-evening program.

The adult classes of the Sunday school are fully organized, having their own benevolent objectives and occasional week-day social activities. The church has no gymnasium, but its Sunday-school boys play basket-ball in other gymnasiums. The five young women's classes are united in a somewhat loose organization representing the all-around interests of dawning womanhood. In general, however, there is no full organization of a week-day program for young people comparable with that in many of the churches studied, and the church is in doubt whether its particular constituency needs one.

Table IX summarizes the numerical data relating to the Sunday school.

TABLE IX—SUMMARY OF SUNDAY-SCHOOL STATISTICS

Department	Pupils		Teachers	
	Age	Enrollment	Male	Female
Total		540	10	42
Cradle Roll		25	...	...
Kindergarten	3–5	47	1	5
Primary	6–8	52	0	11
Junior	9–12	100	0	16
Young people	13–20	157	7	9
Adults	21 & over	159	2	1

The addition of seven officers to the 540 pupils and 52 teachers gives a grand total of 599. Pupils in the attending departments number 515, and attendance averages 59 per cent. of enrollment. The approximate age-distribution in the attending departments is as follows:

	Number	*Per Cent.*
Children	238	46
Adolescents	118	23
Adults	159	31

A summer Daily Vacation Bible School is held for five weeks in coöperation with the neighboring Christian Church.

Growth and Conservation

The annual average of accessions to the membership of the church for the last decade has been about 6 per cent. of the total membership. Of 107 persons received during 1925, 59 per cent. were transferred by letter from other churches (of whom only sixteen were previously of the church's denomination), and 41 per cent. were received on confession of faith. Fifty-eight per cent. had been resident in the community more than one year, while 42 per cent. were newcomers within that period.

Ranked by order of numerical importance, the most important sources of new members are:

(1) People newly moved to the city who belong to churches elsewhere. No other church studied showed anything like the same ratio of reception from other denominations.

(2) Sunday-school pupils. A total of thirteen were received from the Sunday school during the year studied. It harmonizes with the compactness of the church as a social group that there was no extensive drawing on remotely related adherents for church-membership. The church goes after newcomers directly and takes them all the way into church-fellowship if it gets them at all.

(3) Not more than one-tenth of the total number of accessions were persons who were not transferred from other churches, or who had neither come up through the Sunday school nor attended church services for a considerable period prior to uniting. In other words, the capacity of the church to win recruits immediately from the community appears to have been rather limited. The church appears, however, to be recruiting about proportionately from the entire parish area in which the constituency lives. Considerable numbers of new

members are being secured from territory remote from the church.

The occasions of forty-three losses of church-members during the same period are as follows:[11]

Total 43

Death 13
Transfer 25
  In city... 4
  Out of city 21
Dropped 5

Relationships

Including the local charities of Church Z, the financial support of which has already been reported under the heading of benevolences, the combined reports of the church and subsidiary organizations and a check of the lists of staff and officers of the recognized social agencies of the city reveal a total of forty-three stated contacts with such agencies during the year, as follows:

Type of Contact	Number of Agencies
Contributions toward financial support.......................	12
Church-members on staff or governing boards (38 persons)....	19
Practical coöperation..	6
Publicity and advocacy (in printed bulletin).................	6

These contacts are entirely interdenominational and non-sectarian in character. Judged by the nature of the agencies with which it coöperates, the church appears as most interested in health, character-building and civic movements; that is to say, in preventative and normalizing social effort rather than in the alleviatory and remedial sort.

The pastor is a director of the Welfare League and the Anti-Saloon League of his state and of the Urban League of his city, and a member of the advisory committee of its Neighborhood House.

Relations to the denomination through financial contribution to the extent of about $20,000 for the year 1925 have already

[11] For the last decade, as a whole, there have been about four losses for every seven gains; so that the ratio of the year (four losses for every ten gains) is more than usually favorable.

been reported. Church Z is represented in denominational affairs nationally by two members on the Commission on Missions; regionally by the pastor's trusteeship in Chicago Theological Seminary; and within the state through eight members serving as trustees of denominational colleges or academies, as well as by frequent elective officers in local ecclesiastical bodies. As one of a very few outstanding churches of a denomination that is relatively weak in the southwest, Church Z has naturally come into an established ascendancy in the fraternal councils of its churches in the entire region.

As expressions of its interdenominational coöperation, Church Z has five directors on the central body of the Church Federation (including the two ministers) and three directors on the board of the Young Men's Christian Association of the city, and it is actively related to the leadership of the Community Training School for Sunday-school workers.

Adaptations

As was forecast at the outset, Church Z has not been found to present a marked case of urban adaptation in the sense that it shows many radical departures in principle from the average behavior of the church, and especially of the more prosperous church, in the city.

Its most obvious and outstanding qualities—its progressive and influential pulpit; the active social life of the parish; its amply sustained and ably managed parochial organizations; its generally excellent and well-operated plant; its very satisfactory financial management and results; its strong denominational leadership and interdenominational activity—all these impress one as the expressions of a fine tradition carried out somewhat opulently and with noteworthy good taste, rather than as marked by originality or great individuality.

The majority of the most significant recent changes as viewed by the church itself—its modernized by-laws, especially the centralizing of administrative responsibility in a Church Council representing all subsidiary interests; its enlarged provision for and policy of religious education, including the attempted unification of all aspects of work for children and youth; its highly successful mid-week social and religious service; the revision of its basic statement of faith—all seem to have occurred in response to general viewpoints and considerations acquired from current progressive religious thinking and practice. At least they reflect only remotely any modeling of the church upon its local environment.

THE REFLECTION OF A TYPICAL URBAN SITUATION

Church Z, however, reflects with considerable accuracy of detail an actual urban situation which is also typical.

It gets its relative immunity from environmental pressure by finding and removing itself to a highly homogeneous parish area, inhabited on the average by exceptionally well-to-do people, people enjoying a wide margin of resources by means of which they are able to operate an exceptionally efficient religious organization.

Even within this select area, the church deals selectively, keeping in greatest actual contact with the most desirable population, economically speaking.

Its parish quite definitely thins out in areas occupied by less well-to-do people, but is especially drawn out in the direction in which live adherents of its characteristic sort—possibly even beyond the distance of most effective service to them.

It has developed a very closely knit group of adherents whose central core, composed of people with numerous relations to their church, is notably large; while its outreach to remoter adherents is small. In other words, the church has shown great powers of assimilation with respect to its selected material.

The constituency is dominated by the family element, and the constituent families have a large quota of children. This is a clear mark of the residential portions of cities in contrast with downtown centers.

The church organizes a varied social life for its constituents and has projected the outlines of a balanced church program "from the infant in the cradle to all ages of life," but without being sure whether the measures taken to this end constitute a "real accomplishment" or what limits are set by the character of the constituency that the church serves, and particularly by the fact that this constituency is already well served by other social and educational agencies.

Summarizing from the negative viewpoint, one may say that this version of adaptation has left the church with a relatively large but generally conventional week-day program; with relatively few detached individuals in the constituency, and with no loosely related groups that are associated with the church through service rendered them but that are not yet fully assimilated; with a staff only one member of which represents a high degree of specialization; with a plant not even well suited for the more technical educational processes that the church has already undertaken; without the marks of acute environmental pressure and the effect of characteristic urban conditions.

All told, Church Z illustrates one way, and for it and many other churches a very serviceable and successful way, of fitting an institution into a certain type of urban situation—serviceable and successful, provided the right situation can be found and provided that it lasts.

PREPARATION FOR PROSPECTIVE CHANGE

An explicit acknowledgment of the church's anticipation of radically different conditions in the future is found in a sentence from the last report of the Trustees with respect to the endowment fund: "As the city changes, the church will from year to year become more of a down-town church, as the center of our residential section will eventually be farther and farther west." The report goes on to argue: "The church should continue to minister to the territory in which it is now situated for many years to come. In order that it may do this, it is necessary that our Endowment Fund be greatly increased." This argument presumes the ultimate substitution in the near vicinity of the church of a less well-to-do population than is now resident there. This prospect is entirely in line with environmental trends as revealed in the introduction of the study.

Church Z's solution of its problem of adaptation, namely, the finding of a good environment, is so genuinely successful, on the one hand, while, on the other hand, its success on present lines is so dependent upon the environment's remaining good in the present sense, that the most obvious recommendation for the future concerns means of discovering whether contrary changes are impending, and, if so, how rapidly they are coming on.

It seems, therefore, pertinent to suggest specifically that the church continuously study the changes of the next few years, first, in its environment, and, secondly, in itself, along the lines of this study.

This may seem but superficial counsel, relating merely to institutional fortunes. Even so, why is it too much to hope that a scientific grasp upon the measurable, external aspects of its problem, and their periodic reëxamination, may suggest to the church ways of marshaling and directing its more vital energies toward profounder ends?

Case II

ROSEVILLE METHODIST EPISCOPAL CHURCH, NEWARK, N. J.

The story of this church is an episode in the expansion of the metropolitan community of Greater New York. This colossal process of city building first made and prepared soil favorable for the church to grow in. Now, however, in its later stages, it has begun to strain and twist ominously at the church's roots. The church meanwhile has been busy and enterprising; alarmed at some of its newly experienced difficulties, but not clearly conscious of the larger forces moving beneath it. It has derived a hopeful and progressive spirit from the general atmosphere of forward-looking Christianity rather than from an understanding of urban trends or of those of its particular environment—like a plant drawing food from the air rather than from the earth.

The psychological timeliness of the present study lies in the fact that now at length the possibility is dawning upon the church that it may be forced to make more radical and deliberate adaptations to match the very massive processes of urban change to which it is being subjected. As yet there is nothing to record of fundamental or conspicuous response to this discovery. The church has simply grown rather more selective in its dealings with the community. The following story is therefore primarily a description and diagnosis of a transitional situation, which may perhaps be of practical help to the church as it stands, in all likelihood, not far from the parting of the ways.

History

It would take nearly 90 per cent. of the total population of Chicago to people the metropolitan area of New York outside the city proper. And Newark, the fifteenth city of the United

66

States in population, would enjoy the much greater reputation and prestige that its size and industrial and commercial position deserve but for the dwarfing proximity of the greater city.

Newark's period of most rapid growth in population was the decade preceding the Civil War. At that time it was a booming center of some 40,000 people between which and the semi-rural villages skirting the Orange and Watchung Mountains incipient suburbs were already developing. One of these bore the rather idyllic name of Roseville. The decade that saw its first cluster of neighborhood stores, its school and group of churches marked the beginnings, in 1854, of a Methodist Episcopal church in the establishment of a Sunday school situated within a short distance of the church's present site.

As Roseville Church has evolved with the community, the chief epochs in its career are clearly marked by its successive church structures. The first building of simple village type was occupied for nearly thirty years. Next, in 1886 came the present main structure of stone, reflecting growing suburban prosperity and solidity. A little more than twenty years later an unusually ample parish house was built, embodying the most acceptable Sunday-school architecture and equipment of its time. The Roseville community had by then become one of the most desirable residential sections of Newark, which was enjoying another period of very rapid growth with a population approaching 375,000.

Twenty more years of life followed for the church as a leading Christian enterprise of Newark, strong, prosperous, enviable and munificent. Meanwhile, however, virtually everything that can happen in the development of a great city had been taking place on the Jersey side of the metropolitan community. Stated in terms of the social composition of Newark, there had been a series of eruptive transformations, accompanying expansions and redistributions of population and of the functions associated with various districts of the city. Again and again race had driven out race. On the other hand, the structure of the city was becoming increasingly set, industrial districts permanently defining themselves along railways, and business along axial streets. Major thoroughfares and permanent improvements had been fixed, while parks and topographical barriers tended here and there to stay or deflect the streams of change. About these obstructions the tides of population eddied. In the general outcome the main body of the more prosperous American populations had been driven beyond the city limits of Newark and even beyond its immediate suburbs to the skirts of the "first mountain." Those remaining within the boundaries of Newark, together with the older populations of foreign origins, had been reduced to a slight fringe in the farthermost wards.

As the result of these movements, Roseville has now become scarcely more than an atoll of residential territory surrounding a business center of increasing size and, in turn, almost entirely surrounded by industry and foreign populations tributary to it. The balance of the internal character of the neighborhood has been correspondingly changed. Occupancy by stable families has given way to transiency and to numerous conflicting social tendencies. There are fewer homes; many more apartments and tenements. In the immediate past there has been very rapid drainage away of older and more substantial population to the farther suburbs. Yet there are more people than ever in the district and a certain reënforcement of desirable population is being introduced through the erection of a better class of apartment houses in limited areas. By reason of their relative newness in an acute phase these changes had impaired the church but slightly up to the date of the study. It has virtually held its own in numbers, in Sunday-school enrollment and in total constituency. On the other hand, the character of its community and of its prospects is radically altered and its future must obviously be planned along different lines of development.

I. MAJOR ASPECTS OF THE CHURCH

Among the twenty-six churches studied, Roseville Methodist Episcopal Church ranks slightly below the median in the magnitude of its service-program, measured by total annual attendance upon its organizations and stated activities. But it stands appreciably higher in variety and scope of program. In other words, its work is highly developed considering its bulk.

The distribution of emphasis between formal religious services and the other elements of the program throws the Sunday school into high relief. While all activities are strongly sustained, this is the outstanding emphasis of the church.

The following sections describe the church in the aspects formally investigated.

Members and Constituents

Twenty-four hundred and seven persons are definitely connected constituents of the Roseville Church. Of the entire constituency, 1,507, or 63 per cent., are members of adherent families (one or more adults of which are included in the enrolled constituency), while 900 are individuals whose families as such are not attached to the church. This ratio marks the church as still belonging essentially (though not in a pronounced degree) to the "family" type, in contrast with the "down-town" city church which tends to build up much more largely out of detached individuals.

AGE OF ADHERENTS

The 2,407 recorded adherents of the Roseville Church are divided by age as follows:

TABLE X—CONSTITUENTS BY AGE

	NUMBER			PER CENT. DISTRIBUTION		
AGE-GROUP	Total	Family Group	Individuals	Roseville Church	Newark	26 Churches
Total	2,407	1,507	900	100	100	100
Adults (21 and over).......	1,660	1,135	525	69	67	73
Adolescents (15-20)	333	145	188	14	11	8
Children (5-14)	406	221	185	17	22	19
Minors (age unknown)......	8	6	2	*	*	*

* Less than one-half of 1 per cent.

The three last columns of the table compare the per cent. distribution of the adherents of the Roseville Church according to age with that of the population of the city of Newark to which it is assumed the Roseville community roughly corresponds, and with that of the adherents of the twenty-six churches included in this series of studies. The comparison shows that Roseville tends to be an adolescents' church. The age that is generally supposed to be most aloof religiously has been drawn by this church more successfully than any other.

Adult constituents tend strongly to come from family groups; children to a less extent. Adolescents naturally include many self-supporting workers living away from home, and adolescence is the age that breaks away from the family. Consequently it is no surprise to find a high percentage of adolescent adherents not belonging to family groups.

MANNER AND DEGREE OF ADHERENCE

In what ways are these 2,407 adherents attached to the Roseville Church? Examining the varying ties that bind them, one finds more than two-thirds belonging exclusively to some one of the church's major divisions. They are church-members only, or Sunday-school pupils only, or members of subsidiary organizations only. Of the less than one-third that remain, much the largest group belongs to the church and to one or more subsidiaries. Five per cent. of the total constituency belongs to church, Sunday school and subsidiaries, all three, and this group constitutes a sort of core of the entire constituency.

The particular groupings of adherents, the aggregate memberships of the major groups and their overlapping memberships are shown in Chart IV.

Considering further the overlapping memberships of the several groups, approximately one-third of all church-members (Sections F and G) are found to belong to subsidiaries, and nearly one-third of all Sunday-school pupils (Sections B and G) to belong to the church.

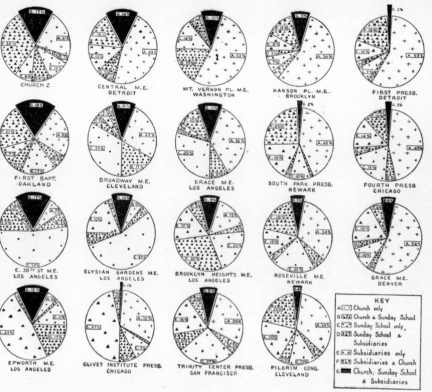

CHART IV

Composition of Constituencies of Nineteen City Churches

ADHERENTS FROM FAMILY GROUPS

Sixty-three per cent. of all members' of the Roseville church are drawn from adherent families. Adherents from this group tend to show two kinds of attachment: namely, through church-membership only, or through multi-connections with church, Sunday school and subsidiaries. These divergent tendencies are probably explained by the fact that family solidarity may work in two opposite ways. Thus a person may become a church-member, though an inactive one, merely because his family maintains a nominal allegiance to the church; or, if his family is active, he may find himself making many attachments and undertaking many responsibilities. Individual adherents tend rather to be found in Sunday school alone or in the subsidiary organizations alone. To state the case more specifically, while the church draws virtually two-thirds of its members from family groups, the Sunday school draws only one-half of its pupils from this source. But the subsidiaries also find two-thirds of their members here. It is thus only the Sunday school that reaches out beyond the church's other departments into the otherwise unattached community to win the lone individual.

The total situation may be summarized thus: Gathered around a small core of exceptionally active members are three major church constituencies, partially overlapping one another, but in very large degree composed of different individuals. Some of these individuals in turn belong to adherent family groups, while others show a merely individual attachment at one or more points. Altogether they constitute the social group identified with the Roseville Church.

PLEDGED SUPPORT AND REGULAR ATTENDANCE

Pledged financial support and regular attendance on formal services are important additional forms of participation in the life of the church group. In the Roseville Church about two-fifths of all constituents of all kinds and degrees are found to be pledged contributors (including those pledging through the Sunday school). Of church-members only, nearly two-thirds are pledged contributors. This is the best record for the eleven cases compared on this point. The church is below average, however, in the proportion of its adherents detached from families who pledge. It may have to look more largely to them in the future for financial support.

Only about one-fifth of the constituents—including 30 per cent. of full church-members—are regular attendants on formal services. These regular attendants are drawn with greatest frequency from among persons connected with the church in numerous other ways. Seven-eighths of those who have the largest number of memberships in different activities are also pledged contributors. Constituents from family groups furnish more than their quota both of pledged contributors and of regular attendants. This adds a further item to the discovery of the core of the church.

Regular attendance and pledged contribution correlate more completely than any other two factors investigated. The church has very few non-contributing attendants.

NUMBER OF CONNECTIONS

In the last paragraph the discussion passed over from a consideration of *how* constituents are related to the church to the question of how *much* they are related. In the calculation of the number of connections, the fact of pledged financial support is added to those of membership in church, Sunday school or one or more subsidiaries. Classified on this basis, the 2,407 adherents to the Roseville Church are distributed as follows.

The most typical situation is one in which an adherent is attached to the church in only one or two ways. This accounts for over three-fourths of all cases. Roseville has, however, fewer "oncers" than the average of ten other churches com-

TABLE XI—NUMBER OF ADHERENTS' CONNECTIONS WITH CHURCH

NUMBER OF CONNECTIONS	NUMBER OF ADHERENTS		
	Total	Family Group	Individual
Total	2,407	1,507	900
1	1,103	535	568
2	740	526	214
3	347	274	73
4	129	95	34
5	41	34	7
6	17	14	3
7 or more	5	5	0
Not reported	25	24	1

pared on this point, but more "twicers"; so that the per cent. age of those having more than two connections is about the average. Adherents who belong to adherent families tend to have more connections than those who do not. Adults furnish proportionately more adherents with many connections, probably because there are more organizations to which adults are eligible and because adult leadership is commonly necessary in organizations of minors.

A comparative distribution of adherents by number of connections and according to age showed that only 13 per cent. of all adherent children have more than one connection with the church, and only 43 per cent. of adherent adolescents, although two connections are more characteristic of adults than one.

MAXIMUM ATTACHMENTS

Since membership in organizations, however frequent, does not in itself guarantee regularity of attendance, and since no information was available as to the individual's attendance upon subsidiary organizations to which he belonged, a study was made of the names listed by the church (1) as regular church attendants; (2) as pupils in the Sunday school; and also (3) as having at least two other connections with the church. The result of this study was to identify the particular group of constituents that are more highly connected than any other. It consists of ninety-three persons. Judged by the sample, the much-connected person is an adult somewhat oftener than an adolescent, and is likely to be a woman. Eighteen women were found related to the Roseville Church in five or more ways. If the making of a pledged contribution is substituted for Sunday-school attendance and a count is made of adherents who attend church regularly, pledge and have three or more other connections, the list is reduced to sixty-six names. These few adherents are found whichever way the church turns.

Whether this is a normal proportion, considering the ratio between leaders and followers in all human groups, or whether it indicates a poor distribution of service and responsibility, are questions which it would be going beyond the bounds of the study to attempt to answer. It is at least debatable whether the much-connected person is not sometimes over-connected.

How the entire constituent group thus identified is organized by the church appears in detail in a succeeding section.[1]

Environment

How are the 2,407 constituents of the Roseville Church related to the urban community in which it is located, and especially to that part of the community in which most of them reside? Within a radius of one mile from the church building are the homes of probably 60,000 people, and within this area approximately 84 per cent. of the constituency lives. It is therefore fair to regard this radius as the effective environment of the church.

As already discovered, the area does not present, and has not for a considerable period, presented a consistent social evolution. Among its more outstanding characteristics are the following: (1) It is not politically unified. About two-thirds of it lies in Newark and one-third in the more distinctly suburban municipality of East Orange. (2) It includes one of

---

[1] Children under five years of age belonging to constituent families constitute a normal addition to the constituent total which should be brought into the total picture; but their number has not been ascertained. There is also a small psychological margin of people who do not adhere to the church in any stated way, but with whom the church feels some connection and for whom it assumes pastoral responsibility. Their status will be dealt with in connection with cases where they are so numerous as to constitute a problem for interpretation.

the most "American" localities in Newark, though having fewer native white than the average of East Orange. Yet 51 per cent. of the population is of foreign birth or origins and 4.5 per cent. is Negro. (3) With respect to the proportion of rented homes (seventy-two in every hundred), its rank is intermediate between Newark and East Orange. (4) The line of greatest westward expansion of the central business and industrial district of Newark is directly toward the church, and this district now penetrates to within a mile of the church. (5) The Lackawanna railroad adjacent to which the church is located creates a natural pathway for further industrial expansion from the direction of the city. (6) Most of the residential area left between the church and the central district is in the zone of acute deterioration and is occupied by Italians and Negroes. (7) In the three other directions considerable areas remain which are zoned for residential use but which are, in Newark, open to apartment- and tenement-house construction. (8) A belt of industries separates the church's immediate vicinity from the more carefully restricted residential zone in East Orange.

The Roseville Church is thus increasingly being hemmed in. It is still fortunate in that the intricate and changing structure of the community leaves it, for the present, three considerable areas (in three directions and all within one-half mile of the church) which are essentially residential and are not penetrated by foreigners to any great degree. The largest of these lies to the northeast, and beyond it extends a very recently developed region of single- and double-family houses primarily suited to the contiguous industrial populations. The creation of the new and the decay of the old thus occur side by side. Again, the portion of the area that lies nearest to the Roseville Church has a certain independence of Newark because it affords excellent means of commutation to New York City. The whole situation is thus highly complex. In the large it exhibits the familiar process of encroachment of commercial and industrial developments, with their tributary foreign population, upon a residential area once predominantly American. Beyond this it is a thoroughly typical urban situation in that all sorts, degrees and stages of development are mingled within a small area making the total rate of social change acute.

Relationship of Constituency to Environment

Eighty-four per cent. of all the church's constituents live within a mile of the church building. Only 6 per cent. live farther than two miles. In other words, the Roseville Church is closely related to Roseville. Of the cases studied, only the small churches included in the City Parish, Los Angeles, have more compact parishes.

There is no significant difference between constituents from family groups and detached individuals with respect to distance of residence.

DIRECTION

The distribution of constituents as to direction corresponds with great accuracy to the social pattern of the community as described in the discussion of its structure and functional areas. The parish is cut off to the southeast by the expansion of the central business and industrial area in this direction; and to the northwest by the corridor of industry stretching along the East Orange line—probably also by the psychological factor that East Orange "feels" like a separate community in spite of its proximity.

The parish is correspondingly elongated from northeast to southwest; but three members live to the northeast of the church to every one living to the southwest of it. This lack of balance reflects the larger area and more desirable residential character of the territory lying in the former direction; also the fact that this territory has been less unfavorably affected by social changes.

In general, though closely identified with the Roseville community, the church thus draws upon it in a highly selective manner. It shows marked directional affinities and avoidances.

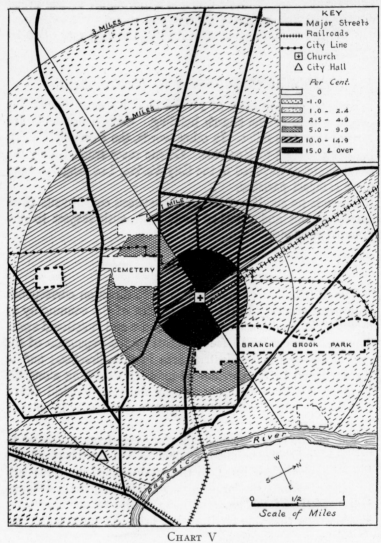

KEY
Major Streets
Railroads
City Line
Church
City Hall

Per Cent.
0
-1.0
1.0 - 2.4
2.5 - 4.9
5.0 - 9.9
10.0 - 14.9
15.0 & over

3 MILES
2 MILES
1 MILE

CEMETERY

BRANCH BROOK PARK

River

Passaic

W N
S E

0   1/2
Scale of Miles

CHART V
Parish of Roseville Methodist Episcopal Church, Newark

Of course this means that the church appeals to certain classes or types of people more than to others.

VARIATIONS IN DIRECTIONAL DISTRIBUTION

There is considerable variation with respect to directional distribution among elements of the church's constituency.

Constituents of two classes, *viz.* (1) those belonging to adherent family groups and (2) church-members, are less numerous, relatively, in the industrial and foreign section to the southeast, but more numerous over the East Orange line.

Non-members as a group—all ages being considered—are drawn most heavily from the area to the northeast which is especially desirable from the commuting and residential standpoint.

The eighty-eight officers are drawn with very disproportionate frequency from the direction of East Orange. This seems to imply that the chief brains and leadership of the church (together with a disproportionate fraction of family adherents) tend to be found in a different direction from that in which the bulk of the constituency lives.

Curiously, regular attendants turn out to be drawn disproportionately from the southwest which is in general an older section and one on a humbler economic level than those either of the northeast or of the northwest.

Considering directional distribution in terms of age-groups, one finds that of adults corresponding most closely to the total distribution of constituents (of whom they make up much the largest proportion). Adolescents and children are both drawn disproportionately from the direction in which non-members live and from the generally avoided section to the southeast. This is, of course, simply another way of saying that these two age-groups constitute a larger proportion of non-member constituents. It is exceedingly striking, however, to find only 11 per cent. of children coming from the direction of East Orange in which officers so strongly tend to be found. This result is probably natural in view of the difficulty that children traveling alone would find in crossing the industrial barrier at the East

Orange line, and probably also in view of the proximity of excellent Sunday schools in East Orange itself.

DISTANCE AS AFFECTING NUMBER OF CHURCH CONNECTIONS

For the total constituency and for each age-group, distance of residence beyond the first mile definitely reduces closeness of attachment to the church as measured by the average number of the constituents' connections with it.   Such a result, though not exhibited by the twenty-six churches as a group, might naturally have been expected in one which was so recently a neighborhood church.   The degree to which distance reduces closeness of attachment is summarized in Table XII which shows the per cent. of adults, adolescents and children respectively who have more than two connections with the church.

TABLE XII—PER CENT. OF ADHERENTS LIVING AT SPECI-
    FIED DISTANCES FROM THE CHURCH WHO HAVE
    MORE THAN TWO CONNECTIONS WITH IT

DISTANCE	PER CENT. OF ADHERENTS			
	Total	Adult	Adolescent	Child
Total	23	30	11	2
Less than ½ mile.....................	17	31	12	2
½ to 1 mile.........................	22	33	17	4
1 to 2 miles.........................	20	27	6	0
2 to 3 miles.........................	16	20	0	0
3 to 4 miles.,.......................	8	9	0	0
4 to 5 miles.........................	0	0	0	0

For all classes the second half-mile zone shows more many-connected adherents than the first.   It does not carry one beyond walking distance and in this instance constitutes no handicap to closeness of connection.

No children with more than two connections live beyond the first mile, and distance has highly deterrent influence upon the closeness of the connection of adolescents also.   For adults, however, the reduction in the number of connections as distance increases is more gradual.

The significance of this phenomenon would seem to be that the Roseville Church is not able to furnish the average advantages of the church to the constituents that it draws from beyond a mile radius. For the majority of them, the availability of transportation facilities does not fully make up for loss of proximity. The distant adherent gets less out of his church than the nearer one.

SUMMARY

It is clear that the relation of the church to its environment is close, vital and probably more profound than the church recognizes in its conscious planning. As a social group the church is definitely molded on the structure of the community. It maintains no effective occupancy of territory more than a mile from Roseville, and when it attempts to serve at a greater distance, it generally fails to extend its full values to its members. On the other hand, its marked avoidances of certain territory within the distance-limits of its intensive parish show that at present it does not know how to serve many of the elements resident in Roseville itself. Its greatest catholicity of adaptation is with childhood and youth. From these age-groups it can draw adherents from areas where it cannot get adults. This is the most heartening aspect of the showing as related to future prospects.

II. AGENCIES, RESOURCES AND METHODS

Organizations and Stated Activities

On the basis of average attendance as counted or thoughtfully reported by the church staff and the officers of the various organizations, and the number of weeks per year that each activity is in operation, an estimated aggregate annual attendance on regular activities of 71,304 is reached.[2] No method was discovered of making a comparable estimate of attendance upon the numerous occasional and strictly seasonal activities.

The estimated attendance on the regular program is divided as in Table XIII.

---

[2] For definition of regular activities, see p. 449.

TABLE XIII—ESTIMATED ANNUAL ATTENDANCE ON SPECI-
FIED OCCASIONS AT ROSEVILLE M. E. CHURCH AND
AT 26 CHURCHES

	ATTENDANCE			
	ROSEVILLE CHURCH		26 CHURCHES	
			Approx. Median	*Range of Variation*
OCCASION	*Number*	*Per Cent.*	*Per Cent.*	*Per Cent.*
Total *	71,304	100		
Formal religious services (Sunday and week day)..........	34,840	49	51	15–75
Sunday school..................	20,180	28	24	9–38
All other stated activities......	16,284 †	23	22	9–51

* Sunday, 83 per cent.; week day, 17 per cent.
† Includes meetings of church officers and committees.

The ratio between Sunday and week-day activities indicates
that the church has not gone very far toward becoming a
"seven-day-a-week" church in the radical sense.

Of the twenty-six churches studied, only four report a
higher proportion of the year's attendance as furnished by the
Sunday school. This is in part a reflection of the unusual fact
that the Roseville Sunday school has three sessions weekly.
It also harmonizes with the fact of the large adolescent constituency, though it would be hazardous to guess which is
cause and which effect.

The estimated attendance of 15,854 upon activities other
than church services and the Sunday school is divided between
age- and sex-groups as shown in Table XIV.

TABLE XIV—ESTIMATED ANNUAL ATTENDANCE ON SUB-
SIDIARY ORGANIZATIONS AND STATED ACTIVITIES

ORGANIZATIONS		ATTENDANCE	
No.	*Type*	*Number*	*Per Cent.*
12	Total	15,854	100
1	Mixed adults	300	2
1	Adult men	1,800	11
4	Adult women	2,750	17
2	Mixed young people *....................	3,120	20
0	Young men	0	0
0	Young women...........................	0	0
2	Mixed boys and girls....................	3,984	25
1	Boys	1,040	7
1	Girls	2,860	18
0	Mixed children	0	0

* Between 15 and 23 years of age.

Summarizing the attendance by sex, the distribution is as follows:

	Per Cent.
Mixed of both sexes............................	47
Men and boys...................................	18
Women and girls................................	35

The preponderance in the above showing of activities of the two sexes meeting together is largely due to the varied young people's organizations and the junior church. Roseville is not characterized by a pronounced differentiation of subsidiary program according to age- and sex-groups as many of the cases studied are.

NOTEWORTHY CHARACTERISTICS OF SUBSIDIARY ORGANIZATIONS

Formal worship and religious education have separate discussion in later paragraphs. Of other organizations, the most exceptional features are perhaps the following:

(1) Each of the traditional missionary organizations for women has a separately officered evening division for business women who cannot attend meetings during the day.

(2) A large mothers' club, meeting semi-monthly, is regarded as the "threshold of the church" and helps to assimilate women who have little natural contact with the social group that constitutes the core of the church.

(3) The traditional Methodist organization of young people in the Epworth League has been modified in favor of a Sunday night forum and social and a corresponding weekly young people's gathering called "The Racqueteers."

(4) As a modification of the traditional prayer meeting, a series of short courses covering teacher-training, mission-study and leadership are held in connection with devotional addresses given on Tuesday nights.

(5) There are strongly developed organizations of Boy and Girl Scouts, including three troops of the latter organization.

A rather striking but deliberate omission, considering the size and type of the church, is that of a regular choir.

The announcements of the week of November first, 1925, list sixteen services and subsidiary meetings of parish organizations. This is fairly representative of church life during the active season.

The study of the printed church calendars for a year reveals the following round of church activity:

There are a Vacation Bible School and extensive camping activities during the summer.

The pulpit is supplied with outside preaching during July and August. On the second Sunday in September the pastor is back in his place. The church council is reorganized; Sunday-school officers are installed and the Sunday-school training school begins.

Throughout the active months of the year a succession of denominational and Protestant interests outside of the local parish are advocated, expressive of the extensive participation of the Roseville Church in general religious activity.

During the year studied, about every third Sunday of the winter months the evening service had the ostensible character of a forum and was addressed by an outside speaker.

The church year culminates after Holy Week and Easter services, with the annual meetings of church and Sunday school.

How few of the total constituency are engaged in more than one or two church activities in spite of their large number and variety, and how very few indeed enjoy the privilege and bear the burdens of numerous and intimate connections, has already been discovered. The program as a whole, in the largest sense, may belong to the constituency as a whole, but the average of individual participation is pretty low.

Staff

The paid staff of the Roseville Church consists of the minister, a minister of education, a deaconess, a secretary and a parish visitor. A part-time clerical assistant is also employed for the minister of education.

A summary of the preparation, experience, tenure and remuneration of all members of the staff is given in Table XV.

TABLE XV—ANALYSIS OF PAID STAFF

	Pastor Male	Minister of Religious Education Male	Deaconess Female	Parish Visitor Female	Secretary Female
Sex	Male	Male	Female	Female	Female
Degree of education					
Academic	College	College	High school	High school	High school
Professional or special	Theological Postgraduate	Theological	Religious training Drew (1yr.)	...	Secretarial course
Years of employment					
Prior to this position					
Secular work	...	7	...	6	8
Religious work	6	5	...	1	...
In this position	5	1	15	2	13
Present salary					
Cash	$4,800	$3,000	$360	$720	$1,440
Perquisites					
Nature	Parsonage	...	Christmas and vacation $100 Living $400	...	...
Value	$700	...		...	...
Entitled to ecclesiastical pension	Yes	Yes	Yes	...	No
Length of vacation	6 weeks	1 month	1 month	1 month	1 month

WORK OF STAFF

In order to show the amount and distribution of total work of the staff, individual records were kept by each member for the week of November 25, 1925.

As shown by these records, administrative and pastoral work take up much more of the total time of the staff than all other kinds of work, and much more than any other one kind.

The kinds of duty which tend to fall to workers in the different positions in the staff are clearly marked in the data. The minister of religious education, deaconess and secretary all spend more time in administrative than in any other aspect of work. The pastor's primary emphasis, on the other hand, is pastoral work, which also naturally takes most of the time of the parish visitor. The pastor's secondary emphasis is upon administrative work, followed by that upon the preparation of sermons and conduct of public ministries. The secondary emphasis of the secretary is naturally upon clerical work.

The deaconess' work is almost equally divided between pastoral and administrative functions. She is the unofficial leader of types of women's work that require special executive attention and has particular pastoral responsibility for the sick.

All women workers spend considerable time attending meetings for which they are not directly responsible, a fact which appreciably reduces the time in which they are available for directly productive work. All members of the staff, during the week studied, worked from two to three hours longer than the prevailing business or office day in Newark, and the two ministers worked overtime every day without exception. The pastor was on duty all seven evenings of the week.

It is not known just how far the week recorded was representative, but it undoubtedly shows the actual tendencies of the work-habits and distribution of time of the Roseville staff.

In the internal practice of the Roseville Church, an extra-disciplinary agency, namely, the Church Council, composed of representatives of all major departments and organizations, tends to become the functioning executive body. A system of committees reporting to this council has been effectively developed and the major bulk of church business is conducted through them.   The pastor is not a presiding officer of the council; neither does he habitually meet with officers having charge of property and finances.   The situation signifies that the church has evolved its own machinery and methods of administration somewhat apart from the ecclesiastical scheme.

Within the paid staff weekly conferences are held which attend to many administrative issues and are characterized by intimate discussion of many detailed problems.   Work, by mutual agreement, is assigned to the person best qualified to undertake it, the pastor being included in the results of this staff procedure.   Beyond this, the actual method of internal administration consists of informal conferences between the pastor and members of the staff.   The pastor takes a hand in any matter as occasion demands.   In the last analysis, he is responsible for recommending his associates for dismissal or employment, and for intervention in case of unsatisfactory work; but he makes few direct assignments except to the secretary as his immediate clerical assistant.   The staff is admirably and habitually coöperative.

RELATIONS OF STAFF TO SUBSIDIARY ORGANIZATIONS

A crucial question in any highly organized church is the degree to which the leadership of organizations and activities, which traditionally lie within lay responsibility, is taken over by the paid staff.

In the Roseville Church, only the deaconess is a personal leader of boy- and girl-groups, and unofficially of certain women's organizations.   The other paid women-workers are expected to be members and occasionally hold office in women's organizations, but are not charged with extensive official responsibility.   The total number of social calls and visits of mercy reported by members of subsidiary organizations is about 2,500 per year.   This would seem to indicate that the supply of lay talent in the Roseville Church is still adequate for the range and variety of work developed, and that its technical requirements are not yet beyond the capacity of the average church member.

Plant and Equipment

The site of the church measures approximately 160 x 120 feet. The plant consists of church with attached parsonage (the latter valued at $8,000) and detached Sunday-school building. The buildings are of durable and dignified material and have been kept in excellent condition. Their placement on the site was fixed in the more suburban days of the neighborhood. They are set moderately back from the street, the line of which is planted with shrubbery, and thus the location has acquired a spacious effect as the city has grown up tighter about it. Both church and Sunday-school buildings are of ample size and suitable furnishing. Their lack of physical connection, however, makes it inconvenient to use them in conjunction.

Of the twenty-five church plants studied, that of Roseville Church ranks eighteenth, scoring 554 on the Interchurch thousand-point scale.[3] The median for the twenty-five churches is about 600.

TABLE XVI—SUMMARY OF SCORE OF PLANT

ITEM	STANDARD SCORE	POINTS SCORED		RANK IN 25 CASES
		Number	Per Cent.	
Total	1,000	554	55	18
Site	130	85	65	19
Building or buildings.........	150	107	71	18
Service systems...............	160	66	41	21
Church rooms................	170	111	65	21
Religious school rooms........	200	125	63	9
Community service rooms.....	190	60	32	17

The most radical deficiencies of the Roseville Church, as shown by the table, are in its lack of modern service systems and community service rooms, while the general character, quality and condition of its property are still above the average.

Nine-tenths of the shortcomings of the plant are due to the laxer standards and architectural deficiencies of the periods in which the buildings were erected. They simply were never intended for many of the uses to which it is desired to put them, and their lack of adaptability happens to be rather extreme.

---

[3] For explanation, see p. 451.

The entire property has a reported valuation of $150,000, but its actual replacement value is much greater.

Finances

RECEIPTS

The annual receipts for the current local operation of the Roseville Church are reported at about $26,000, of which a very small proportion (about $700) consists of subscriptions for permanent endowment. Nearly three-fourths of the total (more than $19,000) comes from weekly pledges, and only 13 per cent. from loose collections taken at public services. There is a very small endowment income. In other words, the church has few resources except the out-and-out contribution week by week by a minority of its constituency.[4] All told, income averages about $11.00 per constituent annually. The church studied as Case I receives nearly three times as much relatively. Roseville's expenditures have to be on a correspondingly moderate scale.

A sum of more than $17,000, all told, is raised for benevolences, nearly one-fifth of which comes from women's organizations.

EXPENDITURES

Expenditures for current operation, of which about 40 per cent. goes for the salaries of the paid religious staff, are summarized in Table XVII.

TABLE XVII—FINANCIAL EXPENDITURES OF THE CHURCH

Item	Amount	Per Cent.
Grand Total	$26,410	
Total Current Account	25,810	100
Salaries	10,560	41
General administrative expenses	1,813	7
Music	2,653	10
General operation and upkeep of property	6,808	27
Expenses of departments specially budgeted—church school	1,200	5
Publicity	1,048	4
Ecclesiastical connections	884	3
Miscellaneous	884	3
Investment Account Building and Loan investment	600	

[4] The rental value of the parsonage is not considered in the above financial picture.

The distribution of expenditures shown in the table reveals no striking departures from the average. Benevolent expenditures are almost entirely for parochial and denominational objects. The amount charged to parochial benevolence, $1,676, was actually used for the improvement of the church property, thus making its larger community uses possible. Undenominational benevolences cover eleven objects, of which the Anti-Saloon League and the County Council of Religious Education are the major ones. A rather broad contact with local social institutions is maintained by the rotation from year to year of non-denominational objects of benevolence. This results in giving rather small amounts to a large number of causes.

The approximate total expenditures [5] of the church for its last fiscal year were:

	Amount	Per Cent.
Total	$43,730	100
Current expenses	26,410	60
Benevolences	17,320	40

Public Services and Worship

Although, measured by total attendance upon all organizations and activities, public services constitute about one-half of the total stated program of the Roseville Church, only a small minority of the total constituency, as has already been noted, are actually regular attendants at services.

The morning service averages about 300 worshipers. On the Sunday covered by the study, about ten women were present for every six men; and a total of about sixty children under twelve years. Some impressions of the service and its setting follow.

The auditorium is ample and dignified, with decorations and appointments in good taste, though not of special ecclesiastical merit. The ushering is courteous and efficient. The mood of the congregation as it gathers strikes a happy medium between reverence and social cordiality. The music, rendered by the congregation under the leadership of a precentor and

[5] In addition to the total given, numerous subsidiary organizations raised and expended, but did not account for, small sums for their own operations.

accompanied by organ, violin and bass viol, seems not quite on a par with the service as a whole. Ritual elements include the Apostles' Creed, psalter and Gloria. Verbal announcement from the pulpit supplements the printed bulletin. The Junior Department of the Sunday school shares the first twenty minutes of the service, then passes out to its own "children's church." On the Sunday of the survey communion was served. A brief meditation is substituted for the sermon. The communicants go forward to the altar on either side of the church in alternating groups of about twenty. The service is rendered acceptably and sincerely according to Methodist form and naturally produces impressions corresponding to the taste and antecedents of the worshipers. While not strikingly a unity, the service as a whole is harmonious and consistent and reaches a definite climax.

The composition of the audience at the evening service is 83 per cent. adult, the remainder consisting of adolescents and a handful of children. Women and girls comprise nearly three-fourths of it. The tone of the service is not essentially different from that of the morning.

Though there is active greeting of strangers at the door, neither service falls into a well-marked social mood at the close. Visiting in the pews and aisles is not prolonged.

A study of the weekly bulletin for a year indicates that the preaching of the Roseville pulpit is about evenly divided between religious themes approached doctrinally and devotionally and practical ethical discussions in which the value of the church to society and the special needs of the youth of our day seem to have rather marked place. The announced topics have a popular ring, but are not sensational. Little place is given in the pulpit to the special advocacy of causes either denominational or public, but the two inside pages of the weekly bulletin carry news stories of Methodist work, especially in the realm of missions. The bulletins reveal that there were nine addresses in the year by outside speakers, and ten marking religious or national anniversaries, while communion was celebrated six times.

Religious Education

The Roseville Church stands near the top rank of the cases studied with respect to the proportion of Sunday-school attendance relative to total attendance on all stated activities. No church of the group has more clearly defined or given broader practical scope to the idea of religious education. The consideration of this topic involves, accordingly, more than the Sunday school.

The entire interests of children and youth are conceived as being embraced in the young people's department of the church, which desires to occupy an educational point of view toward the problem of youth in all its aspects. The director of this department is called Minister of Education, and under this broad concept a successful integration of the several phases of work for youth is actually in operation.

Three separate sessions of the Sunday school are held each Sunday apart from the inspirational session of the Men's Brotherhood. The time schedule is as follows:

Time	Department	Length of Session
9.45 A.M.	Junior and Junior High School	2 hours
10.30 A.M.	Beginners and Primary	1 hour
2.30 P.M.	"Teen-age" Young People and Adult	1¼ hours

Following an instruction period, the Junior group shares the worship of the morning service for twenty minutes, then passes into a separate room for a "memory period" and for its own fully organized morning worship. The children's church is completely officered and carries out the major procedure of an adult church. In their departments, worship is carefully developed by the committees of high-school and young people's groups, and there is a thoughtfully prepared course in worship for juniors. All told, a very complete development of the devotional and liturgical side of religious culture is provided.

Each department of the Sunday school has a week-day program of expressional and social activities. This is most adequately carried out by the young people's group and by the

Junior group through strong Scout organizations. The difficulty of formally assimilating the Scout program to the church's general scheme of religious education was noted in a recent annual report of the Religious Education Committee. Each Sunday-school department has also a highly organized series of projects in social service, partly concerned with denominational benevolences but including also numerous forms of assistance to the church itself and still more to individuals and agencies of the community.[6]

No church studied has so fully integrated service-activities of this sort with the concept and practice of religious education, nor so definitely unified them under official supervision. The church's system of training teachers and leaders has been broadened and deepened to match the enlarged conception and program of religious education. Three concurrent courses in leadership are carried on weekly for eight months of the year.

SIZE AND COMPOSITION OF THE SUNDAY SCHOOL

Counting a Cradle Roll of 130 and a Home Department of eighty-five, the Roseville Sunday school enrolls about 900. The attending departments at the date of the study reported 695 pupils, with an average pupil attendance of 387, or 56 per cent. Enrollment by departments is shown in Table XVIII.

TABLE XVIII—SUMMARY OF SUNDAY-SCHOOL STATISTICS

DEPARTMENT	PUPILS		TEACHERS	
	Age	Enrollment	Male	Female
Total		910	17	60
Cradle Roll		130	...	...
Beginners	4–5	89	0	6
Primary	6–8	100	0	20
Junior	9–11	166	4	20
Junior high school...........	12–14 }			
"Teen-age"		122	6	8
High school.................	15–17 }			
Young people	18–28	152	5	5
Adult	Over 28	66	2	1
Home Department		85	...	...

6 For further detail, see p. 97.

With fifteen officers, in addition to the 910 pupils and seventy-seven teachers, the grand total of Sunday-school enrollment comes to 1,002. Pupils in the attending departments number 695, and the average attendance is 56 per cent. of the enrollment. The approximate age-distribution in the attending departments is as follows:

	Number	Per Cent.
Children	416	60
Adolescents	213	31
Adults	66	9

Each department possessed its own assembly-room and departmental superintendent. Twenty-three individual classrooms are in use, and forty-eight of the seventy-seven classes are seated at tables or desks during the class period. Up to the "teen-age" department International closely graded lessons are used. Above this point numerous elective courses are chosen from a long list offered. Among texts found in use in the high-school and young people's classes were Fosdick's "Twelve Tests of Character" and "Manhood of the Master" and Slattery's "Highways to Leadership." Two of the adult classes had returned to the use of the International lessons. One was following topical studies with the Bible as the only text.

Rather an ample use is made of printed material. The Sunday school issues a monthly mimeographed periodical and presents an extensive annual report in print.

The Sunday-school finances total about $3,000 per year, of which about $1,000 is spent for supplies and incidentals, $1,500 for benevolences and the rest for departmental activities. The finances are completely assimilated with those of the church and figure in the total receipts and expenditures reported.

The ultimate control of the Sunday school and virtual responsibility for the entire young people's program is vested in a Committee of Religious Education, which meets monthly during ten months of the year and has actively functioning sub-committees.

All told, the Roseville Church presents a well-balanced and

elaborate program of religious education, including not a few original and noteworthy features. The church plant, though not very suitable for this purpose, is successfully utilized by the device of holding sessions at different hours. The plan of integrating all phases of youth's interests in a single program is working with considerable smoothness. The development of lay leadership is making good progress. There is competent professional leadership and an adequate basis of organization backed by the intelligent sympathy and confidence of the church.

Growth and Conservation

During the twelve months previous to the survey (November, 1925) the Roseville Church received 141 new members and lost 156.

Nearly as many new members were received by transfer from other churches as on confession of faith. Eighty-eight of the 141 received had been resident in the community for a year or more, and fifty-three for less than a year. This reflects the considerable mobility of the neighborhood, but indicates, at the same time, that the Roseville area is being reënforced by new populations which the church is in position to assimilate.

Of the eighty-eight new members resident in the community for a year or more, fifty-three had been brought into some previous relation to the church. Thirty-three of these were already in the Sunday school and twenty-five of them had been probationary church-members. Seventeen others who were members of churches elsewhere had been brought into established contacts with the Roseville Church, through attendance or the Sunday school, before they came into formal membership-connection.

It is evidence of moderate evangelizing energy that during the year the church should have won thirty-five persons already established in the community but not previously related to it in any way. Many of these came through friends or through marriage into church families, and a few through contacts originating in bereavement or other crises.

In addition, to have found out and assimilated thirty-five newcomers holding church letters, and to have won eighteen other newcomers for allegiance to the church, is strong evidence of the active values of the church in helping strangers to get adjusted to new social relationships as well as of evangelizing energy.

Sixty per cent. of accessions from previous church-memberships were Methodist, while 40 per cent. came from eight other denominations. This number included thirteen Presbyterians. Most of them were former members of the Presbyterian church located to the southeast of Roseville, whose neighborhood had been overridden by a Negro population and whose church property was sold to Negroes.

The phenomenon of gaining new members thus throws important light upon movements of population within the city, as well as testifying to the catholicity of the Roseville Church.

The phenomenon of loss of membership is equally significant. The 156 members lost during the year were divided as follows:

```
Died .............................................   28
Transferred to other churches.......................   97
Removed from rolls..................................   31
```

The total losses of the year slightly exceeded the gains. This reflects a fairly heavy turnover of members, and points to one of the basic problems confronting the church: namely, whether in this substitution of new members for old there shall be sufficiently complete assimilation of new material so that the work of the church may proceed unimpaired, whether the newcomers bring as good financial support as was given by those lost, and whether or not the general atmosphere and tradition of the church shall be unfavorably modified.

Measurable Relations of Church and Community

As already noted, the social service work of the church is organized and programized in detail as part of the process of religious education. It is also accounted for in a unique printed summary of the hundreds of organizational "good turns" performed by the various branches of the church during the year.

This very elaborate and impressive record may be summarized as follows: In addition to regular church benevolence already reported in the section on finance, there have been contributions toward the financial support of six agencies of the community by subsidiary organizations of the church.

Forty-four church members have served on the administrative boards or as active volunteer or paid workers in eighteen out of the fifty-one agencies participating in the Newark Community Chest. This measures the very wide contact of the church through its laity with the constructive forces of the community.

The church has official delegates in two interdenominational religious agencies.

Practical coöperation was recorded between Sunday-school departments or subsidiary organizations of the church and fifteen social agencies, thirteen of which were non-denominational. The most frequent forms of coöperation were providing holiday gifts, contributions of clothing and of institutional supplies and furnishings, the giving of entertainments and the conduct of religious services for institutions. There was a definite alliance with the local branch of the Public Library in its extension work; and agencies like the Church Federation and the Young Men's Christian Association, which attempt corresponding extension services in various districts of the city, used the church as a base of operations.

The interests of five community agencies other than denominational have been advocated in the printed calendar of the church during the year.

All this is in addition to numerous helpful services undertaken by the church for individuals within its own constituency. It registers a deliberate and significant projection of the church into the community beyond the widest circle with which the church itself is directly related.

Adaptation

It must now be asked more definitely how its changing environment has affected the Roseville Church, what its directions of adaptation have been, what specific changes have occurred, and what, if any, re-definitions of objective and purpose have accompanied its external adaptations.

RECOGNIZED PROBLEMS

The current problems of the Roseville Church, which it believes to arise out of changes in the community, were formulated by the minister at the time of the survey as follows:

"Our neighborhood is rapidly changing and the swiftness of the change is steadily accelerating. There is the constant departure of individuals of financial and personal strength. This weakens the church's financial resource and personal leadership. In some of the activities, the annual turnover of leadership is as high as 75 per cent. The very folks the church has given many years to training depart when they are needed, apparently, to the greatest extent. In six years' pastorate, out of the 932 accessions, 928 dismissals took place.

"There is also the resultant change in the business interests of the community. The fine old businesses on Roseville Avenue are being transformed into business and professional homes or are transiently occupied. The number of apartment houses is rapidly increasing; numbers of new stores of the one-story variety are being built. The Italian population is on the increase to a marked extent; the Jewish element is coming in, but not so rapidly; while the Catholic element is dominant in the community. In spite of the rapid changes and the acute problems, our workers are alert to the changing conditions and are honestly striving to keep abreast the changing currents. We have some anxiety as to the future financial support of the church, and institutional endowment does not seem possible to attain at the present time in amount sufficient to relieve the situation. While the plant is a fine one, there are many particulars in which it is not adapted to the work that we wish we could undertake.

"The denomination does not regard the changes that we are experiencing with a sufficient sense of their acuteness to come to our rescue with their already over-burdened budgets. We are left to ourselves to work out our own destiny. The scope of our work is so large and our resources so inadequate that we often have to look for community response and be guided by that in directing our emphasis. We want to keep our church an educational institution with an appropriate program. With regret we have not been able to make certain advances which manifestly ought to have been developed."

Behind the attitude of the church, as thus expressed, one sees with a fair degree of clearness the directions that its adaptive impulses have taken. These may be stated as follows:

DIRECTIONS OF ADAPTATION

The church has developed the skeleton of an all-around program of church life and activity for its inner constituency. This life it desires to share with any and all who can become virtually assimilated to the basic common ideals of the group. This development of a varied program has been coincident with the decline of single-family homes in the Roseville community, the passing of its roomier suburban conditions and the decline of its economic and cultural standards. What is probably indicated is the subconscious sense on the part of the church that its constituency has now come into a more intensive version of the urban mode of life, one in which individual families cannot provide so complete and satisfactory a range of cultural and recreational experiences for their members as they formerly did.

In the church's week-day program (which, comparatively speaking, is an outline rather than a fully developed scheme) the social and expressional activities of the constituency and their directed social service are assimilated to worship and instruction as aspects of the religious life. In other words, there is a conscious attempt to unify the broadened and elaborated version of Christianity that has been adopted.

These opportunities, however, are primarily adapted to the church's own constituency. That is to say, in order to be served by the Roseville Church, a population has to be essentially assimilated to it. The church has no frequent and systematic series of occasions which draw "outsiders" in large numbers. This is in contrast with the broad provision which more radically socialized churches make for the use of the plant by groups seeking constructive self-expression, even though they may be of other faiths and have no special sympathy for the church as a religious agency.

The geographical analysis of the parish shows its definite avoidance of certain areas, the characteristics of whose people are not in general harmony with those of the church.

While newcomers to the community, irrespective of denomination, are assimilated with considerable rapidity if they are Protestant, the church thus shows a selective and limited approach to the community as a whole.

These are somewhat formal statements of the most common of experiences: namely, that when a church develops an active group-life it must, on the whole, draw like-minded people. It cannot do much for those who are not relatively like-minded, except as it manages to win secondary constituencies, who are themselves like-minded, and whom it practically segregates in separate sets of services and activities.

ADAPTIVE CHANGES

In effecting this significant but limited degree of adaptation, the church has made rather moderate changes in the following lines:

(1) *Organization and Staff:* The denominational ecclesiastical system has received a local adaptation and more paid workers have been employed.

(2) *Plant:* A willingness has been shown to adapt and use the church plant for the new aspects of the program, but its actual modifications have been small and inexpensive. Battleship linoleum has taken the place of carpets in the chapel, and basket-ball goes on in rooms intended for sociability and prayer meetings.

(3) *Finances:* Money has been forthcoming for these limited increases in staff and plant. It is significant of the church's tentative attitude toward its more novel activities that the expense of equipment for community work has been, prop-

erly enough, viewed as a phase of benevolence instead of as an ordinary current church expenditure, and has been so charged in the budget.

(4) *Program and activities:* In addition to the fairly complete social and recreational program for age-groups organized in the church school, the following items have already been noted as showing adaptation to specific urban situations: There are missionary organizations of business women meeting in the evening; there is a mothers' club consisting primarily of women who do not come fully within the social and cultural tradition of the church and who are felt to stand somewhat outside the central group; there are a Daily Vacation Bible School and camp activities reaching beyond the church's fully assimilated constituency.

RE-DEFINITION OF OBJECTIVES

These additions and elaborations are not so extensive as to compel any formal restatement by the church of its reason for being or of the major objectives of its work. Nothing in its older formulations is particularly challenged. The pulpit and church-school platforms furnish many progressive restatements of Christian ideals and duty, but these are too occasional and too individual to be cited as authoritative evidence of any re-definition of the essential purpose of the church, though it has doubtless moved with the general movement of liberal Christian thinking.

One may find, however, some suggestions of the re-definition of objectives in statements that attempt to set forth the enlarged conception of religious education. Thus the Charge to the Church-School Faculty, incorporated in the service of installation and dedication at the opening of the new Church-School year in September, 1924, states: "The Church School exists that those who are members thereof may have a progressive experience in Christian living through their active participation in Worship, Instruction, Service and Recreation, and that it may be a center of influence for the stimulation of the higher life of the Community."

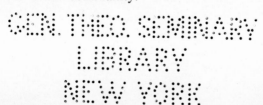

The major elements of this statement may be defined as follows: Active participation is indicated as the chief means of
grace.   Wide ranges of activities and many-sided aspects of
life are comprehended within the field of organized participation.   All this is undertaken with conscious regard to the
community as the ultimate object of service.

These ideas, if not extremely novel, are at least highly significant as indicating the lines along which the church is now
moving in its basic thinking.

SUCCESS OF ADAPTATIONS

The adaptations just catalogued are not so radical nor so
extensive as to dominate the fortunes of the church.   Their
specific effects cannot therefore be segregated from the results
of the total institutional process.   Though it is believed that
they have helped the church, it is probably unfair to assert
that they are solely or distinctly responsible for any particular
aspect of its success or failure.

The most that can be asserted is something like the following:

Whether because of or in spite of these emphases and policies, the old constituency of the church is not being fully held,
though the losses are not extreme in view of the overlaying of
the old community by such a complex of new elements, and
the magnitude of the shift of population.   Loyalty, however,
continues to hold a good many distant families who are probably not now in a position to get full value out of their church
relationships.   Many removals from the community are so
recent that the ultimate readjustments of those concerned have
not been reached.   It is at least uncertain whether the church
can keep as much of its old constituency as it has done up to
now.

On the other hand, shifts of population are bringing new
constituents into the community and the assimilating energy
of the church has been able to make its gains just about offset
its losses numerically.

The former resources of finances and leadership are so far

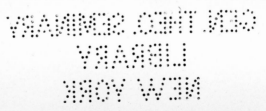

being fairly well held, but new resources are probably not being gained proportionately to the number of new people.

Broader ministries to the church's inner constituency have been developed but not appreciably broader ones to the community at large. There is no extensive provision for serving the community on its own terms.[7]

The religious spirit of the constituency and the degree of lay participation in the church's activities have at least not diminished.

No notable improvement is to be noted in interdenominational relations or in local coöperation with social agencies; but social-mindedness has undoubtedly a larger place in the church's outlook.

The Methodist denomination has not been intimately related to the church's evolution, and probably needs to acquire a new understanding of the church's prospects and future possibilities.

Compared with the other churches studied, and in view of its particular problems, the achievements and prospects of the Roseville Church unquestionably rank above average, though not with the very highest group. The story as a whole shows some of the things that a church may do when it is somewhat pressed by environmental change, but not so hard pressed as to have been compelled to transform itself radically to meet its situation.

---

[7] No assumption is implied that there necessarily ought to be such provision.

Case III

FIRST BAPTIST CHURCH, OAKLAND, CALIF.

In this series of case studies of significant churches, the great metropolitan communities that have grown up at the western gateway of the nation, around the Bay of San Francisco, are represented by Trinity Center Presbyterian, on the San Francisco side (Case XII), and the First Baptist Church, in Oakland.

Two Cases Compared

When it is attempted to arrange the cases in a series showing degrees of institutional development, both of these churches are difficult to place. Measured, as to breadth and variety of program, by a list of sixty organizations, activities and practices found in city churches, Trinity Center ranks in the lowest fourth, while the First Baptist stands as next to the lowest case. On the other hand, measured by total annual attendance upon all regular organizations and activities, Trinity Center ranks much above the average of the cases studied, while the First Baptist is the fourth from the largest. In brief, both are large enterprises; but, like the two preceding cases, they disclose narrow programs measured by those of the other churches with which they are being compared.

This unusual ratio between the total magnitude of the program and its breadth is in itself worthy of investigation. Otherwise the two churches are significant generally for very different reasons. Trinity Church is located at a secondary center of a large city; the First Baptist Church at the primary center of a small city.

Trinity Center has strikingly reversed a downward trend in its institutional fortunes by means of radical innovations in ecclesiastical relationships, involving a large measure of denominational aid and control. The First Baptist Church has somewhat accelerated a continuously upward trend which has

104

been closely associated with the almost spectacular growth of Oakland.

Trinity Church has rebuilt itself and its work out of a community that has suffered extremely from adverse change; the First Baptist Church, by a highly selective attitude, has built itself up almost regardless of particular changes in the character of its community. As a result, Trinity Church is characterized by a very strong week-day program; the First Baptist Church has followed, with successful ingenuity, essentially traditional church methods and is lacking in real innovations in spite of its adoption of strikingly distinctive devices.

Both churches succeed in getting people to attend their services in large numbers. The constituency of Trinity Church consists largely of detached individuals drawn from non-church families, chiefly children and young people. The constituency of the First Baptist Church, on the contrary, consists chiefly of church families and their children, though it also includes a disproportionate number of constituents in the younger age-groups.

Most of the adherents of Trinity Church are attached through membership in some single activity, as the Sunday school or one of the subsidiaries. The First Baptist Church, on the contrary, has a very large core of people with many attachments to the church, bound together in an exceedingly strong and highly centralized organization. The staff of both churches has been greatly enlarged in recent years, and their finances correspondingly increased. In the case of Trinity Church, however, the new resources have been primarily denominational subsidies, while in the case of the First Baptist Church they have come from the constituency itself. Both churches have greatly enlarged the amount and proportion of their loose collections as a result of success in securing large congregations. Both church plants have had moderate improvement, but neither has been radically changed.

The recent development of both churches has definitely been the result of experimentation, conceived, in the case of Trinity, by overhead denominational officials, and in the case of the First Baptist Church, by the type of business mind that is engaged in boosting Oakland.

To summarize: Results, in the case of Trinity, have been revolutionary both in the work and in the outlook of the church. Internally it has reconstructed itself to meet its newly conceived and accepted task, though, as already indicated, without a really representative enlargement of program.

In the case of the First Baptist, on the other hand, the outcome of recent development has been essentially incidental. The church is promoting itself in new and successful ways which, however, involve but slight inner adaptation to anything distinctively characteristic of Oakland as a city. It shows fresh resourcefulness in making a winning approach to a very general urban situation, unconsciously limiting itself to the middle- and upper-class constituencies, but without radical departure from old lines of service.

Both churches thus present significant attempts to solve the problem of the church in the city. The First Baptist has been carried ahead with the momentum of a rapidly growing city, and as yet has experienced only minor difficulties of adjustment. Trinity Church has suffered a complete reversal of environmental fortunes, though not such extreme and obliterating change as has driven many churches out of existence. The story behind these striking alternatives of circumstances and method is told for the First Baptist Church in the following paragraphs.[1]

History of First Baptist

The First Baptist Church was founded in 1854, four years after California was admitted to statehood and when Oakland was a mere village of a few hundred people.[2] By 1869 the church had already moved twice before settling down to a long career of average growth at the corner of Fourteenth and Brush Streets, then considerably removed from the central business development of the city. Oakland at this time had about 10,000 people.

The dramatic turning-point in the career of both Trinity Presbyterian and the First Baptist churches was physical ca-

---

[1] For the study of Trinity Church, see p. 319 ff.
[2] The first Federal enumeration of 1860 gave Oakland a population of 1,543.

tastrophe. After thirty-three years at the corner of Fourteenth and Brush, fire destroyed the First Baptist Church in 1902, and before removal and occupancy of the new building on the present site were accomplished, came the earthquake of 1906 which almost totally wrecked the partially completed building. It was, however, reconstructed with nation-wide aid from the Baptist denomination and occupied in 1908. This reëstablished the institution as the central church of its denomination in Oakland, and its leading church in the entire Bay district. Oakland at this time was approaching a population of 150,000.

The present study of the First Baptist Church was made after more than twenty-five years of continuous growth in the present building. Its records prove notable institutional advance for the period as a whole. They particularly show the renewal of progress from the beginning of the ministry of the present pastor, after a period of hesitancy and appreciable decline which immediately preceded.

I. MAJOR ASPECTS OF THE CHURCH

Members and Constituents

Fifteen hundred and eighty-four persons are reported on the books of the church as its definitely connected constituency. Forty per cent. of these are males, and 60 per cent. females. Fifty-four per cent. come from families, one or more adults of which are also enrolled constituents, while the remaining 46 per cent. are individuals from families not attached to the church.

As compared with the population of the city of Oakland, and the combined constituencies of the twenty-six churches, the composition of the First Baptist constituency according to age appears as follows:

	PER CENT.		
	Adults (21 & Over)	Adolescents (15-20)	Children (5-14)
Constituencies of:			
First Baptist Church..............	65	12	23
26 Churches	73	8	19
Population of Oakland	75	9	16

Thus in its composition the First Baptist Church tends to be a young people's church.

MANNER AND DEGREE OF ADHERENCE

The different ways in which the 1,584 constituents adhere to the church are shown in Chart IV.[3]

Seven hundred and thirty, or 46 per cent. of the total constituency, belong either to the church alone, to the Sunday school alone or to the subsidiaries alone. The remainder represent different kinds and degrees of overlapping membership. The total overlapping equals 53 per cent. of the total constituency. Only one church of the twenty-six has a larger body of adherents related to it in more than one way—and the triple overlapping memberships in church, Sunday school and subsidiaries (19 per cent.) are more numerous in the First Baptist Church than in any other.

NUMBER OF CONNECTIONS

Thirty-seven per cent. of all the constituents of the church belong in only one way, but this group includes almost half of the individual adherents. There is not a wide difference in the percentages of family adherents and of individual adherents that belong in two ways, but many more of the former than of the latter belong in more than two ways, and age is less of a factor in the former class. Nearly one-fourth of all adults and adolescents, but only a little more than one-tenth of children, are connected in four or more ways.

A special tabulation was made of the 257 persons that constitute the highly connected core of the church, as defined by attendance at services, enrollment in Sunday school and at least three other relations. Adults from adherent families furnish the largest element in this group, and there are relatively a few more men than women.

Environment

The very rapid growth of Oakland has been accompanied by those general and typical social changes that one learns to

---

[3] Page 71

expect in any urban community. These changes are now
coming to affect the prospects of the First Baptist Church in
fundamental ways. First of all, the expanding business center has caught up with and now embraces the church's property. Growth has been accompanied by the relocation of
various types of population, and most of the area immediately
surrounding the church is residentially less desirable than
formerly.

THE CHURCH'S NEIGHBORHOOD

As Chart VI shows, the First Baptist Church is located on
the northern edge of the central business district of Oakland,
about half a mile north of the city hall. All the older sections
of the city are included within a radius of two miles, while
a circle drawn at three miles touches the Berkeley line on the
north and includes the separately incorporated communities of
Alameda, Emeryville and Piedmont. Except for the narrow-
ing coastal plain extending along the Bay to the north and
southeast, permanent limits are set to metropolitan development at about this distance by the Bay on two sides and foot-
hills on the other two.

Within the half-mile between the church and the City Hall
lies the city's zone of most acute transformation, where the
expansion of the central district is rapidly taking over an area
of homes and formerly outlying institutions. Beyond the central business district in the second half-mile to the south falls
the area of wholesale business and light industry, together
with the more concentrated quarters of the Chinese and Japa-
nese. The major part of Lake Merritt lies within this distance to the east, and its inner margin within a half-mile of
the church includes the newly developed zone of hotels and
many-storied apartments which now for the first time are becoming characteristic of the city. Except for the area reserved
for this type of development, most of the territory to the south
and east is open to industry and is likely to be increasingly
surrendered to it as retail business moves north.

Within half a mile to the southwest of the church lie secondary business streets and then residential areas gradually
passing into the Negro and foreign colonies of West Oakland

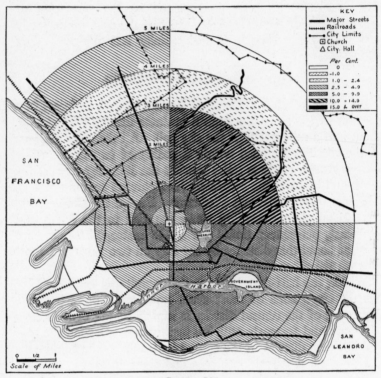

CHART VI
Parish of First Baptist Church, Oakland

and on to the concentrations of heavy industry along the Bay. From the northeast and northwest come the major thorough-fares of the city converging at the City Hall. In the narrow angles between these streets new buildings are exceedingly few. Population is congested and the area within a mile of the church is generally deteriorating. Immediately to the northeast along the line of the city's chief expansion, business has already gone beyond the church and will undoubtedly rapidly surround it, cutting it off from the desirable residential area even more than at present. Only to the northeast does the barrier of hills, together with the park at the head of Lake Merritt, leave any large area of desirable residence within a mile of the church. Such are the main aspects of the church's immediate environment in its present location at the corner of Telegraph and Twenty-first Streets.

But this is not the whole truth as to environment. When most of a church's constituency lives in its immediate vicinity, as happens, for example, in the case of Trinity Center, environment may be sufficiently defined in terms of proximity. The constituency of the First Baptist Church, however, is so widely scattered that it is necessary to consider its environmental relations to the entire city of Oakland.

The sphere of the church's influence is little localized. Standing near the center, but not particularly identified with its vicinity, it must adjust itself to an exceedingly varied area, including all the mass of social, racial and occupational differences that occur in Oakland. Confronted by so rich a total environment, and favored, as has been seen, by the peculiar topography and structure of the city, the church has only dealt with it selectively.

Parish

The First Baptist Church has a very scattered parish. It is exceeded in this respect by only four of the twenty-five churches studied,—all of which are located in much larger cities.

The parish is also very lopsided, finding the majority of its adherents to the north and especially to the northeast in the direction of the nearest desirable residential territory; while it conspicuously thins out in the industrial and foreign districts to the southwest. (Chart VI.)

The church draws more following from the second and third miles to the northwest than from anywhere else. It naturally shows few members in the central business section where population is inevitably scant. Apart from the variations due to this physical barrier and to the social attractions and repulsions previously indicated, the constituency spreads out thinly but fairly evenly throughout most of the area of the city and its adjoining municipalities.

Disregarding 122 persons whose addresses were not recorded, and one who lives outside the metropolitan area, 14 per cent. of all constituents are found living within half a mile, and 36 per cent. within one mile of the church; while 11 per cent. live more than four miles away. This leaves more than half of the constituency living beyond one mile but within four miles of the church. Within the area thus defined, the church shows extraordinarily widespread drawing capacity.

The distribution of constituent families differs radically from that of detached individuals. Many more of the latter are drawn from within one mile, and especially from the first half-mile; while there are relatively more adherents from families in almost every zone beyond a mile.

The probable explanation of the inequalities of parish distribution has already been offered. This explanation is strengthened when one imposes the parish map upon a map showing characteristics of population by similar zones and sectors. The church registers in almost exact detail an avoidance of business, industrial and strictly foreign areas, with some slight exception in the direction of its former site. In general, in sectors of equal distance, constituents are numerous in proportion as the area is residentially desirable and exclusively American. In other words, the church shows a high degree of selection when viewed from the standpoint of the total parish area. Upon the better grade population to which it appeals it has a more than city-wide hold, covering most of the metropolitan area east of the Bay.

So great is this hold that (unlike Case II) there is no determining relation between distance of residence and closeness of connection with the church for any age-group of constituents. The proportion of adolescents and children that are related to the church by more than two connections is greater for the constituents living from three to four miles from the church than it is for those living at any lesser distance.

The same thing is true for adults living from one to two miles and from two to three miles. This is at variance with what has been considered to be the general fact: namely, that remoteness of residence cuts down closeness of connection. It shows how successfully a centrally located city church, making a genuinely attractive appeal, can overcome the handicap of a scattered constituency.

II. AGENCIES, RESOURCES AND METHODS

Organizations and Stated Activities

The total annual attendance on all organizations and stated activities of the church is estimated at 127,443. The ratio of the week-day to the Sunday program is smaller than in any other church studied. This is shown in Table XIX.

TABLE XIX—ESTIMATED ANNUAL ATTENDANCE ON SPECIFIED OCCASIONS AT FIRST BAPTIST CHURCH AND AT 26 CHURCHES

	ATTENDANCE			
	FIRST BAPTIST CHURCH		26 CHURCHES	
			Approx. Median	Range of Variation
OCCASION	Number	Per Cent.	Per Cent.	Per Cent.
Total *	127,443	100		
Formal religious services (Sunday and week day).........	73,060	57	51	15–75
Sunday school................	24,492	20	24	9–38
All other stated activities......	29,891 †	23	22	9–51

* Sunday, 92 per cent.; week day, 8 per cent.
† Includes meetings of church officers and committees.

Compared with other churches studied, formal religious services have much greater emphasis in the First Baptist Church, the Sunday school considerably less than average emphasis, and subsidiary organizations slightly more.

The estimated attendance upon activities other than church services, Sunday school and officers' meetings is 29,015, divided between age- and sex-groups as shown in Table XX.

TABLE XX—ESTIMATED ANNUAL ATTENDANCE ON SUB-
SIDIARY ORGANIZATIONS AND STATED ACTIVITIES

	ORGANIZATIONS	ATTENDANCE	
No.	Type	Number	Per Cent.
	Total	29,015	
12	Classified by Age and Sex...............	25,895	100
0	Mixed adults	0	0
2	Adult men.............................	16,768	65
1	Adult women..........................	1,287	5
2	Mixed young people *.................	3,016	12
1	Young men	240	1
1	Young women	360	1
3	Mixed boys and girls.................	3,000	12
0	Boys	0	0
2	Girls	1,224	4
0	Mixed children......................	0	0
	Classified by Function		
	Choir	3,120	

* Between 15 and 23 years of age.

Numerically, the outstanding feature of the subsidiary program is the John Snape Class, ostensibly a non-denominational Sunday-morning group meeting in a theater, but founded and led by the pastor of the church and obviously in effect a subsidiary organization. Counting this class (together with the church's men's brotherhood) gives the church a men's program about six times as large, relative to the total, as was found in any other church studied. Mixed organizations for young people and for boys and girls consist of three grades of Baptist Young People's Unions. Organizations for adult women, though an exceedingly strong factor in the church's life, are carried on primarily through the meetings of limited groups rather than through central gatherings representing all the women of the parish. The significance of the organized women's work is not adequately represented by its attendance per cent. in the recorded program.

Staff

The composition, qualifications, experience and salaries of the church's staff are summarized in Table XXI.

TABLE XXI—ANALYSIS OF PAID STAFF

	Pastor	Director of Religious Education	Church Secretary	Treasurer *
Sex	Male	Male	Female	Male
Degree of education				
Academic	Secondary school	College	High school	High school
Professional or special...	Theological seminary	Theological seminary and Postgraduate	...	...
Years of employment				
Prior to this position				
Secular work	...	6	2	25
Religious work	26	2	...	...
In this position	6	1	1	2
Present salary				
Cash	$8,000	$3,000	$1,500	$520
Perquisites				
Nature	...	Automobile expenses	...	...
Value	...	$120	...	...
Entitled to ecclesiastical pension	Yes	Yes	No	No
Length of vacation	6 weeks	2 weeks	2 weeks	None

* Part time.

The size of the staff is very moderate considering the total magnitude of the church's work. This is obviously due to the fact that the constituency is handled in large audiences rather than divided into numerous small groups requiring paid leadership. Again, the strong and unusually good supply of lay leadership makes it unnecessary for the staff to undertake certain responsibilities often falling to paid workers.

Finances are adequately handled by lay trustees and a paid treasurer, so that the pastor does not have to concern himself directly with them. He has created an extra-constitutional advisory committee, consisting of the deacons, trustees and three members at large who are called in to advise on basic policies.

There is an actively functioning Sunday-school council with

which the Director of Religious Education immediately works; also a committee on religious education, including the heads of all the organized youth-groups of the church. This latter organization looks in the direction of an inclusive departmentalization of all young people's work, but the idea is not completely carried out.

Relations of members of the staff to one another are highly informal. There are no set office conferences, but much incidental consultation. The secretary assists all three of the principal members of the staff.

WORK RECORDS

Of a total of 216 hours of work performed by the four members of the staff (including the part-time treasurer) in a sample week during the study, for which records were kept, 28 per cent. went to administration, which ranked first, 18 per cent. to pastoral work, 12 per cent. to strictly technical functions, primarily the bookkeeping of the treasurer, and 10 per cent. to clerical work. This distribution reflects the fact that the pastor comes to the church office for only a few hours per week. His sermon preparation is done at home, and much of the minor detail of administration is thrown upon the secretary. Consequently her time spent in administrative duties nearly equals her clerical work, and she has a considerable proportion of virtually pastoral responsibility in office conferences.

The pastor gives more of his time to homiletical preparation than to any other function, ranking high in comparison with pastors of the other churches studied in this respect. He gives an equal amount of time (19 per cent.) to pastoral and to strictly ministerial functions, both largely outside of his own stated constituency. In his judgment, 70 per cent. of all such ministries are performed outside of the parish proper.

The combined work of the staff averages thirty-one hours per day. There is the usual wide discrepancy between the time spent by the secretary, who has a stated work-day, and ministers who are on duty at all hours. On five of the seven days, the pastor worked more than ten hours.

Plant

The plant consists of a large stone church occupying a corner lot approximately 100 x 188 feet in dimensions. On the rear of the lot a two-story double apartment has been remodeled for social and supplemental Sunday-school use. The church offices are here also.

Among the twenty-five churches studied, there are eighteen plants judged superior to this. It scores 553 on the Interchurch standard.

On account of the substantial material of the structure and the ample and attractive, though not essentially churchly, auditorium, the plant ranks high with respect to structure and church rooms. Its strategic location, and its numerous, though extremely ill-arranged, Sunday-school rooms place it above the average with respect to site and to religious education plant. But it ranks very low indeed with respect to service systems and facilities for community service.

Table XXII shows the advantages and deficiencies of the plant in fuller detail.

TABLE XXII—SUMMARY OF SCORE OF PLANT

Items	Standard Score	Points Scored		Rank in 25 Cases
		Number	Per Cent.	
Total	1,000	553	55	19
Site	130	86	66	18
Building or buildings.........	150	110	73	16
Service systems	160	57	36	22
Church rooms................	170	120	71	15
Religious school rooms........	200	128	64	7
Community service rooms.....	190	52	27	21

Of special equipment should be mentioned the exceptional facilities for electric illumination. In the auditorium a spotlight is played upon the choir, soloists, preacher or baptismal ceremony, in turn, at evening services. The electric sign on the front of the church, forty-four feet high and four feet wide, surmounted by an illuminated cross, is locally believed to be the largest church sign in America. It is of steel construction, weighing about 900 pounds, and valued commercially at $900. The letters on the sign are eighteen inches high.

From this sign the church has assumed its designation, "The Church of the Radiant Cross."

The adjacent apartment building furnishes unusually good office space, ample in size and well-lighted.

Finances

Receipts for current expenses of the church for the fiscal year preceding the date of the study were approximately $32,300. Individual pledges of nearly $19,000 furnished 59 per cent. of the total and came from 700 subscribers. Twenty per cent. of all receipts were from loose collections (only two other churches studied at all approximate this ratio) ; and 7 per cent. were raised and expended by the subsidiary organizations, including the Sunday school.

The church's trend to large Sunday audiences as its outstanding form of ministry makes it economical in financial costs, as well as in demands upon a paid staff. The annual expenditure is approximately $24.00 per hundred attendants. Only two other churches of those studied cost less. Measured by cost per adherent, however, economy is not so pronounced. In this respect the church stands on the border line between the less expensive and the least expensive groups of churches.

Benevolent receipts of nearly $18,000 came mainly from 324 pledged subscribers and from the women's auxiliary. The grand total of receipts was about $50,000.

Current expenditures were about $30,500, divided as shown in Table XXIII.

TABLE XXIII—FINANCIAL EXPENDITURES OF THE CHURCH

Item	Amount	Per Cent.
Grand Total	$30,537	
Total Current Account	28,042	100
Salaries	12,345	44
General administrative expenses	650	2
Music	3,465	13
General operation and upkeep of property	5,697	20
Expenses of departments specially budgeted	3,087	11
Publicity	2,114	8
Miscellaneous	684	2
Investment Account		
Permanent improvement	2,495	

This distribution does not involve any special peculiarities, except that only one church studied spent relatively more for publicity.

Benevolent expenditures were chiefly for the authorized national and foreign missionary bodies of the Baptist denomination, and secondarily for the local Baptist churches and missions, not more than 3 per cent. going for individual and family relief within the parish.

Public Services

Attendance on public services has been greatly increased as the result of a deliberate policy of advertising and popular sermonizing. The services have been made varied and entertaining, and they have been skillfully promoted through publicity devised by professionals. Their most telling features have been: first, an ingenious and pleasing type of preaching in which personal narrative plays a large part, often through a long series of sermons in which public interest is skillfully drawn out from week to week; and, secondly, numerous "big" occasions, such as the attendance of clubs or fraternal orders *en masse*. Attendants at the evening congregations are largely not members of the church, though, as evidenced by a show of hands at one of the services attended, they are mostly church people. In considerable degree, attendants are also drawn from the transient population inhabiting the church's immediate neighborhood.

A careful count for the year preceding the study gave an average attendance of 541 at morning services and 804 at evening services. These were gains of 22 per cent. and 27 per cent. respectively over the previous year.

The pastor characterizes the morning service as his "sheepfold," and the evening service as his "fish pond." On the morning of the study, the congregation was overwhelmingly adult. Adolescents and children comprised not more than 12 per cent. of the total. Before the opening, conversation and sociability were actively carried on in the lobby and the rear of the auditorium. The service followed the conventional order. It was supported by a competent chorus choir, but lacked any striking liturgical feature. The chief innovations were a somewhat deliberately reiterated expression of friendly intimacy between pastor and congregation; a similar reiteration of the importance of size—"this magnificent gathering," "our great membership," etc.—a not unpleasant but repeated reminder, both directly and indirectly, of the need of securing financial support from casual attendants.

The pastor had just returned from his vacation of seven weeks in Alaska. The sermon was the first of a series of seven based on this experience. It was entitled "Ships that Pass in the Night," the ships being, first, the literal ship itself, then fellowship, friendship, courtship (in view of the diminishing population of Alaska), statesmanship (in view of its political needs) and worship. Members of the party who took the Alaskan cruise were made to rise and be introduced. The sermon was saturated with scriptural references and sustained by pleasant diction and rhetoric which appeared to be rather deliberate than passionate.

At the close of the service, the pastors remained in front of the pulpit and were greeted by from seventy-five to one hundred of the congregation. Most of the audience dispersed immediately in long lines of automobiles of inexpensive make, but fifty or sixty remained visiting for a considerable period.

The more largely attended evening service does not differ greatly in order or atmosphere from that of the morning, except for congregational singing at the opening and the usual inclusion of a musical specialty. During much of the year the evening sermon was preceded by a brief pulpit editorial on some popular issue.

THE JOHN SNAPE CLASS

This men's class is held an hour and a quarter before the morning service in the Franklin Theater, with an average attendance of over 300, which ranks it among the major services. On the day of the study, the audience consisted of middle-aged business men of the lunch-club type, who "checked

in" under signs announcing the theater offering of films for
the afternoon as "Kiss Me Again" and "The Beast at Bay."
The service was conducted by lay officers and opened with an
organ prelude and community singing from music thrown on
the screen and conducted by a song-leader with characteristic
men's club "pep." These features were applauded in theater
audience fashion. A brief address by a lay speaker representing a civic club in a neighboring city then followed. Notices
of employment desired and help wanted were included in the
announcements. The pastor's address took its clew from, but
was not narrowly limited by, the International Sunday-school
lesson of the day.

The general trend of sermonizing may be judged from the
examination of the announced topics of a year. The morning
sermons included three series of five or six each on the Lord's
Prayer, "The Place of the Jew in History and Prophecy" and
"What I Believe After Thirty Years." Ample use was made
of the special celebrations, but no strong emphasis is laid upon
Lent. The nearest approach to sensationalism in the morning
sermons was found in such topics as "Clean Your Wind-
shield." The special window-dressing of the experts, as applied to the evening topics, gave an appearance of sensa-
tionalism rather beyond the performance. Besides the series
based on the previous summer's vacation, the longest series
was based upon the fact that "Rupert Hughes Has Quit
Going to Church," followed on successive Sunday nights by
"Who Is Rupert Hughes?" "Is It the Fault of the Church?"
"What Can the Church Do About It?" "What About Rupert
Hughes' Boy?" Other titles were "Walter Johnson and the
World Series," "Cecil de Mille's Ten Commandments and the
Ten Commandments Given by God to Moses," the climax
capped by "The Woman Who Turned to Rubber and Then
Turned to Salt."

The evening sermons also included a considerable number
of reviews of popular books.

A sample of the advertising of the services of this Sunday
follows:

"CHURCH OF THE RADIANT CROSS"

FIRST *BAPTIST* CHURCH
John Snape, D.D., Pastor

"Glaciers, Icebergs and Spouting Whales"

DR. JOHN SNAPE
will tell about them and his Alaska vacation to-morrow

11 A.M.—"Fifteen Days on Shipboard, or Ships That Pass in the Night."

7.45 P.M.—"Totem Poles or Superstitions and Traditions of Indians and Others."

Dorothy Dukes Dimm, Cello Solos
Two Sermons in series of 8 on Alaska—don't miss one.
Both Services Radiocast by KGO.

21st & TELEGRAPH AVE.   One block from Y. M. C. A.

Religious Education

The Sunday school is of average size relative to the membership of the church, but, measured by attendance on the total annual program, the place occupied by the Sunday school is below the average.

The school, in form, is a thoroughly departmentalized and effective modern one under a lay superintendent and the technical direction of a professionally trained Director of Religious Education.   General statistical data appear in Table XXIV.

TABLE XXIV—SUMMARY OF SUNDAY-SCHOOL STATISTICS *

DEPARTMENT	PUPILS		TEACHERS	
	Age	Enrollment	Male	Female
Total	...	824	15	19
Cradle Roll	...	106	..	..
Beginners	4–5	63	0	1
Primary	6–8	70	1	5
Junior	9–12	107	4	5
Intermediate	13–15	45	3	3
Senior	16–24	148	3	3
Adult	24 & over	245	4	2
Home Department	...	40	..	..

* The Sunday schools of the branch churches, viz: Columbian Park, with 68 members, and the Mexican Sunday school, are not included in the above figures.

The addition of nineteen officers to the 824 pupils and thirty-four teachers gives a grand total of 877. Pupils in the attending departments number 678, and attendance averages 58 per cent. of enrollment. The approximate age-distribution in the attending departments is as follows:

	Number	Per Cent.
Children	240	35
Adolescents	153	23
Adults	285	42

Two adult Bible classes constitute organized social groups and carry on an active week-day program once a month. The Boy Scouts and Girl Reserves of the church are recognized as affording supplemental values in character-training. A denominational junior missionary society is sustained. The theory is officially accepted that all these agencies (including also the very active series of Baptist Young People's Unions) are to be considered educational, that they should all be related and that through them all-around activities should be provided for youth. That the theory is not fully carried out is due partly to the disinclination of the organizations to be coördinated and partly to lack of sufficient leaders and facilities.

An active Sunday-school workers' council is maintained, consisting of officers and teachers and heads of organized classes. A continuous training course for teachers, including twelve weeks of practice teaching in the year, is operated, and departmental councils of teachers are held monthly. The inadequacy of Sunday-school facilities was indicated in the section on plant. At least fourteen small classrooms are inadequately lighted. Modern seating facilities for classrooms are not available. These are serious handicaps upon the excellent organization and effective leadership.

The continuous process of religious education is supplemented by the summer Daily Vacation Bible School, which enrolled 135 pupils in 1925. The majority were from the immediate vicinity and were already in the Sunday school of the First Baptist Church, but about 8 per cent. were Orientals.

Growth and Conservation

It is impossible to isolate particular winning elements within the total life and ministry of the church. The general processes by which recruits are secured are, however, revealed by a study of 161 new members received in 1924-25. This shows that the church is growing chiefly by the transfer from other churches. Compared with this major source, accessions as a result of direct evangelism or through the church's own preparatory processes were quite secondary, comprising only 29 per cent. of the total.

Judged by the residences of its new members, the church shows capacity to draw recruits from virtually the whole of the wide area over which its membership is scattered.

Gains by transfer are, however, not immediate and not always easily won. A majority of persons thus received seem to have settled down in the community without forming church connections. They therefore have to be reëvangelized before being brought into active fellowship. One evidence of this is the considerable proportion of persons admitted on "experience" who were formerly professing Christians but have no church letters.

Behind the gains of the church one plainly sees the extraordinary growth of Oakland. The movement toward Oakland as a suburb is represented by twenty-nine transfers from other Baptist churches in the Bay region. The position and prestige of the church gives it the first call on newcomers of its denomination over a wide territory, though it is significant that detached individuals are recruited from greater distances, on the average, than are families.[4]

Current Church Life

The peculiar climate of the San Francisco Bay region fixes the opening of the active church year, with Sunday-school Rally Day, early in August. Only a slight seasonal letting-down of activities occurs at any time. This is preceded by the pastor's vacation, when the preaching is done by the associate pastor and resident Baptist officials. The pastor then returns and the regular series of sermons on his vacation experiences starts the year with a boom. From this date forward the subsidiary organizations begin to bring off their recurrent special

---

[4] The church recognizes the significance of Christian home influence upon infants and uses a "form of service for the parental dedication of little children" with a certificate of such public dedication devised by the pastor.

programs and the church finds itself actively participating in numerous religious occasions and interests, denominational and interdenominational. Training-schools of religious education and a school of missions occupy several weeks. In keeping with the character of the church, numerous representatives of denominational enterprises are heard, though usually not in the pulpit.

The most frequent meetings of the year are those of the various circles of the Women's Association, of which five or six are held weekly. This organization combines all women's interests of the church and is carefully departmentalized. It divides the parish into twelve groups of about forty women each. These groups are created arbitrarily by a chance drawing from four lists: namely, those of leaders, active participants, contributors to women's work who are not participants, and "shut-ins." This device mixes up, in predetermined proportions, all types of women in the church, prevents cliquishness and keeps groups changing year after year. It has been definitely chosen in contrast to a system of geographical grouping. This is a definite symptom of a church with a city-wide viewpoint rather than localized attitudes and affiliations.

Relations to Community and Denomination

The breadth and variety of responsible contacts between the church and organized community welfare are indicated by the connection of eleven of its members with regional interdenominational enterprises in some official capacity, and of twenty-one members with civic and local social agencies in the same way.

The pastor is the President of the Lions Club of Oakland and takes active part in the commercial and civic affairs.

Beyond the small direct gift from the Women's Association to the Community Chest, financial support of social agencies appears, however, to be personal rather than institutional.

The major emphasis of the community work of the church is denominational. The Columbian Park Mission in a new residential district in East Oakland and the Mexican Mission south of the business center, though primarily under the administration of the district Baptist Extension office, are regarded as branches of the First Baptist Church and the members are enrolled with the parent church. A Negro church, the Chinese Orphanage and a new suburban church all received significant financial assistance from the church throughout the year. More than 75 per cent. of all the church's benevolent expenditures within the community went to these budgets.

Important state and regional offices of the Baptist denomination are located in San Francisco with which twenty-three members of the church were connected by salaried or elective positions, in addition to six connected locally with denominational work. The pastor is a member of the governing board of the Northern Baptist Convention, a trustee of the more important denominational schools of the Pacific Coast, and a lecturer in the Baptist Divinity School of Berkeley.

Adaptations

As indicated at the outset of the study, the First Baptist Church is in most respects a large and prosperous church of the traditional type. Favored by incoming religious population, it has exhibited special enterprise and ingenuity, and stands in many and important relationships with the community. It makes a city-wide appeal, and thereby has so far escaped the necessity of becoming intimately related to its immediate environment or of being greatly influenced by the rapid changes taking place in its immediate vicinity. In all this it is typical of numerous central churches in the smaller cities. It lives and serves as do many others under similar conditions.

Its more conspicuous advances are clearly to be ascribed to general influences in the modern ecclesiastical world rather than to anything local or particularly urban. The rising standards of the denomination as officially promulgated by officials who belong to the church, the newer ideals of religious education as taught in its near-by theological seminary, furnish examples and explanation of the impact of such general ideas.

Even so limited and superficial a version of adaptation to an urban situation as the church shows nevertheless involves numerous interesting and significant points.

(1) Its sense of responsibility has definitely been increased by the removal of nearly all the other old-time central churches of Oakland to the still remoter margins of the central business district. The church describes itself as the "downtownest" one in Oakland and feels that it is incumbent upon it to assume the part of the permanent church at the center.

(2) The lay leaders of the church include some of the city's outstanding figures in civic enterprise. Their vision of a bigger and better Oakland includes that of a bigger and better First Baptist Church as aspects of a single vista. The style and effectiveness of the church's publicity and public appeal have very close affinities with the peculiar promotional sort of city-mindedness of these well-marked types.

(3) The presence of handicapped and under-privileged elements in the population of Oakland has been definitely recognized by the church in the assumption of responsibility for branches and missions, and through the financial assistance of feebler enterprises. Mexicans, Orientals, Negroes and humbler suburbanites are continuously helped indirectly through general denominational agencies dealing with such problems. There is, however, essentially no community work under the church's own roof for people of the immediate neighborhood.

(4) The existence, throughout the rapidly growing city of Oakland, and in the church's own vicinity, of a large element of religiously unplaced people has been discovered; and the availability of this population to a church with attractive services, special publicity and distinctive methods of pulpit cultivation has been demonstrated.

(5) It has been demonstrated, too, that persistent financial appeal to miscellaneous audiences, reënforced by the transient element, can greatly add to the support of the church.

(6) The development of a large radio audience interested in the atmosphere and content of services is another earmark of an urban church adapting itself to the performance of central functions. This audience reaches into the sparsely settled mountain regions of several western states.

Of outstanding innovations or enlargements, the addition of a Director of Religious Education to the staff, important developments along the lines of denominational objectives, the departmentalized and sectionalized organization of women, and the increased budget would probably have come to any church of equal size and permanence that was open to current tendencies and moods.

But the immense and flashing sign, the equally striking newspaper publicity, the employment of professional publicity agents, the drive for a popular type of preaching, the expert accounting applied to all efforts and expenditures in these directions and the study of their results, numerical and financial, the paid treasurer, the opening of the church office, the Daily Vacation Bible School, the active civic contacts of the pastor, radio broadcasting and, less consciously perhaps, the growing demand for casual pastoral work among the unchurched, all of these are distinct omens of the church's awareness of and adaptation to certain characteristic urban moods and forces, though often minor ones. Not less so is the indirect service to special needy populations through denominational methods and channels.

Finally, the whole prospect of the church is conditioned by a somewhat unique urban situation topographical in nature: namely, the fact that there is a large area of elevated land within easy reach inhabited by a large body of well-to-do people. The fact that the church draws so heavily upon this available area is obviously an expression of its instinctive adaptation to an advantageous fact.

Other definitely territorial expressions of adaptation are strikingly lacking. The church belongs less to the immediate vicinity than it does to the city at large, and this appears to the present observer to be its chief shortcoming, in view of the crying needs of a neighborhood of depreciated physical character, occupied by an exceedingly varied and transient population.

The church has grown, has increased its prestige, its city-wide appeal, its audiences, its funds, its remoter community ministries. Why can it not also send stronger and deeper roots into the immediate neighborhood and devise suitable special ministries in its behalf?

CASE IV

HANSON PLACE METHODIST EPISCOPAL CHURCH, BROOKLYN, N. Y.

After ten years of obscure and unstable missionary effort beginning with 1847, the Hanson Place Methodist Episcopal Church took permanent root in that part of Brooklyn which now shares with Manhattan the central congestion of the world's greatest metropolis.

The church and Brooklyn grew up together for half a century, during which the city was the chief refuge of Protestant population from the foreign invasion of New York, a place of American homes and families and, in popular fame, the "city of churches." For much of this period the Hanson Place Church was under distinguished pastoral leadership and bore a recognized and honorable part in the city's religious development.

Finally came the vast sweep of population that made Brooklyn more populous than Manhattan itself. In the last two decades the church has seen the movement of city-building carried far beyond it, first into Brooklyn's own outlying regions and then into the remoter boroughs. This movement carried along much of the older type of population, leaving the old centers to be occupied by New York aliens and by the expanding business and industry of the increased community.

The most significant omen of this outspreading population movement was the extension of the subway beyond its Atlantic Avenue terminal opposite the church. During the subway operations, a corner of the church building was undermined and fell into the excavation. The church was thus dramatically challenged to decide whether to move on with the population flood or to stay and take the consequences of changed conditions. Moreover, the new transit facilities had greatly increased the sale value of its site, so that it would have been very easy to go.

But the church decided to stay. Its location was at what was becoming an almost unequaled focus of transportation, the very best spot to which to draw crowds from a distance. At the same time, as the structure of the city was working itself out, the best sections (in the sense of having the most valuable improvements and being occupied by the wealthiest people) were three rather small areas lying in three different directions, but all within one mile of the church. Consequently there remained enough population of the sort to which the church had been accustomed in the past to support it while it was developing capacity for a larger outreach.

The statistical history of its last decade shows that the church has succeeded measurably in making the transition. Its membership averages about 7 per cent. larger for the last five years than for the previous five, in spite of rather drastic revisions of the roll in both periods. The Sunday-school enrollment is about 17 per cent. less over the same periods. But current expenses have increased about 75 per cent. Benevolences doubled during the Methodist Centenary Movement, and have since been kept at that level by special endeavor in behalf of local philanthropies. The church's property values, as now estimated, are two and one-half times those of 1915. All this signifies that it is making more than moderate institutional headway against conflicting currents.

General Characteristics

Measured by total attendance on all stated organizations and activities, the church, though not quite ranking with the group of largest cases among the twenty-six studied, stands well above the average. Its Sunday program absorbs 84 per cent. of its total ministries, which is appreciably more than the average proportion. Only two of the twenty-six cases lay relatively greater numerical stress on formal religious services. In short, Hanson Place Church is, first of all, a series of well-attended preaching services and cultural occasions. Only two cases, relative to total attendance, have smaller Sunday schools;

while, in the relative strength of its subsidiary organizations, the church stands at about the average.

The great audiences bring into the constituency of the church a decidedly unusual proportion of detached adherents, people who either do not have families [1] or whose families do not themselves belong to the constituency. Only one other of the twenty-six churches has relatively more adults in its total following. Compared with the numerous and varied ministries found in many of the twenty-six cases, those of Hanson Place show only conservative tendencies either as to number or character. Ranked according to a list of sixty current church practices, only three of the twenty-six cases have a narrower program.

The specific means by which the church is adjusting itself to its situation, and the noteworthy aspects of its service, are the theme of the main body of this study.

I. MAJOR ASPECTS OF THE CHURCH

Members and Constituents

Naturally the occasional and transient following of such a church as has been described is much larger than the sum of the recorded constituency which the church has attached to itself in any determinate way. The latter, however, is the only aspect in which churches can be accurately compared. The reported total constituency [2] numbers 1,845, only 39 per cent. being male. This ratio expresses a considerable exaggeration (especially in the adult constituency and particularly among adults who do not belong to adherent families) of the church's often-noted tendency toward feminization. The excess of adults and the shortage of children in the constituency is still greater compared with the total population of New York City than compared with the composition of the constituencies of the twenty-six cases, as is shown in the following tabulation:

---

[1] Many of the Brooklyn assembly districts adjacent to the Hanson Place Church show excess populations either of adult males or of adult females—thus revealing the presence of an unusually large number of people not related to families in the same areas.

[2] For exact definition and method of calculating, see p. 447.

Constituencies of:	PER CENT.		
	Adults (21 & Over)	Adolescents (15-20)	Children (5-14)
Hanson Place Church	88	3	9
26 churches	73	8	19
Population of New York.............	69	11	20

It is noteworthy, too, that the shortage of adolescents is relatively greater than that of children. Besides, the following that Hanson Place Church succeeds in winning to definite adherence by means of its great audiences is one in which adult women, religiously detached from family groups, form a very disproportionately large fraction.

MANNER AND DEGREE OF ADHERENCE

The constituency is less unified by means of its organized activities than in the majority of the churches studied. As shown by Chart IV, 71 per cent. of all adherents are connected with the church in only one way, and that way, for 56 per cent. of adherents, is full membership. Only one church of those studied exceeds at this point. There remains 29 per cent. of the constituency to make up the entire overlapping membership of church and Sunday school, church or Sunday school and subsidiaries, or all three. The proportion of adherents who belong to all three is, however, beyond average. Nearly twice as many of this group come from adherent families as from the ranks of detached individuals. One finds consequently, on the one hand, a proportionately large central core of adherents closely related to the church, and, on the other, an undue proportion (practically all adults and predominantly women) belonging to the church only. The overlapping of church and Sunday school is about average, as is that of church and subsidiaries, leaving that of Sunday school and subsidiaries much below average. All told, however, the Sunday school is pretty well integrated with other aspects of the church's life, the proportion belonging to the Sunday school alone being relatively slight.

NUMBER OF CONNECTIONS

Hanson Place Church shows a larger proportion than the average of adherents who have more than one connection.[3]

---

[3] For method of calculation, see p. 447.

Still more striking, however, is the great excess of adherents who have an extreme number of connections—in some cases as high as five or seven each. Of eleven churches studied in detail on this point, only one appears to be putting equal or heavier burdens upon a few specially faithful supporters; and in Hanson Place Church most of these highly burdened adherents are adult women.

The church reports 1,825 pledged contributors, of whom two-thirds are women or girls, and nearly two-thirds adult. The number of contributors comprises 56 per cent. of the church-membership, 44 per cent. of the Sunday-school enrollment, and 57 per cent. of the membership of the subsidiaries; but 75 per cent. of the membership of church, Sunday school and subsidiaries. This is striking proof that those who are carrying the heavier burdens of service are also most frequently involved in support. But, relative to their numbers, only a few more financial supporters come from adherent families than from the ranks of detached individuals.

The total picture presented on the basis of these data is that of a social group, about 6 per cent. of whose constituents are bound to it in an extreme number of ways (five or more) within a nucleus of about 9 per cent. who form a central core by virtue of overlapping memberships in church, Sunday school and subsidiaries; with a Sunday school largely identified with these overlapping memberships; but, on the other hand, with a very large per cent. of "oncers" who belong to the church only. The nucleus, the fringe, and the intervening areas contain each a disproportionate number of women.

Parish and Environment

The church is located about three-quarters of a mile southeast of the Brooklyn Borough Hall, immediately opposite the Flatbush terminal of the Long Island Railroad, just below the convergence of the most important through routes over the Brooklyn and Manhattan Bridges, and at a focal point of the subway, surface and elevated systems. It stands toward the eastern end of the central business district of Brooklyn, and from it business streets radiate in all directions.

DISTANCE AND DIRECTION OF RESIDENCE OF CONSTITUENTS

Of 1,610 resident constituents whose addresses were known to the church, 31 per cent. live within one-half mile, and 48 per cent. within a mile of the building. On a typical Sunday, just about half the members of the congregation walk to church. So heavy a concentration of following in the immediate vicinity indicates a parish of medium density rather than of scattered dispersal. But, on the other hand, only one other church of the twenty-six has a higher proportion of adherents living at a distance of from four to five miles. In other words, while there is a heavy concentration about the church, there is also a distinct zone of distant adherents,—or not at all an even dispersal throughout the parish.[4]

The parish, too, is exceedingly lop-sided. More than one-half of the total constituency lives in a single sector to the southeast in the line of Brooklyn's major development, while slightly more than a third lives to the southwest, being largely massed along the margins of Prospect Park. This leaves only 13 per cent. living in that half of the parish lying toward the northwest in the direction of business, industry and foreign sections, the river and the city of New York.

ENVIRONMENT

The fact that virtually one-half of the constituency lives within one mile of the church, but only 13 per cent. on the New York side of it, raises the question of what environmental influences have been at work in distributing its adherents. These may easily be traced in the characteristics of the area. Adequate analysis is difficult, because this is one of the most complicated districts of Greater New York; but the more outstanding characteristics may be indicated as follows: (1) More than half of the area within a mile of the church, and outside of the central business district, is associated with industries which make Brooklyn, even regarded apart from New York, one of the greatest productive communities of the nation. The other half of this area is primarily residential. Here the church is at home.

---

4 Extreme distance makes some difference with the closeness of the adherents' relations to the church, but not much in the case of adults.

(2) The economic distance between the two halves of the area is equally clear-cut. A line drawn through the church roughly following a northeasterly and southwesterly direction divides nearly all the adjacent population that has less than average wealth from that which has more. In the areas toward the water front, a standard of living next to the lowest in the city prevails ($2,000 average family income), while the dominant standard in the area away from the water front, where the constituency is strong, is that of from $4,500 annual family income up.[5]

(3) These broad contrasts are complicated by the fact that the Brooklyn Heights section, lying northwest of Borough Hall, and overlooking the water front, is one of the three wealthiest of the city. It is, in turn, surrounded by the city's most heavily populated foreign-born colonies; and the native-white population of native parentage constitutes only one-fifth of the population in the sector toward the water front, while it averages one-third in the adjoining sectors away from it.

With respect to the areas ·thus described, Hanson Place Church presents one of the more extreme cases of geographical unrelatedness to one-half of its nearest environment, in contrast with very complete relatedness to the other half. This is almost equally true of families and of detached individuals, and of all adherent age-groups. Except as they may be served by its popular preaching services, almost nothing in the church's direct program betrays the presence as immediate neighbors of any of the populations who present Brooklyn's most outstanding social problems. The church's ministry to these elements is indirect and through other agencies.

FUTURE ENVIRONMENTAL PROBABILITIES

The structure of the older parts of Brooklyn now seems fairly well established, and the stabilizing influences of city planning, combined with reduced foreign immigration and lessened pressure from Manhattan Island, are likely to leave the situation gradually to better itself. Population declined

---

[5] Data as to economic districts from the *Survey of the New York Market,* New York University Bureau of Business Research for Daily Newspaper Advertising Managers' Association, New York, 1923.

slightly between 1910 and 1920 in a large proportion of the more congested of the adjacent census districts, and the better areas are now markedly reënforcing themselves by high-class improvements reflecting increased land values.   In certain areas also the comeback of depreciated districts is rapidly going on, in ways analogous to, and promising to duplicate, that which has transformed the Greenwich Village section of Manhattan.   The erection of great apartment hotels adjacent to the central business district is also bringing in new elements of high-grade population.   All told, therefore, the area within a mile of Hanson Place Church has probably seen its worst days; and the institutional prospect of the church, so far as this is based on the character of this area, should grow better, particularly as combined with the increasing prestige of the central business district and the multiplication of transit facilities.

II. AGENCIES, RESOURCES AND METHODS

Organizations and Activities

A careful estimate of annual attendance on all stated organizations and activities of the church is presented in Table XXV.

TABLE XXV—ESTIMATED ANNUAL ATTENDANCE ON SPECIFIED OCCASIONS AT HANSON PLACE CHURCH AND AT 26 CHURCHES

	ATTENDANCE			
OCCASION	HANSON PLACE CHURCH		26 CHURCHES	
			Approx. Median	Range of Variation
	Number	Per Cent.	Per Cent.	Per Cent.
Total *	106,370	100		
Formal religious services (Sunday and week day)	69,480	65	51	15–75
Sunday school	15,600	15	24	9–38
All other stated activities	21,290 †	20	22	9–51

* Sunday, 83 per cent.; week day, 17 per cent.
† Includes meetings of church officers and committees.

In a church whose transient constituency is so large, and which uses so many special occasions to attract chance attendants, comparison based upon stated activities is scarcely just. But if attendance on occasional public gatherings were included, it would only emphasize the fact that the organized life of the church in its subsidiary societies and groups is still less than the 20 per cent. of the total regular attendance which it comprises according to the above estimate; whereas in certain of the churches of the group studied it reaches 50 per cent. or more.

Analyzing further this important, though minor, aspect of the Hanson Place Church, over three-fourths of the subsidiary program is found to consist of the activities of the Epworth League and the choir. This is shown in Table XXVI.

TABLE XXVI—ESTIMATED ANNUAL ATTENDANCE ON SUB-
SIDIARY ORGANIZATIONS AND STATED ACTIVITIES

ORGANIZATIONS		ATTENDANCE	
No.	*Type*	*Number*	*Per Cent.*
	Total	21,100	
11	Classified by Age and Sex.................	12,988	100
0	Mixed adults	0	0
0	Adult men	0	0
4	Adult women	1,164	9
1	Mixed young people *..................	8,240	63
0	Young men	0	0
1	Young women	360	3
2	Mixed boys and girls..................	1,760	14
2	Boys	1,152	9
1	Girls	312	2
0	Mixed children	0	0
	Classified by Function Chiefly choir	8,112	

* Between 15 and 23 years of age.

In only five of the twenty-six churches studied is the organized work of women numerically less developed, while, except for the Boy Scouts, there are no outstanding activities for young men or young women or for boys and girls organized separately. Comparatively speaking, therefore, the subsidiary program is little differentiated, as well as slightly developed.

The Epworth League, with 279 members, gets an average of 140 in attendance on its Sunday evening sessions, seventy-five of whom come, on the average, to a light supper served before the devotional meeting. This is an outstanding group. The choir also, with 225 enrolled members, is an exceedingly strong social organization, as well as a notable musical group. It is believed to be the largest in the United States.

Staff

In spite of the large volume of business carried on by the church, it is operated by a staff of only four paid religious workers, supplemented by an unusually outstanding director of music, and by strong lay backing.[6]

This is possible primarily because the church's program deals so largely with constituents massed in audiences rather than with smaller and more actively participating groups that call for technical leadership and close supervision.

In composition, the staff reflects (though it does not precisely square with) the most frequent and logical arrangement of four workers,[7] namely, a pastor, a general assistant specializing to a certain degree in religious education, an inside secretarial assistant, and an outside pastoral assistant. In the present case, the general assistant is a deaconess whose work corresponds so exactly with the characteristic duties of assistant pastors as found in the twenty-six churches that her position logically falls into that class. The work of the secretary and visitor respectively corresponds closely with the average of these positions.

The preparation, experience, tenure and remuneration of the staff is summarized in Table XXVII.

TABLE XXVII—ANALYSIS OF PAID STAFF

	Pastor	Church Secretary	Deaconess	Church and Sunday-School Visitor *
Sex	Male	Female	Female	Female
Degree of education				
Academic	College	College	High school	Elementary school
Professional or special ...	Theological seminary	Postgraduate	Postgraduate Deaconess training school	...

---

[6] There are also two recreational instructors employed for a few hours per week.

[7] Determined by an analysis of sixty-eight four-worker staffs.

TABLE XXVII—*Continued*

	Pastor	Church Secretary	Deaconess	Church and Sunday-School Visitor
Years of employment Prior to this position				
Secular work..........	...	1	8	...
Religious work	22	...	9	...
In this position..........	3	1	1	...
Present salary				
Cash	$6,000	$1,500	$360	$180
Perquisites				
Nature	Rent	...	Room, board, laundry, ear fare	...
Value	$1,470	...	$1,000	...
Entitled to ecclesiastical pension	Yes	No	Yes	No
Length of vacation.........	2 months	1 month	1 month	2 months

* Part time.

TIME AND CHARACTER OF WORK

During a sample week for which the staff kept detailed records of its work, the pastor was on duty fifty-eight hours, or four hours less than the average for pastors of the twenty-six churches. The time occupied by his duties was divided as follows: conduct of services and sacraments, 10 per cent.; sermon preparation, 28 per cent.; pastoral duties, 19 per cent.; administrative duties, 40 per cent.; cultural pursuits, 3 per cent. On this showing he fell into the sub-group of executive-preachers, these two aspects of his work being outstandingly stressed. With respect to pastoral duties, he stood considerably below the average, and to public ministerial functions just at the average.

The deaconess worked sixty-three hours during the sample week, which was just the average for assistant pastors in the churches studied. She put in three days of seven to ten hours, and three days of over ten hours each, but took one holiday. Her work showed wide variety, including preparation for, and conduct of, the Sunday morning junior congregation, administrative and pastoral duties being primary.

The secretary worked forty-two hours (two hours less than the average of the secretarial group), but under average conditions which included a half holiday and no excessively long days.

The visitor's forty hours was much below the average of the visitors' group and included an unusually large percentage of time spent in attendance upon meetings relative to active visitation.

The average week's work-time of the four workers was a little over fifty hours each. One-fourth of this combined service was given to pastoral duties, one-fourth to administrative, and one-fifth to clerical work. This distribution of time agrees very closely with the median cases of the twenty-six studied; but the pastor's emphasis upon pulpit preparation, and the time spent by the deaconess in preparation for the junior church, caused homiletical preparation to be stressed much more than the average.

The work of the music-director, in addition to the above, includes the unusually painstaking administration of the choir as a social and business organization, as well as technical leadership.

Plant

The staff works, and the church works and worships, in a plant erected in 1874 which ranks twenty-second among the twenty-five cases compared. It scores a little more than 50 per cent. on the Interchurch World Movement thousand-point score-card. Considering the magnitude of the church's enterprise, this is decidedly the most inadequate plant studied.

The building, a brick structure of the rigidly ecclesiastical architecture of a half-century ago, occupies a corner site. Its spacious auditorium, with two galleries, suggests the music-hall of its time. It has been recently improved by a great organ with choir-loft filling the entire front; and, though, to the writer's eye, it fails in essential beauty, it is a good place in which to speak and to hear.

The particularly weak points of the plant are its service systems and its religious education and community service rooms, which reach respectively only 34 per cent., 46 per cent. and 32 per cent. on the standard score. This is only to say that the plant is old and mainly unmodernized, that the religious education facilities are much behind present day ideas; and that, in spite of the recent provision of a usable gymnasium secured by the excavation of the basement and cutting into the first story, the total structure has no all-around provision for the week-day activities or for the administration of a modern church.

A summarized score of the plant appears in Table XXVIII.

TABLE XXVIII—SUMMARY OF SCORE OF PLANT

Item	Standard Score	Points Scored		Rank in 25 Cases
		Number	Per Cent.	
Total	1,000	503	50	22
Site	130	88	68	16
Building or buildings	150	91	61	24
Service systems..............	160	54	34	24
Church rooms................	170	118	69	17
Religious school rooms........	200	91	46	21
Community service rooms.....	190	61	32	16

Finances

The total amount raised during the last year for local parish purposes approximated $40,000, of which about $30,000 were from strictly current sources. About $37 was spent for each one hundred of aggregate attendance, or $22 per determinate constituent. Two-thirds of the cases studied cost more than this, relative to attendance; half cost more relative to the size of the adherent group. (Still larger churches which put equal stress on preaching are, however, still more economical.) Hanson Place is not a church of great wealth and tends to be limited in program to the types of service that are least expensive.

As for the church's sources of income, a very unusual proportion (approximately one-fifth) comes from loose collections at public services. This reflects support from its great audiences of transients who contribute casually without subscribing. A small amount is obtained from pew rents. The proceeds of an annual church fair are a definitely established resource recognized in the church budget. Outside of income

TABLE XXIX—FINANCIAL EXPENDITURES OF THE CHURCH

Item	Amount	Per Cent.
Grand Total	$39,649	
Total Current Account............................	30,876	100
Salaries	10,050	32
General administrative expenses.................	848	3
Music	3,852	12
General operation and upkeep of property.........	13,821	45
Expenses of departments specially budgeted.......	213	1
Publicity	1,800	6
Ecclesiastical connections	292	1
Investment Account		
Endowment or permanent improvement	8,773	

of current origin, the rent of the old parsonage (after a large deduction for taxes) is an important item.

Expenditures on current account are shown in Table XXIX.

The per cent. of expenditures devoted to salaries is not far from average. In spite of the outstanding musical features of the church, expenditures on this account are not beyond the average by reason of the absence of paid singers and the rather low pay of the director, supplemented as it is by income from a music-school which he is allowed to hold in the church building. The upkeep and operation of the property, however, takes a very much more than average proportion of expenditures (45 per cent. of the total), largely on account of the items of taxes, fuel, power and light. This reflects the constant use of the organ, the necessary pushing of an inadequate heating plant, and the excessive need of illumination in a dark church.

Expenditures on property account consisted of payments on a small mortgage remaining on the church property, including items of both principal and interest.

Public Services

Except during the two summer months, the average attendance at the Sunday morning services is 450, at the evening services 1,000, and at the mid-week service, 125. On the morning covered by the study, females formed nearly 75 per cent. of the congregation and, in spite of the presence of the junior congregation, some 92 per cent. were adults. One hundred and eighteen of the choir's 225 members were present, and constituted more than one-fifth of the congregation.

The church auditorium is used for the Sunday-school session just prior to the morning service. Transition to the morning worship is therefore gradual, accompanied by rather vigorous movement and conversation. The vested junior choir takes its place in the rear gallery with considerable informality. With the organ voluntary, the great adult choir enters from front doors on either side of the pulpit and ascends the choir seats tier by tier until the entire front of the church is filled. The gowned minister takes his place. During the hymns, the musical-director acts as precentor. The order of service has no unusual features, except that the junior congregation's recessional follows the offertory anthem. Preceded by banners, the children march down from the gallery and down the center aisle, passing out at the front of the church into their own further service.

Judged by the year's topics, the characteristic sermon for at least a third of the time is one of a series of discourses based upon some scriptural episode or history. These carefully prepared studies are expanded with competent scholarship and fidelity to the text, and are applied with brilliance and aptness to exceedingly specific current situations. Two such series were presented during the current year, one on the personalities behind the New Testament, the other entitled, "On the Mountain Tops with Jesus." A goodly proportion of the announced topics sound original or challenging, as, for example: "The Little Lost Arts of Life"; "Jesus Christ, Citizen"; "When Conscience Is Eclipsed"; "The Biography of a Backslider." The pulpit, both morning and evening, is opened with rather generous frequency to advocates of special causes or interests.

The larger evening attendance is secured by methods not differing in principle from those used in the morning. The choir is augmented in size, and solo artists are imported from Sunday to Sunday. Sermon topics are popularized but never get further toward sensationalism than, for example, in "Flim-flamming the Flimflammer." The impressive and uplifting effects of the chorus choir, direct and attractive preaching in the graphic narrative style, with pertinent applications, are the more superficial explanations of the large attendance. Pageantry, however, should also be mentioned. It is somewhat frequently used, has been developed to a high degree of excellence in connection with public services, and brings out very large gatherings on special occasions.

Through the winter season, the public evening service is followed by an informal social period entertained by radio.

Religious Education

A numerical summary showing the structure and enrollment of the Sunday school appears in Table XXX.

TABLE XXX—SUMMARY OF SUNDAY-SCHOOL STATISTICS

DEPARTMENT	PUPILS		TEACHERS	
	Age	Enrollment	Male	Female
Total	...	577	14	21
Cradle Roll	...	40	..	..
Beginners	3–6	50	0	3
Primary	7–9	31	1	3
Junior	10–12	56	3	5
Intermediate	13–15	43 }	5	5
Senior	16–18	32 }		
Adult	21 & over	203	5	5
Home Department	...	122	..	3 *

* Visitors, not included in total.

The addition of eighteen officers to the 577 pupils and thirty-five teachers gives a grand total of 630. Pupils in the attending departments number 415, and attendance averages 64 per cent. of enrollment. The approximate age-distribution in the attending departments is as follows:

	Number	Per Cent.
Children	180	43
Adolescents	32	8
Adults	203	49

These data show that the preponderance of the adult constituency carries through into the Sunday school, and that there is the meager attendance of children often characterizing the down-town church—a situation less intelligible in the case of Hanson Place than when the constituency is geographically more remote. The shortage of adolescents in the constituency is probably reflected in the absence of any young people's department as such.

The adult department includes several organized Sunday-school classes which serve as social units and provide a partial but important substitute for the rather small subsidiary program of the church. They also carry out specific pieces of church work that lie beyond the sphere of religious education as such.

Methods of Growth and Conservation

In 251 cases examined of recent accessions to the church, 55 per cent. were by letter from other churches, and 45 per cent. on confession of faith. Four-fifths of those coming by letter were from the Methodist denomination, quite an appreciable number being transferred from other Methodist churches throughout Brooklyn.

By what concrete means were these recruits secured? In spite of the characteristic mobility of urban populations, only about 15 per cent. appear to have been strictly newcomers into the community secured after only brief preliminaries. Of established residents in Brooklyn, six-tenths of those who came by letter had been previously related to the church, chiefly by somewhat regular attendance upon services. As might be expected in a church with a relatively weak subsidiary program, the minor organizations are not very important as recruiting agencies—except that the choir brings in a considerable number through its membership. Pastoral ministries consist most largely of the cultivation of the existing membership, and responses to calls of need or for assistance in obtaining employment. A few persons helped in such crises are brought into church-membership. But the great recruiting ground of the church is its public services. Much is made of the communion. On account of the larger congregation at the evening service, communion is held then in addition to its celebration at the morning service. A record is kept of non-members who commune as well as of members, the ratio over a period of months equaling one-fourth of the members. After the habit of anonymous attendance and fellowship through communion has been established, it proves not difficult to get large numbers of persons to come forward with their letters in response to invitation from the pulpit.

Of those who joined the church on confession of faith during the period studied, the great majority had been associated with it through previous probation or through the Sunday school.

The new member is asked to sign an interesting questionnaire telling about his previous experience and present interests. This is intended as a means of placing him accurately in his new church relationships.

Besides the attempt to get the newcomer definitely enlisted in some form of church work, there is a systematic general cultivation of the whole constituency through postcard announcements of special occasions and interests.

The growth of the Hanson Place Church thus appears to be related to determinable and fairly effective processes of assimilation. These processes, however, after membership is secured, do not carry the majority of adherents into the more intimate organizational contacts. Indeed the church's knowledge of and hold upon its own membership can hardly be said to be close. About 30 per cent. of the total membership will be present at the average communion service. This is undoubtedly characteristic of much church work in great cities.

Church Life and Work

A more vital and adequate sense of the life of a church is gained by following its consecutive currents from week to week than is possible when it is approached topic by topic; and the former approach tends to supplement if not to correct the latter at certain points.

It is something of a discovery to find how largely a church that is relatively weak in formal subsidiary organizations finds a substitute for the usual work of such organizations in the systematic assignment of special responsibilities to such subsidiaries as exist and in the appointment of special committees for carrying on its very extensive program. The program is planned in detail for the whole church and for a year in advance. The observer gets the impression of unusually intense lay activity. He finds this activity expressing itself in something very like the modern project method. All departments of the church unite to take a long look ahead and are prepared to accept specific undertakings not nominally growing out of their objectives as conventionally announced. The result is an unusually unified program. The subsidiaries do not, as they do in so many churches, function almost independently of the church itself. Moreover, this policy is not ineffective. For example, of the churches studied, no other that was making so intensive a use of dining-room and kitchen facilities was without a paid housekeeper. In Hanson Place Church, the monthly depreciation and breakage of these facilities is simply inventoried by a women's committee and the cost assessed proportionately against the organizations using them.

Again, the interpretation of the church in terms of its permanent structural organizations does not fully reckon with the largely attended and popular cultural events that color and characterize the impression the church makes upon its community. A prime example is the annual series of Happy Saturday Night Entertainments. A limited number of tickets for these occasions is sold in advance in order to underwrite the bare cost, after which they are thrown open to the public free except for a voluntary collection. These events command great audiences. Again, as is natural in a church with so notable a choir, the occasional and seasonal concerts and oratorios constitute very distinct features of the year's activities.

Internally, Hanson Place Church impresses one by reason of the widely diverse elements and planes of experience for which it makes room within its constituency. Thus, one finds simultaneously occurring a class-meeting, the rehearsal of the great choir, and active gymnasium work—all in a church not at all insulated for sound. The class-meeting is characterized by testimonies and songs of genuine gospel-hall flavor, with hearty audible responses. The choir is conducted as a great musical and social organization, light refreshments following each rehearsal. (It also maintains monthly dances, but not in the church building.) The gymnasium is full of shouting children. There is no apparent sense of disharmony between these variant expressions of church life. This in itself is a happy achievement.

In not a few cases of highly adapted churches, ecclesiastical machinery originally devised for a system of rural circuits has not been found adequate for urban needs, and has actually been subordinated to that especially devised for the case. In Hanson Place Church, on the contrary, the traditional internal organization of a Methodist church is not overlaid nor subordinated. This may go with the fact that the church has attempted only a moderate departure from the traditional program; at any rate the local Methodist system is being carried out in faithful detail and is working well.

Hanson Place Church shows intimate participation in and is itself a striking expression of denominational life. While, in relation to its larger public, such expressions are not unduly stressed, the church does not allow itself or others to forget that it is one of the great denominational enterprises of the metropolis. The advocacy of current Methodist activities is emphatic and such practical Methodist interests as hospitals, institutions and methods of denominational cultivation of the constituency are continuously at the fore.

Such a strategic place in the denomination, and such broad responsibility as Hanson Place Church bears, results in a somewhat more determinative denominational consciousness than is evidenced in most of the other churches studied. The church aspires to be the official denominational center for the entire eastern half of the metropolis and its suburbs and to erect a great and many-storied central edifice, to serve both as a denominational shrine and as the administrative focus of its operations. Such a proposal is now actively before the larger Methodist body of Brooklyn and vicinity.

Urban Adaptations

In the case of Hanson Place Church, the features habitually associated with the more obvious and pronounced forms of adaptation to urban situations, as found in the twenty-six cases studied, are not largely in evidence. The church lacks that all-around and highly differentiated organization and program of activity along age and sex lines, associated with an expanded week-day program, which is one of the major trends in other cases. It lacks the technical phases of community service that attempt to meet distinctive urban situations and serve the populations whose fortunes present outstanding social problems. It lacks the special facilities and the varied technical staff that usually go with either of these tendencies in their maximum developments.

It is not easy to say, and probably a translation of the church's own inner consciousness could not show, how far its present limitations of program are due to limitations of its plant and finances. Probably the church has never thought through the question of what it would do if it had ampler means.

The social changes it has experienced in constituency and environment have been radical, but not so complete as in many cases; and the adverse aspects have been counterbalanced by advantages. By no means all of the church's kind of people have moved away, and the church itself has become increasingly popular, central and accessible.

Some of the characteristics of the resulting situation may be summarized as follows:

There has been a notable conservation of the older habits and atmosphere of the church. In a changed situation it has retained a large number of essentially unchanged people. The structure and characteristics of a Methodist church of the old time have not been superseded nor buried.

To the traditional program of a great church of the old type, many modern improvements have been added within the limits commonly accepted by the denomination, and involving but small additions to staff or slight modifications of plant. Besides the vast choir, there is a modernly organized Sunday school, a children's church, an unusual use of pageantry, the successful appeal of popular preaching.

Certain characteristics of urban civilization have been utilized, or at least fallen in with, to a noteworthy degree.

The church is largely basing its policy upon its accessibility.

It is getting increased support from the loose collections of casual attendants.

It is building upon the basis of urban individualism. A large and probably increasing proportion of its adherents come to it singly and not from otherwise adherent families.

It has managed to create a genuine religious life upon the basis of anonymousness. Large numbers of people who have no organized fellowship with the church habitually attend and doubtless receive many of the continuous benefits of a religious institution.

Among the outstanding impressions arrived at upon the basis of the entire study are those which show a hard-working minority of aggressive lay supporters, coöperating with a somewhat limited professional staff, and showing great resourcefulness within limited resources. The use of the project method to supplement feeble subsidiary organization, and the large measure of unification of the church in its entire program, strikes one as somewhat brilliant achievements.

The proposed center for Brooklyn Methodism on the Hanson Place site ought to materialize. The land values represented by the property justify nothing less than very intensive improvement. With adroit business intelligence in command, it should be possible to finance the enterprise and to get much bigger and better results along present lines. Such a consummation would get for the church a larger and wider hearing in an imposing urban setting. Organized religion, as now expressed in Hanson Place's great congregations, would make an enlarged appeal to the city's imagination. It could become a central institution, as few churches have opportunity to be.

May one not, however, venture the conviction that the welfare of its immediate neighbors ought always to be part of a church's most intimate moral consciousness and part of the atmosphere of its daily living, whatever be the particular agencies that carry on localized community work? In this sense, at least, one would like to see Hanson Place a local church as well as a central one, with very specific and traceable relations to the vicinity in some of its aspects.

CENTRAL METHODIST EPISCOPAL CHURCH, DETROIT, MICH.

Originating in itinerant evangelism while Detroit was but a frontier outpost, the incorporated organization which became the Central Methodist Episcopal Church three times relocated its house of worship before the city had a population of 75,000. It then found a desirable site at what was to be the permanent structural focus of the city (at that time well beyond the business district) ; and there it has stood ever since. After sixty years, the church, as technically rated by these studies, has the best location of all the twenty-six representative cases investigated.[1] Yet scarcely 12 per cent. of its constituency lives within a mile of the church, while two-thirds live over three miles away, and more constituents live over five miles away than in any nearer mile-zone. Furthermore, nearly the entire constituency lives on one side of the church.

How can any one think that a location so to one side and so remote from the homes of its constituency, is good, not to say best? That such a belief is held, certainly indicates something novel and unprecedented in the urban religious situation as relating to the church and its people. Fortunately, in the case now under consideration, the steps by which the church reached its conclusion are clear and have been recorded with unusual fullness.

The church still thought that it had the best location when, after thirty years, business was encroaching upon it and membership had dwindled (going to "heaven and the suburbs," as the contemporary phrase ran) along with the growth of Detroit to the quarter-million size. In this crisis it first definitely came to identify itself as a "down-town church"; and elected to remain in its old place on the theory that "all down-town

---

[1] For the grounds of this judgment, see p. XVIII.

churches must be maintained by up-town people," their maintenance being regarded as "a phase of missionary work" demanded by the exigencies of the modern city.

After twenty years more of experience with the problem of conscious adaptation in a limited form (but without radical modification of plan or equipment), the church still thought it had the best location; this in spite of the fact that by this time it could have sold its site for a million dollars and moved elsewhere. All the exigencies to which the church in the modern city is heir were naturally greatly intensified as Detroit, surpassing all of the other large cities in rate of recent growth, leaped toward and beyond the million mark. The answer of the church was to erect, in 1914, a supplementary six-story plant, with rooms for religious education, social life and community service, surmounting a ground floor of stores. This addition, with the modernization of the old plant, cost nearly $375,000. And still later, additional adjacent property was purchased with a view to future expansion.

The theory of the church's proposed ministry by means of the new plant was clearly defined and recorded. It was set forth that the vicinity of the church building had come to be a region of hotels, boarding-houses and rooming-houses. In addition to its already established ministries, it was the duty and task of the church to provide proper opportunity of human intercourse, social life and some rational recreation for the homeless young people living under conditions such as these.

The present study was made after there had been nearly a decade of operation under this new policy, and after considerable evolution of the policy itself. Probably no one assumed that success under the changed conditions would be easy. A study of statistical trends shows that, in the second half of the preceding decade, the church averaged smaller in membership by nearly one-fourth, and the Sunday school by about one-ninth, than in the first. (These figures need interpretation because the vast deflation of 1,000 members is far greater than normal and would seem to show that there was undue padding of the figures of the earlier period. Even so, however, some real numerical reduction seems to be indicated.) The great cost of additions to property was more than offset by increased land values; but the unparalleled standards of benevolent giving during the Centenary period have been found difficult to maintain. The scale of local expenditure, however, has been largely and permanently increased. Manifestly the church is not beyond difficulties, the common penalty of those that resolve to stand their ground in a down-town center.

But deeper than these relatively external conditions, lies the fact that the church that has evolved on the old site bears internal marks of a changed composition and of altered prospects.

It is composed, to a disproportionate extent, of detached individuals whose families are not also related to the church. Only seven out of the twenty-six churches studied have relatively so few adhering family groups.

Again, the church contains a very excessive proportion of adults. Only four of the twenty-six cases have relatively more, and only four have relatively fewer children.

Two additional points will serve to place the church in the series of the twenty-six cases. First, it is one of the largest cases, only six out of the twenty-six reporting a larger annual attendance on stated organizations and activities. Second, its program does not show really radical modifications such as many churches have undertaken when confronted with equal environmental change. On an identical list of sixty church practices, only seven out of the twenty-six cases are found to have narrower programs; and the range, as well as the number, of church activities is only medium. What a church with such general traits turns out to be in structure and in behavior is revealed step by step in the following sections.

I. MAJOR ASPECTS OF THE CHURCH

Members and Constituents

The total constituency listed as in actual connection with the church and all its organizations and activities numbers 2,626. As has been noted, the distribution according to age is strikingly distorted in favor of adults. This appears more fully in the following comparison, which shows that age-distribution of constituents in the twenty-six churches as a group corresponds closely to the age-distribution of Detroit's population.

| | PER CENT. | | |
	Adults (21 & Over)	Adolescents (15-20)	Children (5-14)
Constituencies of:			
Central Methodist Church	84	5	11
26 churches........................	73	8	19
Population of Detroit................	72	10	18

In comparison, the Central Methodist Church is strikingly deficient in children, and proportionately even more deficient in adolescents. The sex-distribution of the constituency, however (forty-three men to every fifty-seven women), agrees exactly with the strongly modal tendency of the twenty-six churches. From the standpoint of sex, then, the church is not more one-sided than the majority.

MANNER AND DEGREE OF ADHERENCE

The introductory section has already noted the extraordinary average distance of the homes of the constituency from the church building. But this has not prevented extraordinary closeness of connection. The constituency includes more than an average proportion of persons belonging to more than one of the church's major departments. The per cent. of those who belong by church-membership only, while above the average of the twenty-six cases, is not extreme; and the proportion of those who belong to the church, the Sunday school and the subsidiaries (14 per cent.), is not only well above average but is beyond that found in any other down-town church save one. The one-way overlaps of church and Sunday-school memberships and Sunday-school and subsidiary memberships, do not vary greatly from the median case, while the overlap of the church and the subsidiaries is very high. This condition (which is graphically portrayed in Chart IV) reflects, it will be found, the unusually developed cultural program of the church.

The total picture then is of a remote constituency that nevertheless is better integrated than is, on the average, one living much nearer its church.   And the fact holds for every age-group in the constituency.

Church-members come with considerably greater frequency from family groups than from the ranks of detached individuals, though detached individuals preponderate in the constituency as a whole.   Especially is this true of the membership of subsidiaries.   The subsidiary organizations, in other words, tend to serve the non-family adherent.   This was their first intention.   On the other hand, nearly two-thirds of those who belong to the church, the Sunday school and the subsidiaries, all three, are from adherent families.   This element still furnishes the more intimately connected core of the church.

While of the total constituent body the proportion connected with the church in only one way is just above the average, the proportion connected five, or six, or seven, or more ways is exceedingly high.   Almost all of those who are thus rooted in the church in an extreme number of ways are adults, their sex-ratio being about seven women to one man.

Out of 782 pledged contributors reported, nearly two-thirds, also, are adult women.   Contributors include 38 per cent. of the membership of the church (which is considerably below average on the basis of eleven cases in which this point was covered), and about one-third of the enrollments of the Sunday school and the subsidiaries; but they constitute 76 per cent. of those who are members of church, Sunday school and subsidiaries, all three.   Thirty-eight per cent. of constituents belonging to adherent families are pledged contributors, but only 22 per cent. of detached individuals.   This is simply to say that the workers (as identified by the number of their connections) are also the givers, and that members of adherent families bear more than their proportion of financial responsibility.

Experience shows that virtually every church has a core of hard-working and responsible adherents.   One may picture this core as surrounded by successive layers of adherents whose relatedness to the church is less and less complete.   In the Central Methodist Church the core is unusually large and the relatedness of the remainder thins out less rapidly than usual.

Detached individuals supply an unusual proportion of the church's total numbers; but adherent families are the chief source of its closely related workers and of its financial support. These closely related workers are women in an overwhelming proportion of cases, though the sex-ratio of the total constituency is just normal. The ratio of all contributors to the total constituency is below average.

Parish and Environment

The central business district of Detroit has the form of a pyramid. Its base rests upon the zone of industries and railways bordering the Detroit River. Its apex is about one mile north of the river where Woodward Avenue crosses the Grand Circus, a small semicircular park. All the major north and south streets of the business section bend to a focus upon this park. The radiating major thoroughfares, which determine the chief characteristics of Detroit's physical structure, converge within the few blocks below it; and, as the center of gravity of the business district has moved northward, the most important transit routes increasingly tend to draw in toward this point.[2] Here at the corner of Woodward Avenue, opposite the Grand Circus, stands the Central Methodist Church. Several of the city's largest hotels and amusement places are immediately adjacent, and the vicinity is marked by the presence of numerous central institutions, like the Young Men's and Young Women's Christian Associations, and the leading clubs.

Within a mile of the church lives a population of approximately 95,000 people, 22 per cent. of whom live in single-family dwellings, 36 per cent. in two- and four-family flats, and 29 per cent. in tenements housing four families or more.[3] The area shows marked aberrations with respect to the composition of its population, males exceeding females to the extraordinary degree of 22 per cent., and roomers exceeding

---

[2] The widening of these major thoroughfares, already authorized by the voters, will constitute one of the most extensive improvements ever undertaken in a city's basic street plan. The completion of this project will still further fix the distinctively focal character of the plan.

[3] Character of housing of 13 per cent. of population unreported.

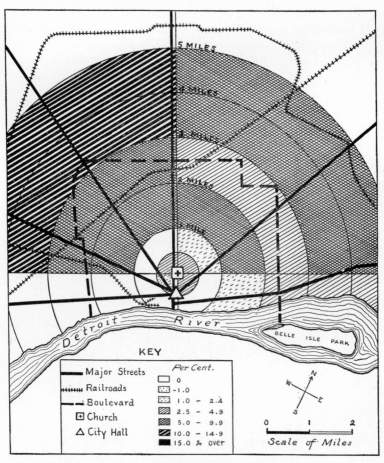

5 MILES

4 MILES

3 MILES

2 MILES

1 MILE

Detroit River

BELLE ISLE PARK

KEY

		Per Cent.
▬ Major Streets	□	0
┼┼┼┼ Railroads	▦	-1.0
┄┄ Boulevard	▨	1.0 — 2.4
⊞ Church	▨	2.5 — 4.9
△ City Hall	▨	5.0 — 9.9
	▨	10.0 — 14.9
	■	15.0 & over

N
W — E
S

0   1   2

Scale of Miles

CHART VII
Parish of Central Methodist Episcopal Church, Detroit

families by one-sixth (whereas in the city as a whole there are twice as many families as roomers).

Socially speaking, the area is extremely complex. However, its most general characteristics may be briefly summarized.

Railways and industries occupy the river front, and the pyramidal business district lies across the central axis.

Within a mile to the southeast of the church falls the site of the oldest settlement of the city, originally French. From this early center, the main movement of foreign population has gone forward by successive racial waves, as it has done from similar points of original settlement in most American cities. This sector is now the home of people of various races, Greek, Syrian, Rumanian, Mexican and West Indian Negro. Only 14 per cent. of the population is native white. Two-thirds of the population are male. There are sixty-one roomers to every thirty-nine families. The tenement type of habitation is strongly prevalent, and home ownership stands almost at zero. All these foreign and Negro populations show that heavy excess of males which indicates that they belong to the ranks of the most recent immigration.

In striking contrast with the southeastern sector, that lying within one mile to the southwest of the church has 57 per cent. of its population native-born (though largely of mixed parentage); but the population is still two-thirds male, and there are even more roomers per family. The flat gains on the tenement as a type of housing, but there is still virtually no home ownership. The chief foreign-born elements consist of little, well-marked groups from Spain, Malta, Turkey, China and Japan.

Turning now away from the river and the central business district, one finds the main zone of foreign occupancy resting on the river front to the southeast. Here native-born population declines again to 27 per cent. Getting away from the water front, however, there is less congestion. Flats equal or exceed tenement-houses in the second half-mile zone, and almost supplant them on the edge of the area. There are just about as many roomers as families, and a little home ownership begins to occur. Here are the heavily populated Italian and Jewish districts. The sector also includes part of the solidly Negro district. The male excess is now only 16 per cent., and is especially marked in the Italian and West Indian Negro population.

Northwest from the church is the direction of the city's major desirable growth. Within a mile of its building, native whites constitute two-thirds of the population. But there is a 20 per cent. excess of male over female population, and there are fifty-five roomers to every forty-five families. This is the chief habitat in Detroit of young Americans living away from home in boarding-houses and furnished rooms.

For the northwestern sector in general, the type of housing is more mixed, small single-family houses occupying a good many blocks. Home ownership begins to appear on the margins of the mile zone. The foreign element is still polyglot, consisting of small clusters of various races rather than of solid masses of one-race groups.

Considered in its entire circumference, the area within a mile of the Central Methodist Church contains one of the most cosmopolitan social situations in America, a situation made more striking and exigent by the exceedingly rapid growth of Detroit and the consequent newness, transience and instability of so much of the population.

The mile immediately west of the church includes also the area of most active and radical physical change. Here the advancing city is first rendering the existing structures undesirable from the standpoint of their former uses; it next fills them with transient occupants, and then gradually replaces them with business, apartment hotels and institutions of the newer and more expensive types.[4]

To this entire area, lying within a mile of it, and of which it is the geographical center, the Central Methodist Church is related, by residence of constituents, only to the extent of 1 per cent. living within one mile to the southwest and 3 per cent. in each of the other sectors.

The less than 2 per cent. of the constituency which lives in the second half-mile, mainly to the northeast and northwest, is not much better off as to environmental fortunes than is that within the first half-mile. Aside from these few constituents

---

[4] Data from *1925 Detroit Census,* Board of Education, with coöperation of the Federal Bureau of the Census, Detroit Educational Bulletin, October, 1925.

(12 per cent. of the total), the church avoids, by a sort of natural selection, all the more undesirable sections of the city.[5] In sharpest contrast are the environmental fortunes of people living in the third and fourth mile zone to the northwest, where the constituency is most numerous, as shown by Chart VII.

An examination of a group of typical precincts in this vicinity shows the prevalence of native population living in normally distributed sex- and age-groups; a predominance of single-family dwellings (though, in much of the area, the flat is the predominant form of urban habitation, and high-grade apartment houses are springing up in a few sections); more than half of the homes owned by their occupants. It is true that colonies of the more prosperous Jewish and Negro population have joined the migration into this most desirable direction; but the area occupied by them is relatively small. Roomers are numerous, but are mainly confined to structures specializing in keeping them as a business rather than diffused throughout the general population.

Taking the city as a whole, while the constituents of the church are sprinkled throughout all middle-class districts, their numbers are found to thicken up noticeably wherever there is an area that is especially high-grade from the economic and social standpoints. Moreover, with constituents of this sort, distance is not found to interfere with closeness of connection in any age-group except that of children. The scattered following appears to be served as well as merely held.

Besides being little localized, it is seen that the church models itself upon the city selectively. Its affinity for certain types of population is well marked; its repulsions from other types are equally marked.

II. AGENCIES, RESOURCES AND METHODS

Organizations and Activities

The ratio of the church's Sunday program to its activities of the week days is about that of the median case. This manifestly means that between Sundays this church draws a much larger proportion of its characteristically remote constituency

---

5 For statistical table showing parish distribution in detail, see p. 253.

than many churches draw from constituencies that live much nearer.

Table XXXI shows that preaching services and the Sunday school occupy about a median proportion of the total program, while the program of the subsidiaries is considerably, though not extremely, above the median.

TABLE XXXI—ESTIMATED ANNUAL ATTENDANCE ON SPECIFIED OCCASIONS AT CENTRAL METHODIST CHURCH AND AT 26 CHURCHES

	ATTENDANCE			
	CENTRAL METHODIST CHURCH		26 CHURCHES	
OCCASION			Approx. Median	Range of Variation
	Number	Per Cent.	Per Cent.	Per Cent.
Total *	131,640	100		
Formal religious services (Sunday and week day).........	65,612	50	51	15–75
Sunday school................	31,060	24	24	9–38
All other stated activities......	34,968 †	26	22	9–51

* Sunday, 75 per cent.; week day, 25 per cent.
† Includes meetings of church officers and committees.

In order of magnitude, the largest division of the subsidiary program is that for adult women, followed by those for young people, for adult men, for young women and for boys and girls. The lack of sex differentiation for younger groups probably indicates the relatively small number of children which has already been discovered. This is shown in Table XXXII.

TABLE XXXII—ESTIMATED ANNUAL ATTENDANCE ON SUBSIDIARY ORGANIZATIONS AND STATED ACTIVITIES

	ORGANIZATIONS	ATTENDANCE	
No.	Type	Number	Per Cent.
	Total	33,778	
33	Classified by Age and Sex.................	31,163	100
4	Mixed adults	2,000	6
4	Adult men	3,908	13
7	Adult women	9,387	30
2	Mixed young people *..................	8,424	27
3	Young men	956	3
10	Young women	3,032	10
1	Mixed boys and girls..................	2,536	8
0	Boys	0	0
2	Girls	920	3
0	Mixed children	0	0
	Classified by Function Summer camp	2,615	

* Between 15 and 23 years of age.

The church has one of the strongest programs for adult women found in the twenty-six cases studied. The young people's program also ranks high, while that for adult men is equaled or exceeded in only two cases.

The most striking aspect of the subsidiary program, however, is the large number of organizations through which it is carried on. Besides the traditional parish and missionary societies of the Methodist church, these consist chiefly of educational classes and cultural groups meeting throughout the active church year in connection with the mid-week church night, and of a number of organized Sunday-school classes maintaining a week-day program of sociability and practical service. Extensive gymnasium and camping activities are also to be noted.

Staff

The staff of nine paid religious workers is above average in size, with reference both to the total magnitude of the church enterprise and to the variety of its activities.

Its organization is logical and clear-cut. Besides the pastor, there are three male departmental associates called, respectively, directors of pastoral, of educational and of physical activities. A deaconess supplements the pastoral workers, particularly in service to constituents in the immediate vicinity. The church has a clerical force of four workers, consisting of a general church secretary, an office assistant in charge of the switchboard and subordinate to the church secretary, and two secretarial assistants each related to two of the male executives.

The preparation, experience, tenure and remuneration of the staff are shown in Table XXXIII.

During the sample week (which is not assumed to be absolutely representative), the combined staff was on duty exactly 500 hours. With respect to length of work day, it fell into two strongly contrasting groups, the male executives and deaconess working from sixty-five to sixty-nine hours each, and the four clerical workers observing the ordinary commercial week of from forty to forty-three hours. Except the church secretary, none of the clerical workers attended meet-

TABLE XXXIII—ANALYSIS OF PAID STAFF

	Pastor	Director of Pastoral Activities	Director of Educational Activities	Director of Physical Activities	Deaconess	Church Secretary	Secretary	Office Clerk	Stenographer
Sex	Male	Male	Male	Male	Female	Female	Female	Female	Female
Degree of education									
Academic	College	College	College	High school	High school	High school	High school	...	College
Professional or special	Theological Post-graduate Elocution	Theological Business	Theological Religious education	Physical training	Deaconess school Normal	Business	Business	...	Business
Years of employment									
Prior to this position									
Secular work	6	6	7	14	3½	6⅔	7	14	2
Religious work	22½	5	10	2	2	...	...	16	1
In this position	5½	3 months	2	1½	21	6	3	1¼	1
Present salary									
Cash	$9,500	$3,000	$4,500	$2,750	$360	$1,680	$1,440	$1,010	$1,320
Perquisites									
Nature	...	Auto	...	Summer maintenance	Room, board, etc.	...	...	...	...
Value	...	$385	...	$250	$624	...	...	...	...
Entitled to ecclesiastical pension	Yes	Yes	Yes	No	Yes	No	No	No	No
Length of vacation	2½ months	1 month	1 month	1 month	1 month	2 weeks	2 weeks	2 weeks	2 weeks

ings of the church as part of the recognized duties of their offices.

The length of the pastor's work time was about five hours beyond the average of the pastors of the churches studied. With respect to the proportion of time spent in sermon preparation, he stood at the head of the list, and ranked with the upper fifth with respect to time spent in pastoral ministries. While in no church was a pastor found with his hands more definitely upon the details, as well as upon the major policies, of church business, relatively little of his time in the sample week had to be given to administration, especially in view of the smooth running system of departmentalized responsibility. The distribution of his time thus definitely classifies him as belonging to the preaching type of minister, to which his well-established pulpit reputation would undoubtedly assign him.[6]

The work of the staff, as a whole, is characterized by an unusual concentration upon the major lines of work clearly indicated by the nature of the particular positions. The Director of Pastoral Activities is primarily a pastor, with functions much less mixed than those of most assistant ministers. In keeping with the type, the Director of Religious Education is primarily an executive, though related to the junior congregation on the side of worship. The Director of Physical Activities represents a type of departmentalization infrequently found in the cases studied. He is primarily a supervisor of the gymnasium with secondary executive work in managing the department, and with special relations to a departmental committee on physical activities and various athletic organizations.

Though she is primarily engaged in pastoral work, teaching is unusually emphasized by the deaconess as a secondary function, largely in connection with the Chinese Sunday school and English classes for Chinese.

While the church secretary shows small amounts of pastoral and administrative work, the presence of a large group of male executives in the staff does not make it natural for the

---

[6] Of course the bare amount of time spent in any given phase of the minister's work is not in any case a direct measure of its importance or of his effectiveness. For further discussion of the time records, see p. 450.

clerical assistants to absorb the significant share of other functions that they often do in smaller staffs. The other secretaries are almost purely clerical in function.[7]

All told, the staff presents a highly efficient organization of well-coördinated specialists.

Considering the total work of the staff, clerical duties occupy about twice as much time as either pastoral or executive ones, which rank next. Preparation of sermons, in turn, takes about half as much time as pastoral or executive work; and preaching and officiating at services take about half as much time as homiletical preparation. This shows the large place in a modern highly organized church which secondary means of communication (operated through an office by printing, telephone, correspondence, etc.) have assumed in the cultivation of a religious constituency, especially a remote one; and also suggests the increased importance of records in a complicated organization.

Plant

The auditorium was erected in 1867, and the much larger parish house in 1914. In only three of the twenty-five cases studied do the plants rank higher. All of these are modern plants, designed as units, and having all the structural parts erected at the same time.

Both buildings of the Central M. E. Church are of stone. The modified Gothic of the older building is dignified, though it scarcely appeals to modern taste. The adaptation of the Gothic style in the parish house in order to achieve measurable harmony with the older structure, and, at the same time, to serve the ends of property to be rented for commercial purposes and also of a modern church house, is notably successful. The total plant, now valued at three million dollars, natural'y has to occupy the entire site; but it avoids giving the impression of being crowded by occupying a corner and having its long frontage facing a park. In view of the mixed architectural and structural qualities, it is impossible to rate the plant above medium in these aspects. The older portions of the

---

[7] For contrasting case, see p. 116.

structure, however, had their interiors thoroughly modernized in connection with the addition of the parish house; and the church ranks third with respect to facilities and service systems. The auditorium has been architecturally modified with excellent results; but the limited number of rooms given to the accessory uses of services of worship brings the church down to tenth place on the item of church rooms. It stands at the top of the list, however, with respect to Sunday-school facilities and equipment, its problem here being somewhat simplified by its relatively small numbers of children. The strength of the plant is in its provision for cultural and social ministries, rather than in that for technical social service; in spite of a most excellent gymnasium and handball courts, it ranks only eighth in community facilities.

All told, the plant clearly shows that it was specially designed or reconstructed for the program it is desired to carry out: namely, one chiefly of large gatherings for public worship and an active cultural and social program for a relatively homogeneous constituency.

The score by items, compared with the standard score of the Interchurch World Movement 1,000-point score-card, is shown in Table XXXIV.

TABLE XXXIV—SUMMARY OF SCORE OF PLANT

Item	Standard Score	Points Scored		Rank in 25 Cases
		Number	Per Cent.	
Total	1,000	745	75	4
Site	130	105	81	6
Building or buildings..........	150	125	83	8
Service systems	160	131	82	3
Church rooms	170	129	76	10
Religious school rooms........	200	161	81	1
Community service rooms.....	190	94	50	8

Finances

The total amount raised for current expenses during the year preceding the study was approximately $115,000, including about $54,000 for benevolences. This puts the church well toward the top of the list in the total of its financial operations. The cost is just about average relative to the magnitude of the program as measured by aggregate annual attendance or by number of constituents.

About one-sixth of the annual income for the church's own support was received from other than current sources. Rents on property (the stores under the parish house and an adjoining business and office building) bring in about $9,000, in addition to which a little comes from endowment.

Of income from current sources, about 60 per cent. was from pledges contributed in weekly envelopes; while nearly one-fifth was from loose collections. Only one other of the churches studied received so large an amount from pledges, and only two others got anything like the same proportion from loose collections (which now run beyond $10,000 annually). Loose collections have tripled in ten years, while receipts from pledges have nearly quadrupled. The pledged receipts come from 660 subscribers, out of a total of about 1,100 giving units (families and single individuals) as estimated by the church.

The distribution of expenditures is shown in Table XXXV.

TABLE XXXV—FINANCIAL EXPENDITURES OF THE CHURCH

Item	Amount	Per Cent.
Total	$60,540	100
Salaries	18,624	31
General administrative expenses	6,348	10
Music (including salaries)	8,232	14
General operation and upkeep of property	15,726	26
Expenses of departments specially budgeted	7,258	12
Publicity	3,179	5
Miscellaneous	1,173	2

In spite of the large staff, the per cent. paid on salary account is not beyond average. Music costs considerably more than the average per cent. of the total expenses budgeted. Publicity takes about an average amount of the budget. The proportion going to departments separately budgeted is low because, under the church's type of organization, there are not the usual semi-independent enterprises.[8]

---

[8] The organized Sunday-school classes constitute an exception to this statement. They handle their own finances, which are not reported in any of the above figures. The total, however, is relatively small.

There are about 360 benevolent pledges, leaving some 740 giving units not taking stated responsibility for benevolent contributions.

A relatively small debt of about $100,000 rests upon the property, and there is a very slender endowment which the church is striving to increase.

Public Services

The estimated average attendance at stated public services during the active season is 800 at the Sunday-morning service, 550 at the evening service and 175 at the mid-week service. The last is conducted as a religious lecture by the pastor following an evening of sociability and educational classes.

The public services have an atmosphere of reverence and hospitality without undue formality. They are presided over by the pastor, assisted by one or two of the departmental directors. The vested choir is a mixed double quartet. The order of service is fairly elaborate, including the Apostles' Creed, a chant after the prayer, the psalter and Gloria and two anthems, with frequent choral responses. Printed notices of the week are reënforced verbally. The pastor (whose work record has designated him as belonging to the pulpit type) enjoys international reputation for the brilliance and literary quality of his preaching. His representative homiletic material is turned into published books year by year.

The evening service is usually preceded by an organ recital, and is regularly broadcasted by the Detroit Free Press. It follows a somewhat simplified order of service. Musical attractions given by the male and female quartets of the choir are featured.

The character of the congregations was ascertained in detail by means of cards signed by most of those attending morning and evening services on two successive Sundays in March, 1925. Forty-two per cent. of the morning congregation were members of the church, but only 13 per cent. of the evening congregation. Church-members from all sources, including Methodists from other churches and members of other denominations, made up three-fourths of the congregation in the morning and two-thirds in the evening. Methodists, all told, constituted more than half of the audience in the morning, but only one-fourth in the evening services. At either service, from one-sixth to one-fifth of those present were strangers living outside of Detroit. At least one-fourth in the morning, and one-third in the evening, were not church-members at all. This indicates the difference so frequently found between the morning and the evening congregations, but also shows the unusually varied hearing which the message of Central Methodist Church gets. In its public ministries, the church is functioning largely for the members of other churches, including those of other Methodist churches of Detroit; also, to a less extent, for strangers in the city, and to about an equal extent for the unchurched.

Religious Education

The enrollment, organization and age-distribution of members of the Sunday school appear in Table XXXVI. The relatively small number of children in the Sunday school has already been noted. A large proportion of the more distant families of the church are presumably using the neighborhood Sunday schools for their children.

TABLE XXXVI—SUMMARY OF SUNDAY-SCHOOL STATISTICS

Department		Pupils	Teachers	
	Age	*Enrollment*	*Male*	*Female*
Total	...	904	10	35
Cradle Roll	...	138	..	..
Kindergarten	1–5	45	0	2
Primary	6–8	35	0	8
Junior	9–11	40	0	6
Intermediate	12–14	52	3	3
Senior	*	76	2	4
Adult	*	418	5	12
Home Department	...	100	..	..

 * Range of ages not given.

The addition of five officers to the 904 pupils and forty-five teachers gives a grand total of 954. Pupils in the attending departments number 666, and attendance averages 88 per cent.

of enrollment. The approximate age-distribution in the attending departments is as follows:

	Number	Per Cent.
Children	120	18
Adolescents	128	19
Adults	418	63

The Sunday services of the junior congregation parallel
those of the church, but are not formally related to the Sunday-
school worship which follows; nor is the Epworth League
administratively unified under a common scheme of religious
education. The Wednesday night cultural groups, however—
clubs for debating parliamentary practice and for the discussion of current events, the Browning Club, and courses in
world-citizenship and "our Bible"—are under the Director of
Education, and are regarded as a broadening of the process of
religious culture. The entrenched position of some of the
long-established adult Bible classes, and their rather independent spirit, create something of an administrative problem.

All told, the agencies of religious education are numerous,
but not fully integrated into a departmental organization.

Current Church Life

As lived out by the church, the phases of organized life
which have been noted actually flow together as part of the
stream of weekly, monthly and seasonal events. After a
rather long summer vacation (during which various camping
activities are carried on), the major features of the church's
program get under way, centering in the Sunday services, religious and cultural activities of the mid-week church night,
the gymnasium schedules, and the regular and special programs of the minor organizations.

The seasonal interests of the holidays of the Christian year
supply the recurrent high lights of the picture. Other types of
special activity are the Sunday-afternoon organ recitals, the
occasional hospitality shown to various lodges and clubs that
become the church's guests at services Sunday night; the
timely, recurrent special emphases on civic interests and duty;
and the occasional ministries that express the special flavor of

the pastor's outlook and genius, such as his annual series of historical or literary lectures and his recommendations of books for reading. The pastor religiously reserves the bulk of the active church year for consecutive ministries to his own parish; but is in great demand, especially as a preacher at universities. An unusual number of notable foreign religious leaders are heard in the Central Church pulpit. All the outstanding religious and cultural enterprises of the city at large are heartily exploited. On account of the church's superior location, many interdenominational gatherings are held in its building. Throughout the year, the manifold interests of the Methodist denomination are systematically promoted and carried out.

For its own distinctive constituency, the church performs a strongly marked type of service by means of quite characteristic methods.

The literary flavor of the pulpit is reënforced by a strong supplementary educational program which is more extensive, for the adult body of the church, than in any other case studied. This notable emphasis exists, however, within a total program that is only moderately broad and by no means outstanding by reason of the range or originality of most of its undertakings.

The church is organized as an efficient machine, its departments quietly supplementing the central work of the pulpit. It functions through an amply paid staff, which is largely occupied with organization and group activities, and in the creation of indirect contacts and appeals not involving face-to-face relationships. The extent to which these phases of the organized life of the church have evolved is much greater than the enlargement of older functions that has taken place during the same time. While no time-records of the church's work of the past are available, unquestionably a different balance of ministries has come about and would now be revealed.

It follows that, in the actual functioning of the church, the constitutional denominational system of local church life has been largely overlaid by types of organization immediately reflecting the church's current program. With no change in the theory of internal organization, a distribution of actual work very different from that of the past would be found between the staff and the lay officers and active members of the church group and between the constitutional officers and the new departmental committees. At the same time, the new departmentalization has not yet gone so far as considerations of logic and efficiency may carry it in the future. Not infrequently the church appears to be doing virtually the same thing twice for the same group of people, because old habits and ways of accomplishing results have not been fully substituted for.

It is to be recognized that one of the most vital and primary of the types of human association is that which gathers a group of followers about persons with natural capacity for leadership. Such natural leaders often create or take possession of some of the numerous, flexible subsidiary organizations of the Protestant church. Spontaneous clusterings of this sort would appear to be the real explanation of a portion of the existing organizations of the Central Methodist Church. But organizations that center in personalities do not always fall in or correlate with those based on the efficient division of functions. This is an entirely normal situation, which explains much in both the form and the actual ongoing of the institution.

Gains and Losses

Both the current activity of the church and its organized characteristics as they appear at any given time, concern and are attributes of an ebbing and flowing of a constituency that has to be recruited continuously, because it is always suffering the losses incident to all institutions, together with the peculiar ones growing out of its special circumstances.

An examination of 187 cases of recent accessions to the church shows that 79 per cent. were received by letter from other churches, 59 per cent. being formerly Methodists and 20 per cent. from other denominations. Only 21 per cent. came on confession of faith. The small ratio of recruiting other than by letter, doubtless reflects the limited representation of youth in the constituency of the church, and the great flood of reënforcements that comes from other communities. Other down-town churches showed the same general tendency; but none of those studied had it to the same extent.

The usual method of organized recruiting is to make a collection of a large number of "prospect" names. Lay committees then undertake to solicit these persons in behalf of church-membership, supplementing the work of the paid staff. The presentation of letters is then invited at the end of the public services; but the pastor believes that eight out of ten who come forward in response to such appeals from the pulpit have previously been subject to pastoral cultivation, and that their coming is foreseen.

The Director of Pastoral Activities visits every home of the church at least once a year. A small Saturday catechetical class is also held between New Year and Easter.

In 152 cases of recent losses, seventeen members were found to have died, while five were dropped and 130 transferred by letter. The church recognizes that the proportion of those who were dropped is unusually small, but feels that this is evidence of an exceptionally close pruning of the church rolls. Of the 130 transferred, 115 went to other churches. Eighty-seven were dismissed to churches outside of the city, but forty-three, or nearly one-third, went elsewhere within the city. The reasons given showed that about three-fifths of these had moved and found some other church more convenient. Three or four merely stated that they had moved, while two changed their church allegiance for family reasons. Fifty-five of the 130 persons granted letters had been members of the church less than five years, forty-five for from five to nine years, and thirty for over ten years. This shows a large per cent. of loss occurring in the ranks of long-time members.

Relation to Social Agencies

In addition to the support of denominational and parochial benevolences, 1,153 contributions—as revealed by a recent circularization of the church—were made by its members within a year to civic and social agencies. The largest number of contributors was naturally that supporting the group of broadly civic agencies, 225 of which were to the community fund for the joint budget of the city-wide welfare interests. The largest numbers of contributions were received by the following types of agencies:

Hospitals and prevention of sickness.....................	160
Non-denominational religious agencies (including Young Men's and Young Women's Christian Associations)...	140
Family relief agencies....................................	108
Educational and character-building agencies.............	68

The women's organization of the church contributed supplies and clothing to a wide range of philanthropies, and the church's publicity continuously stressed civic and social interests. While the data for the other churches studied are not easily made comparable on this point, the number of officers of social agencies seems to be relatively less than from certain other churches, but the deep involvement of the church in the community and its far-reaching services are clear.

Adaptations

The Central Methodist Church of Detroit, in its present phase, is built upon the extraordinary freedom from local attachment of select religious populations in cities, and their easy transportability. It is defined by the movements of its constituents rather than by their places of residence. But the constituency of a church of this sort is not a cross section of a general population. With respect to age, nativity, economic status, family relationships and general intelligence, it is clearly a peculiar group. Such a group indeed can largely substitute accessibility for proximity in the determination of its church location and exchange "freely chosen associates for the predetermined community group" as the principle of its group organization.

Rapid gains and losses show the instability of a group with such characteristics; but under urban conditions it is continuously renewable from new-coming populations and from members of each generation as they grow up into the status in which the Central Church has the greatest appeal for them. This latter is evidenced by the fact that the Central Church is drawing detached individuals away from their families in all the residential parts of the city in almost the same proportions that it draws families.

On the other hand, the church is distinctly limited in its local appeal. The neighborhood Daily Vacation Bible School, the Chinese and Greek work, though considerable relative to the population of these nationalities in the community, are but diminutive phases of its total program. It has almost no direct relation, through means that are parochially organized and carried out, to local problems. The sense of social difference between the neighboring down-town populations and the church almost entirely outweighs the fact of contiguity. On the other hand, the church is in massive and varied relations to all manner of specialized agencies dealing with the problems of these populations. It is one of the responsible centers of earnest and large-minded advocacy and interpretation of civic and social problems that must underlie all concrete efforts for the solution of those problems. But it does not deal with them itself. Its impressive city-wide appeal is to a specialized constituency. It has not brought a dual or a triple set of adherents under its immediate ministries within a single organization and under a common roof.[9]

Besides the far-coming regular constituency and the small local following, there is the transient constituency drawn from out of town, from city-wide areas, and to some extent, probably, from the locality. The contribution of the transient constituency, through loose collections, to the expenses of the church is significant and increasing. On the other hand, financial responsibility has not been so well diffused throughout the entire constituent group as in the average of the churches studied.

In the present case, as probably in every similar one, the strength of the church's situation is greatly reënforced by the psychological advantages that go with prestige of location, reputation of success and high standards of expression. Here is something in the religious realm which is among the big and beautiful things accessible to a popular following in down-

---

[9] In contrast, compare the other Detroit cases, IX and X.

town Detroit. The extraordinary increase in property values, especially as these have been made currently productive through the inclusion of rental properties in the church plant, has constituted a double insurance of the venture in its financial aspects. It has also made possible an adequacy of facilities and a consequent competitive advantage. While an analysis of the congregation proves that there is no more, at least, than a grain of truth in the local pleasantry that the Central Church evening service exists upon the overflow of the movies, it is a noteworthy fact that what the church has to offer equals the best that the city provides in any other realm for the crowds who throng its down-town centers.

Perhaps the most suprising aspect of the church's success is the fact that, with such remote geographical relations with its stated constituents, and with a constituency of such an unusual character as has been shown, it has secured the more than average integration of its adherents into a social group. The active core of Central Church is proportionately larger, its numbers belong to the church in more ways, come oftener and stay longer, than is true of many parishes based upon close proximity.

This version of the major aspects of the church goes somewhat beyond the formulas, and perhaps differs from the theories, which it uses in self-interpretation. It may have "more families than ever before" (as was claimed in 1914), but the texture of the social group as a whole is decidedly not the same; neither, probably, is the composition even of the constituency coming from family groups. What the case proves is that a down-town church can maintain itself by transporting adherents from long distances. It does not prove that this can be done without a selective appeal to distinctive urban traits and habits, with the consequent marked distortion of the normal proportions of a population group. These far-coming adherents no longer think of the support of a down-town church by up-town people as a "missionary" proposition. It is rather the normal expression of the essential functions of a city center in urban life and of the natural relations of certain classes of population to it.

Again, the major argument used a decade ago for enlarging the church in its present location and for the particular content of its program in connection with the new plant, is actually a very secondary aspect of the church's present ministry. The church does draw an appreciable number of sound and promising American adherents from the contiguous non-family areas of the city. But the proportion is by no means great enough to characterize the church as one dealing largely with the transient rooming-house and boarding-house problem. The people for whom it really exists are those whose religion has a sort of civic aspect, who have a sense of city-wide responsibility and of the prestige of maintaining a commanding central institution. They are reënforced with a perhaps even larger group of detached individuals who may be characterized as down-town-minded; that is to say, the central area of the city where they work and play is the focus of their imagination and the natural arena of their religious expressions and fellowship.

CASE VI

MOUNT VERNON PLACE METHODIST EPISCOPAL CHURCH, SOUTH, WASHINGTON, D. C.

When an important denomination undertakes to erect a church building as its national monument in the nation's capital city, and when the local church which is to occupy the structure aspires to live up to the resonant designation "the representative church," the results of the effort ought to be instructive. Such a case of superlative urban enterprise, reared against such a background of nation-wide endeavor, is presented by the Mount Vernon Place Church.

Numerically considered, it is one of the largest organizations studied. Measured by attendance, it puts most of its emphasis, and considerably more than is usual, upon formal religious services; about average emphasis upon the Sunday school; and a little less than average upon subsidiary organizations.

Only four of the twenty-six churches studied have relatively smaller week-day programs. Largely as a reflection of this fact, Mount Vernon Place Church ranks in the lowest fourth of the cases with respect to number of activities—rather a small number indeed for its size. But in the attempt to meet the pressure of local needs, while at the same time living up to its representative character, the church has undertaken certain very infrequent activities. The result is a somewhat unusual combination of elements—pretty sure evidence that a forcing process of some sort has been at work.[1] In other words, the church's adaptation to its situation, although in some aspects more deliberate and self-conscious than in most cases, has been uneven. This fact greatly heightens the interest of the study.

---

1 Though, as the present study will show, the church is fairly conservative in most of its activities, the unusual ones were sufficient to classify it with the "widely variant" type according to the technical method developed in the author's previous study *1000 City Churches* (New York; Doran, 1926).

178

Historical Background

The Mount Vernon Place Church originated in the years following the division of Methodism into its northern and southern branches prior to the Civil War. At that time the Baltimore Conference, to which Washington churches were attached, remained in the northern division. In an effort to regain a footing in the capital city, the southern church established there a missionary enterprise which had a struggling existence till the close of the war. During the following forty years, having built a house of worship upon a site adjacent to the present structure, the church enjoyed moderate growth along with the city. Sectional animosities gradually faded, and it became, if not one of the outstanding churches of Washington, at least among the leaders of the second rank, and the mother of a thriving group of churches of its own denomination.

With the new century came the gradual unfolding of an idea (shared both by local and national Methodist leaders) that the denomination needed an enterprise in Washington more commensurate with its growth nationally, and with the rapid progress of the section which it peculiarly represented. It was said that when Southerners in high political office came to Washington, they were not finding a church with such standing as Southern Methodist churches enjoyed at home among their constituencies. The proposal for the erection of a "monumental" church in the capital city having finally been formally made by the local conference, was endorsed by the General Conference of the denomination in 1906.

There followed more than ten years of promotion and campaigning for financial resources under specially created machinery of the denomination. The corner stone of the "representative church" building was laid in 1917; and, in spite of great financial difficulties incident to the World War, the building was occupied in 1918.

The building was completed just at the time of the maximum expansion of the personnel of government during the war. A state of mind unusually favorable to the interests of religion existed throughout the nation. Mount Vernon Place Church had also a pastor of very conspicuous pulpit ability. These conditions coöperated to bring about exceedingly rapid growth. But they also served to create an acute problem when the deflation of the post-war period set in. Annual accessions had come to be from six to eight times the average of the preceding fifteen years. This peak of achievement, however, was soon passed. The accessions of 1922-24 were only half those of 1918-20. But by 1925-26 the largest gains of the past had again been exceeded, and the per cent. gained on confession of faith had become larger than ever before. Losses, however, were still great, so that net gains remained below the war-time maximum. The church roll also continued to carry a large number of non-resident members.

The present study of the church came in the midst of a period of readjustment and at what promised to be the turn of the tide. A church of moderate size had suddenly become a great one; but, with the shifting conditions, was naturally unable to maintain the unprecedented rate of growth set by the war period. Its immediate concern is consequently the consolidation of its net gains and the stabilization of the situation for a new period of effort, less spectacular but possibly even more constructive.

I. MAJOR ASPECTS OF THE CHURCH

Constituency

Although reporting 3,226 members, the church listed for the purposes of the study a total active constituency of 2,877. Thirty-five per cent. of these were male and 83 per cent. adults. Only two of the twenty-six churches had fewer male adherents, and only five had more adults.

The following tabulation compares the age-distribution of constituents with that of the twenty-six churches and with the general population of the city of Washington. It shows a rather serious skewness in the constituency, both reflecting and exaggerating the characteristics of the capital city, which also has relatively many adults and few children. The sharp excess of females, too, is partly to be explained by the disproportion of the sexes in Washington.

	PER CENT.		
Constituencies of:	*Adults* *(21 & Over)*	*Adolescents* *(15-20)*	*Children* *(5-14)*
Mount Vernon Place Church........	83	6	11
26 churches	73	8	19
Population of Washington............	75	10	15

Just half of the total number of adherents come from families in which one or more of the adult heads are also related to the church. This proportion is somewhat below the median.

MANNER AND DEGREE OF ADHERENCE

Over two-thirds of the adherents of the Mount Vernon Place Church are connected with it through only one relationship. But 32 per cent. have overlapping memberships. This ratio corresponds exactly to the median found in the twenty-six cases. There is, however, a decided excess of adherents who belong to the church only. On the contrary, almost none belong to the subsidiaries only, a category which, in a number of cases of those studied, included a fifth of the church's constituency and sometimes over a half of it. This is to say that the church is almost without that group of loosely related activities which many city churches foster and which often appeal to constituencies different from those attracted by the traditional program. On the other hand, no other church has so high a proportion of Sunday-school pupils who are also church-members. It is the overlapping of memberships at this point that explains the church's total showing as to manner of adherence; since the overlaps of church and subsidiaries and of subsidiaries and Sunday-school memberships are below or much below average, and the overlap of all three is but slightly above average. All told, then, the Mount Vernon Place Church consists, to the extent of 70 per cent. of its total constituency, of people who belong to the church alone or to the church and Sunday school, leaving only 30 per cent. to account for all the other ways of adherence. This showing probably reflects the unusually small week-day program. The predominance of adults in the constituency, on the contrary, doubtless tends to reënforce the Sunday program of formal worship.

Parish and Environment

LOCATION

The church faces on Mount Vernon Square (the site of the Washington Carnegie Library) on which converge six streets, including two of the chief business thoroughfares and three great avenues. The older business district lies in the quadrilateral formed by the Capitol, the White House, the Union Station, and Mount Vernon Place; and, after these three most outstanding buildings, the church enjoys probably the most focal point in the structure of the older city.

PARISH DISTRIBUTION

The constituency is widely scattered throughout the city, only 36 per cent. living within a mile of the church building, while 10 per cent. live beyond five miles. Its distribution is largely toward the northwest, in the line of the city's major growth. Just one-half of all adherents live in this direction.

Why is so large a fraction of the church's constituency more than usually remote from it, and why is the distribution, both of its total and of its near-by adherents, so asymmetrical? The situation suggests that rather profound environmental attractions or pressures may have been at work, and raises the question of the probable effect of these same influences upon the future of the church.

ENVIRONMENTAL CHARACTERISTICS STATISTICALLY DETERMINED

Washington contains relatively few foreigners, but one-fourth of its population is Negro. (Both of these elements of population are gradually declining relative to native-born

whites.)   The civil subdivision in which the church is located
includes most of the public buildings, as well as the main business section.   It has the heaviest foreign-born population of
the city (8.7 per cent.) and next to the heaviest Negro population (35.9 per cent.).   It includes also the oldest and most
congested housing.   These elements are naturally socially uncongenial or impossible from the standpoint of the church.

EVIDENCE OF ENVIRONMENTAL INFLUENCE

Confronted with the data of parish distribution by zones
and sectors, one sees at a glance the modeling of the parish on
the social characteristics of the city.   Within the first half-
mile, few constituents live to the northwest, the area being
chiefly occupied by the Negro quarter; nor to the southwest
(the direction of the Capitol) where foreign and transient
populations infiltrate the business section or live in the depreciated structures of the older city.   Constituents are naturally
few also in the more solidly built-up business section to the
southwest (the direction of the White House).   Conversely,
the near-by strength of the church is most conspicuous in the
older aristocratic area clustered about and between the famous
residential "Circles" so characteristic of the capital city.

Beyond the first mile the parish definitely follows the area
of the city's most prosperous growth, especially to the heights
on either side of Rock Creek Park and into suburban Mary-
land.   It is also strong in the middle-class residential district
beyond the Capitol and Union Station, and moderately strong
in all the newer middle-class subcenters east and west of the
Soldiers' Home, besides having an appreciable constituency in
the Virginia suburbs.   In spite, then, of the marked one-
sidedness of the parish geographically, the church has succeeded conspicuously in maintaining a city-wide appeal upon
its constituency.

Within a half-mile of the church, and in much of the territory within the next mile to the northwest, all the areas that still remain residential are undergoing very rapid transition toward ultimate use for business structures and apartment-houses. South and west of the church the period of depreciation of old housing, before it comes into its new uses, is likely to be fairly brief. Here deterioration is already more than offset by improvement. But north and east of the church (though here the city's zoning plans have set apart large areas for ultimate business uses) the rate of change promises to be slow. This prospect leaves the way open for a long period of further depreciation of property and general cheapening of living conditions. Such a situation may ultimately demand additional special adaptations on the part of the church. In brief, while one part of the immediate environment shows prospects of growing better quickly, the other half is very likely for a time to grow worse.

But the genuinely city-wide appeal of the church has already been attested; and its central position, structurally as well as geographically with respect to the city as a whole, appears to be impregnable. The more extreme phase of Washington's expansion to the southwest is likely soon to exhaust itself, so that it remains doubtful whether any other site in the city could be more suitable permanently for a church serving the entire District of Columbia.

II. AGENCIES, RESOURCES AND METHODS

Organizations and Activities

An estimated annual attendance of 154,576 upon all stated organizations and activities of the church is divided as shown in Table XXXVII, which also compares Mount Vernon Place Church with the median of the twenty-six cases and shows the range of variation on the items indicated.

TABLE XXXVII—ESTIMATED ANNUAL ATTENDANCE ON SPECIFIED OCCASIONS AT MOUNT VERNON PLACE CHURCH AND AT 26 CHURCHES

	ATTENDANCE			
OCCASION	MOUNT VERNON PLACE CHURCH		26 CHURCHES	
			Approx. Median Per	*Range of Variation* Per
	Number	*Per Cent.*	*Cent.*	*Cent.*
Total *	154,576	100		
Formal religious services (Sunday and week day).........	87,100	56	51	15–75
Sunday school	40,560	26	24	9–38
All other stated activities......	26,916 †	18	22	9–51

* Sunday, 86 per cent.; week day, 14 per cent.
† Includes meetings of church officers and committees.

The program of subsidiary organizations falling under "all other stated activities" is carried on under the following arrangement:

	Per Cent.
Organizations for men and boys...................	20
Organizations for women and girls...............	14
Mixed sex organizations.........................	66

No other church studied has so slightly differentiated its activities according to sex. This is presumably because so unusual a part of its program is made up of the relatively passive exercises of public worship and instruction in which men, women and children habitually meet together.

The further subdivision of the subsidiary program according to age and sex is shown in Table XXXVIII.

The showing of the following table confirms the general analysis already made. Measured by attendance, the development of organizations for young men, for young women, for boys, and for girls is in each case below the average of the churches studied. Though women are generally the most highly organized element in the church, but two churches of the twenty-six give relatively less stress to their program, judged

TABLE XXXVIII—ESTIMATED ANNUAL ATTENDANCE ON SUBSIDIARY ORGANIZATIONS AND STATED ACTIVITIES

No.	ORGANIZATIONS Type	ATTENDANCE Number	Per Cent.
	Total	25,668	
19	Classified by Age and Sex..............	14,748	100
1	Mixed adults........................	360	3
2	Adult men	1,440	10
2	Adult women	1,080	7
4	Mixed young people *	7,096	48
3	Young men	860	6
3	Young women	1,080	7
3	Mixed boys and girls...............	2,208	15
1	Boys	624	4
0	Girls	0	0
0	Mixed children	0	0
	Classified by Function Chiefly choir	10,920	

* Between 15 and 23 years of age.

by relative attendance, than does Mount Vernon Place Church. Certain types of subsidiary organizations, on the other hand, greatly exceed the average: namely, those of young people (two Epworth Leagues, a dramatics club, two young people's missionary societies, an Intermediate Missionary Society, besides several organized Sunday-school classes maintaining programs of work and sociability beyond the usual scope of Sunday-school interests). Mixed organizations for boys and girls (the Intermediate Epworth League, missionary organizations and the Daily Vacation Bible School) also make more than average provision for this age within the range indicated.

All told, this is a rather slender total program of age- and sex-subsidiaries. Relative to it, the subordinate activities which are classified by function bulk large, comprising two-fifths of the total. To this showing, the chief contributor is the choir of seventy voices. The choir is a strong social, as well as a musical, organization.

Staff

Types of church programs that deal with large numbers of constituents massed in passive audiences are found to be economical of paid staff, as compared with those that involve varied, technical and often individual work with small groups. No church studied has so many hundred constituents per paid worker as Mount Vernon Place. From this standpoint, its staff is small. On the contrary, relative to the number of items in the church's program, the staff is about average.

It consists of: (1) a pastor; (2) an ordained minister as an all-around assistant; (3) a woman assistant for inside secretarial work; and (4) a woman who, at the time of the study, was just working over from secretarial duties to those of an outside administrative and pastoral assistant. This is the most frequent and obvious distribution of positions found in four-worker staffs, though in this case distinctions as to function are not so clear-cut as the above statement would indicate.

The pastor's age, and his length of total experience, are somewhat below the average of the pastors of the churches included in the study; but his education is beyond the average. He has occupied his present position for a briefer time than the average. The male assistant represents about the average age of his group, but his previous fifteen years' pastoral experience is somewhat unusual. It is entirely characteristic of the general tendency with church staffs that two of the four workers have been in their present positions for less than a year.

TIME ON DUTY

The work of the staff as a whole for the sample week equaled about seven and three-quarters hours per day for seven days. The pastor was on duty sixty-three hours, slightly more than the average of the pastors' group; the male assistant for fifty-six hours, slightly less than that of the male assistants' group; the secretary-visitor for nearly fifty-eight hours, in contrast with an average of fifty-four hours for visitors and forty-four hours for secretaries; and the secretary forty-three hours. Both male workers reported more work-days of average length, and fewer of extreme length, than was characteristic of the group as a whole. The secretary was the only member of the staff who took a holiday outright.

CONTENT OF WORK

Interpreted on the basis of the distribution of his work-time during the sample week, the pastor seems to belong to the "preacher-executive" type represented by only two of the twenty-four pastors studied. Forty per cent. of his time went to homiletical preparation, compared with 20 per cent. for the group as a whole; and 26 per cent. to church administration, as compared with 32 per cent. for the group as a whole. This distribution reflects the special emphasis on pulpit and public services which has already been discovered as characteristic of the church; the fact that although the program of the church is not varied, its absolute magnitude is great; and also, probably, the fact that the pastor has rather ample assistance in outside pastoral ministries and hence does not need to give so much time to them personally.

The male assistant is chiefly concerned with administrative, pastoral and homiletical duties. The general tendency in churches is for the pastor to reserve the preaching function chiefly for himself; but in this case, the assistant has charge of the Junior Church, which brings preaching into the category of his primary duties. His administrative work reflects in considerable measure his functioning as a director of religious education.

The almost exclusive time given to clerical duty by the secretary is characteristic of the secretarial group, while the exceptional combination of duties represented by the secretary-visitor while in process of working over from one position to another has already had comment. Her work, as reported for the sample week, does not correspond closely with that of any type of position found in other churches.

SALARIES

The per cent. of the total church budget devoted to salaries of the paid religious staff is about average. The pastor's remuneration, including perquisites, is placed at $7,200, which is appreciably above the median. That of the male assistant is, with perquisites, $4,260, which ranks him in the highest quarter of male assistants on this item. The secretary-visitor's salary of $1,675 (with perquisites, $1,980) also ranks her in the upper quarter of workers of her type; while the secretary's salary of $1,500 is almost exactly the average. All told, the staff accurately reflects the church in its numbers and in the character of its work. For industry and economy of service, as measured by the number and distribution of work hours, it ranks well with the average. From the standpoint of remuneration and conditions of labor, on the other hand, the church is seen to be doing well by the staff.

Plant

Washington's magnificent system of diagonal boulevards was designed to create focal points of interest at their intersections. Many of them are dignified by public buildings or graced by statuary or landscaping. They are among the well-known marks of the capital city. When the Southern Methodist denomination desired to erect a monumental church building and denominational shrine in keeping with the character of the city, it naturally chose such a triangular site.

Architecturally, the building is a rather ornate example of the Renaissance style. Its material is Georgia marble. It rises from a landscaped and terraced lot graded well above the street level, and fronts directly upon a diminutive park. The site affords a setback of nearly seventy-five feet at the front of the building, and from thirty to forty feet at the sides.

The lower story is entered directly from the lot level. Access to the main floor is by massive stone steps leading to pillared porticos which constitute the most striking architectural features of the structure. An exceedingly spacious front lobby is marble-lined, and contains staircases and galleries treated on monumental lines. The lobby leads directly to the auditorium, which is seventy-five by eighty feet in dimensions, and the elaborate style of which harmonizes with the exterior. The color scheme is dull olive and silver above a rich mahogany paneling and pews. Windows, filled with pictorial glass, occupy most of the wall space on two sides; and virtually the whole front is occupied by a vast organ, which rises above a long and shallow gallery, and an all too cramped pulpit and altar space. The high rear gallery pitches up sharply over the lobby. The total effect is impressive and suitable in a city that takes its style from the nation's public buildings and in a structure designed to be venerated by an entire church.

The remainder of the building is decidedly less satisfactory; and a careful checking of its features, one by one, forces one to the conclusion that almost everything else was sacrificed in favor of a striking auditorium. Although the auditorium is already too small for even average demands, and although it is the deliberate purpose of the church to magnify the pulpit, the balance between public services and the other elements of the church's program is not properly reflected in the design of the building. These shortcomings were shown conclusively when the church was rated on the Interchurch one-thousand-point score-card. In total rank, the monumental building of the representative church turns out to be only about average, compared with the plants even of far less outstanding churches. The most clinching evidence is that the church has felt compelled to purchase two adjoining dwelling-houses for present Sunday-school use and as a step toward a future specially designed addition for the use of its religious education and parish activities. A summary of the score-card is given in Table XXXIX.

TABLE XXXIX—SUMMARY OF SCORE OF PLANT

Item	Standard Score	Points Scored		Rank in 25 Cases
		Number	Per Cent.	
Total	1,000	603	60	12
Site	130	108	83	5
Building or buildings........	150	132	88	4
Service systems	160	82	51	14
Church rooms	170	121	71	14
Religious school rooms........	200	120	60	14
Community service rooms.....	190	40	21	24

Finances

The approximate total of money raised by the church during the last conference year was $83,300, divided as follows:

For current expenses.......................... $35,545
For property account.......................... 15,453
For benevolences 32,324

This total includes a reasonable estimate of the income of subsidiary organizations not formally reported through the church.

The church has no endowment and does not rent pews. The great bulk of its income comes through individual pledges, supplemented by Sunday collections. The payment of over $15,000 on property account finally freed the church property from debt, and the structure was formally dedicated in March, 1926. Financing during the building period was naturally rather strenuous and the pastor, during this time, had to concern himself actively with its promotion. Financial solicitation is largely carried on through pulpit appeals, supplemented by systematic correspondence.

Noteworthy sources of income are: (1) the very considerable amounts raised by the Sunday school, largely through the assessments of budget items against various departments and organized classes. (2) An income of $2,747 was derived from fees for musical instruction. This made possible the employment of a full-time director of music and the operation of a music-school as a somewhat unique adjunct of the church, while at the same time the proportion of expenditure for music was only about average.

Expenditures for the upkeep and administration of the plant are small, partly on account of its newness and generally substantial character, but perhaps more because of the slenderness of the week-day program. Expenditures for special departments are also below average, because (except for the music-school) the church has not developed such departments. A larger proportion of expenditures goes for publicity than in any other church studied; and the miscellaneous category covering expenditures impossible to classify is unusually large. The distribution of expenditures (other than benevolent) appears in Table XL.

TABLE XL—FINANCIAL EXPENDITURES OF THE CHURCH

Item	Amount	Per Cent.
Grand Total	$50,998	
Total Current Account	35,545	100
Salaries	11,609	32
General administrative expenses	876	2
Music	4,174	12
General operation and upkeep of property	6,302	18
Expenses of departments specially budgeted	2,984	8
Publicity	3,053	9
Ecclesiastical connections	672	2
Miscellaneous	5,875	17
Investment Account		
Payment on property	15,453	

Of benevolent gifts of about $32,000, relatively large amounts came through the Sunday school, the Epworth League and the women's societies. They were devoted chiefly to denominational concerns, local, national and world-wide. Of local interdenominational institutions, the Central Union Mission and the Church Federation were generously supported.

Public Services and Worship

The average attendance on the Sunday-morning service is about 900; in the evening 500,[2] and at the mid-week service 150. A fully organized junior congregation, conducted by the ordained assistant pastor, with an average attendance of 145, holds simultaneous morning services.

The assembly of an audience including so many strangers and transient visitors as this one naturally creates something of the atmosphere of the casual public gathering. The introductory morning service definitely attempts to counteract this condition and to make the spirit of worship ascendant. The service is ritualistic to a more than average degree; it includes the Creed, a responsive reading, the Gloria and an offertory response.

A vested choir of eighty-four members, with an average attendance of seventy, presents high-class music in a spirited manner and furnishes one of the noteworthy features of the service.

---

2 It is the conviction of the church that these estimates are too low. No actual count is kept.

The preaching is stimulating and interesting. Its manner is somewhat informal, with oratorical moods interspersed through, rather than continuous in, the discourse. The preacher gives an impression of homely simplicity, and makes effective and perhaps artful use of the Southern vernacular. The sermonic form, with definitely religious themes, is habitual.

At the close of the service, the audience is a long time in dispersing, after much informal sociability. There is much introducing of strangers who frequently are taken about to inspect the church.

Strangers are asked to register in the foyer, and, in addition, ushers take names of all who appear to be newcomers. A monthly total of fifty to sixty names is secured for pastoral follow-up.

The characteristic attitude of the attendants suggests that they are considerably impressed by the dignity and metropolitan atmosphere of the church. One senses, too, some of the conditions of crowd psychology in the vast audience occupying every inch of space that police regulations will permit, and regularly including a group seated within the altar-rail.

Religious Education

The total enrollment of the Sunday school in all its departments is nearly 1,300. Half of the pupils of the attending departments are adults. The outstanding characteristic of the school is perhaps its group of highly organized young people's and adult classes. These classes are notable for their strong organizational consciousness. They command important financial resources and conduct active service programs.

A summary of the organization and attendance of the school appears in Table XLI.

The addition of sixty-four officers to the 1,086 pupils and seventy-three teachers gives a grand total of 1,223. Pupils in the attending departments number 1,061, and attendance aver-

TABLE XLI—SUMMARY OF SUNDAY-SCHOOL STATISTICS

DEPARTMENT	PUPILS		TEACHERS
	Age	Enrollment	
Total	...	1,086	73
Cradle Roll	2–3	55	5
Beginners	4–6	43	6
Primary	7–8	90	20
Junior	9–12	58	9
Intermediate	13–15	59	7
Senior	16–18	60	7
Young people	19–27	183	10
Adult	28 & over	513	9
Home Department	...	25	..

ages 52 per cent. of enrollment. The approximate age-distribution in the attending departments is as follows:

	Number	Per Cent.
Children	286	27
Adolescents	140	13
Adults	635	60

The inadequate provision of the new building for such extensive operations in religious education has already been indicated. Makeshift partitions have had to be put up to divide the attic into classrooms, while dark closets and storerooms under the stairs are also in use. No fewer than five such rooms are inadequately lighted and ventilated. This condition is in flagrant contrast with the spacious marble vestibule and the lofty and impressive auditorium.

The church's narrow range of subsidiary organizations (compared with the average of the twenty-six cases) is somewhat counterbalanced by the numerous and essentially independent Sunday-school groups. A religious fraternity of young men, originating in the Sunday school, has developed chapters in many places throughout the country. There is little integration, however, of Sunday school and other subsidiary activities, although some of the classes accept service-assignments proposed by the Senior Epworth League. Putting the matter in another way, the Sunday school is modernly organized, departmentalized and supervised, so far as its children's groups are concerned, and has in addition several mass-classes of adults. An excellent experiment is under way in the organization of parents and teachers in the interest of youth; and the standard teacher-training courses of the denomination are conducted on an extensive scale.   Among educational methods, dramatization of religious material has had exceptional use.

Besides a Daily Vacation Bible School during the summer, the most notable supplemental agency of religious education is the afternoon school for Chinese and Latin peoples.   This school has had a notable and devoted history of sixteen years. It is now thought of as primarily a contribution to Christian Americanization, but has also close affiliations with the Central Union Mission, an interdenominational gospel agency. Teachers are drawn from several denominations.   Forty-nine Chinese, twenty-eight pupils from the Latin races, and thirty-five teachers are enrolled, with an average attendance of eighty.

Current Church Life

The small week-day program, relative to the mass of the church's total enterprise, was noted at the outset.   The midweek prayer meeting, with a probable missionary service, and an occasional social with luncheon or dinner once a week on the average during the active church year, make up the meetings of the typical week.   Besides these, an active service program of the young people's organizations and Sunday-school classes goes on, chiefly taking the form of the lay-conduct of services in institutions and missions.   An incidental, but well-marked, social ministry is that of helping constituents and strangers to secure employment.   Another important development is that of summer outing facilities, for which the church maintains a camp on the Potomac River.

Still another noteworthy feature of the church's enterprise is the variety of its publicity matter.   Several departments and classes issue their own bulletins, and the appeal to the constituency through print and correspondence is unusually well developed.

A well-organized system of parish calling by lay workers results in 500 or 600 calls per month in the effort to reach the entire congregation at frequent intervals.

One of the most unusual aspects of the church's program is the music-school already alluded to. It has now been in operation for five years. Instead of merely furnishing studio facilities in order to allow the music-director to supplement a part-time salary, the church pays the director in full and receives the income from his teaching which, as already noted, makes the net cost of music very moderate. One of the purposes of the school is to train church musicians competently and according to worthy standards. The average number of private lessons given per week is forty-six. Choir concerts are given monthly during the active church year; and a small chorus selected from the larger church choir has a regular extra rehearsal in preparation for singing at the Thursday evening service. Two additional choirs of subsidiary organizations also rehearse weekly.

In most of its aspects, the work of the church is continuous throughout the year. No such long summer let-down occurs as one finds in many other cases.

Growth and Conservation

In the year preceding the study, losses from church-membership equaled 26 per cent. of the gains as against 35 per cent. for the previous ten years as a whole. Sixty-five per cent. of accessions were by letter (as against 73 per cent. for the previous ten years), and 35 per cent. on confession of faith. This changed ratio indicates the diminishing flood of migration to Washington, but still leaves the church making substantially two-thirds of its gains from the ranks of those already members elsewhere. Of those coming by letter, 77 per cent. were former Southern Methodists. Of the remaining 23 per cent., the majority were Northern Methodists, leaving only 5 per cent. actually from non-Methodist sources. Three per cent. came from other churches in Washington. The great majority were from the South, about equally divided between states adjacent to Washington and the lower South, with scattering recruits from Oklahoma and Texas. An examination of a limited number of cases showed 35 per cent. living near the church, 32 per cent. coming from an average distance, and 33 per cent. from an exceptional distance. This seems to indicate that the active current appeal of the church is city-wide, just as its total distribution of membership is. New recruits were gained about equally to the northeast and north-west, the directions of the city's major growth. About 30 per cent. of those newly received into membership seemed to have been previously drawn to the church through regular attend-ance or membership in some subsidiary organization. The first contact in recruiting, however, is generally the result of pulpit invitation, or through pastoral work in following up the names of strangers secured at the public services.

With the diminishing but still rapid and probably perma-nent migration of population to Washington, and the estab-lished prestige of the church as a national institution of the denomination, the securing of new members has been pretty much the shaking of a plum tree. At least the highly favor-able situation of Mount Vernon Place Church is in immense contrast with that of churches in deteriorating communities from which population is moving away, and with those that receive only local support. The names of a good many people moving to Washington are sent in by pastors and friends from all parts of the South. Such prospects must, however, be ac-tively followed up, and are generally secured one at a time. This necessity is reflected in the fact that the whole constitu-ency contains less than an average number of adherent families.

Of recent losses of membership, 19 per cent. were by death and 81 per cent. by transfer to other churches. There has been no recent revision of the roll, a circumstance that leaves a considerable discrepancy between book-membership and the active list.

The church recently established a system of affiliated mem-berships permitting Southern Methodist congressmen or other office-holders temporarily resident in Washington to ally them-selves with it without breaking their established connections with home institutions; and the system was subsequently adopted by the denomination at large.

Relations to Social Agencies and Denomination

An exceptional proportion of the social ministries of the church is carried out in connection with a varied group of social institutions of Washington. Thus the Epworth League holds monthly meetings in the Tuberculosis Hospital, the Home for Incurables, the Hospital for Insane, the Home for Aged Women, and Central Union Mission; and bi-monthly services at the District jail. As already indicated, the church is one of the main financial supporters of the interdenominational Central Union Mission. It is also an important supporter of the Washington Federation of Churches; and, as the mother church of its denomination in the city, it exerts responsible leadership in all Southern Methodist connectional movements and affairs. It is not, however, conspicuously related to the general coöperative movements of social agencies, nor concerned in the more recently developed forms of constructive work. But its sentimental standing in the eyes of the denomination as a whole, and the central location and symbolic significance of its building, serves to create a peculiarly influential atmosphere for the entire round of the church's life. No fewer than eight outside organizations, largely denominational ones, use the building as a meeting-place with some regularity.

Summary and Interpretation

The experience of Mount Vernon Place Methodist Episcopal Church, South, constitutes an episode in the growth of Washington as the capital city. It marks the concrete realization of an impulse for group expression on the part of a great denomination, such as could only have been satisfied in such a capital city. During the decade preceding 1920, slow-growing Washington suddenly found itself near the front rank of rapidly expanding cities; and Southern Methodism was first to carry out the dream of a sort of national cathedral church which numerous denominations have since adopted.

The sudden conspicuousness and success which thus came to the church have involved a real test of character. In spite of an inevitable growth of self-consciousness, it has remained essentially simple, industrious and sincere. Consequently it has not been unduly disturbed by the slowing up of its rate of growth in more recent months. It remains true, nevertheless, that, in very unusual degree, the present church is the product of special circumstances and of the operation of external forces. It is a ship borne on the waves rather than a growth of the soil. The ship is being skillfully navigated and has a course of its own. But this is not the same thing as to have sprung from the deep roots of strongly localized experience. Under these circumstances, it is no surprise that the church's objectives are not absolutely clear-cut, and that its future prospects have been regarded from the standpoint rather of loyal emotion than of keen analysis and diagnosis.

The study makes it clear that the involuntary adaptations of the church to its situation have been considerable. The characteristics of its constituency reflect the city of Washington in the abnormal proportions of the different age-groups of population, in the excess of women, and in the numerical frequency in the constituency of the individual away from home, the transient resident, the job hunter and the casual visitor.

The scattered distribution of constituents in the parish also reflects the shifting movements of Washington population, though the shifting has come gradually and is not yet extreme. Washington, as a city, is exceptionally and permanently centralized by its character as the national capital. The focalization of prestige about the central public buildings has left the city's subcenters unusually feeble. The church is thus practically justified in taking a non-territorial attitude toward its mission. Its city-wide appeal enables it largely to ignore environmental changes in its immediate locality. Its city-wide appeal, however, as evidenced by the distribution of its constituency, is essentially limited to middle- and upper-class populations, as classified from the economic standpoint.

The deterioration of much of the territory in the church's immediate vicinity is likely to be quickly offset by the increase of apartment hotels and the improved character of business structures in the neighborhood. Consequently there is good chance that the church's constituency may be rapidly reënforced from near-by sources—this partly offsetting the tendency of the parish to scatter.

The more conscious and voluntary factors of the church's life and work chiefly follow traditional patterns slightly modified by the church's rather mild idiosyncrasies. Numerically, the outstanding phase of the total church life is its great preaching services. Notable audiences crowd the auditorium Sunday after Sunday at the morning service. The church and the Sunday school have a larger overlap than in any other case studied. But there is almost no subsidiary constituency apart from that already comprehended either by church or Sunday school. This is in immense contrast with many of the churches studied, which have thrust themselves out into the community far beyond the frontiers of their strictly religious organizations. The relative feebleness of the subsidiary program is, however, partly made up for by the strength of the organized classes of the Sunday school. The strong leadership and marked independence of some of these groups contribute greatly to the exceptional amount of lay work which is carried out in the church's name. Both the amount and the variety of service going on from week to week under lay initiative and control are bound to impress the observer.

There is also to be noted a strongly marked church tradition of local philanthropy, deeply rooted at certain points in the circumstances and needs of the immediate local community. The voluntary ministries of the church in down-town missions and institutions, and particularly in the Chinese Sunday school, are evidences on this point.

The more recently developed and conspicuous aspects of the church's progress reflect, however, a response to denominational expectations more than they do a clear-cut adaptation either to parochial or to community needs. The church building is a monument to denominational ideals and purposes more than it is an instrument for the church's own work. It is an excellent building for visitors to worship in, but much less satisfactory for the Sunday school. The most distinctive and unusual features of the church's program, such as the music-department, strike one as admirable embellishments of the situation more than as profound reflections of the responsiveness of the church to the challenge of the city.   What one must so greatly approve in the ample development of religious education, missions and general parish life, is, on the whole, just a fine carrying out of denominational standards and an evidence of conformity and of living up to the character created for the church rather than of originality and profound local insight.

Real organizing ability and an excellent adaptation to conditions is seen in the machinery for finding, assimilating and keeping in touch with the army of incoming members with which the church has recently been blessed.   The increasing use of publicity methods, and of stimulation from a central office of the large and widely scattered constituency, is also good modern church business.   All told, then, if one asks why the Mount Vernon Place Methodist Episcopal Church, South, is what it is, the answer must primarily be found in tradition, determining the building up of a program and life largely through a process of accretion, with some interesting touches of institutional individuality; but, in the main, with still greater evidence of docility and loyalty than of radical adaptation to the particular situation.

FOURTH PRESBYTERIAN CHURCH, CHICAGO, ILL.

The Fourth Presbyterian Church is one of the most conspicuous religious enterprises of its city, a church nationally famed as great and successful. It justifies its reputation by standing first among the twenty-six churches studied in total annual attendance. Its numerous lines of endeavor include many activities of impressive size.

But since unusual size may easily be unduly impressive, it is particularly important in any large organization to see the parts in their true proportions. Relative to the distribution of annual attendance among the major divisions of the church's program as presented by the average of the churches studied, the Fourth Presbyterian is characterized by very large public services, an average Sunday school and a small subsidiary program. For breadth and variety, its activities are not proportionate to its size; while it is above average in these respects, it is not beyond the middle third of the cases studied.

Again, the church lacks the unity of a strongly knit natural group of people who know one another and are related in many ways. Its nucleus of members who are tied to it through many connections is relatively small. The church tends rather to fall into three distinct constituencies, viz., the church-attending constituency, the Sunday school, and the adherents of subsidiary organizations. The overlapping margins of these constituencies are unusually narrow; and the members of subsidiaries obviously do not constitute a unified group.

Into the make-up of the constituencies thus tenuously related, there enters an unusual proportion of adherents who are either without families in Chicago, or detached from their families in their religious relationships. Consequently the

202

THE EXTERIOR OF THE FOURTH PRESBYTERIAN CHURCH, CHICAGO, ILL.

THE INNER COURT AND FOUNTAIN OF THE FOURTH PRESBYTERIAN CHURCH, CHICAGO, ILL.

EXTERIOR OF THE MANSE OF THE FOURTH PRESBYTERIAN CHURCH, CHICAGO, ILL.

AUDITORIUM OF THE FOURTH PRESBYTERIAN CHURCH, CHICAGO, ILL.

THE WOMEN'S CLUB RECEPTION ROOM OF THE FOURTH PRESBYTERIAN CHURCH OF
CHICAGO, ILL.

THE DOMESTIC SCIENCE LABORATORY OF THE FOURTH PRESBYTERIAN CHURCH,
CHICAGO, ILL.

THE RELIGIOUS SCHOOL ASSEMBLY ROOM FOR THE FOURTH PRESBYTERIAN CHURCH,
CHICAGO, ILL.

THE GYMNASIUM OF THE FOURTH PRESBYTERIAN CHURCH, CHICAGO, ILL.

THE MEN'S CLUB AND RECEPTION ROOM OF THE FOURTH PRESBYTERIAN CHURCH OF CHICAGO, ILL.

THE MEN'S CLUB LIBRARY OF THE FOURTH PRESBYTERIAN CHURCH, CHICAGO, ILL.

loosely organized church does not have the closely knit home to fall back upon. Its units are largely single individuals.

Still again, the composition of the Fourth Presbyterian Church reveals in extreme degree that excess of adults which one learns to expect in down-town churches attracting city-wide followings—with the corresponding shortage of adolescents and children.

Its parish is exceedingly scattered in spite of deliberate and persistent efforts to keep in close contact with the immediate locality.

As a result of this whole series of rather striking departures from the average of churches, any characterization of the church assuming that what is true of part of it is true of the whole is bound to be misleading. Classified by the more unique elements entering into its program, the Fourth Presbyterian Church is highly developed and strikingly adapted to its particular situation. But this special uniqueness and adaptability relates in the main to a rather small minority of a highly non-typical constituency. Reflecting its constituency the church is a network of enterprises loosely knotted together rather than a closely woven fabric. Its unity is administrative rather than social.

This condition is an extreme expression of tendencies generally shown by the group of churches under examination. It is not therefore to be regarded as abnormal in the sense of being unwholesome or mistaken. These tendencies merely reveal the necessary nature of the city church under the more acute and distinctive of urban circumstances, and the terms upon which organized religion may serve the city in the most conspicuous fashion.

Background in Recent History

After forty years of growth along with that of Chicago, the church reached a crisis consequent upon the extreme depreciation of the area surrounding its building and the removal of much of the population of the type that had furnished its previous support. But after a careful social survey of the vicinity, and an analysis of the possibilities of a localized ministry under the changed conditions, the church decided to stand its ground. It selected a more advantageous site within a short distance of the earlier one and, some fifteen years ago, proceeded to erect an almost unrivaled plant.

Since then its story has been one of outstanding institutional success. Its numerical growth in membership in the decade 1911-21 was five times that of the previous decade. Its average church-membership of the last three years has been 29 per cent. greater than for the first three years of the last decade. Average enrollment in the Sunday school, however, has been only about the same. This is to say that the departments did not all grow equally. Naturally, too, some of the church's more experimental projects had to be modified time after time. But the church's expenditures in virtually all lines have been very much larger and the total enterprise has gone forward at an impressive rate.

I. MAJOR ASPECTS OF THE CHURCH

Constituency

The combined card-index of the church's definite constituency in all organizations and departments lists a total of 4,103 persons. Forty-four per cent. belong to constituent families; 56 per cent. are detached individuals. This shows decidedly fewer from constituent families than was the average of the churches studied. The constituency is 43 per cent. male, 57 per cent. female, which is the exactly modal situation. The age-distribution is shown in the following comparison.

	PER CENT.		
	Adults (21 & Over)	Adolescents (15-20)	Children (5-14)
Constituencies of:			
Fourth Presbyterian Church........	85	5	10
26 churches........................	73	8	19
Population of Chicago...............	70	10	20

The ratio shows a much higher proportion of adults and relatively fewer adolescents and children than in the corresponding age-groups in the city of Chicago, and a generally similar variation from the average of the twenty-six churches. Of these cases, only three have a higher per cent. of adults. (The data, unfortunately, do not reveal the further age-grouping of adults. Undoubtedly the trend is toward younger adults, who occur in excess in the population of Chicago, rather than to elderly people.)

MANNER AND DEGREE OF ADHERENCE

Over three-fourths of the constituents of the Fourth Presbyterian Church belong to it in only one way. Only three of the twenty-six churches have a smaller overlap of membership. Considerably more than the average proportion of constituents belong to the church only or to the subsidiary organizations only. On the contrary, the church ranks in the lowest quarter of the cases studied with respect to the overlap of church and Sunday school, of Sunday school and subsidiary, or of church and subsidiary memberships. (See Chart IV.) The church thus has three definite constituencies with relatively a very small core of overlapping memberships. (The overlap of church and Sunday school consists chiefly of adult men; that of church and subsidiaries chiefly of adult women.)

In the median case studied, about half of the church's total constituency has but one connection. "Oncers" do not greatly exceed the average in this case, but there is a great deficiency in adherents belonging to the church in two or more ways. Thus not only is the institutional nucleus small, but the average of integration is low for the constituent body as a whole.

Environment and Parish

LOCATION

The church, as is shown by Chart VIII, is located one and one-quarter miles north of the center of the Loop; three-quarters of a mile north of the Chicago River, and the same distance south of Lincoln Park.

Thirty-nine per cent. of the resident membership (whose

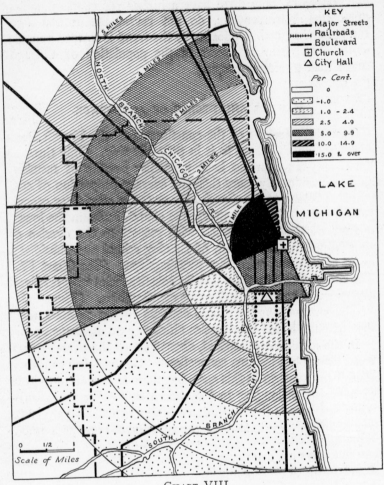

CHART VIII
Parish of Fourth Presbyterian Church, Chicago

location was reported) lives within one-half mile of the church; 24 per cent. lives over five miles from the church in northern and western suburbs and south side residential areas; the remainder is widely scattered. Directional distribution is as follows: north, 32 per cent.; east, 4 per cent.; south, 19 per cent.; west, 45 per cent. This identification of the church with the immediate locality to the extent of nearly 40 per cent. of the constituency, coupled with the fact of its deliberate purpose to maintain strong contacts with the vicinity, requires that a study be made of the environmental factors presented by this area.

CHARACTERISTICS OF THE "LOWER NORTH SIDE"

The district immediately north of the Chicago River and between the river and Lake Michigan is locally known as the "Lower North Side." In the immediate vicinity of the church, its outstanding features are the recent northward thrust of the central business district across the Chicago River and the expansion of the industrial zone paralleling the river, with vast consequent changes in the character of the district.

Considered in detail, these changes constitute no less than a classic example of the processes that unmake and make again such areas of cities as stand in the path of their central expansion. In this case, moreover, these processes are shown in their most acute phases. The expansion of industry and business has caused the invasion both of the high-class residential district, formerly the best in Chicago—along major streets leading north from the Loop—and also of residential areas occupied by industrial population, paralleling the river. An extreme physical deterioration of the district has taken place. Colonies of lately come foreigners have penetrated inward from the river and have pushed the former occupants farther north; while retail business has furrowed through the wealthy section and created a transitional zone between it and the slum; a zone occupied by all varieties of transient and unrooted people—homeless men from the ranks of casual labor to the south, and white-collar workers occupying furnished rooms and lodging-houses on the north and south streets. Wealth has been pushed back to the streets immediately fronting on the Lake and into the small angle formed by Lincoln Park and the Lake. Here it is concentrated as in few areas on earth. In this one small spot are said to live 2,000 of the 6,000 fortunate individuals whose names appear in the Social Register of Chicago and suburbs. Furthermore, the return to residential use of near-in locations has come about in spectacular fashion through an aggregation in an immediately adjacent area of vast hotels and expensive apartment houses, located largely on land reclaimed from the Lake. These reënforce the "Gold Coast"; and their influence is gradually working back into the deteriorated area, much of which will rather promptly be pressed out of its transitional phase into more or less permanent character in the new cycle of urban development.

In relocating, the Fourth Presbyterian Church set itself on North Michigan Avenue just between the district to the southeast in which hotels and apartment houses are concentrated, and the older established mansions of the "Gold Coast" on the north; but with the zone of acute deterioration beginning sharply almost at its back.

Census statistics for the political areas roughly identified with the Lower North Side (Wards 21 and 22) reveal the general composition and characteristics of population.[1] It numbers approximately 114,000 persons, 62 per cent. of whom in Ward 21 are of foreign antecedents, as are 88 per cent. in Ward 22. The population of Ward 22 is 12 per cent. Negro. Ward 21, which includes the church, has in its population about 7,000 excess males, half of whom are foreign-born. This roughly measures the casual worker element. Its chief foreign element belongs to the older immigration (German, Swede, Irish); but it contains over 2,000 Italians. Ward 22, lying toward the west and bordering on the Chicago River, has 2,000 excess males, also chiefly foreign-born. Its major foreign elements represent newer immigration—6,000 Italians, 4,000 Hungarians, 1,800 Austrians, besides 4,500 Germans, 1,000 Swedes, 500 Poles.[2] Nine per cent. of the population over ten

---

[1] 1920 Census, Vol. III, p. 275.
[2] The last three belong to the neighborhood of Olivet Institute, the subject of Case Study XVI.

years of age is illiterate. Housing in Ward 22 includes many
one- and two-story single-family houses. Its excess of families
over dwellings is 39 per cent., compared with over 46 per cent.
for Chicago as a whole, and 54 per cent. in Ward 21. This
greater density of population, in spite of much superior general
conditions, reflects the vogue of the apartment-houses already
alluded to.

RELATION OF PARISH TO ENVIRONMENT

Within the first half-mile of the church, where 39 per cent.
of its constituents live, they are most numerous to the north
and the west; but the distribution is fairly symmetrical relative
to the distribution of population which is cut off by the Lake.
(Chart VIII.)

Within the second half-mile, there are almost no constituents, on account of the almost exclusive occupancy of the area
by industrial, transient and foreign elements. The church has
little direct contact with the problems of these populations.

A second zone of constituents is found from three to four
miles distant from the church to the north and west, their location roughly corresponding to the Boulevard System. Other
distinct concentrations of adherents are found more than five
miles to the north, west and south and out in the suburbs. In
general, the distribution of the constituency, except in the immediate vicinity of the church, is that of the higher-grade
population of Chicago; and all areas of poorer or foreign
population are untouched except within the first half-mile.

The church is thus highly selective in its city-wide appeal.
In its local ministry and program it is socially more inclusive.

Constituent families live at a slightly greater average distance than detached adherents; and there are relatively more
detached adherents who live immediately to the south of the
church.

Church-members, also, are relatively more numerous than
the total constituency in the fourth and fifth miles from the
church, and beyond five miles.

Pledged contributors also live at a greater average distance than non-subscribing adherents. Officers of the church live at a considerably greater average distance than total constituents, and are more frequent on the north side.

These comparisons reveal that, in general, the geographical distribution of all elements in the constituency follows essentially the same pattern, though with minor variations as noted.

Increasing distance of residence does not decrease the closeness of constituents' relations to the church, measured by numerous connections with it. Among such adolescents and children as the church gets at all, the remote ones are as often closely related to it as near-by ones. This measures the ability of well-to-do populations commanding transportation facilities to ignore distance in their organized religious life.[3]

II. AGENCIES, RESOURCES AND METHODS

Organizations and Activities

The church's estimated total annual attendance on all stated activities is 182,593, divided as shown in Table XLII.

TABLE XLII—ESTIMATED ANNUAL ATTENDANCE ON SPECIFIED OCCASIONS AT FOURTH PRESBYTERIAN CHURCH AND AT 26 CHURCHES

	ATTENDANCE			
	FOURTH PRESBY-TERIAN CHURCH		26 CHURCHES	
OCCASION			Approx. Median Per Cent.	Range of Variation Per Cent.
	Number	Per Cent.		
Total *	182,593	100		
Formal religious services (Sunday and week day).........	113,700	62	51	15–75
Sunday school................	36,400	20	24	9–38
All other stated activities......	32,493 †	18	22	9–51

* Sunday, 82 per cent.; week day, 18 per cent.
† Includes meetings of church officers and committees.

Only eleven of the twenty-six churches have smaller week-day programs, and only four have smaller subsidiary programs, relative to their totals. Attendance upon public religious services, on the contrary, ranks relatively very high. The absolute

---

[3] See parallel condition in Cases V and IX, but contrasting one in Case II.

magnitude and importance of the other departments being fully acknowledged, here lies the church's preëminent strength and success.

The division of attendance upon subsidiary organizations classified according to age- and sex-groups is shown in Table XLIII.

TABLE XLIII—ESTIMATED ANNUAL ATTENDANCE ON SUB-
SIDIARY ORGANIZATIONS AND STATED ACTIVITIES

| | Organizations | Attendance | |
No.	Type	Number	Per Cent.
	Total	29,331	
28	Classified by Age and Sex..............	27,973	100
1	Mixed adults	1,680	6
1	Adult men	1,802	7
6	Adult women	3,659	13
2	Mixed young people *	5,390	19
1	Young men	1,188	4
2	Young women	4,230	15
0	Mixed boys and girls	0	0
9	Boys	7,264	26
6	Girls	2,760	10
0	Mixed children	0	0
	Classified by Function		
	Summer camp	1,358	

* Between 15 and 23 years of age.

Two noteworthy aspects of the above showing are the large number of separate organizations and their unusual degree of sex-segregation.

Of the total subsidiary program, 37 per cent. is carried on through male organizations, 38 per cent. through female organizations, and 25 per cent. through mixed organizations.

CHARACTERISTICS OF PROGRAM

Each of the twenty-eight subsidiaries has an interesting and significant story; but, in order to keep this study within proper proportions, only their most general aspects can be mentioned.

Women's work in the Fourth Presbyterian Church is not unified, but is rather carried on through numerous groups reflecting age, occupation, and probably also certain social cleavages in the constituency. Active boys' work is developed through numerous organizations with strong recreational programs. There are two young people's societies of the Christian Endeavor type. Notable club-work is maintained for young business women and students of the vicinity, with varied social and recreational, educational, and religious programs. There is a smaller amount of club-work for girls. The recreational ministry for young men includes one or two foreign groups.

Staff

The staff consists of fifteen paid workers (other than musicians and janitors) giving half-time or more. The organization of the staff is as follows: minister, assistant minister, assistant minister (director of men's work), secretary of young women's club, gymnasium superintendent and director of boys' work, director of girls' work, two parish visitors, three secretaries (respectively for the minister, for the director of men's work—in his capacity of executive secretary of the church— and for the other three department executives), benevolence secretary, missionary secretary and librarian, bookkeeper, switchboard operator. In addition, there are two relief switchboard operators and an instructor of women's and girls' gymnastics employed for several evenings per week.

This is a relatively large number of workers considering the variety of the program, but not more than average relative to total attendance. The per cent. of total budget devoted to religious workers' salaries is above average, but not extreme. This indicates a willingness to make somewhat opulent expenditures for the sake of extra quality in results.

The average work-day of the nine full-time workers reporting was between six and one-half and seven hours long on a seven-day basis. This falls below the average of the twenty-six churches on account of the large proportion of workers observing fixed hours which are almost always fewer than those of independent workers. The major types of work, measured by time expended, are administrative, pastoral and clerical. The proportionate amount of time spent in administrative and pastoral work approximates the median of the twenty-six cases.

(It would probably reach or exceed the median if the pastor's work record had been included.) Thirty-nine per cent. of the total work-time is given to clerical work; this is the highest ratio found in any of the cases. No other church studied has made so plentiful a provision of clerical assistants.

The musical staff includes two organists.

Plant

The church possesses one of the notable church plants of the United States. It is a stone structure in the Gothic style, occupying a spacious site and consisting of a well-balanced group of buildings surrounding a court and connected by an arcade in front. The interior of the church proper is particularly beautiful and dignified, and the variety of appointments, as well as their quality, is most unusual.

The plant is valued at over $750,000. It ranks first in the twenty-five cases studied, scoring 840 on the Interchurch thousand-point standard. The score is subdivided as shown in Table XLIV.

TABLE XLIV—SUMMARY OF SCORE OF PLANT

Item	Standard Score	Points Scored		Rank in 25 Cases
		Number	Per Cent.	
Total	1,000	840	84	1
Site	130	114	88	3
Building or buildings	150	146	97	1
Service systems	160	141	88	1
Church rooms	170	151	89	2
Religious school rooms........	200	150	75	3
Community service rooms.....	190	138	73	1

It would be hard to find an actual church plant more nearly approaching the highly exacting ideal embodied in the standard.[4]

---

4 Athearn, *The Indiana Survey of Religious Education,* Vol. I, pp. 107-110, compares the plant of the Fourth Presbyterian Church with those of eleven other exceptionally housed city churches and also rates it first on the Interchurch scale. The actual scoring, however, reveals an interesting difference between the judgment of the Indiana surveyors and that of the present study. The present study credits the plant with only 840 points out of 1,000 to Athearn's credit of 924. The discrepancy falls almost entirely in the rating of Sunday-school and community service facilities. As to the former, Athearn's implied criticism of the

Finances

The current receipts of the year 1924-25 were approximately $110,000; and benevolent receipts $88,000—a total of approximately $200,000. This amount far exceeded that raised by any other church studied, except one or two immediately engaged in building operations.

The distribution of sources of current income was: pew rents, 34 per cent.; endowment, 23 per cent.; individual pledges, 18 per cent.; special gifts, 14 per cent.; fees and dues, 8 per cent.; all other, 3 per cent. The proportion derived from pew rents and endowment was much beyond the average. An unusually large per cent. of expenditures went to music and to "departments specially budgeted" (including summer camp and work of clubs for age- and sex-groups).

The distribution of current expenditures is shown in Table XLV.

TABLE XLV—FINANCIAL EXPENDITURES OF THE CHURCH

Item	Amount	Per Cent.
Grand Total	$112,485	
Total Current Account	111,760	100
Salaries	32,875	29
General administrative expenses	7,522	7
Music	16,517	15
General operation and upkeep of property	24,383	22
Expenses of departments specially budgeted	23,376	21
Publicity	4,065	4
Ecclesiastical connections	629	*
Miscellaneous	2,393	2
Investment Account		
Permanent improvement	725	

* Less than 1 per cent.

Compared with the average of the churches studied, these expenditures represent a high cost relative to the size of the constituency, and also relative to attendance; but the per cent. of constituents who make stated financial pledges is low.

---

basic plan of the Sunday-school layout in the Fourth Presbyterian Church in saying that the partitioning off of classrooms surrounding the main Sunday-school auditorium provides "reasonably adequate isolation for the separate classes" (op. cit., p. 143), does not seem consonant with so high a rating as that allowed. Again, the probably over-exacting Standard calls for about twenty types of rooms for "community service"—and even the elaborate equipment of the Fourth Presbyterian Church hardly comes as near the ideal as the Athearn score suggests.

Benevolent expenditures, not included in the above, were. chiefly devoted to the national and world-wide missions of the Presbyterian denomination, local Presbyterian interests absorbing most of the small remainder.

Public Services

There is an average attendance on the Sunday morning worship of 1,250, of which 60 per cent. is female. The young people's service, held at the same time, has an average attendance of 125 additional. The Sunday-afternoon service runs throughout the year with an average attendance of one hundred, 70 per cent. of which is female. The evening service has an average attendance of 650, with 60 per cent. female; the midweek service an average attendance of one hundred, with 50 per cent. female. Public services are moderately ritualistic and take somewhat ornate color from their very sumptuous setting. All have high-grade and expensive music. The preaching is simple, direct, practical and frequently evangelistic. The pastor generally preaches on Sunday morning and evening. One assistant pastor conducts the young people's service, the other the afternoon service. The pastor analyzes his morning attendance as consisting of one-third of regular members, one-third of transient visitors in Chicago, and one-third of an irregular and floating constituency from all over Chicago.

The reënforcement of these outside elements saves the services from the summer slump so characteristic of city churches. Attendance runs about the same the year round.

Religious Education

The Sunday school is supplemented by Bible and mission-study classes conducted by subsidiary organizations. No director of religious education as such is employed. Organized Sunday-school classes are promoted by, and in part identified with, the clubs and organizations of the men's and women's departments. The total overlapping membership of Sunday school and subsidiaries, however, is less than the average.

Sunday-school enrollment reaches about 1,200, or, with the

non-attending departments, over 1,400. The enrollment is two-thirds adult. Classes usually rated as "senior" and "young people's" are associated with adult departments. The school is fully departmentalized and very adequately housed. A summary of enrollment and attendance is shown in Table XLVI.

TABLE XLVI—SUMMARY OF SUNDAY-SCHOOL STATISTICS

DEPARTMENT	Age	PUPILS Enrollment	TEACHERS
Total	...	1,395	23
Cradle Roll	...	75	..
Beginners	3–5	82 ⎫	
Primary	6–8	80 ⎪	
Junior	9–11	100 ⎬	13
Intermediate	12–14	80 ⎪	
Young People's Dept.	*	300 ⎭	
Adult Department	*	558	10
Home Department	...	120	..

* Range of ages not given.

The addition of four officers to the 1,395 pupils and twenty-three teachers gives a grand total of 1,422. Pupils in the attending departments number 1,200, and attendance averages 53 per cent. of enrollment.

The relatively small per cent. of children, and the low average attendance (55 per cent. in the children's department and 53 per cent. in the total school), is characteristic of down-town churches bringing pupils over long distances.

Current Church Life

Carried along on the vital stream of the church's life, such activities as have now been described recur from day to day, or weekly or monthly as the case may be. Their course is accented by large numbers of special or occasional affairs.

Sunday brings a round of eight or nine services or religious group-meetings, with perhaps 3,000 in attendance. For the eight to ten months of their active operation, three or four clubs or gymnasium groups, particularly for boys, girls and employed young women, will gather in the church daily during the week days, with an aggregate attendance of about one hundred per day. This is in addition to the Wednesday mid-week service, the Friday-night Bible class and numerous regular meetings of officers and committees.

The more usual type of women's organizations meet monthly, and there are monthly social events of the young people's societies.

Extras naturally include a numerous round of special events or programs fostered by these numerous organizations, together with very continuous participation in denominational or interdenominational gatherings and projects. There is an intensive period of mission study during the winter, during which eight graded classes operate. Groups of boys and girls meeting separately receive instruction in preparation for church-membership. A series of congregational dinners is held. The Men's Club holds four notable social affairs. And in the summer more than fifty boys, who have worked loyally in the church during the year, enjoy a camp outing. Behind all these activities go on the persistent labors of minister, staff and lay workers.

Gains and Losses

The ratio of losses to gains—78 per cent. for 1925—has stood at about their average for a considerable period of years.

A study of 245 cases of recent accessions shows 46 per cent. received by letter, and 54 per cent. on confession of faith. Compared with many city churches which get most of their accessions by letter, this indicates the church's evangelistic emphasis and very distinct appeal to the unchurched.

Of accessions by letter, 43 per cent. came from other than Presbyterian churches. This indicates the feebleness of denominational bonds in determining the religious affiliations of city populations. Forty-seven per cent. of the accessions consisted of persons who had been resident in Chicago for more than one year; 53 per cent. for less than one year. This shows the renewal of the church by streams of population from other communities. Fifty-three per cent. of the new members lived near the church, 22 per cent. at an average distance, and 25 per cent. far distant. Of those resident in the community more than one year, 87 per cent. had been previously related to the church through attendance or belonging to some of its organizations. This tends to prove that the subsidiary organizations function to an important extent as reservoirs on which the church draws for members.

In brief, Fourth Church not only receives members by transfer, but wins converts. It gets many not previously Presbyterians. It tends to assimilate older residents into church life and subsequently to win them for church-membership; but it wins a still higher proportion of newcomers directly. The proportion of new members recruited from near-by is somewhat higher than the proportion of near-by members in the total constituency. But the church also shows marked ability to win new members from long distances.

Of 204 recent losses, 45 per cent. were caused by transfer of members to other churches; 47 per cent. were dropped; 8 per cent. died. Seventy per cent. of the letters granted were to other Presbyterian churches; 64 per cent. were to churches outside of Chicago and suburbs. Two-thirds of those granted letters had belonged to the church less than five years, indicating fairly brief connection; but 60 per cent. of those dropped from the list had belonged to the church more than five years, apparently indicating that the church is not in position to keep closely in touch even with members of long standing.

Relation to Social Agencies and Denomination

Eighty members of the Fourth Presbyterian Church are known to be on boards of directors or paid staffs of thirty-one social institutions of Chicago. A total of sixty-one relations with social agencies was recorded during the year previous to the study, including financial support given, publicity in church literature and practical coöperation. The major cultural interests of Chicago are frequently advocated; likewise its general Christian enterprises. The church's predominant interest, as implied in the number of contacts, is in hospitals and children's homes; but it is also influential in general civic and social movements in the city. Two-thirds of the above reported connections with social agencies are with those affiliated with the Presbyterian denomination. Besides very large financial support of general denominational missions, the church bears particularly close relation to three former branch churches (now in charge of the denominational City Extension Society), maintains auxiliary committees for the Presbyterian Hospital and Presbyterian Home, and has close relations with McCormick Theological Seminary. The high place which it occupies in the national counsels of the Presbyterian denomination is well known.

Summary of Adaptations

The Fourth Presbyterian Church erected its present plant and devised its program about fifteen years ago, after a thorough technical survey of the local field; and it has ever since maintained the attempt to adapt its ministry closely to the needs of that field, with settled conviction and commendable conscientiousness. The results are particularly manifest in the proportion of adherents drawn from the immediate vicinity of the church, and in the services of specialized type devised for employed girls, students, and a few foreign groups. There is also a significant approach to the child life of the neighborhood, and thoughtful ministry to the poor and unfortunate.

The immediate environment has changed continuously throughout the period of the church's present policy. In the material sense, and for the district as a whole, change has been for the good. Improvements of the harbor and the Chicago River front are among the outstanding examples of American municipal progress. Business and industry of the highest class are occupying previously very undesirable areas. The erection of great hotels and apartment houses furnishes a modern type of residence for desirable populations close to the church and to the center of the city. This, to a considerable degree, offsets the deterioration of the older parts of the neighboring residential section. Apparently the area of acute deterioration in the immediate vicinity has spread about as far as it can. The major streets of the district are increasingly going over to retail business and will more and more constitute extensions of the central business district and transit corridors for access to the Loop.

These changes have continuously affected the localized program of the church. In general, the week-day program appears to be smaller than formerly, and the variety of the church's contacts with the neighborhood is not increasing. Meanwhile the chief success of the church: namely, as a great city-wide institution, is so conspicuous that it might, with little institutional loss, abandon all special efforts for the immediate neighborhood, as similarly situated churches have frequently done. Such a solution would itself be a capital case of non-localized adaptation to an urban situation. Fourth Church is commanding enough, probably, to keep a permanent nucleus from the desirable classes, to which it could add large numbers of transient attendants from the down-town and near-by hotels and from the great mobile population of the city in general. To make a church out of such elements, even without any localized adaptation, is one significant way of modeling a religious institution upon the characteristics of the modern city.

The outstanding mark of the Fourth Presbyterian Church is that it has conspicuously made both local and non-local adaptations.

These studies do not undertake to indicate what any church ought to do. What Fourth Church has done proves what can be done. The church is officially fixed in the opinion that it should continue to make both sorts of adaptations. This was definitely voiced in the pastor's fiftieth anniversary sermon. One gets the impression that as the difficulties of localized adaptation continue, or at least do not grow less, doubts may arise, if they have not already arisen, with respect to this aspect of the church's ministry.

The future, then, is likely to hold not only the prospect of a continuous series of environmental changes which will make necessary the continuous readaptation of the localized program, but also a challenge to the church's fundamental position. The answer to this challenge will have to be found outside of any evidence drawn from specific data, somewhere in the realm of fundamental insights and convictions as to the purpose of the church and the nature and special genius of its service to the world.

CASE VIII

SOUTH PARK PRESBYTERIAN CHURCH, NEWARK, N. J.

Measured by the size of its constituency, the South Park Church ranks about midway in the list of the twenty-six cases studied. But total attendance on all organizations and activities ranks lower relative to the number of constituents, and the church's total program is relatively narrow.

Yet with the small numbers to deal with and the limited bulk of the total program, the church has entered upon a few unusual ministries. This renders the balance and proportion of its internal structure highly exceptional. Even though the total program is narrow, in order to cover its unusual features, the constituency has to be spread out especially thin at other points.[1]

Stated more concretely, public services of worship represent about an average proportion of the constituency; the Sunday school attracts a very small proportion; while organizations usually regarded as subsidiary comprise a very large proportion. These subsidiaries are also exceptionally numerous, reflecting, as one discovers, diverse and little-related elements in the constituency.

Still again, in these subsidiary organizations are found a very disproportionate number of adolescents.

And this one-sidedness of organization and composition exists in a church that lacks a strong and unifying nucleus of members related to its several departments through overlapping memberships. Instead the members tend toward three separate constituencies, identified respectively with the church, the Sunday school and the subsidiaries. The subsidiaries in turn are a collection of largely unrelated organizations, so that

---

[1] Contrast the previous case (Case VII), in which a much larger block of unusual activities cuts small figure because the rest of the church is so much larger, with this in which a small block cuts a large figure because the rest of the church is relatively smaller.

the fabric of the church is even of looser texture than the above showing suggests.

In all this the church very clearly reflects its origins, the changes through which it has passed, and the results of very definite and resourceful attempts to adapt itself to its situation and serve its community.   This constitutes the significance of the church for the present study.

History

South Park Church was founded in 1853 during the decade of Newark's most rapid growth.

The city, then boasting some 40,000 inhabitants, was bursting its former boundaries in all directions and founding many churches.   The presence of a somewhat rowdy and religiously neglected population in the vicinity of a railroad station in the then southern outskirts of the city (about three-fourths of a mile from the center) led a group of influential citizens to organize there, first a Sunday school (held in a railway car on a siding), later an incorporated religious society, and finally a Presbyterian church.   Apparently, however, the movement had little denominational atmosphere.   It is not inaccurate to say that the church was conceived in a spirit of local accountability and community service.

Two notable pastorates by distinguished ministers of the old school carried the church through more than four-fifths of its history and into the period of the World War.   It grew up into a distinguished place in the city.   Its exceedingly dignified house of worship has long been a landmark among the galaxy of palatial residences formerly grouped about Lincoln Park.

Throughout this long period (which witnessed the growth of Newark in population from 40,000 to nearly 400,000), work for the poorer elements of the population, for whose sake largely the church had originated, was continued, along with that of the church itself, in a chapel located south of the railroad tracks.   In the late eighties, the chapel's ministries had developed something of an institutional phase.   Paid workers were employed and a three-story building provided as a mission center.   It was operated largely by volunteers from the Christian Endeavor Society.   Contemporary descriptions of it particularly stressed the reading-room as "a substitute for a saloon."   Later a new building was erected, and the separation of the chapel constituency into an independent church was discussed.

The early nineties saw radically new elements introduced into the situation.   Newark took its share in the fortunes of metropolitan New York in being the nation's first dumping ground of the "new immigration"—that from southern and eastern Europe.   These new people settled down in great numbers, at the back doors of the city's most desirable residential sections.   This movement was later followed by a great invasion of Negroes, especially during the World War.   The inevitable result was the removal of the chief elements of the older residential population to outlying sections of the city and a considerable weakening of the church.   The expansion of the area of business also cut into the neighborhood, while the vicinity of the chapel became almost solidly Catholic and largely Italian.

These changes radically affected the church's policy and prospects.   Consequently, in 1917, the work and constituency of the chapel were consolidated with the work at the church. This brought together in one organization and under one roof rather diverse social groups.   The consolidation, though still reflected in the slenderness of connection shown by a large part of the constituency, was on the whole successfully effected. About the same time the church received a very valuable re-enforcement in the persons of a remnant of former members of St. Paul's Methodist Episcopal Church, which was removing from the neighborhood.   Its program was broadened, the staff increased and a gymnasium with other improved facilities added to the church structure at the cost of $26,000.   The declining condition of the church prior to, and its decidedly upward trend under, the new policy are statistically established by an examination of ecclesiastical reports for a decade.

At the end of the decade the ratio between losses and gains was more favorable and there had been an increase in accessions to membership on confession of faith.

I. MAJOR ASPECTS OF THE CHURCH

Members and Constituents

Fourteen hundred and one persons constitute the definitely connected constituency of the church.[2] Of these, 706, or slightly more than one-half, belong to constituent families; namely, those with one or more adults included among the enrolled constituents; while the remaining half are individuals from families not attached to the church. This ratio marks the church, though not yet an extreme case, as belonging essentially to the "down-town" type, in contrast with the "family" type consisting chiefly of "believers and their children."

AGE AND SEX

The following comparison shows the age-distribution of the 1,401 constituents, of the twenty-six churches studied, and of the city of Newark.

	PER CENT.		
	Adults (21 & Over)	*Adolescents* (15-20)	*Children* (5-14)
Constituencies of:			
South Park Church	69	15	16
26 churches	73	8	19
Population of Newark	67	11	22

The constituency is about 39 per cent. male and 61 per cent. female. This is the exact ratio between the sexes shown for members by New York City churches in the Federal Religious Census of 1916; but the cases now studied (which are for constituencies) average 4 or 5 per cent. more men. The above comparison shows adults constituting 69 per cent. of the total for South Park Church, which is 2 per cent. greater than in the city as a whole. The church is thus to a slight degree an old folks' church with respect to its city, but not an old folks' church as compared with the twenty-six cases. It has far more than the proportionate number of adolescents, especially of girls. On the other hand, it tends not to be a children's church. Here lies its greatest departure from a normal distribution of constituency.

Sixty per cent. of the adults belong to constituent families, but only 33 per cent. of the adolescents, and 31 per cent. of

---

[2] For definition of constituents and method of calculating, see p. 447.

children. This showing corresponds to the common experience that the child or youth can be lifted out of the family group into some sort of church connection more easily than the adult can.

MANNER AND DEGREE OF ADHERENCE

How are the 1,401 constituents related to the church? About 66 per cent. belong to the church only, the Sunday school only, or the subsidiaries only; that is to say, they have but one line of connection per adherent with the church; while the remainder represent numerous varieties of overlapping memberships. The overlaps of church, Sunday school and subsidiaries, of church and Sunday school, and of Sunday school and subsidiaries involve but little more than 5 per cent. of the total constituency. Chart IV shows this graphically. In no other case are the sectors representing these relationships so slender. On the contrary, the overlap of church and subsidiaries is exceptionally large. On the whole, however, South Park Church tends to tie its adherents to itself in but few ways. This leaves the highly organized core for the church (represented by the black sector on the chart) relatively diminutive; while the outreach to various slenderly related constituencies is relatively large. In short, the church has pushed out well into the community, but in so doing has not closed up its own ranks to an average degree. It is a loosely related body, doubtless reflecting the somewhat divergent and non-homogeneous elements which its history has brought together. Only time can tell whether their tenuous ties can be woven into strong and enduring ones.

Environment

From the standpoint of massing of population and the crowded occupancy of land within Greater New York, Newark and its immediate suburbs rank second only to Manhattan Island and Brooklyn, and ahead of the city's other three boroughs. On the other hand, its greater average distance and more distinct physical separation from the center, its somewhat divergent interests and more independent history and development unite to give Newark very definite and almost unique character as a secondary metropolis. The ultimate environment, on whose influence the study of South Park Church throws light, is thus that of Greater New York; the immediate environment remains to be more fully described.

South Park Church is located somewhat more than a half-mile southwest of the business center of Newark.[3]

Characterizing in the simplest possible terms the area within a mile of it, one notes first that the church stands just at the end of the highly developed business district, at the point of divergence of the two most important arterial thoroughfares to the southwest. The semicircle south and east of the church is almost entirely filled by heavy industry and business, with Italians and Negroes as the fill-in population. This sector includes, however, one large solidly foreign residential district of Italians and Slavs.

The quadrant to the north of the church is about equally divided, within the first half-mile, by industry stretching back from the main business axis, and by an area of greatly deteriorated residences occupied by very mixed populations, predominantly foreign and Negro. Within the second half-mile in this same direction lies the main foreign business section, surrounded immediately by massed polyglot populations, by secondary belts of industry along the railroads, and by large areas occupied somewhat solidly by Italians and Negroes.

The western quadrant is cut into along both margins by industry and by foreign retail business; and more successful foreigners have filtered into it in such numbers as to suggest recently a mass movement. The major part of it, however, zoned for residential occupancy, reflects a higher economic level, and remains mainly in the hands of white American population.

CENSUS DATA

The ward data of the United States Census for 1920 reveal a total population in the area closely related to the church as

---

[3] The cost of providing maps showing the environment and parish distribution of every church discussed went beyond the funds available for the graphic illustration of this work. The reader of the verbal descriptions must therefore try to imagine himself as standing at the church in the center of such a diagram as is used in charts on pages 51 and 78. By turning himself about in mind he can follow the rather brief description with sufficient accuracy.

of about 143,000 persons, over two-thirds of whom are of foreign origins, and 6 per cent. are Negro. Only a little over one-fourth are native white of native parentage, and 30 per cent. are actually foreign-born. Six per cent. are illiterate—these consisting mainly of adult foreigners. Only 13 per cent. of all habitations in the area are owned by their occupants. In spite of the fact that the characteristic industrial housing of Newark is a two-story dwelling, and that the area treated as the church's environment covers two outlying wards, the excess of families over dwellings equals 52 per cent. of all families. Native whites of native parentage are 1 per cent. fewer, and foreign-born whites 39 per cent. more numerous than in Newark as a whole.[4]

ENVIRONMENTAL PROSPECTS

A continuance of the present rate of growth of population will give Newark three-quarters of a million population in 1950—twenty-three years hence.

By that time the cutting down of foreign immigration (unless the national policy is again changed) will have greatly reduced the percentage of foreign-born and of near-foreign antecedents.

There is likely to be also a return of residential population to the vicinity of the center as apartment-houses replace present structures owing to the high value of the land. This, the common tendency of congested cities approaching the half-million population line, is already coming into evidence in Newark. Rising land values are almost sure to put back a

---

[4] The most available recent evidence as to the distribution and relative strength of population of foreign antecedents in Newark is that secured in a city-wide school survey of 1922 (*Nationality and Age-Grade Surveys, Public Schools of Newark, N. J.*, Monograph No. 11, Board of Education, June, 1923). Thus, when children in thirty-six public schools located within a mile of the church were classified by nationality of father, native whites ranked first sixteen times, or about one-half of the time, second nine times, third six times and fourth four times.

Native white preponderance, however, was found only in areas to the west of the church; and, even in this direction, in six schools there were more Russian-born fathers (known by the parallel study of language spoken at home to be Jews) than there were native whites, while to the northeast and southeast Italian parentage ranked first. Slavic parentage predominated in two schools, while Negroes were second in four schools and third in two more. South Park Church is thus ringed about by preponderant foreign populations on two sides, and faced by very strong foreign minorities in the remaining directions. It is believed, too, that there has been further rapid invasion of the American section by Jews since the date of the report.

higher-grade population of some sort into the vicinity of the church. Moreover, the increasingly strategic character of its location, from the standpoint of the business center and transit facilities, greatly improves its opportunity for making an effective city-wide appeal. Such is the environment, present and prospective, to which the church has adjusted and will have to adjust itself.

Parish

The church's present relation to this environment was carefully measured. Disregarding twenty-four persons whose addresses were not recorded, but including thirty-three whose addresses were outside of Newark and immediate suburbs, virtually all of whom, however, lived within the New York Metropolitan area, 25 per cent. of all constituents are found to be living within half a mile of the church, and 44 per cent. within a mile, while 20 per cent. live beyond three miles. This constitutes a fairly scattered parish, though less scattered than those of several of the twenty-six churches studied, most of which were located in larger cities and perhaps possessed greater drawing capacity.

The distribution of constituents from constituent families is radically different from that of detached individuals. Many more detached individuals are drawn from the first mile, and relatively more families from almost every zone beyond a mile.

DIRECTION

The constituency (that resident in Newark and immediate suburbs) lives 30 per cent. to the east of the church and 70 per cent. to the west in the direction of the immediately contiguous high-grade residential population. Adherents are almost absent in the second half-mile to the northwest where the parish runs into the solidly foreign section, but become relatively numerous again in the second and third mile in that direction. Another notable jump is across the business and Italian section to the northeast to the Forest Hill section between two and three miles distant, where relatively numerous adherents are found.

DENSITY OF OCCUPANCY

Considering the relative density of the constituency with reference to the church building by distance zones and directional sectors, the heaviest adherent population is found within half a mile to the southwest. As between the other three sectors, adherents are most numerous within this distance in the direction of the former chapel. In the second half-mile to the northeast there is distinct lack of adherents on account of the intervention of the business section. Within this zone also the neighborhood of the old chapel furnishes the next to the most adherents. In general, the parish tends strongly toward the southwest, the church finding 42 per cent. of all adherents in this direction. Suburban adherents, however, live most largely to the northwest.

The probability of the explanations of parish distribution already suggested for the several sectors is strengthened when one superimposes the map of the total parish upon a city map showing the characteristics of population by similar zones and sectors. Judged by these basic social data, South Park Church registers in quite exact detail an avoidance of foreign, industrial and business areas except in the direction of its former chapel work. In general, in equal sectors, the relative number of constituents increases just in proportion as the area is residentially desirable and populated by Americans. In other words, the church draws selectively from the surrounding parish area. This explanation is still further supported when the distribution of suburban members is considered. The same situation was shown by Cases II and IV, and has now become an old story.

II. AGENCIES, RESOURCES AND METHODS

Organizations and Stated Activities

A careful estimate of attendance on all organized or regular activities gives a total of 34,028 for the year.[5] Only three of the twenty-six churches studied intensively have smaller programs than this.

---

[5] Attendance on church services—much the largest single item—was arrived at by actual count.

The ratio between Sunday and week-day attendance marks a definite variation of South Park Church from the average in the direction of a week-day program, and the following analysis of the program will show that it runs to innovations rather than to conventional development.[6]

The estimated attendance is divided as shown by Table XLVII.

TABLE XLVII—ESTIMATED ANNUAL ATTENDANCE ON SPECIFIED OCCASIONS AT SOUTH PARK CHURCH AND AT 26 CHURCHES

Occasion	Attendance					
	SOUTH PARK CHURCH A		B		26 CHURCHES	
					Approx. Median	*Range of Variation*
	Number	*Per Cent.*	*Number*	*Per Cent.*	*Per Cent.*	*Per Cent.*
Total *	34,028	100	34,028	100		
Formal religious services (Sunday and week day) ..	18,539	54	18,539	54	51	15–75
Sunday school	5,025	15	6,125	18	24	9–38
All other stated activities...	10,464 †	31	9,364	28	22	9–51

* Sunday, 71 per cent.; week day, 29 per cent.
† Includes meetings of church officers and committees.

Column B in Table XLVII adds the attendance on certain Sunday morning Bible classes to that of the Sunday school proper, although these classes are not organically a part of it, and subtracts their attendance from "all other stated activities." This procedure makes the South Park Church more nearly comparable with the other churches studied. On this basis, the percentage of time the church gives to formal services is appreciably greater than the average; that given to Sunday school is distinctly less than the average; while that given to subsidiary organizations and programs is decidedly more than the average. If the Sunday school is defined strictly, the church falls into the lowest quarter of the ranking scale on the size of this item.

---

[6] For contrasting case with about the same proportion of week-day activity, see p. 161.

Attendance on "all other stated activities" (including the Bible classes) is divided between the organized age- and sex-groups as shown by Table XLVIII.

TABLE XLVIII—ESTIMATED ANNUAL ATTENDANCE ON SUBSIDIARY ORGANIZATIONS AND STATED ACTIVITIES

No.	ORGANIZATIONS Type	ATTENDANCE Number	Per Cent.
21	Total	10,159	100
2	Mixed adults	189	2
1	Adult men	350	3
6	Adult women	1,174	12
4	Mixed young people *	3,924	39
1	Young men	260	3
2	Young women	720	7
0	Mixed boys and girls	0	0
3	Boys	1,062	10
2	Girls	2,480	24
0	Mixed children	0	0

* Between 15 and 23 years of age.

Numerically measured, the major stress of this subsidiary program is upon the four young people's organizations.

About 43 per cent. of the total subsidiary attendance consists of women and girls attending separate organizations, 16 per cent. of men and boys attending separate organizations, and 41 per cent. mixed attendance of the two sexes on the same organization. Only one church devotes a higher per cent. of its program to women and girls.[7] This corresponds with the more than average proportion of women in the total constituency.

Staff

South Park Church was pastorless during the period of the study. The normal staff, implied by present arrangements with other paid workers, would consist of:

(1) *Pastor,* in general administrative charge of the church, performing all functions traditionally restricted to the clergyman; responsible for the conduct of public services and for general pastoral activities.

(2) *Director of Activities,* related to all subsidiary organizations as general advisor, and in particular charge of the

[7] Not included in the case studies.

Sunday school, young people's work and utilization of the gymnasium and community facilities.

(3) *Secretary,* also in charge of the "department of visiting," performing the current duties of an office secretary but not primarily responsible for the keeping of church records; responsible for organizing volunteer workers to carry on visitation within the parish.

While generally carrying on previously established arrangements, the working relations of the paid workers to the lay authorities of the church and to one another have naturally reflected the abnormal conditions of a church without a pastor and the special experiences of the current period. They are therefore not significant as throwing exact light upon permanent methods of staff relationships or functioning.

Plant

Among the twenty-five plants studied, that of South Park Church ranks twentieth on the Interchurch thousand-point scale, scoring a total of 551 points. The median of the twenty-five churches is about 600 points.

The church occupies a conspicuous site at the junction of Broad Street and Clinton Avenue. The strategic relation of its location to the structure of the city has had earlier comment. The church building proper is a substantial structure, Renaissance in design, and said to follow closely a model by Sir Christopher Wren. It is located on a slightly wedge-shaped lot. The Sunday-school and parish rooms are elongations at the rear of the auditorium, to which the recently erected gymnasium has been somewhat arbitrarily attached. The result is an irregular structure with parts not so well related as though they had been designed at one time.

Largely on this account, the church ranks only twentieth among the twenty-five churches studied with respect to its site, while it ranks thirteenth with respect to the general type and esthetic quality of the edifice, considered both as a whole and in its decorative detail. Its room for worship is a distinguished example of a consistent Renaissance interior. Administrative facilities provided for in connection with the erection of the gymnasium are fair.   On the other hand, the church has scarcely a vestige of a modern Sunday-school plant, and its service systems lack much of being modern.   Relative to the standard fixed by the score-card, its provision for community service is just average in spite of the very excellent gymnasium and shower and locker rooms.[8]

The strong and weak points of the plant are systematically shown in the summarized score in Table XLIX.

TABLE XLIX—SUMMARY OF SCORE OF PLANT

ITEM	STANDARD SCORE	POINTS SCORED		RANK IN 25 CASES
		Number	Per Cent.	
Total	1,000	551	55	20
Site	130	84	65	20
Building or buildings.........	150	116	77	13
Service systems	160	78	49	17
Church rooms	170	108	64	23
Religious school rooms.......	200	92	46	20
Community service rooms.....	190	73	38	12

Fortunately the fact that the church has a second frontage on a back street makes further additions quite feasible without serious modification of the existing structure.[9]

Finances

The receipts of the church during 1925 for its current expenses (including those of the Sunday school and the subsidiary organizations) were about $20,000.   There was also a balance of about $1,100 on account of the year 1924.   Less than half ($9,399) came from individual pledges, and about 17 per cent. from pew rentals, but only about 7 per cent. was received in loose collections.   Some 5 per cent. came from entertainments.   The percentage received from loose collections is so small as to be nearly negligible as a source of support.   This is rather contrary to the tendency of down-town churches to capitalize their appeal to transient attendants.

[8] The proposed remodeling of the rooms above the chapel will add definitely to Sunday-school facilities and should give the church a notable dramatic equipment; but the lack of clubrooms is extreme.

[9] Additional rooms for Sunday school and clubs could easily be constructed over the present locker and furnace rooms without visible relation to, and consequently without clashing with, the rather exacting architectural lines of the front.

Fees and dues for the use of social facilities do not figure as sources of support.

The benevolent total of about $6,750 includes the miscellaneous benevolences of the subsidiary organizations and special gifts of the Women's Missionary Society. Of the total, about 45 per cent. came through this society. The grand total of current and benevolent receipts was thus approximately $26,750, and the church closed the financial year with a slight balance.

Twenty thousand four hundred and twenty-five dollars was budgeted for 1926 by the church alone, not counting probably $1,000 expenses of subsidiary organizations. This implies a very low rate of expenditure per constituent, compared with that of the other cases studied; but a more than average rate relative to the total annual attendance on organizations and activities.

The distribution of 1925 expenditures was rendered distinctly abnormal by virtue of the absence of the normal item for the pastor's salary. It is more singificant therefore to consider the distribution of the slightly larger authorized budget for 1926, shown in Table L.

TABLE L—FINANCIAL EXPENDITURES OF THE CHURCH

Item	Amount	Per Cent.
Total	$20,425	100
Salaries	12,500	61
General administrative expenses	830	4
Music	1,940	10
General operation and upkeep of property	3,555	18
Expenses of departments specially budgeted	....	..
Publicity	1,100	5
Miscellaneous	500	2

In no other case studied is the per cent. of the total expenditures devoted to salaries so high. This is the result of a relatively broad program including considerable supervision of the work of small groups carried on as part of a relatively small enterprise.[10]

10 This budget includes no item covering the expenses of subsidiary organizations. In view of the considerable sums raised by these organizations and the relatively large share occupied by their activities in the total program of the church, a really inclusive budgeting of all receipts and expenditures would seem desirable.

Of benevolent expenditures of approximately $6,750 in 1925, all but 3 per cent. went to denominational objects, primarily the authorized missions and educational institutions of the Presbyterian Church.

Public Services and Worship

Measured by the total annual attendance, public services and worship (including the mid-week services) constitute somewhat more than half of the total operations of the church to which the staff, plant and budget are devoted. Church attendance is carefully counted. There was an average at Sunday-morning congregations of 256 for the forty Sundays of the year when the church is felt to be in normal operation; and an average evening congregation of 185.

On the Sunday morning covered by the study, about one-fourth of the audience appeared to be composed of men, and three-fourths of women. On a rough count over 80 per cent. were adults and only 8 per cent. children. While the congregation was assembling, an atmosphere of moderate social cordiality prevailed. The ushering was dignified and courteous. The service occupied an hour and a half. It was only slightly liturgical in character, with the Apostles' Creed and Gloria following a responsive reading, but with the organ and a soprano soloist substituted for the usual church choir. The ministers were gowned. Children representing Sunday-school groups were seated in the gallery. The service was conducted by the director of activities (not an ordained minister) and the sermon presented by a supply preacher. At the close of the service there was active visiting for about fifteen minutes among the attendants.

THE SECOND SERVICE

Only about seventy persons attended the evening service on the Sunday studied; but young people were a noticeable element in the congregation. The service was briefer, but of the same general character as in the morning.

Religious Education

Measured either by attendance upon the Sunday school or upon the Sunday school and other organizations for Bible study, the church puts less than average emphasis on religious education. In theory, it is intended to gather up all church activities of children and young people under the idea of religious education; but, as the director of activities confesses, "Few recognize the theory, and the existing relationships of organizations do not carry it out." There is a small Young People's Society of Christian Endeavor maintaining a Sunday-evening service and supper, and a very active young people's Bible class, with full organization and an independent social life, meeting Sunday mornings.

Since the Sunday school is a relatively separate instrument of religious education, it is fair to report upon it separately and to summarize independently other phases of education which are not integrated into this single department.

The Sunday-school session is held on Sunday afternoons and lasts one hour. The enrollment of pupils and teachers and the average attendance of pupils are shown in the upper part of Table LI.

TABLE LI—ENROLLMENT AND ATTENDANCE IN RELIGIOUS
EDUCATIONAL ORGANIZATIONS

		PUPILS		TEACHERS		
	Age	Enrolled	Average Attendance	Total	Male	Female
Grand Total	...	285	160			
Sunday School Total	...	179	97	13	0	13
Beginners and Primary...	3 to 8	67	26	4	0	4
Junior	9 to 12	47	36	6	0	6
Senior	13 to 18	65	35	3	0	3
Other Bible Classes Total	...	106	63	..	..	..
Young People's Bible Class	19*	87	56	..	..	..
Adult Bible Class	Over 21	19	7	..	..	..

* Average age.

In addition to the Sunday-school pupils, officers and teachers and the Bible classes reported on in the table, there is a cradle roll of fifty-six and a home department of fifty-four. Attendance in the Sunday school proper is 55 per cent. of enrollment. This is a very low percentage.

The age-distribution of the 285 persons statedly enrolled in religious education is as follows:

	Number	Per Cent.
Total	285	100
Children	114	40
Adolescents	152	53
Adults	19	7

Only four of the churches studied had more adolescents in religious educational organizations relative to the size of their adult constituency, but only five had fewer children. This showing agrees with the age-distribution of the total constituency.[11]

Each department of the Sunday school has a separate departmental assembly-room. Only two or three of the classes, however, enjoy isolated space for class purposes through the use of the balcony of the gymnasium. Classes generally sit at desks or tables during the instruction period. The range of instructional material has been somewhat wider in the past, but is at present confined to the Uniform International Graded Lessons.

Growth and Conservation

Gains and losses in membership from January, 1925, to April, 1926, were intensively studied.

SOURCES OF NEW MEMBERS

Of 117 new members received, fifty-three, or 45 per cent. of the total, came by profession of faith, twenty-five by reaffirmation of faith, and thirty-nine by formal letters of transfer. The proportion coming on profession of faith is well beyond the average.

---

[11] Page 224.

Records as to former church connection of those coming by letter or reaffirmation were accessible in fifty-six cases. Of this number, thirty-five were members of Presbyterian churches, and twenty-one recruits from six other denominations, notably from the Methodist and Lutheran. This means that more than one-third of these recruits from former church-membership were not of the same denomination as the church. A noteworthy source of accessions by letter is a Scotch Presbyterian element in Newark, probably showing the advantage to the Protestant church of the new type of immigration now coming to the United States.

A study of the geographical distribution of the residences of the 117 new members revealed that the area from which the church draws members corresponds quite accurately with that over which its constituency is spread. This is not always true with churches.

For the period studied, the losses of membership equaled 36 per cent. of the gains, which was slightly above the average rate of the previous three years, leaving a net gain of seventy-five. Twenty-nine per cent. of the losses were by death—a considerably larger proportion than the average of the previous three years—and 71 per cent. by transfer of members. There was no general clearance of the roll. In the absence of this process, the ratios between total losses and gains and the several occasions of losses and gains do not appear to have changed significantly over a period of ten years.

Current Church Life

Following Easter, the church lets itself down into the vacation period through a gradual diminution of activities. Those of most of the subsidiary organizations are limited to about nine months. For the three summer months, union Sunday services are held in coöperation with two neighboring churches. The Sunday school, however, is continued.

With the middle of September the church is working back toward normal functioning. Rallies of the Sunday school and a "loyalty day," in which all organizations march in procession to a church service, help to get up momentum. Church life then largely follows the pattern of the Christian year with its festivities and seasons.   Virtually every week brings forward the social events of some organization, and there are certain special occasions in which the church at large is interested. Among the more colorful interests are plays and pageants. Numerous denominational, or interdenominational, or civic interests are announced to the church or participated in by it. This keeps alive the sense of belonging to the larger world of Christian affairs.   The annual meeting of the church occurs in January.

The most striking characteristic of the church's current life is the large number of relatively small organizations which it has as units of activity and expression.   The total constituency not exclusively related to church and Sunday school is about 700.   This number is divided among twenty-one subsidiary organizations.   So exceptional a number of subsidiaries reflects the many sources from which the church has gathered up its constituency in the past and the many diverse groups with which it is still in contact.

Six of these organizations are for adult women.   Their purposes do not go beyond the ordinary range of women's activities in conventional churches; yet they are broken up into societies reflecting the original church group, the chapel group, a group that more conveniently meets at night than in the afternoon, and special circles of acquaintances and friends. Such a situation is in sharp contrast with the tendency in many churches to unify and departmentalize all women's interests in a parish under one central organization.

There are four young people's organizations, each representing a group of special origins or interests.   The Young People's Bible Class, for example, had an almost spectacular beginning in the revolt of about thirty young people from a Lutheran church located in the residential district about a mile southwest of South Park Church.   The grounds of the revolt were theological and cultural.   The Lutheran church still maintains preaching in German, and the young people felt that it took an unduly repressive attitude with respect to conduct. They therefore withdrew and for a time maintained an independent Bible class of their own which met in a Jewish synagogue. Their original contacts with South Park Church were through the dances of the Saturday Night Club in the gymnasium, which some of them attended. They became an acknowledged subsidiary of the church in 1925, but naturally remain a group largely independent in feeling and spirit.

Organizations for young women reflect rather the differences between the more passive and more active athletic temperaments than they do diverse origins; but boys' organizations are essentially based upon different groups; one, for example, coming from the old chapel district.

Community Relations

The local charities of Newark do not receive financial support from the church as such; most of them being financed through the Community Chest. The combined reports of the church and subsidiary organizations, and a check of the lists of staff and officers of the city's social agencies, revealed, however, a total of twenty-two stated contacts with the community-serving agencies during the year as follows:

Type of Contact	Number of Agencies	Number of Members
Contributions toward financial support	1	..
Church-members on staff or governing board	15	23
Practical coöperation	5	..
Publicity and advocacy (in printed bulletin)	1	..

The Presbyterian denomination has few philanthropic institutions of its own in Newark; consequently contacts of the South Park Church with agencies were almost entirely interdenominational and non-sectarian in character. Measured by these contacts, the church appears to be most actively interested in health, child-caring and character-building agencies; that is to say, in preventative and normalizing social efforts rather than in merely alleviating or remedying individual ills.

Denominational Relations

South Park Church is not now directly operating or financing any branch mission that might involve it in denominational coöperation or oversight. Its benevolences are almost entirely denominational, and it maintains all normal denominational relations. But it appears to have only a moderately intimate connection with the organized affairs of the denomination in the city. However, periodic discussions of realignment in Presbyterianism have kept the church's fortunes and plans in the mind of the denomination, and whatever the church proposes on its own account, the question of its relationships to other churches is sure to be raised recurrently. For, in spite of removals and amalgamations, there are obviously still too many Presbyterian churches within a mile of the center of Newark for the available Protestant population. This inherent fact of being deeply involved in the denominational situation must be set down as of basic significance, however it may be temporarily disregarded.

Adaptations

How did South Park Church come to be as it is? As was discovered at the outset, it has been experiencing for a good many years a rather exigent set of changes, both in its immediate and in its total environment, which may well have resulted in radical departures from the average behavior of the church in the city. As a matter of fact, it turns out to present a rather clear-cut case of urban adaptation under environmental pressure.

The following section attempts to summarize the major findings of the study from this viewpoint.

TYPICAL EXPERIENCES OF THE URBAN CHURCH

The general series of changes through which the South Park Church has passed, particularly in the last two decades, is essentially typical. It has been repeated in all fundamental respects by the central religious institutions of every large American city that has grown rapidly.

The relation of the church to the structure of the city is changed. Its building, standing on the same and original site, has seen the outskirts of the city develop into the gateway to the center.

New and largely alien elements have come into the city until three-fourths of the population are not of American origin.

Business and industrial expansion have crowded upon the immediate neighborhood of the church, and the outward aspect of the entire region has been changed with the erection of new types of structures.

The older constituency has largely died off or removed.

Changes equally striking have befallen the poorer area south of the tracks which was the former scene of the chapel work.

These changes have created an acute zone of deterioration in the neighborhood of the church; but this has been quickly followed by striking physical improvements due to an era of high land values and to some tendency of population to return to the center and live in apartment-houses.

The more prosperous of the partly assimilated alien populations have broken away from racial colonies and filtered into the outlying residential districts formerly held by American population.

There has consequently been a steady retreat of the most prosperous classes out of the city altogether and into the suburbs.

On the whole, therefore, while the changes have not been without their compensations nor have they been driven to blighting irrecoverable extremes, they have made the church's situation vitally and permanently different. Incidentally they have given it an increasingly strategic location with respect to the city as a whole.

The total effect of these changes upon the church is summarized in the fact that it has less available human material left in its vicinity and probably a permanently smaller Sunday-school constituency, but greater capacity for outreach toward a city-wide ministry, and more people open to its selective approach.

THE CHURCH'S REACTIONS TO CHANGE

For reactions probably traceable to these changes, one must look first below the surface of the situation. Deeper down one finds a constituency continually evolving away from its former family basis, ending with a higher proportion of detached individuals, and occupying a larger parish area selectively rather than uniformly.

In policies deliberately adopted, one traces the reassertion of the old tradition of local responsibility and service, the stimulating effects of experiments in outreaching ministries undertaken during the War, and the controlling influence of strong leadership. The work of the church has been consolidated at one location; and it has been internally adapted to what is intended as a program of community service. The elements of this program have been varied. They have constituted definite adaptations of service to the types of people found in the constituency; but perhaps not in every case the most profound and significant adaptations.

The chief institutional changes have been the extension of the week-day program, an enlargement of church plant, the employment of a director of activities with special reference to community work for varied groups, and a considerable increase of the financial budget in order to support these new features.

The large adaptation of the tone and spirit of the church to the character of the community as a whole has been less pronounced.

MODIFICATIONS OF OBJECTIVE

Changes in the thinking of the church have probably been less extreme than those in its program and institutional life. There has not always been the most thorough-going understanding of what the church was heading for. Members of the survey committee testified that changes as they came "were not much talked about." The general trend was felt to be rather an evolution of an attitude implicit in the church from the beginning. Yet the adoption of the title, "Community Church" must have been accompanied by some enlargement of the concept of the church's mission. The issues involved, however, were faced concretely, one at a time, rather than theoretically. This may very well be the best method of sound thinking.

What was finally arrived at is locally expressed in the formula, "A community church meeting community needs." This is a resonant slogan and the specific measures by which it has been supported have been proved generally good in the test of experience.

SUMMARY OF SUCCESSES

Under the community-church conception and policies, the South Park Church has grown conspicuously (in striking contrast with many neighboring churches) and at a moderately accelerated rate. The bulk of the old constituency has remained loyal and has found new motive for effort and new pride in their institution. As one of the Survey Committee remarked: "The church is like a college with a good football team; even those not actively participating feel a share in its victories."

The church has enlarged the range of its parish, though not to an unusual extent. It does not yet make a strictly city-wide appeal; but exhibits rather symptoms of growing ability to make one, with, at present, a strong regional trend of parish to the southwest.

The church has repeatedly absorbed new constituencies from other sources (for example, the chapel group, the St. Paul's Methodist Episcopal Church group and the young people's group from the Lutheran church), though sometimes without altogether assimilating them.

The financial support necessary to bring about these changes has not been lacking nor skimped. The envelope system is said to have widened the basis of support, and the church's financial outlook is hopeful.

The immediate neighborhood of the church is still somewhat strongly held by it. Here especially it gets its detached adherents.

While no institutional realignments have taken place as between the church and other churches of its denomination, the situation as related to all of them has been faced and will be faced again.

There is no intimation that the religious spirit of the church has grown less, and it is probable that in connection with the multiplication of organizations the absolute amount of lay service has been somewhat enlarged, though this is a point that may need watching.

All told, the church's recent development presents an excellent example of the fusion of old and new objectives and processes. It has come to relatively radical modification of method and outlook without very clear foresight or perfect sense of balance, but, on the other hand, without any essential break with the past. In other words, there has been real continuity of development. One who reads the old documents of the church and then talks with its present Survey Committee cannot fail to note that the two do not speak exactly the same language. But one must also feel that, in this case, loyalty to the past is inextricably bound up with loyalty to the present and with hope for the future.

FIRST PRESBYTERIAN CHURCH, DETROIT, MICH.

Three neighboring religious organizations, located on Woodward Avenue within a mile and a quarter of Detroit's central business district, have more widely scattered constituencies than any other of the twenty-six cases studied. They are the Central Methodist Episcopal, St. John's Protestant Episcopal and the First Presbyterian Church. The explanation is, in general, that these churches have stuck to their present locations under circumstances before which others might have moved.

This digging-in of these and other similar down-town churches is one of the striking phenomena of the contemporary urban religious situation in America. But each case represents a special version of the attack upon the same general situation, and each solution reflects a unique atmosphere in the church concerned.

The First Presbyterian Church, with which the present case study deals, is one of the oldest, richest and most influential Protestant enterprises in the city, and has been particularly famous in the life of its denomination. After three changes of site reflecting the earlier evolution of the city, it has maintained itself in its present location for thirty-eight years.

Its position lacks the extreme strategic advantage of that of the Central Methodist Church, but, from the standpoint of opportunity for a local ministry, the character of its immediate environment is slightly better. With respect to external method, the two churches have approached an essentially common situation in the same general way. Each has erected a large parish house as an adjunct to its former plant, where it carries on a varied program supplementary to its historic tradition. On the whole, the mood of the First Presbyterian Church has been the more opportunistic, and its procedure, though not less thoughtful, has borne a somewhat less theoretical stamp.   The erection of the new church house, in 1910-11, was an attempt to meet the transformation of the immediate locality into a rooming-house district, and to serve the numerous young men and women living away from home; but, as the present pastor modestly testifies, the church did not know how to operate and utilize the new plant, and had to learn by experience.   Its present policy is the result of a series of experimental trials and shifts which are themselves most instructive.

The results of the church's total effort, statistically measured, are that its membership has shown virtually continuous growth from year to year and is now 50 per cent. more than it was a decade ago; that the Sunday-school attendance averages somewhat larger, and that the permanent level of local expenditures is about two and one-half times greater.[1]

Ranked with the other churches included in these case studies, the First Presbyterian Church stands ninth in total annual attendance upon all stated organizations and activities. Its program is still primarily one of religious activities.   Only three churches have a higher ratio of attendance on Sundays compared with that on week-days.   This is in striking contrast with the trend of the Central Methodist Church toward a stronger week-day program.   In other words, the modifications with which the First Presbyterian Church has attempted to meet its new situation are not essentially radical.   Its parish is slightly localized and its work somewhat broader than formerly.   But out of a list of sixty activities and practices of modern churches, its program includes just thirty, which is the median number in the twenty-six cases studied.   As compared with city churches as a whole, the program has more than average range, but not anything like that of the broadest and most adventurous cases.

The particular secret of this moderate broadening of program is found in the fact that the First Presbyterian Church

---

[1] In this study of the First Presbyterian Church, the extensive work of the Dodge Community House in Highland Park, adjacent to the Dodge Motor works, is not statistically included, because, although the church has title to the property and controls the enterprise through an appointment of the majority of its trustees, the community house has a distinct constituency and is separately staffed and financed.

has developed a second constituency. Church life as lived by the older adherent elements is not greatly altered, but new things are undertaken for the sake of the new people. This has resulted in giving the total program an appearance of all-roundedness. There is what seems like effectively graded provision for a wide variety of interests on the part of each age- and sex-group, when in fact a given constituency is served by one part, and sometimes by a fragmentary part of the program.

This is the major fact that appears from the more detailed study of the case.

I. MAJOR ASPECTS OF THE CHURCH

Constituency

Ranking ninth in total annual attendance, the church ranks third in the number of its recorded adherents in all stated organizations and activities, the figures being: attendance, 111,487; adherents, 2,576. The variation of its showing as between these two viewpoints is due to the very small amount of duplicatory membership. Overlapping members constitute only 20 per cent. of the total. Only six of the twenty-six cases make a feebler showing on this point.

AGE AND SEX

The constituency of the First Presbyterian Church is 88 per cent. adult. Only two other churches of the cases studied have more adults.

Compared with the twenty-six churches and with the population of Detroit, the extreme deficiency of the constituency in children, and its even greater shortage of adolescents, is revealed in the following comparison. (Exactly the same tendency has already been seen in the Central Methodist Church.)

	PER CENT.		
	Adults (21 & Over)	Adolescents (15-20)	Children (5-14)
Constituencies of:			
First Presbyterian Church..........	88	3	9
26 churches	73	8	19
Population of Detroit....:..........	72	10	18

Such is the cost of staying in a down-town location without any commanding means of making local appeal to youth.

The constituency has forty-three men for every fifty-seven women—a condition that agrees exactly with the strongly modal tendency in the twenty-six churches. That is to say, the disproportion between the two sexes is not exceptional; and it is somewhat strange that it exists to a greater extent in the minor than in the adult group.

Fifty-three per cent. of all constituents come from adherent families, one or more adults of which also belong to the church in some way. This proportion puts the First Presbyterian Church in the median position of the twenty-six cases studied. In other words, its family character, the threatened loss of which was made the keynote of its new policy, is as well maintained as in the average of all the cases, and much better than in the Central Methodist Church. This fact may explain certain of the more conservative characteristics of the present case.

MANNER AND DEGREE OF ADHERENCE

Fifty-seven per cent. of the total constituency is composed of members of the church only. Only one case has a higher per cent. falling in this class. Out of the total small overlap of membership, that of church and subsidiaries is high, which leaves that of church and Sunday school and that of Sunday school and subsidiaries unusually small. Only four cases have a smaller per cent. of adherents belonging to the Sunday school only. In other words, the Sunday school is largely integrated with other aspects of the church's life; but its relations are numerous so that the overlap in any one direction is not great.

Only two churches of those studied have relatively so small a number of constituents who belong to church, Sunday school and subsidiaries, all three.

Behind these various ways of adherence one discerns such distinct major constituencies as those that belong to the church only, those that belong to the church and subsidiaries and those that belong to subsidiaries only. Exclusive memberships in church or in Sunday school or in subsidiaries make up 80 per cent. of the total. This means that the enterprise as a whole has an unusually small common core.

Adult women make up the majority of adherents belonging to the church and subsidiaries. Adult men, on the contrary, preponderate in the group that belongs to subsidiaries only.

DEGREE OF ADHERENCE

Considering each separate organization to which constituents belong, and including the making of a pledged financial contribution as a method of adherence, 53 per cent. of all constituents are found to belong to the church in only one way, and 31 per cent. in two ways. Only 1 per cent. of the total have four or more connections, which is in striking contrast with 8 per cent. in the same category in the Central Methodist Church, and obviously goes with the separate and loosely united constituencies already discovered and with the small central nucleus.

The most highly connected age-group in the church is the adolescent, 19 per cent. of whom have more than two connections, compared with 16 per cent. of adults and 11 per cent. of children.

Of 829 pledged contributors reported, 46 per cent. are male, and about four-fifths adult. They comprise 35 per cent. of the church-membership, 25 per cent. of the Sunday school and 32 per cent. of the subsidiary membership; but there are 52 per cent. of those belonging to church, Sunday school and subsidiaries, all three. The per cent. of each separate constituency that pledges is below average, but that of the triple allegiance group is high, showing that this little group takes more than proportionate financial responsibility, as well as being more closely related to the church through memberships.

All told, the data relating to the constituency of the First Presbyterian Church reveal an extreme tendency to form separate and distinct constituencies. In spite of its fears, and beyond any formula of procedure that it possessed, the church has been successful in conserving its original church-going constituency. It has evolved a second smaller church-belonging constituency (probably largely from new elements) which uses the parish house. Finally, it has gathered a still smaller group, largely of men, who belong to the subsidiaries only.

Parish

The church is located at the corner of Woodward Avenue and Edmund Place, about half a mile beyond the Central Methodist Church. It stands surrounded by a large area of once fine homes now cut up for occupancy by several families, or turned into rooming-houses. In a word, it is exactly in the zone of most active deterioration and most rapid evolution of character.

Eighteen per cent. of the constituency lives within a mile of the church, as compared with 8 per cent. for the Central Methodist Church, and 10 per cent. for St. John's Protestant Episcopal Church which is located between the two. In other words, while these three have the most scattered parishes of the twenty-six churches studied, each half-mile of additional distance from the center of the city provides slightly more opportunity for a localized ministry under an actively adapted program.

In measurable factors, the environment of the First Presbyterian Church averages slightly better than that of the other two.[2] "Flats" greatly predominate over the tenement type of housing; largely, however, on account of the cutting-up of old single-family houses. Along Woodward Avenue an enormous proportion of roomers is found, but the number, on the whole, is smaller and much less generally diffused than in the area farther south. The presence of excess males in the population is not general nor so extreme as in the areas previously discussed. Especially along Woodward Avenue there has been a more rapid substitution of apartments and apartment-hotels for the old, run-down type of single-family housing. The area thus benefited, however, is very limited. Beyond it lies a very different region occupied by middle-class and industrial populations, largely living in single-family houses and exhibiting a very considerable per cent. of home ownership. Both in

---

[2] For a general description and characterization of the area adjoining the church, see Case Study of the Central Methodist Church, p. 156 ff.

the apartments and in the family residential area American whites predominate and there are few Negroes.

Analysis of the 18 per cent. of the church's constituency that comes from the immediate locality shows that here both church-members and non-member adherents are drawn disproportionately from the non-family group; and that this is true both within the first and second half-mile distance. This definitely registers the relatively small, but still significant contact of the church with the rooming and light-housekeeping populations.

The officers of the church show a distribution of residence essentially the same as that of the membership at large.

Distance of residence is no barrier to regular attendance and to close relations with the church. Relative to the total constituency, a higher proportion of regular attendants is found in the zone from one to five miles from the church than in either the nearer or the farther zones. In other words, in this case, immediate proximity does not aid regular attendance, and only very extreme distance reduces it. This is true for all age-groups, though with some variations.

Considering both distance and direction of the constituents' homes, there is a most amazing agreement between their distribution and that of the constituencies of the Central Methodist Church and of St. John's Episcopal Church, as shown in Table LII.

This table shows that, with no significant exception, all three of these neighboring churches are strong where any is strong and weak where any is weak. That is to say, they reflect the same affinities and repulsions. They have fitted themselves to the city in the same way: namely, by drawing a following from the best areas, however remote, and, in the main, avoiding the poorer ones, however near. This demonstrates that, whatever their differences in theology, temper or particular programs, the three churches make virtually identical social and economic appeals.

As a phenomenon of the rapid growth of Detroit, extreme decentralization has probably had its day. As with virtually all still larger cities, there is pretty sure to be an extensive return of desirable population to the vicinity of the center through the development of new areas occupied by hotels and apartment-houses. This tendency is already well marked, and its probable future acceleration will improve the immediate

TABLE LII—DISTRIBUTION, BY DISTANCE AND DIRECTION, OF CONSTITUENTS' RESIDENCES IN THREE NEIGHBORING DETROIT CHURCHES

Direction	Total	Under ½ mi.	½ to 1 mi.	1 to 2 mi.	2 to 3 mi.	3 to 4 mi.	4 to 5 mi.	Over 5 mi.
Total								
Central Methodist	100	10	1	13	12	22	22	20
St. John's Episcopal	100	8	7	13	19	20	13	20
First Presbyterian	100	13	7	17	16	21	15	11
Northeast								
Central Methodist	34	3	1	7	3	8	5	7
St. John's Episcopal	31	2	2	3	4	7	4	9
First Presbyterian	32	3	2	7	9	7	3	1
Northwest								
Central Methodist	48	3	0	5	6	11	14	9
St. John's Episcopal	45	4	4	9	7	9	7	5
First Presbyterian	42	5	3	7	5	8	9	5
Southeast								
Central Methodist	17	3	0	1	3	3	3	4
St. John's Episcopal	22	1	1	1	7	4	2	6
First Presbyterian	21	2	1	2	2	6	3	5
Southwest								
Central Methodist	1	1	0	0	0	0	0	0
St. John's Episcopal	2	1	0	0	1	0	0	0
First Presbyterian	5	3	1	1	0	0	0	0

environment and ought to bring additional available populations within the fields of the down-town churches. For, even when non-home-owning and relatively transient, it is possible to capitalize the economic strength of such populations for the support of the church (as already shown by the Central Methodist Church) in the great increase of its loose collections. The type of ministries carried on through community houses may easily be adapted to the peculiar psychology and needs of this group. For the First Presbyterian Church, therefore, there should be better times ahead locally, at the same time that, in its more general constituency, it continues to share the growth of the city.

II. AGENCIES, RESOURCES AND METHODS

The estimated total annual attendance on all stated organizations and activities of the church is shown in Table LIII.

TABLE LIII—ESTIMATED ANNUAL ATTENDANCE ON SPECIFIED OCCASIONS AT FIRST PRESBYTERIAN CHURCH AND AT 26 CHURCHES

	ATTENDANCE			
	FIRST PRESBYTERIAN CHURCH		26 CHURCHES	
OCCASION			*Approx. Median Per Cent.*	*Range of Variation Per Cent.*
	Number	*Per Cent.*		
Total *	111,487	100		
Formal religious services (Sunday and week day).........	60,100	54	51	15–75
Sunday school	28,308	25	24	9–38
All other stated activities.....	23,079 †	21	22	9–51

* Sunday, 89 per cent.; week day, 11 per cent.
† Includes meetings of church officers and committees.

This showing is by no means complete, since the church house alone, including its irregular and merely occasional functions, has an attendance of some 30,000 per year; but it affords the most systematic method of comparing church with church in regard to the major elements of program. The First Presbyterian Church, it will be observed, agrees quite closely with the median case in the proportion of attendance given to formal religious services, Sunday school and other activities respectively. The most striking variation is that it has a far smaller subsidiary program than the more extreme of the churches studied, in some of which this phase of the program comprises half of the total.

The division of attendance between major types of subsidiary activity is shown in Table LIV.

A further analysis of the subsidiary program shows that it is carried out through a large number of organizations, supplying something for every age- and sex-group. Only two other churches have a more complete differentiation and grading of activity.

TABLE LIV—ESTIMATED ANNUAL ATTENDANCE ON SUBSIDIARY ORGANIZATIONS AND STATED ACTIVITIES

No.	Organizations Type	Attendance Number	Per Cent.
25	Total	22,201	100
1	Mixed adults	1,360	6
4	Adult men	1,809	8
4	Adult women	1,530	7
2	Mixed young people *	8,400	38
4	Young men	1,830	8
2	Young women	1,438	7
2	Mixed boys and girls	2,184	10
2	Boys	1,640	7
1	Girls	360	2
3	Mixed children	1,650	7

* Between 15 and 23 years of age.

But the largest factor in the subsidiary program is the activities of mixed organizations not differentiating between the sexes. This is to say that age- and sex-differentiation, while present, relates to minority aspects of the program, and probably, as already suggested, to only part of the constituency.

The young people's organizations constitute by far the largest proportion of the program. All the other age- and sex-agencies are relatively weak because the total program is divided among so many kinds. For example, two-thirds of the cases studied exceed the First Presbyterian Church in the relative strength of their programs for adult women.

Without naming particular organizations, one notes as an outstanding fact about a number of them that they are under the leadership of remarkable personalities. Several that take the form of Sunday-school classes carry on supplemental social and philanthropic programs. They also frequently organize themselves into athletic classes in connection with the church-house program. The four divisions of the young people's circles carrying on religious programs of the Christian Endeavor type are small organizations showing careful grading by age. The church tends to put local names and its own stamp upon its minor societies. Few national movements, either denominational or other, are utilized as units of its subsidiary program.

The characteristic all-aroundness of the resultant scheme of church life is explained by the fact that the subsidiary groups are so numerous rather than by the working out of any logically designed subsidiary program. The groups, on the whole, have been independently promoted and are maintained through a strong self-perpetuating instinct.[3]

Staff

The paid staff, consisting of four full-time and one half-time religious workers, is just about average in size, considering the magnitude and scope of the church's program. It includes a pastor, an ordained assistant pastor who is specifically designated as superintendent of the church house, and three women-workers: namely, a secretary and treasurer, an assistant to the assistant pastor (both in clerical work and in church-house activities) and a Bible-school visitor working on half time. These are supplemented by two gymnasium instructors giving a few hours per week.

The preparation, experience, tenure and salaries of the staff are summarized in Table LV.

WORK TIME

On the average, the members of the staff worked fifty-seven hours each during the sample week for which records were kept. The pastor's working week of eighty-four hours was longer than that of any other pastor of the churches studied, the group average being sixty-two hours. It involved exceed-

---

[3] Small groups with much the same psychology are characteristic of the Central Methodist Church. See p. 172.

ingly long hours every day and a large number of meal-times encroached upon by engagements. It included seven weddings.

The staff as a whole showed a very high proportion of time given to pastoral duties, only four churches exceeding it in this respect. The amount given to clerical work was about median, but that given to administrative work was notably low. The explanation of these differences is found in the tendencies of the individual workers. During the sample week only one other

TABLE LV—ANALYSIS OF PAID STAFF

	Pastor	Assistant Pastor	Bible-School Visitor *	Assistant to Superintendent of Church House	Treasurer and Secretary
Sex	Male	Male	Female	Female	Female
Degree of education					
Academic	College	College	High school	High school	High school
Professional or special	Theological Seminary	Chicago University	...	...	Business Chicago University
Years of employment					
Prior to this position					
Secular work	...	4½	...	4	...
Religious work	23	1	...	5	1
In this position	14	10	4	8	14
Present salary					
Cash	$10,000	$5,000	$500	$1,700	$2,000
Perquisites					
Nature	Parsonage	...	...	...	...
Value	$1,200	...	...	...	...
Entitled to ecclesiastical pension	Yes	Yes	No	No	No
Length of vacation	...	1 month	...	1 month	1 month

* Part time.

of the twenty-four pastors studied gave so much time to pastoral work as the pastor of this church. His homiletical preparation and administration, on the contrary, took less than average time; the latter apparently because original office contacts with the public and the administrative details of most of the activities are assumed by the assistant pastor.

In contrast with the pastor, who exemplifies the strongly pastoral type of ministry, the assistant pastor belongs to a mixed type which may be named pastoral-executive, both these lines of duty being of primary rank in his case.

Instead of keeping the general church office, the secretary-treasurer works in relative isolation, functioning as private secretary to the pastor and giving her time almost entirely to this clerical work and to the bookkeeping of the treasurer's department.

The assistant to the assistant pastor combines large elements of executive and teaching duties with clerical ones in connection with the activities of the church house.

The Bible-school visitor is naturally a pastoral worker, but includes in her duties some teaching and minor administrative functions, particularly in the dispensing of charitable aid, and also serves as a group leader.

The departmentalization of fields is less sharply defined in the staff of the First Presbyterian Church than in many others. The assistant pastor is a general understudy to the pastor, and two of the three women workers have decidedly mixed functions.

There is no formal weekly staff conference, partly on account of the pastor's frequent absences from the field in connection with the administration of national denominational affairs.

Plant

The main church structure of the First Presbyterian Church is a massive and exceedingly imposing Romanesque building of brown stone set well back from Woodward Avenue. It was erected in 1888. The four-story parish house, built in 1910-11, is a plain brick structure, with excellently designed interior, set on an inside lot cornering on that of the church, with tennis courts in the rear.

The estimated value of the total plant is $1,500,000.

It ranks eighth among the plants of the twenty-five churches studied, its deficiencies being due primarily to its age, to lack of unity in design and to the rather strongly utilitarian quality of the parish house. A comparative summary of its score by items, as reached by the use of the Interchurch thousand-point score-card, is shown in Table LVI.

While the church's location is most strategic, and while the purchase of the cheaper inside lot supplementing the original site is a capital case of real estate strategy which many churches might with advantage imitate, the total site, even with the tennis courts, is not ample and does not afford the church the spacious setting that the more fortunate cases possess. The interior architecture is not so distinguished as the exterior. Completely modern service systems have not been substituted for those installed nearly forty years ago. The relatively higher standing of the church with respect to the religious school rooms is due to those provided by the new church house

TABLE LVI—SUMMARY OF SCORE OF PLANT

Item	Standard Score	Points Scored Number	Per Cent.	Rank in 25 Cases
Total	1,000	676	68	8
Site	130	94	72	11
Building or buildings.........	150	112	75	15
Service systems	160	95	59	10
Church rooms	170	122	72	13
Religious school rooms........	200	127	64	8
Community service rooms.....	190	126	66	3

rather than to those included in the original plant which are not of modern design. The church house, however, ranks very high with respect to facilities for community service, which it was especially designed to afford.

A comparison of this showing with the facilities of some of the less commanding churches of the group studied provides ample argument for the enlargement, now under consideration, of the First Presbyterian church house.

Finances

The church is rather amply supported at a cost of about $66 for every hundred of attendance upon stated organizations and activities. In only six of the twenty-six churches studied is the relative cost greater. The current receipts of the last reported year approximated $61,000, of which one-fifth was from endowment. Of about $48,500 from current sources, one-half came from pew rentals, one-fourth from supplemental

individual pledges and special appropriations from the benevolence funds of the church for the support of the work of the
church house, and the rest as the undifferentiated income of
subsidiaries and from miscellaneous sources. The total known
income of the subsidiaries available for their local current support totaled about $6,000 more than was reported in the church
budget ($1,500 in one single instance), while a number of or-
ganizations made no accounting.

A balance of $10,000, accumulated over a series of previous
years, was also expended, making the total available for expenditure about $71,000.

Local expenditures for current objects amounted to approximately $53,640, and there was an additional expenditure for
improvements of a permanent character in the shape of the
general reconditioning of the interior of the church building
proper, costing $17,000. The approximately $70,640 expended
is accounted for in detail in Table LVII.

TABLE LVII—FINANCIAL EXPENDITURES OF THE CHURCH

Item	Amount	Per Cent.
Grand Total	$70,640	
Total Current Account	53,640	100
Salaries	19,450	36
General administrative expenses	1,187	2
Music	7,780	15
General operation and upkeep of property	17,599	33
Expenses of departments specially budgeted	4,042	8
Publicity	2,958	5
Ecclesiastical connections	624	1
Investment Account		
Permanent improvements	17,000	

Within the strictly current expenses the proportion going to
salaries was not far from the median. Publicity expenditures
were also about average. Those for music and the operation
of the plant were both high. The employment of artists of
reputation would explain the former circumstance, and the
necessary operation of two separate buildings, in one of which
an active week-day program goes on, explains the second.[4]

---

4 Under "departments specially budgeted" the above accounting disregards the
fact that the church reports separately on the expenses of the church house, be-

In its total expenditures for its own support, the First Presbyterian Church ranks fifth from the largest case.

Public Services

The estimated attendance at Sunday-morning services is 900, at evening services 400, and at the mid-week service fifty. The last service is commonly preceded by a congregational dinner.

The Sunday-morning service, as conducted by the pastor and his assistant, is devout and dignified. On the Sunday studied, the congregation appeared to include about 5 per cent. of children and 10 per cent. of adolescents. The male element was about 25 per cent. The service was preceded by an organ recital, and the whole was broadcast by the Detroit News. At the same time as the service a nursery for infants and a kindergarten for young children are operated. The music by organ and quartet is of the highest artistic quality. The preaching is direct and practical; sermon themes, habitually, are definitely scriptural. The pastor is president of the denominational Board of National Missions and practical interests of the church have very frequent pulpit presentation.

The Sunday-evening service is briefer but not radically different from the morning service. Its much smaller attendance is felt to constitute an urgent problem.

Religious Education

The organization and enrollment of the Sunday school is summarized in Table LVIII, page 262.

The addition of fifteen officers to the 951 pupils and forty-two teachers gives a grand total of 1,008. Pupils in the attending departments number 951, and attendance averages 88 per cent. of enrollment. The approximate age-distribution in the attending departments is as follows:

---

cause the expenses set forth under this head are chiefly those incidental to the operation of a supplemental plant rather than for the cost of special activities. Accounting, as carried on by the church, is therefore one between buildings rather than between distinct aspects of program. It is, however, noteworthy that the reported cost of the operations roughly covering the newer program of the church is approximately about one-fifth of the total.

	Number	*Per Cent.*
Children	368	39
Adolescents	92	10
Adults	491	51

The Sunday school groups itself into six departments, though the senior and adult classes are not actually managed under a departmental system and report individually. A complete new enrollment is made annually. As previously noted, the twelve classes recognized as being organized include a number characterized by long histories and outstanding lead-

TABLE LVIII—SUMMARY OF SUNDAY-SCHOOL STATISTICS

DEPARTMENT		PUPILS	TEACHERS	
	Age	*Enrollment*	*Male*	*Female*
Total	...	951	17	25
Cradle Roll class	2–3	12 *	0	2
Beginners	4–5	42	0	2
Primary	6–8	124	0	10
Junior	9–12	120	4	4
Intermediate	13–15	100	4	4
Senior	18–20	62	2	2
Adult	21 & over	491	7	1

* Total Cradle Roll, 172.

ership, one teacher having served for nineteen and another for twenty-three years. A number of these classes maintain strongly developed philanthropic and community-service work. A forum is held in the church auditorium following the morning service with an average attendance of one hundred. It hears a wide variety of eminent speakers, largely upon topics of civic interest. During the summer a Daily Vacation Bible School, largely composed of children of the immediate locality, with an enrollment of over one hundred, supplements the work of religious education, and a Saturday religious and craft school in four divisions, with eleven teachers and an enrollment of about 120, is carried on during the active church year. This school is beginning to reach numbers of foreign children. The assistant pastor is Sunday-school superintendent and has general charge of the other activities of religious education. It is characteristic of the church, however, that those engaged in religious education tend to fall apart into distinct and largely independent groups not easily united under a traditional scheme of modern Sunday-school organization.

As with other down-town churches, the ratio of children and adolescents in Sunday school to the church's adult constituency is much below average.

Gains and Losses

Sixty-one per cent. of the accessions to church-membership during the year prior to the study were by letter, and 39 per cent. on confession of faith. On this showing the First Presbyterian Church mediates between churches that exist under disadvantageous circumstances, and so cannot easily attract any large number of members by letter, and the extremely popular down-town churches (of which the Central Methodist Church is an example) into which memberships by letter flow so fast that such churches can scarcely be expected to keep up a normal proportion of gains from other sources.

Three-fourths of those coming to the First Presbyterian Church by letter were already Presbyterians, but one-fourth came from other denominations. (This is approximately the ratio found in the Central Methodist Church.) The proportion of newcomers to the community (resident less than one year) was 43 per cent., a very high ratio though not the most extreme. All but two of those received into membership during the year who had been permanently established in the community had also previously become related to the church, 42 per cent. through attendance upon services, 42 per cent. through the Sunday school, and 16 per cent. through the subsidiaries. In other words, the characteristic method of recruiting employed by the church involves a prior process of somewhat definite assimilation. There is no short-cut evangelism, and the pastor testifies that his church would not respond to any, no matter from what source.

Upon careful estimates, 86 per cent. of all new accessions reside at a considerable distance from the church building. This tends to show that the church is actually recruiting from the general areas in which its members live, in contrast with certain other churches that recruit only near-by and then find their memberships subsequently scattered by removals of residence.

The losses in church-membership for the year previous to the study were seventy-two by transfer, nineteen by death and sixteen by revision of the roll, the latter including nine who were dropped in consequence of joining the Christian Science denomination. Of the seventy-two dismissed to other churches, sixty-four went to Presbyterian churches and eight to others; thirty-seven transferred out of the city and thirty-five within its borders. This shows rather large drainage to outlying churches, but was partially in accordance with the church's long-time policy of colonizing members to form new Presbyterian organizations, a considerable number of members in this case being dismissed to the Ferndale church.

The losses of the year equaled about two-thirds of the gains. This ratio has been prevalent for a decade and was characteristic of each five-year period separately calculated. It may, therefore, be regarded as rather firmly established.

Aspects of Current Church Life

Church life from week to week takes its form from the regular public services and the meetings of the large number of organized groups. The church house accommodates an average of three or four formal meetings each week-day, organized social events alone aggregating 265 during a recent year. The tennis courts are systematically operated during the season and are flooded for skating during the winter. The gymnasium as such has relatively small use, fewer than 2,000 persons per year in the aggregate being counted in organized athletics.

The types of recurrent interest indicated by the published announcements of the church imply its large intellectual and practical interest in denominational, interdenominational and civic affairs. In addition to an average of $30,000 per year of benevolent contributions, chiefly denominational, the church exerts very continuous leadership in regional denominational affairs, and, in view of the relation of the pastor to the national organizations of the denomination, puts large stress in its publicity upon broader interests.

Similar stress is laid upon those religious affairs of the city that are fostered interdenominationally. The church's bulletin includes very frequent and specific announcements of the needs of local community agencies. Appeals are also made for contributions of supplies, or opportunities of work for needy persons are presented.

Beyond its own organizational relations, the church has projected itself extensively into the organized life of the community. Seventy-six of its members occupy places upon the directing boards of thirty-three social agencies listed in the Detroit Handbook of Social Work. This representation is particularly strong in settlement-house, hospital, children's aid and general civic types of organization.

Though not formally reporting it as part of its work, the church stands in particularly close relation with the Dodge Community House, having title to the plant and holding an endowment of more than $160,000 for it. This institution, provided by members of the Dodge family, exists primarily for the service of the heavy foreign-born population employed in the automobile industry. It has a model three-story plant, erected in 1925, adjacent to the Dodge factory, with an average attendance of over 5,000 per month enlisted in more than thirty types of social activity, of which playground, music-school, sewing and dressmaking classes, clinic and the Sunday school have the most numerous enrollment. A Daily Vacation Bible School and a wide program of summer camps and outings are also provided.

Adaptations

In the First Presbyterian Church of Detroit, institutionalized Christianity shows another case in which a church is successful in spite of having a remote constituency. The church has grown rapidly during the time that this condition has prevailed, and has greatly increased its resources. Obviously the present sources of financial support will ultimately be reduced with the dying-off of the present disproportionate adult constituency whose children, as has been shown, are not actively enlisted in the church to the same degree that their parents have been. But this contingency is largely being discounted by the securing of endowment funds while the present generation lives.

Informal estimates by the pastor put more concretely than impersonal statistics can the major peculiarity of the church: namely, its separate and distinct constituencies. Not 5 per cent., he says, of adherents using the church house are from the older elements. There is a very complete gap between the children of the older families and the present young life of the church, which is recruited from other sources. This separateness of constituencies is shown statistically by the small dimensions of the central core of the church as measured by overlapping affiliations and by the small average number of connections per individual.

By reason of the distinctness of the several constituencies, the broadened program of the church nevertheless leaves that of the majority of its adherents relatively unchanged. The elaboration that the program has received since the erection of the church house applies to the second constituency rather than to the original one. The value of the program of the church house to the new elements is profoundly related to the fact that they are frequently from a less favorable economic level than the original ones; people whose crowded homes really need to be supplemented by the facilities and social opportunities of the church plant.

While the general situation confronting the church is shared by its neighboring churches in the city, the rather slight difference in total environment caused by its location somewhat farther from the center, registers itself in the greater degree to which its program is localized. It can get a larger proportion of its following from the immediate vicinity than more central churches can.

Apart from this circumstance, the notable unanimity with which the down-town Detroit churches are enabled to stick to their posts is due to the fact that they have all reached essentially the same solution of their problem: namely, a selective appeal to the more desirable populations of the entire city. The almost absolute correspondence of parish distribution between the three neighboring churches covered by the study has already been pointed out as most amazing. Socially speaking, the three conform to exactly the same pattern.

Considering how the present adaptations of the church to its situation came to be, it is evident that its basic characteristics arose through operation of underlying forces worked upon by rather general instincts; not primarily through deliberation. The church's program is consequently the result of a series of accretions, not of any radical reorganization on a reasoned-out basis. Just as a second building was added to the original plant, so second and third organizations and devices have been added to the essentially unchanged original program.

The older elements of the program are perhaps relatively even more successful than the new. To have created and maintained the loyalties that bring large numbers of attendants over great distances to religious services, even once on Sunday, is as striking as anything that the church has done for near-by populations in its week-day program; and, as between the two, the Sunday aspect of the work is still exceptionally large by comparison with the churches of the group being studied.

The rather simple relations between the members of the paid staff, their decidedly mixed functions and the minimum in their work of what has to be labeled administration are further evidence that clear-cut organization as such does not express the prevailing genius of the church. On the contrary, the very strong stress upon pastoral relationships which the work records reveal, provides exceptional opportunity for the influence of personal leadership to permeate the entire situation. That the staff can so largely give itself to pastoral duties is undoubtedly due to the characteristic ability of the subsidiaries to manage their own affairs under strong unpaid leadership.

No one that likes to build churches according to plans and specifications would think of sitting down and organizing *de novo* a church like the First Presbyterian Church. Its remote constituencies loosely related to the church and to one another, its little integrated subsidiaries, its almost complete lack of internal reorganization in connection with the great extension and elaboration of the church's program, will not appeal to the mechanical mind. But the church's way has succeeded. It broadens its influence, keeps replenishing its members, makes net growth, carries on an exceedingly extensive and varied set of activities and, on the whole, has made a very great psychological readjustment, considering its deep-rooted habits and the flavor of its past history, in becoming what it is. Without attempting any very clear theoretical re-defining of the church's position, the pastor makes the rather clinching argument that the church is sold to the new order of things or it would not have supported it. Unless, then, one delights in logical arrangements and closely knit systems for their own sake, this will seem not a bad way to succeed in church work.

The church probably will take the next steps of its evolution in the light of fairly conservative experimentation. This will be in keeping with its history and genius. It knows that it needs more room for the activities of its present groups and will therefore undoubtedly enlarge the plant of its parish house. It should get more endowment. One would think that its immediately localized work might be enlarged till it bears a more impressive proportion to the sum total of the church's activities. Thus, without breaking with its present tentative and teachable mood, the church may continue to stand its ground, at the same time keeping ahead of any contingencies that may arise, yet without ever pretending to have reached a complete formula for the solution of its intricate problems.

CASE X

ST. JOHN'S PROTESTANT EPISCOPAL CHURCH, DETROIT, MICH.

When a church greatly enlarges itself, both as an institution and as a social force, by an extension of working alliances; when it establishes such intimate relations with other agencies of constructive effort that at many points it is hard to tell where the one begins and the other ends, it not only becomes a striking and attractive subject of study, but imposes certain difficulties upon investigation. Categories designed to fit church enterprises that are more definitely this and not that, have to be strained and modified when used in interpreting a situation with such blurred outlines.

A case of this sort is presented by St. John's Protestant Episcopal Church of Detroit. Only one other of the twenty six churches studied has so large a program, measured by a list of sixty items of current church practice. It thus classifies technically with the most highly developed urban types in respect to the range and originality of its institutional activities. This standing is the result of a deliberate policy, extensively carried out, of affording a meeting place and facilities to other organizations and becoming the host and backer of their numerous activities. Besides turning over its adjoining rectory rent-free to the Young Women's Christian Association for use as a down-town center, the church also affords this organization gymnasium facilities in its parish house. It is a training and service center for the Boy and Girl Scouts. It is the headquarters for diocesan work for foreign-speaking peoples. It has rendered an especially notable service as a cultural rallying center of Russian refugees. It provides a very worthy development of group social life for deaf mutes.

Turning to characteristics reflecting more general factors of the church's background, one notes first that it shares with its immediate ecclesiastical neighbors in Detroit the distinction of having an extremely scattered parish. The only one of the twenty-six cases that exceeds it in this respect is its still more centrally located neighbor, the Central Methodist Episcopal Church.

Of characteristics somewhat reflecting the Protestant Episcopal communion, the following are important: The church definitely extends a well-defined sense of parochial responsibility to a large body of remote adherents who are not bound to it by any concrete ties recently expressed. At least a third of all whom the church counts as constituents have no present determinate relation. Most of the churches studied do not list any large proportion of these marginal elements. Behind the fact that the Episcopal churches do list them lie certain persistent attitudes that continually color the conduct of those churches.

Again, the distinctive work of the church for the foreign-born is not an attempt to reëvangelize them. The exchange of ecclesiastical recognitions between the Protestant Episcopal and Eastern Orthodox churches makes it possible for local parishes like St. John's to render a very dignified fraternal service to a wide group of eastern races through the recognition of their own church life, and to become of direct assistance in developing it. No other church studied is doing work for foreign-speaking people in so auspicious an atmosphere.

In connection with the magnified function of public religious services characteristic of the Protestant Episcopal communion, it is often natural to enlarge the ministry of music. This also has been done in very distinguished fashion in St. John's Church.

History and Trends

The church originated in 1858, when Detroit had about 45,000 people, in order to meet the religious needs of a then small population growing up north of the Grand Circus Park in what were the semi-suburban outskirts of the city. Its building still occupies the original site.

In its own phrase, the church has changed "from one occupying a fine residential neighborhood into the status of a
down-town church." Baptisms for the first fifty years averaged seventy-five annually and confirmations fifty-four, compared with an average of only sixty-three baptisms and forty-
seven confirmations for the last fifteen years; but the average
number of marriages has doubled, and the average number of
burials increased nearly one-half during the latter period.
These shifts are pointed evidence of the passing away of the
more permanent and stable original constituency and the increased service of the church to transient and shifting populations in the major crises of life.

Of more recent statistical trends, an average of about 200
fewer communicant members during the last five years than
during the previous five must be noted. This is largely accounted for by a clearing from the roll of 421 names in 1923;
but a slight actual decline is probable. The Sunday school
averages slightly larger, and benevolences are more than double, while average total expenditures have risen from $38,000
for the first five years to $61,000 for the last five years of the
period. The total constituency and the volume of the church's
work have been greatly enlarged.

I. MAJOR ASPECTS OF THE CHURCH

Constituency

The combined parish list of the church and its subsidiary
organizations contains 3,107 names, of which 1,370 are those
of communicant members. The Sunday school enrolls 336,
and the organizations an additional 978. Statistical data to
show the exact relations between, and the amount of duplicatory membership expressed by, these figures are lacking. If
the overlap of church, Sunday school and subsidiaries is the
average of the other cases studied, the number of determinate
adherents, that is to say, all who belong to the church as active
communicants or by present membership in any of its subsidiaries, is about 1,775, leaving from 1,325 to 1,350 not concretely related at present except by membership in adherent

families. Many of these are baptized or confirmed church people, and the mutual relations between them and the church are recognized by this study as significant from the social as well as the religious standpoint, although too indefinable to be used as comparative data.

Although it is thus not possible formally to compare St. John's with the other churches studied, because its parish list is made up so differently, the traceable differences consequent to the different method and point of view are very significant. Thus, in its age-distribution, St. John's constituency, as recognized by itself, is much more balanced then that of the neighboring churches. It stands close to the average of the twenty-six churches studied, approximating a cross section of the Detroit population, except for being markedly deficient in adolescents.

	PER CENT.		
	Adults (21 & Over)	Adolescents (15-20)	Children (5-14)
Constituencies of:			
St. John's Church	75	5	20
26 churches	73	8	19
Population of Detroit	72	10	18

Again, the relation between the sexes is more evenly balanced than in many churches, being forty-six male to fifty-four female, as compared with forty-four male to fifty-six female which is the average of the twenty-six cases.

Finally, since whenever its constituents belong to families the St. John's parish roll practically lists the entire adherent family, the proportion of adherents from family groups to detached individuals is very much higher than with any other church save one, which is also Protestant Episcopal.

The foregoing statement takes no account of the constituencies of the organizations using the church's plant and fostered through its administrative processes.

Parish

Only 14 per cent. of the constituency lives within a mile of the church, while 20 per cent. lives over five miles away, being most numerous in the two-to-four-mile zone. A somewhat smaller proportion of adherents from family groups lives within the first half-mile, and slightly more in every zone beyond the mile. This indicates that the relatively few followers that the church finds in the immediate vicinity tend to be detached people presumably of the prevailing boarding- and rooming-house type.

The church is located at the corner of Woodward Avenue and High Street, four blocks north of the Central Methodist Episcopal Church. The description of the environmental surroundings of the former church therefore applies substantially to St. John's Church.[1] The two churches fail to about the same extent to reach the adjoining area. The directional distribution of St. John's adherents, and indeed their density of residence from zone to zone throughout the city, shows extraordinary correspondence with that of the adherents of the Central Methodist and of the First Presbyterian Churches,[2] except that St. John's Church is appreciably stronger from within a half-mile to two miles to the northwest; that is to say, in the older residential section not yet acutely affected by change, and lying within the boulevards. Thus a trace of what is probably an old parochial localization appears in the middle distance and in a single direction; but it is not extensive enough greatly to change the total pattern according to which all three of the neighboring churches studied are strong in the better sections of Detroit and almost entirely avoid the poorer sections.

Distribution of partial constituencies was studied by means of the church's map, locating (1) subscribers and (2) active participants in church work, as of 1923. These data show slight variations from the present ground-pattern of distribution, but not enough to warrant attempted interpretation. A most striking change of total balance, however, appears as having occurred within three years. This is shown in the following comparison.

	Per Cent.	
Location of Adherents' Residences	*1923*	*1926*
Within one mile...........................	20	14
Beyond five miles	15	20

[1] For analysis of environment, see 156 ff.
[2] See Table LII, p. 253.

The above comparison reveals the rapid growth of, and the somewhat challenging shift of adherents to, the outlying regions. While the general success of the church up to date indicates that the appeal of central prestige, owing to modern transit facilities, has been able to overcome the absentee character of the constituency within the average range of two to five miles, it is not known whether these forces would be equally successful if, say, 40 or 50 per cent. of the constituency should remove to beyond five miles.

II. AGENCIES, RESOURCES AND METHODS

The average annual attendance on all stated organizations and activities is estimated at 73,336. Its distribution between the major divisions of church life is shown in Table LIX.

TABLE LIX—ESTIMATED ANNUAL ATTENDANCE ON SPECI-
FIED OCCASIONS AT ST. JOHN'S CHURCH AND AT 26
CHURCHES

	ATTENDANCE			
	ST. JOHN'S CHURCH		26 CHURCHES	
OCCASION			*Approx. Median*	*Range of Variation*
	Number	*Per Cent.*	*Per Cent.*	*Per Cent.*
Total *	73,336	100		
Formal religious services (Sunday and week day)..........	47,450	64	51	15–75
Sunday school	7,000	10	24	9–38
All other stated activities.......	18,886 †	26	22	9–51

* Sunday, 83 per cent.; week day, 17 per cent.
† Includes meetings of church officers and committees.

The ratio of Sunday to week-day phases of the program shows the former being stressed to a much more than average degree. This is accounted for by numerous, rather than by largely attended, services. Attendance on formal religious services as such is also much beyond the average. (This is less true in the other cases of Protestant Episcopal churches included in the study.)   The Sunday school, on the contrary, is proportionately small.

But the proportion of attendance associated with the subsidiary program is well above the average.   Comparing with neighboring churches, it equals that of the Central Methodist Church, and greatly exceeds that of the First Presbyterian Church.

All of the above statements exclude the fostered activities of organizations that are housed and facilitated by St. John's Church.   But it is wholly legitimate to add to the account all the stated and recurrent aspects of this supplemental program; since St. John's Church not only contributes the use of its plant but definitely administers the broader aspects of the total program that is carried on under its roof, supplying prestige, organization, publicity, numerous technical services by the trained staff, and the background of inclusive and directive Christian motive.   Some of these activities stand closer to the church's responsibility than others; some it merely houses, others it virtually sponsors—its capacity to undertake relationships upon many different levels being just the mark of its peculiar genius in service.

The inclusion of an annual attendance of over 22,000 upon the regular and stated activities of the fostered agencies would bring the total attendance on the St. John's enterprise to beyond 100,000 and rank it ninth for total size on the list of the twenty-six cases studied, rather than only a little above average, as it ranks if the strictly parochial program alone is considered. The range of activities, too, would be greatly extended.   Some of the features of this supplemental program receive later comment.

Returning, for the present, to the subsidiary program of the church itself, it is found to be more balanced, and to exhibit more complete differentiation of provision for all ages and sexes, than that of most of the cases.   Attendance upon stated subsidiary activities is 35 per cent. male, 49 per cent. female, and 16 per cent. in mixed groups.   The number of organizations, and the estimated annual attendance upon each, classified by age and sex, are shown in Table LX.

TABLE LX—ESTIMATED ANNUAL ATTENDANCE ON SUB-
SIDIARY ORGANIZATIONS AND STATED ACTIVITIES

No.	ORGANIZATIONS Type	ATTENDANCE Number	Per Cent.
	Total	18,786	
26	Classified by Age and Sex.................	14,276	100
1	Mixed adults	210	1
4	Adult men	2,200	15
6	Adult women	3,320	23
1	Mixed young people *	1,080	8
3	Young men	370	3
2	Young women	1,520	11
1	Mixed boys and girls..................	720	5
3	Boys	2,456	17
4	Girls	2,120	15
1	Mixed children	280	2
	Classified by Function Chiefly the choir	4,510	

* Between 15 and 23 years of age.

Few churches have so all-around a program. Few churches
have relatively such strong organizations for adult men.
Women's, boys', and girls' activities are all well developed, and
there is definite organization of young men and young women
separately. This complete departmentalization of the subsidiary church program by age and sex tends to be characteristic
of the Protestant Episcopal communion, but is unusually
marked in St. John's Church.

Features of highly exceptional interest in the program are
the foreign-language services of the Armenian and Assyrian
peoples conducted by their own priests; services for the deaf
under a diocesan clergyman; the choir and junior choir;
and the Russian men's chorus which constitutes an important
social organization for people of that nationality in the city.

The possession of a program of this character and range,
quite apart from that of the guest organizations, would rank
St. John's Church among those that have developed an elaborated parochial life. The additional cultural, educational and
social ministries of the housed or sponsored organizations give
the church the breadth already noted, and include features that,
under church auspices, are strikingly novel.

Staff

The paid professional staff consists of seven full-time and seven part-time workers (the choirmaster and assistant organist being included).

As judged by the average of the twenty-six cases, this is a very large body of paid workers relative to the magnitude of the church enterprise. It apparently indicates that the church is able to draw less on its lay resources than other churches do, partly perhaps because it desires to put a more professional quality into the more unusual aspects of work. It looks, however, as though the Sunday school, finances and social service, as well as the social direction of minor activities, had fallen into the hands of the staff to a somewhat unusual degree. Manifestly the multiplication of formal religious services requires a proportionate increase of the time of the officiating ministry. The church stands third in the relative time consumed by this function. It ought also to be considered that significant time and direction are spent upon creating the conditions that make the sponsored work of the guest organizations possible. Even so, one must conclude that the case presents a very unusual development of the paid staff.

The composition of the staff is striking. It includes virtually all the variations of functioning presented by the entire body of churches studied. Besides the rector and an ordained general understudy (specializing, however, in religious education), there are two major departmentalizations, one headed by an experienced business man known as the business manager, the other by a woman director of social service. To these major departments is to be added that of choirmaster. Additional specializations defined by the field of service are represented by a part-time worker in pageantry. Specializations defined by the particular sex or class ministered to are represented by a boys' club worker who is on part time, and by the diocesan minister to the deaf.

The usual types of assistants are represented by two clerical workers, one functioning particularly as the rector's private secretary, and the other as general parish secretary and assistant to the business manager; and by three part-time visitors, one for general parish calling, one for the Sunday school, and the third for hospital visitation.

The preparation, experience and remuneration of the major members of the staff are shown in Table LXI.

WORK-TIME

The amount and distribution of the duty-time of the staff for a sample week was somewhat modified by the fact that the week included a holiday. As to the time on duty, however, it is notable that the group falls into three very distinct classes. The rector and the ordained assistant worked sixty-four and sixty-five hours respectively, this being slightly beyond the average of the pastors or assistant pastors of the twenty-six churches. The other department heads and the parish secretary observed practically the commercial week in clerical positions, being on duty from forty-three to forty-six hours. The other workers, most of them employed for part-time, gave from nine to thirty-three hours, the total for the three part-time visitors being considerably less than the average of full-time visitors in the twenty-six churches.

Nearly all of the staff carry certain Sunday duties. On the other hand, a very high proportion of the time of some of the part-time workers was taken up with attendance on staff meetings or religious gatherings for which they were not responsible.

As to the content, the work of the staff as a whole is exceedingly well balanced, the pastoral, clerical and administrative phases all showing approximately a median distribution. Pastoral work for the last recorded year represented a total of 2,680 visits.

The individual members of the staff showed marked differentiations in the nature of their work. Compared with the pastors of the group studied, the rector falls into the executive type, though not to an extreme degree. His pastoral and homiletical functions were well balanced, while he spent a larger proportion of his time officiating at services than any of the

TABLE LXI—ANALYSIS OF PAID STAFF

	Rector	Assistant Rector and Director of Religious Education	Business Manager	Social Service Worker	Sunday-School Visitor*	Parish Visitor*	House-hold Visitor*	Rector's Secretary	Parish Secretary
Sex	Male	Male	Male	Female	Female	Female	Female	Female	Female
Degree of education									
Academic	College	College	College	College	College (1 yr.)	College	High school	High school Business school	High school
Professional or special...	Theological Post-graduate	Theological Post-graduate	Accounting	Social service	...	...	...	...	...
Years of employment									
Prior to this position									
Secular work........	6	6	1½	5	6 months	7	10	6	...
Religious work........	19½	10	...	...	7 years	...	...	...	...
In this position........	3½	2	9 months	3	1	1	1	1	16
Present salary									
Cash	$6,000	$3,500	$2,400	$1,500	$300	$300	$300	$1,500	$1,500
Perquisites									
Nature	Parsonage, car	...	...	...	Carfare	Carfare	...	...	...
Value	$1,400	...	...	...	$31	$30	...	...	...
Entitled to ecclesiastical pension.........	Yes	Yes	No	No	No	No	No	...	No
Length of vacation.........	2 months	1 month	1 month	1 month	...	...	...	1 month	1 month

* Part time.

ministers of the other churches. His work-record showed less concentration than that of the average pastor.

The work-record of the assistant minister clearly revealed the general understudy with pastoral functions predominating. His week included more kinds of work than that of the rector, with primary technical responsibility for the Sunday school and the direction of the Sunday-school visitor.

The business manager's time was virtually all given to the administration of finances, including a campaign for the securing of pledges. He is also office manager, and supervises the parish secretary.

Few churches have departmentalized social service work so distinctly, or defined its character more technically. The director is primarily an organizer of the work of others. Her own work accordingly presents the preponderance of executive functions over pastoral and personal ministries, an unusual combination in workers of this sort. The primary stress of the department is on family case-work, forty-five active and nineteen closed cases being reported for the year previous to the study, in addition to 212 transient cases.

The clerical workers are more exclusively devoted to that type of work than is usual in smaller staffs where such workers have to slip into other phases of service.

Of the three part-time visitors, only one has a second function: namely, that of conducting the junior choir.

The work of the entire staff is unified by a weekly meeting, and is facilitated by the clear-cut departmentalization, specialization and subordination of the minor workers to the department directors.

Plant

The church occupies an ell-shaped site at the corner of Woodward Avenue and High Street, with the chapel at the rear of the main church, and the parish house set at right angles to it fronting on Montcalm Street. The main structure was erected in 1859 and 1861 in the consistent but uninspired Gothic style of that period. The interior is dignified and churchly, and enriched by extensive memorials which the years have blended into a large harmony. The rectory (now used by the Young Women's Christian Association) stands beside the church facing Woodward Avenue.

The estimated value of the entire plant is $1,400,000.

Relative to the Standard for Church Plants developed by the Interchurch World Movement, the church ranks fourteenth in the twenty-five cases, scoring 583 out of 1,000 points. Its deficiencies are owing primarily to the fact that it is old and was built piecemeal. The score by major items is summarized in Table LXII.

TABLE LXII—SUMMARY OF SCORE OF PLANT

ITEM	STANDARD SCORE	POINTS SCORED		RANK IN 25 CASES
		Number	Per Cent.	
Total	1,000	583	58	14
Site	130	92	71	13
Building or buildings	150	97	65	22
Service systems	160	53	33	25
Church rooms	170	131	77	8
Religious school rooms	200	124	62	10
Community service rooms	190	86	45	9

The church ranks highest of all on its facilities for worship, the churchly character of which has just been intimated. Its rather spacious parish house, erected much later than the original church, also affords much more than average facilities for religious education (relative to the size of the Sunday school) and for community service. (The fact, however, that the community service rooms scored only 45 per cent. of the standard, in spite of which the church ranks ninth on this point, shows what inferior facilities most of the other churches had for such work.)

The least satisfactory aspect of the entire plant is its service systems which are much out of date.

The entire plant affords only twenty-five rooms, which are in very intensive use and are not adequate for so large and varied a program.

The widening of Woodward Avenue, contemplated by the vast revision of the Detroit city-plan, and already authorized by the voters, will cut off the entire front of the auditorium and make a complete rebuilding of the plant necessary. Pending this, the church is in the midst of an energetic attempt to provide the parish-house unit of a new structure, so that its great program of activities may not be interrupted during what may be a long-drawn-out building-period.

Finances

The total church budget of the year prior to the study involved about $55,000 for local expenditures, and an additional $18,000 for benevolences. The cost was $76 per one hundred estimated attendance, making it the fifth from the most expensive of the twenty-six studied, if consideration is limited to the church's own program. Relative to the total activities that go on under its roof, the cost would be approximately median.

Of current income, nearly $20,000 came from endowment and rentals of property, including an addition to the principal of the endowment fund. Of the remaining $35,000 received from current sources and for current work, about 44 per cent. came from individual pledges, 15 per cent. from pew rents, 13 per cent. from special seasonal offerings and 10 per cent. from loose collections, the latter item being unusually high. Expenditures of $55,871 are accounted for in Table LXIII.

TABLE LXIII—FINANCIAL EXPENDITURES OF THE CHURCH

Item	Amount	Per Cent.
Grand Total	$55,871	
Total Current Account	51,702	100
Salaries	17,732	34
General administrative expenses	1,193	2
Music	8,078	16
General operation and upkeep of property	10,763	21
Expenses of departments specially budgeted	4,405	9
Publicity	3,146	6
Ecclesiastical connections	1,061	2
Miscellaneous	5,324	10
Investment Account		
Permanent improvement	4,169	

For total expenditures, the church ranks in the upper third of the cases studied. Considering the distribution of expenditures, it is significant that the salary item is only about median in spite of the very large staff. This is made possible by the very low pay of the major workers compared with those of other and neighboring churches, and by the large proportion of women workers.

The relative cost of music is very high, but that of the operation of the plant is rather low, partly because it is small relative to the program.

Approximately $15,000 of the $18,000 reported for benevolences were received for the "forward movement" of the Episcopal church, the balance being raised by the subsidiaries for a well-rounded program of parochial, community, diocesan, national and world service.

The endowment of the church, in 1925, somewhat exceeded $166,000.

Public Services and Worship

The average attendance at the major public services for the year preceding the study was as follows:

```
Sunday morning (11 o'clock)...................... 496
       (Including two summer months................. 462)
Vespers ............................................ 165
Evening service ................................... 129
```

There is also a midweek service of Christian instruction and, during the special seasons of the year, additional eight o'clock and nine-thirty o'clock Sunday-morning services.

The eleven o'clock service is attended by nearly as many men as women. This is good evidence of the actual trend of the constituency toward a balance of the two sexes. Music is furnished by a vested male choir of fifty. The rector and assistant preach somewhat interchangeably and, in connection with the numerous services, the congregation hears many other voices, the proportion of outside speakers being unusually great. The rector officiated at about 500 services during the year preceding the study, making 247 addresses, but preaching only eighty-seven sermons. During the same period there were 288 celebrations of the Holy Communion.

Vesper services naturally stress musical and festival events. Other choirs are quite frequently brought in to participate, including the Russian choir which regularly holds its sessions in the church.

The junior church service precedes the Sunday school, and children's communions are held monthly. The services for the foreign-speaking groups and for the deaf have had earlier mention. There is also frequent celebration of the Holy Communion on week days.

Religious Education

The Sunday school of St. John's Church differs radically from that of its neighboring down-town churches in Detroit in that it is primarily a children's institution. Like the church in its total functions, it does not draw largely on the neighborhood. It also reflects the age-distribution of the constituency in being deficient in young people. It has to depend largely upon transportation, as shown by the fact that the average attendance in the primary department is poor and by the frequent stress upon the necessity of bringing children to Sunday school, which the church feels obliged to register.

The departmentalization, enrollment and age-distribution of the school are shown in Table LXIV.

TABLE LXIV—SUMMARY OF SUNDAY-SCHOOL STATISTICS

DEPARTMENT	PUPILS		TEACHERS	
	Age	Enrollment	Male	Female
Total	...	336	8	14
Cradle Roll	...	70	..	..
Kindergarten and Primary ...	4–8	43	0	5
Intermediate	9–12	78	4	6
High school	13–18	38	2	2
Bible classes	19 & over	107	2	1

The addition of five officers to the 336 pupils and twenty-two teachers gives a grand total of 363. Pupils in the attending departments number 266, and attendance averages 66 per cent. of enrollment. The approximate age-distribution in the attending departments is as follows:

	Number	Per Cent.
Children	140	53
Adolescents	49	18
Adults	77	29

To have a school so largely constituted of children, under such circumstances as the church faces, is a real achievement. The lack of large adult departments, such as characterize neighboring churches, may be ascribed to a difference in policy which prefers for them the cultural influence of numerous formal church services in contrast with the ordinary instructional methods of the religious school. At least here are alternative ways of attempting to reach the common objective of development of Christian character.

The entire Sunday school is organized as a church-school service-league, with a carefully systematized program of community and missionary service, including both personal work and benevolent giving.

There is also an interesting parent-teachers' association, which is attempting to associate the school and the family in the study of the problems of youth, in addition to a well-maintained teachers' training class.

Growth and Conservation

Of 150 recent accessions to the church, whose antecedents were examined, eighty-six were found to have come by letter from other Episcopal churches. Of the sixty-four received by confirmation, only thirty-two had been originally baptized as Episcopalians; twenty-eight came from four other Protestant denominations, three had been Roman Catholics, and one Greek Orthodox.

In two-thirds of the 150 cases, the persons received into the church had been resident in Detroit for more than a year, and in four-fifths of the cases of these established residents, membership had been preceded by an established relation with the church, generally that of attendance upon its services. The Sunday school furnished about one-sixth of the new accessions, and the subsidiary organizations a negligible number. The general showing is that most of St. John's recruits have been assimilated to the church through some of its activities before being received as communicants.

The proportion of newcomers to the community, about one-third of the total of new members, is characteristic of a downtown church.

Accessions were secured from people living at average or great distances from the church slightly more often than from those living near by. This tends to show that the church is able to recruit throughout the whole city, and that the disadvantage of distance is more than outweighed by the affinity of the populations of the more prosperous areas for the church.

Removals from the church during 1925 included thirteen by transfer (all to other Episcopal churches) and eleven by death. There was no formal revision of the roll. Of the thirteen transferred by letter, eight removed from the city, and five went to other parishes in Detroit. While the number involved is small, the proportion of drainage from the church to other parishes is rather high.

Aspects of Current Church Life

The topical consideration of the many phases of the work of St. John's Church fails to reveal its on-going as a total process day by day and week by week, and omits many of the most interesting single features.

Besides three formal services (five during holiday seasons) and the worship of children preceding the Sunday school, there is an average of three other Sunday meetings, and an average of five per week day within the church's own program. There is also an average of approximately seven minor religious services per week in the holiday seasons, the whole amounting to well over 1,000 gatherings per year.

The total annual attendance upon all events held in the parish house is about 65,000. Beyond all this stretches an active program of summer camps and outings.

These are various suggestions of the range and magnitude of the current program. Its most extraordinary aspect, however, is perhaps its extreme catholicity. Among the organizations to which the church is host are such polar opposites as the Detroit Evangelistic Association, a militant gospelizing agency, and the extremely High-church Catholic Club. An interesting venture is the Fellowship Club, providing an inexpensive supper for any strangers who may drop in on Sunday evening. It has been found of chief value to the young women of the boarding-house area. Among other notable enterprises is the Episcopalian and Eastern Church Club with 150 members, affording a social center for representatives of seven Near-Eastern nationalities.

During about one-fourth of the year previous to the study, the church conducted an admirable series of lectures on civic topics by authoritative speakers in many lines. These occurred at six o'clock on Sunday evenings.

The monthly parish paper of the church is a most complete and appealing record of parish happenings. The annual year-book issue furnishes a very complete annual summary of the total work of the church and brings together the combined records of all organizations and activities, as is done in but few cases. The historical records of the church are also of high quality.

Relations to the Community

Community relations constitute a large chapter in the story of St. John's Church. They may be regarded in three divisions:

(1) The activities of constructive organizations which are the guests of, or sponsored by, the church. As already explained, the fostering of these is definitely included in the scheme of church administration. The agencies concerned include some of the larger constructive forces of Detroit. The total community activity brought together through these relationships equals approximately one-fourth of the church's total program.

(2) The social service work of the church itself is carried on under a recognized department with a well-defined policy and technically exact standards. It stands in responsible relations to other agencies for family case-work: the Visiting Nurses Association, Girls Friendly Society, etc. Only a small amount of direct emergency aid is given.

(3) The church projects itself into the constructive community life of the city through the membership of thirty-eight

of its parishioners on the boards of nineteen different organizations. Judged by the number of these connections, the social responsibilities chiefly sensed are the care of the sick, maintenance of philanthropic homes for adults, general civic interests, and child welfare.

Relations to the Denomination

Though drawing its constituency from the same general areas of the city as St. Paul's Cathedral, and without the prestige of being the diocesan seat, St. John's Church is the recognized center of its communion for some of its most valuable foreign work. Its foreign-speaking congregations, and its relations with the Russian, Greek, Rumanian, Syrian, Assyrian and Armenian groups of Near-Eastern peoples, have already been noted. It has been the center of diocesan work for the deaf for forty years. It is represented on the diocesan social service commission by four members, and bears a most responsible place in the type of ministries with which it has been so conspicuously identified.

Summary and Interpretations

The study of the St. John's Protestant Episcopal Church in Detroit discovers still another way in which a city church has met extremely rapid urban change. The situation in Detroit has been greatly exaggerated by the unparalleled rapidity of the city's growth. This, on the one hand, has created a situation in which the church at almost any moment could sell its site at a very high price, while, on the other, it has to face the great expense of reërecting its plant in order to stay.[3]

But the church has no idea of getting away. Entirely apart from sentiment and sense of religious obligation, it feels itself to be a successful social institution fitting in with important phases of the down-town center of the city and decidedly making good, though against odds.

The characteristics of such enterprise are well worth reviewing.

---

[3] This expense may partly be met by damages to be collected from the city in connection with the widening of Woodward Avenue.

In the first place, environmental conditions are already probably as bad as they can possibly get. The older type of well-to-do home-owning population has already been pretty thoroughly evicted. But, with the erection of high-grade apartments and hotels in the vicinity of the church, a more desirable near-in population will be substituted for that now in the lodging- and boarding-houses which utilize the deteriorated older structures. The reënforcement of this newer type of people should aid the church both numerically and financially.

The trends revealed by the statistics of the church over the past decade show that its successes up to date are not absolute. They emphasize the need of digging in more deeply now while the constituents that have the present attitude toward the situation still live. The obvious moral of the situation is to get the new buildings and as much endowment as possible in the near future.

St. John's Church is particularly instructive in that it has met the changed situation without accepting a radical distortion of the natural composition of the constituent group. While, on the one hand, a church may substitute the accessibility and prestige of a central institution for the proximity of the neighborhood church, and may bring adherents long distances to its services, it is really avoiding the issue when it brings a disproportionate number of one age or one sex. Thus to have a successful down-town church with a weak program for the young simply means that the church is to that extent not successful. St. John's Church, on the contrary, is keeping an essential age- and sex-balance in its following, and is still successful.

Again, St. John's Church is actively recruiting in all parts of the city. It draws from near, from middle distance, and from far, though still showing a trace of parish intensification in a single sector.

The data are unfortunately weak in the matter of measuring the different elements of the constituency, and especially in defining the size of the closely related and responsible nucleus of members who are always found at the center of any ecclesiastical enterprise. It is significant, however, that the church shows greater dependence upon the paid professional expert than the majority of those studied, and that some of the most vital and aggressive types of organizational and lay leadership which characterize the neighboring churches seem to be absent.

The organization and development of the staff, however, affords a fine example of distinctly urban specialization in field and function. Not only in the range of work entrusted to paid specialists, but in the complex structure of the church's organization, is there a great departure from the status of the one-man church (which is still characteristic in cities) and from the mixture of professional functions still generally prevalent in churches with as many as four or five paid workers.

In St. John's Church, the well-known tendencies of the Protestant Episcopal communion express themselves through a large number of rather slimly attended religious services. These are strikingly marked by seasonal enrichment and the frequent use of festivals and pageantry.

The church's own total week-day program is not up to the average of the churches studied, though it functions through subsidiary organizations to more than an average degree. Adding, however, the activities of other organizations housed and fostered in the church, the week-day program has a conspicuous development.

The characteristic of the church's own program is its balanced and all-around character. These results are reached through a logical provision of activities for all ages and sexes and not by the mere number of successive accretions to a traditional program, as is conspicuously the case in certain other cases. The elaboration of the program is deliberate rather than accidental.

As a consequence of the specialization of staff, the social service work undertaken by the church itself has reached a technical competency not found in most cases. This phase of the work stands in responsible relations to the other social agencies of the city, and recognizes the accepted scientific standards in family case-work.

St. John's work for the foreign-born represents a happy alliance with the foreigner at his best, and on the side of his strength rather than that of his weakness. It fosters the religious organization of foreign-speaking groups under native leadership, and affords opportunity for their social integration, essentially upon the basis of equality rather than of patronage.

This relation with the indigenous constructive movements of the foreign population is an illustration of that recognition of the inter-relatedness of the social forces which is the particular secret of the church's larger ministries. The question is frequently discussed whether it is better for a church to undertake social work directly or to leave it to specialized agencies. St. John's answer is that it is sometimes better to do neither, but rather to make definite alliances and enter into formal coöperation with a wide variety of constructive enterprises. It thus succeeds in intersphering, without rivalry or duplication of effort, with a large number of city-wide social organizations of Detroit.

Not only does such coöperation greatly add to the size of the enterprise conducted under the church's general auspices, but it creates an outlook and an atmosphere that are both unique and admirable.

Adding up all the work of the church in its community aspects: namely, that which it directly undertakes, that which it houses, sponsors and facilitates, and that represented by the participation of its members in the work of constructive agencies, one reaches a very imposing total. The church's version of religious education, of Christian life and service, is directly correlated with, and greatly enriched by, these manifold and immediate practical expressions of faith at work.

The completeness and thorough-going honesty of the church's devotion to the version and method of Christian service which it has worked out cannot fail to impress the observer. Religion and community service have reached an integration in the life of St. John's Church, so that one is not, as in so many cases, a mere application of the other, an afterthought.

GRACE COMMUNITY CHURCH, METHODIST EPISCOPAL, DENVER, COLO.

Beyond anything else, Grace Church is the expression of an idea: namely, that of projecting organized Christianity into the fields of social and industrial relationships. In the working out of this idea, the relations of the church with organized labor have been accorded greatest publicity. This is the thing that has got into the papers; but the church itself rather regards the labor alliance as a significant gesture than as the central sphere of the application of its ideals. What it thinks of as more fundamental is the adaptation of its program to the needs of a strongly localized parish. In this conviction with respect to relative values, it has labeled itself a "Community Church."

On the other hand, Grace Church defines itself still more broadly than in the mere terms of its labor alliance. It thinks of itself as "enlightening the citizenship of Colorado along the lines of economic, social and religious betterment" through its open forum, its publications, and its organized movement for workers' education. It is thus at once a more parochial enterprise and a more far-reaching idealistic endeavor than its mere labor contacts suggest; and as such it should be judged.

The present characteristics of the church are, to a greater extent than those of most of the churches studied, the reflection of the distinctive genius and purpose of one man, its pastor for seven years, the Rev. G. S. Lackland. What is most unusual in its atmosphere and program is, in large measure, his creation.

Institutionally speaking, and when measured by the conventional items of number of members and amount of money

292

spent, the church constitutes one of the medium-sized cases studied. But it ranks third from the highest with respect to range of program, its work covering forty-two of the sixty items with reference to which the churches were compared.

History

Grace Church shared the comparatively brief history of the Centennial State, and grew up with Colorado as a prosperous enterprise in a desirable residential district of the capital city for nearly fifty years. Its neighborhood, adjoining the capitol site, was one of the most aristocratic in Denver. Between 1900 and 1910, however, the city increased its population by 60 per cent. In connection with this growth, the immediate locality of Grace Church suffered one of those spectacular reversals of fortune so characteristic of American urban development. With the opening of outlying residential sections, it ceased to be desirable. Among the pastors of the church during this period were men of great ability and pronounced genius for publicity, under whose ministries it was able to maintain itself in considerable strength during the first decade of the present century, even after the radical depreciation of the quality of the immediate neighborhood had set in. When, however, the situation settled down to its natural level, the church found itself greatly depleted in strength by removals and associated with an environment that was steadily growing worse. Strong down-town churches were still characteristic of Denver; and those nearer the center were profiting by transient and tourist support. Grace Church was just too far out to share this advantage. Ultimately then it found itself in the midst of what had come to be most distinctively the city's boarding-house and rooming-house district. The former homes of its members were occupied by detached individuals and transient families, and its district was invaded by the expanding Mexican colony.

The church's attempt to meet these changes took the character of a completely radical departure of method, rather than of a gradual evolution. With the coming of Dr. Lackland as pastor in 1918, novel and clear-cut policies were adopted.

First of all, definite objectives of service for the transformed local community were set up. Next an effort was made to provide money for use in publicity. One Sunday-evening's collections per month was specifically set apart for this purpose; and the church undertook to rehabilitate itself by means of a broadened appeal. In 1919 the church opened the Denver Open Forum in its auditorium on Sunday afternoons, and the alliance with organized labor began to develop. At this time also the name, Grace Church, was changed to "Grace Community Church"; and a five-year program was projected in harmony with the new policy. In 1924 associate memberships were established, to "enlist the support of liberal-minded folks and affiliate them with a program which they can honestly aid." Such membership was to involve an annual fee of $10, to be used for the existing educational program of the church, to finance a bi-monthly magazine, and to provide a broadcasting station. Throughout the entire period, however, the difficulties of securing adequate financial support for the program were very great; and shortly after the completion of this study, the pastor resigned.

The study must be regarded, therefore, as a report on a bold experiment that undertook more than it could entirely accomplish. Institutionally, however, the experiment was accompanied by decided growth. Church-membership for the last five years of the decade preceding the study averaged 861, as compared with 459 for the preceding five years; and Sunday-school enrollment 701, as compared with 480. The true level of local financial support is difficult to establish, because the period included the erection of a $65,000 parish house as an addition to the church structure. It also included the great Methodist Centenary drive for denominational benevolence; so that the trend of benevolent giving is also not clear. Apparently, however, the new financial level is at least twice as high as that prevailing at the beginning of the decade. These, on the whole, are conspicuous institutional gains.

In the succeeding sections, the study gets down to some of the more underlying trends of the entire situation. These, obviously, are partly the outcome of the deliberate experimental policies just narrated, while, on the other hand, they still more profoundly express the deeper and somewhat conflicting characteristics of the church and, in turn, set limits to its conscious endeavors.

I. MAJOR ASPECTS OF THE CHURCH

Constituency

The listed constituency of Grace Church at the time of the study showed a total of 1,494 adherents of all sorts.

Considering the total social group that had thus been gathered around the church as a center, the first notable phenomenon is that it is noticeably a man's and boy's church. It has forty-seven male adherents to every fifty-three female, which ranks it, in this respect, in the upper fourth of the churches studied; and there are actually more male adherents coming from non-member families than there are female, in both the adult and the minor-age groups. The ratio of men to women is also above the average in the family group. There can hardly be a question that this preponderant masculinity is the reflection of the church's more novel ideals and program.

On the other hand, the church shows evidence of the strong survival of the family element, 48 per cent. of all adherents coming from families with one or more adult adherents. This is a relatively low proportion; but it demonstrates the presence of an underlying conservative element in the constituency.

Again, Grace Community Church, in the phase of evolution studied, is an adult church, 91 per cent. of its adherents being beyond twenty-one years of age, as compared with 75 per cent. for the comparable population of the city of Denver, and 73 per cent. for the twenty-six churches studied. This preponderance of adults is again a definite reflection of the church's program, alliances and the inclusion of affiliated members. The reënforcements stimulated by these means make the adult element in the church considerably greater than in any other studied. The discussion of public questions, and the attempted application of religious principles to industrial issues, has been chiefly conducted on the adult plane.

MANNER OF ADHERENCE

Grace Church has proportionately a large number of adherents who are church-members only, or members of subsidiary organizations only. In other words, its constituency is not a closely knit body, but rather tends to fall into separate groups.

The proportion of adherents whose memberships overlap in one direction only (as between church and Sunday school, church and subsidiaries or Sunday school and subsidiaries) is next to the smallest in the cases studied.

But in spite of this general tendency of the constituency to thin out, the central core of the church represented by overlapping memberships in church, Sunday school and subsidiaries, all three, is 6 per cent. of the total. About one-third of the cases have relatively still smaller nuclei.

It is, of course, obvious that churches that suddenly branch out in many directions may easily gather distinct groups of adherents in their several activities, and that the task of the integration of the constituency into a unit is likely to be found incompletely performed. In view of this situation, the fact that Grace Church has a considerable nucleus of highly connected members becomes significant as showing that this tendency to separatism has been at least partly overcome.

A consideration of the manner of adherence as affected by the constituents' family relationships reveals that, while only 48 per cent. of the total constituency comes from adherent families, two-thirds of the church-members, and three-fourths of the highly connected nucleus, come from such families. On the other hand, two-thirds of the membership of the Sunday school, and two-thirds of the membership of subsidiaries, are made up of detached individuals. The separation into different constituencies is thus partly a distinction between adherents drawn from families and those who are not.

A study of manner of adherence, as affected by sex, shows that those who belong to the church only, to church and subsidiaries, and to church and Sunday school, are very largely women. That is to say, the more narrowly ecclesiastical aspects of the church in its adult phase do not bear the marks of masculinity that have revealed themselves as characteristic of the enterprise as a whole. The subsidiary organizations, which reflect more particularly the new and experimental aspects of the church's program, have, on the other hand, 50 per cent. more men than women in their memberships, while the triple overlap of church, Sunday school and subsidiary membership shows four men to every one woman.

NUMBER OF CONNECTIONS

The relatively small overlapping membership, and the tendency of the church to fall into distinct constituencies, are revealed from another angle by a study of the number of adherents' connections. Including memberships in all organizations, and the making of a pledged contribution as grounds of adherence, 68 per cent. of the total constituency is found to belong to the church in only one way, compared with 49 per cent. in the twenty-six churches as a whole. Only 10 per cent. have more than two connections with the church, compared with 19 per cent. as the average of the twenty-six cases. Over 90 per cent. of all minor adherents belong to the church in only one way, which explains the small overlap of the Sunday school with other organized activities.

To summarize, the divergent tendencies frequently found between adherents coming from adherent families and detached individuals are more than usually emphasized in Grace Church; while men and women also pull in opposite directions to an unusual degree. The church is highly exceptional in that men predominate in the Sunday school, in the subsidiaries, and in the triply related nucleus of the church.

Parish

The church is located at the corner of 13th and Bannock streets, only two blocks from the recently developed Civic Center of Denver, which, in turn, adjoins the extensive grounds of the Colorado State Capitol. The central business district of the city is limited by these park-spaces, but extends from the Civic Center for about one mile to the northwest where it is limited in turn by the river valley, and by the railways that have utilized this valley as their gateway to the city. The course of the river describes a half-circle about a mile and a half from the church on the west, northwest and southwest; and the valley is given over to transportation and industries, with their associate populations which include foreign colonies, among them the Mexican and Jewish groups that impinge upon the immediate parish of Grace Church. In this structure of the city, the northeast and southeast directions are left for the major residential development of middle-class and upper-class character.

DISTANCE AND DIRECTION

Almost one-third of the constituency of the church lives within half a mile of the building, and just about a half within one mile. In comparison with the entire group of churches studied, this constitutes a median dispersal of parish constituency. Only 10 per cent. of adherents live beyond three miles. This situation is dictated by the fact that Denver is not a large city.

The church has definitely aimed to localize large aspects of its work in the immediate community. The considerable massing of constituents immediately around the church shows that this aim has been in considerable measure realized; it also probably explains in part the strong residuum of adherents from family groups within the church. On the other hand, 60 per cent. of all detached individual constituents live within a mile, showing that the church is also drawing adherents one by one out of non-adherent families in the vicinity.

With reference to the city as a whole, the directional distribution of the parish is unusually symmetrical as follows: northeast, 19 per cent.; northwest, 22 per cent.; southeast, 30 per cent.; southwest, 29 per cent. Within particular sectors, however, the influence of physical and social barriers is very manifest. But all told, while avoiding the more absolutely unpromising areas, the church has modeled itself upon the city without great discrimination as to distance, direction or social quality. Such a result is the more easy in a city with a relatively small proportion of foreign-born and almost no Negro population.

From the standpoint of the constituents' closeness of relation with the church, distance of residence appears to have no consistent significance. More adherents who belong to the church in only one way live in the second and third mile zones than in the first or fourth. More who belong in two ways live near or else beyond three miles. The most highly connected group of all lives in the second and third mile zone, but those who have three or four connections are found in very disproportionate numbers beyond three miles and particularly beyond five miles. The same thing is true of the church's officers. In other words, the people who are most closely related to the church tend to live at a considerable distance from it.

Such are the highly complicated, but on the whole characteristic, parish phenomena of a city-wide church that retains a considerable hold on its original neighborhood area and is attempting to renew a localized ministry there. What its localized ministry reaches is largely a group of children and young people. In a church motivated by a novel and commanding ideal and offering, with a varied and attractive program in a city no larger than Denver, distance has little meaning with the adult constituency. It is somewhat significant, however, that regular attendants upon church services, while not primarily drawn from the immediate locality, do not come from so great an average distance as does the select minority of the constituency that holds office and is otherwise related to the church most closely.

No data were available showing parish distribution over a period of time. It is highly probable, however, that what the new policy has meant is simply that the locality of the church is somewhat more cultivated than it otherwise would have been. Otherwise it is unlikely that deliberate policy has controlled the situation to any appreciable extent. The parish is scattered because the natural constituency of the church has removed from its original locality and has diffused throughout the city. The city-wide appeal of the church's ideals has drawn friends from far away fully as often as its localized ministry has won recruits from the immediate neighborhood. All told, the natural processes of the city's growth have made the parish what it is, and conscious adaptation appears to have played a very secondary part.

II. AGENCIES, RESOURCES AND METHODS

Organizations and Activities

Omitting the Labor College, which is not organically a part of the church though in close practical affiliation with it, Grace Church ranks close to the average of the cases studied, as measured by attendance on all stated organizations and activities. The special and non-recurrent ministries of a church of this type are, however, probably unusually large. A total annual service, through week-day activities, to 77,000 people is claimed.

The features of the program that are formally organized and occur regularly throughout the year or over considerable periods, show a total annual attendance of 78,244 arrived at by a careful estimate. The ratio of the Sunday to the week-day is a little above the average, in spite of the expanded program of community service, because the Open Forum, the largest of the exceptional features of the church's work, meets on Sunday.

The distribution of the program among major fields of activity, as compared with its distribution in other churches studied, is shown in Table LXV.

In the table, formal religious services are shown to be slightly stressed, the Sunday school understressed, and the subsidiary program noticeably emphasized, relative to the medians of the total cases studied. The broadened program of the church thus appears partly in connection with the more traditional forms of the church's life: namely, the church services, as well as in the realm of novel subsidiary activities.

TABLE LXV—ESTIMATED ANNUAL ATTENDANCE ON SPECI-
FIED OCCASIONS AT GRACE COMMUNITY CHURCH AND
AT 26 CHURCHES

| | ATTENDANCE | | | |
| OCCASION | GRACE COMMUNITY CHURCH | | 26 CHURCHES | |
	Number	Per Cent.	Approx. Median Per Cent.	Range of Variation Per Cent.
Total *	78,244	100		
Formal religious services (Sunday and week day)..........	42,172	54	51	15–75
Sunday school	16,380	21	24	9–38
All other stated activities.......	19,692	25 †	22	9–51

* Sunday, 82 per cent.; week day, 18 per cent.
† Includes meetings of church officers and committees.

SUBSIDIARY PROGRAM

The most remarkable thing about the subsidiary program is
that nearly four-fifths of it consists of various gatherings and
activities of mixed groups. In only one case studied does the
adult program for men and women meeting together account
for so high a per cent. of the subsidiary program. This condition in the case of Grace Church is primarily due to the
Sunday-afternoon forum.

The activities of this great mixed-sex organization absorb
so large a proportion of the subsidiary program that most of
the others, in comparison with their development in other
churches, are left relatively weak, and the total picture seems
out of drawing. But the children's program, which is largely
intended for children of the neighborhood, is somewhat beyond the average in development, particularly by reason of
the kindergarten, week-day religious school, story hour, play
school, etc. The relative strength of the young people's program also ranks about average, because of the systematic
week-day program supplementing that of Sunday. But the
women's program is relatively weak.

The number of organizations, and the estimated annual attendance upon each, are shown by age- and sex-classification
in Table LXVI.

TABLE LXVI—ESTIMATED ANNUAL ATTENDANCE ON SUB-SIDIARY ORGANIZATIONS AND STATED ACTIVITIES

	ORGANIZATIONS	ATTENDANCE	
No.	*Type*	*Number*	*Per Cent.*
15	Total	18,722	100
1	Mixed adults	8,320	44
0	Adult men	0	0
1	Adult women	900	5
2	Mixed young people *	2,080	11
2	Young men	792	4
2	Young women	648	3
1	Mixed boys and girls	1,800	10
2	Boys	1,278	7
2	Girls	720	4
2	Mixed children	2,184	12

* Between 15 and 23 years of age.

In spite of the unusual balance of the subsidiary program in the direction of mixed adult groups, this table shows careful and graded provision for every age and sex. The showing reflects a deliberate theory of serving the week-day social needs of the local constituency. How the organized program, as thus analyzed, works out concretely will appear in a subsequent section.

Staff

Grace Church employs the services of four full-time professional workers and two part-time workers. This is a relatively large staff for the size of the church enterprise, as measured by attendance; only six churches ranking higher in this respect. It is obviously accounted for by the breadth of the program, which requires more than the usual range of specialized ability, and particularly by the part of the staff's time and energy that goes into the affiliated work of the Labor College whose enrollment does not enter into the attendance total. It is difficult to compare the churches that have such alliances with those that are strictly separate institutions.

The organization of the staff illustrates the difficulty of fitting even a relatively large number of workers to a still more elaborate program. It consists of: (1) a minister; (2) a director of education, including both religious education in the church and executive management of the Labor College, in addition to the direction of the so-called young people's department of the church; (3) a secretary-visitor, who is an ordained deaconess and is regarded as director of the children's department; (4) a kindergartner in charge also of the play school; (5) a part-time boys' worker, and (6) a part-time girls' worker, the two latter largely concerned with the gymnasium.

The preparation, experience and remuneration of the staff are systematically shown in Table LXVII, page 304.

WORK-TIME AND WORK-CONTENT

During a sample week for which accurate records were kept, the combined staff was on duty 288 hours, 26 per cent. of which time was spent in pastoral work, and 24 per cent. in administration. The time given to the former type of work was above the average, and to the latter below the average. Time given to clerical work was also below the average, there being no exclusively secretarial member of the staff. On the other hand, time spent in attendance on meetings for which the workers were not directly responsible was relatively a high item, while that devoted to preparation for preaching and the conduct of public worship was low. The proportion of time spent in making addresses other than in the pulpit was greater than in any other case of the twenty-six studied.

With respect to hours on duty, the data show an unusually hard-worked staff. But the distribution of duties appears rather unusual, partly because a certain idea of departmentalization by age (for example, as between the young people's and the children's departments) crosses the apparently more fundamental idea of departmentalization by function. The result is that there is a mixture of duties that are usually separated. All of the full-time workers do some pastoral work. None of them have clerical assistants distinctly designated as such. It appears that persons not so highly paid could perform some of the numerous duties now devolving upon these workers. Finally, in view of the very long hours on duty, one wonders whether time spent in attending meetings might not be reduced.

TABLE LXVII—ANALYSIS OF PAID STAFF

	Pastor	Director of Education	Deaconess	Young People's Worker*	Girls' Work Director*
Sex	Male	Male	Female	Male	Female
Degree of education					
Academic	College	College	High school	College	College
Professional or special	Theological, Postgraduate	Theological	Deaconess school	Law school	...
Years of employment					
Prior to this position					
Secular work	1	4	...	1	10
Religious work	8	8 months	9	...	...
In this position	7	2 months	5	2 months	2 months
Present salary					
Cash	$3,600	$1,800	$360	$280	$120
Perquisites					
Nature	Parsonage, weddings, funerals, lectures	...	Room, board, carfare	...	...
Value	$2,200	...	$690	...	...
Entitled to ecclesiastical pension	Yes	...	Yes	No	No
Length of vacation	1 month	1 month	6 weeks	...	...

* Part time.

Plant

The original church structure is architecturally beautiful. Its material is the brown stone characteristic of the older palatial edifices of Denver. Its site and environment still maintain externally the appearance of a residential district. The equally attractive chapel was originally a separate structure. The new parish house was added at the rear of the chapel, and the two were connected with the main church by a corridor and a structure housing the administrative offices.

While the three members of the plant are all attractive, the plant is not a unit either as to exterior or in internal plan, and the older parts are not structurally modern. The parish house contains exceptionally well-designed rooms for modern departmental religious education, and in them beauty and convenience are carried out into fine detail. It has also an excellent gymnasium. The chief lack of the plant is an adequate secondary auditorium which would be particularly desirable in view of the increased "secular" program of the church.

Compared with other churches studied, the plant of Grace Church ranks fifteenth in the twenty-five cases, scoring 580 out of a possible 1,000 on the Interchurch Standard Score. The summary of the score by major items is shown in Table LXVIII.

TABLE LXVIII—SUMMARY OF SCORE OF PLANT

ITEM	STANDARD SCORE	POINTS SCORED		RANK IN 25 CASES
		Number	Per Cent.	
Total	1,000	580	58	15
Site	130	90	69	15
Building or buildings.........	150	108	72	17
Service systems..............	160	69	43	20
Church rooms...............	170	119	70	16
Religious school rooms........	200	122	61	12
Community service rooms.....	190	72	38	13

Except for the item of service systems, the ranking on the several items is fairly consistent. The score of only 38 per cent. of the standard assigned to community service facilities, while at the same time the church ranks on this item above its total rank, shows how far the churches as a group are below the assumed standard on this point.

The most outstanding conclusion from a study of this plant, even with its recently built $65,000 addition especially devised for the housing of the current program, is that a structure built to serve one situation cannot easily be adapted to serve another so radically different as the present one.

Finances

From the standpoint of cost, Grace Church is one of five cases standing at the bottom of the scale. The total budget for the local support of the church as such approximates $20,000. As this works out, the cost is only $27 per one hundred estimated attendance on stated organizations and activities, which is relatively low. Most of the churches that show an approximate or lower cost are those that do most of their work through large assemblies.

The above statement does not include the budget of the Labor College, which is a separate organization, nor an additional benevolent expenditure of approximately $1,900.

A study of the sources of income reveals the most unusual situation exhibited by any of the cases investigated. About 15 per cent. of income during the last fiscal year came from rents for the use of the plant and as payments on pledges for the new building. Regarding the balance received from strictly current funds as a total, only 31 per cent. came from pledged contributions. This is less than in any other case, except those of churches charging pew rents or else primarily supported by denominational missionary subsidies. Twenty-one per cent. came as special contributions chiefly solicited by the pastor. Loose collections brought in 17 per cent. of the receipts. This is a very high proportion to come from such a source, and indicates that the church has tapped a vein of popular financial support in its transient audiences. Finally, about 15 per cent. (some $2,500) was received as a subsidy from agencies promoting labor education, including a sum from the well-known Garland Fund devoted to radical propa-

With so small a proportion of stated support from permanent adherents, such as constitute the financial backbone of most churches, the financial problem of Grace Church has been extra-hazardous and, as already indicated, has proved difficult of solution.

Expenditures for the last fiscal year were distributed as shown in Table LXIX.

TABLE LXIX—FINANCIAL EXPENDITURES OF THE CHURCH

Item	Amount	Per Cent.
Grand Total	$21,704	
Total current Account	21,004	100
Salaries	5,050	24
General administrative expenses	420	2
Music	1,245	6
General operation and upkeep of property	5,251	25
Expenses of departments specially budgeted	5,125	24
Publicity	2,480	12
Ecclesiastical connections	1,433	7
Investment Account		
Permanent improvement	700	

The per cent. of expenditures going for salaries is very low. The pastor's salary, which ranks in the lowest group, has been somewhat supplemented by the proceeds of his lectures. The ratio of expenditures for music is also low; and that for up-keep, about average. The expenses of departments separately budgeted, on the other hand, are relatively higher than in any other church studied. They obviously reflect the character of the program. They include chiefly the cost of the Forum and the localized social work. As already noted, special income is solicited for these particular budgets, to which the annual $10 payments from affiliated members have also been devoted. Again, no other church spends so high a proportion of its income (12 per cent.) for publicity; in a typical week, for ex-ample, $10.60 went for newspaper advertising, $4.40 for the printing and distribution of small cards, and $20 for the printing and distribution of window cards, a total of $35. It should be noted, on the other hand, that the loose collections more than paid for the entire cost of publicity.

Public Services

The average attendance on the morning service is 226. There is a simultaneous session of the children's church attended by about sixty. The evening service for the period of the active church year averages 500, and the Sunday-afternoon forum (held from October to April) 320. Eighty-five persons on the average attend the mid-week church night meetings.

The morning service presents a moderately embellished version of the traditional order. A printed request at the head of the weekly calendar asking that attendants observe a reverent attitude perhaps indicates an effort to maintain an atmosphere different from that prevailing at the more popular and informal services. The pulpit is not infrequently occupied by the director of education. The pastor's sermonizing appears to include three fairly balanced elements: first, the presentation of broadly religious themes (suggested by such a topic as "The Shadow of the Eternal"); second, interpretations of liberal Christian thought, largely from the historical viewpoint, in the attempt to recover the original vital elements of the gospel, as in the topic, "What Early Christianity Stood For"; third, direct applications of Christianity to current life, as in the sermon on "My Brother."

The evening service has a distinctly popular character, and includes a number of somewhat unusual features. Following an organ recital comes the pastor's question box. Questions on the night of the field worker's study were: (1) Should preachers officiate for divorcees? (2) Are communists honest? (3) Was Peter the first pope? (4) Do you believe in fasting? The evening was designated as "Nebraska Night," and the song service was announced as a "Big Sing, Nebraska Favorites." It was concluded with a prayer song and the illumination of the cross in the chancel. From this point on the service became conventional, with anthem, quartet, sermon, and choral benediction during which the congregation was seated in silent meditation. During the year preceding the study, the evening service was characterized by a series of "nights"—miners' night, teachers' night, art night, nights for the various nationalities, states and cities, Dixie night with colored jubilee singers and an address on "The Heroes of the South." There was also a sermon series on "What is the Matter with the American Home?" One sermon was based on 300 letters on this subject received from Denver women. Other frequent sermon features were book reviews, largely concerned with novels presenting current social issues.

The afternoon forum has a two-hour session. About two-thirds of the average attendance of 320 consists of men. Generally it is opened with some special feature, followed by congregational singing from "Songs of the Open Forum." The address occupies about an hour and is followed by questions and answers. There is then an offering, after which there are announcements relative to the community educational and social program of the church.

Forum speakers for the year preceding the study included politicians like Senator Adams, who spoke on "The Teapot Oil Investigation," Governor Sweet and the Attorney-General of Colorado; such outstanding radicals as Clarence Darrow and Scott Nearing; Denver's own Judge Ben Lindsey, and a considerable number of professors from Denver University. Other speakers were Charlotte Perkins Gilman, whose topic was "A Man-Made Civilization," Prof. Chas. A. Elwood on intolerance; and Father Ryan on the Catholic view of labor problems. The average of the talent, with respect to reputation and ability, was exceedingly high; and the points of view presented were notable for variety and catholicity. Occasional formal debates were included, for example, one on the Ku Klux Klan.

A monthly publication, containing synopses of the Forum discussions and advocating the general ideals and interests of Grace Church, is regarded as supplementing and extending the church's public ministries.

Religious Education

The organization of the Sunday school, together with a statistical summary, is shown in Table LXX.

TABLE LXX—SUMMARY OF SUNDAY-SCHOOL STATISTICS

| Department | Pupils | | Teachers | |
	Age	Enrollment	Male	Female
Total	...	481	8	19
Cradle Roll	Under 3	90	..	..
Beginners	3–5	34	0	3
Primary	6–8	86	0	6
Junior	9–11	60	3	3
High school	12–17	86	2	5
Young people	18–30	60	2	1
Adults	30 & over	65	1	1

The addition of nineteen officers to the 481 pupils and twenty-seven teachers gives a grand total of 527. Pupils in the attending departments number 391, and attendance averages 74 per cent. of enrollment. The approximate age-distribution in the attending departments is as follows:

	Number	Per Cent.
Children	·226	58
Adolescents	70	18
Adults	95	24

Unlike many of the churches studied, the Sunday school is primarily a children's and young people's institution, in which, as already noted, the element coming from the immediate vicinity is very large. The school enjoys unusually excellent quarters in the new parish building, there being a total of twenty-six rooms in use for its purposes.

The purpose of the church to relate religion to practice is a deliberate policy in the field of religious education, except in the children's departments which are conducted in an essentially conventional manner. What is recognized as the young people's department of the church includes a Sunday-night meeting of the Epworth League type, and a week-night discussion-group session. The endeavor is to yoke the expressional aspects of education with formal instruction and to supplement both by an active service program in the community. The atmosphere of this phase of the work, and the particular functioning of the work on a typical Sunday, appears in the following announcement:

YOUNG PEOPLE'S SUNDAY SERVICES

Dr. Lackland teaches a college class composed of students in the colleges. Mr. Holwell teaches a mixed class that cuts the Gordian Knot. Mrs. Galbreath has a wonderful class of young ladies. Their program is comprehensive.

Sunday, at 5.00 P.M., "Friendship Tea." Everybody learns to know the other fellow. Real fellowship here. At 6.30 the expressional meeting convenes. Paramount religious, ethical, national and international subjects are presented by capable leaders and openly discussed in the meeting.

The week-day school of religion for primary and junior children meeting one evening per week and the story hour on Wednesday evenings, in addition to the religious instruction of the kindergarten, constitute strong supplementary phases of religious education. As already noted, both religious education and the broader social and community phases of adult extension work (including that of the affiliated Labor College) are under the director of education.

Current Church Life

The organization, into the concrete reality of on-going church life, of all the aspects of program and service that have been discussed topically, is best understood by the printed announcements of a sample week, that of October 25, 1925:

DR. SHIRLEY J. CASE ON "THE LIFE OF JESUS"

Dr. Shirley J. Case is America's outstanding authority on "The Life of Jesus." He is professor of New Testament in Chicago University. He will speak next Sunday evening on "The Re-Discovery of Jesus." He will speak each night, Nov. 2-6, at 8.00 P.M. The Course Tickets are $1.00. Single Admission 35 cents. This is the greatest opportunity Denver has had in Bible Study in seven years. Tell everybody. Only 500 seats.

OPEN FORUM—Dr. L. W. Howerth, head of the Sociological Department at State Teachers' College, will speak this afternoon on "Do the Fittest Survive?" Dr. Howerth gave our best lecture last year. The Fankell Male Quartet will sing. Next Sunday Dr. Shirley J. Case of Chicago will speak on "The Modern Past and the Ancient Present."

MID-WEEK PSYCHOLOGY FORUM—Wednesday, 7.30 P.M. This will be the last of Dr. Lackland's lectures on "Psychology of Christian Healing." His theme will be "The Healing Methods of Jesus." Two book prizes. Clara B. Smith will sing.

STORY HOUR for children Wednesday evening at 7.30 in the Primary Room. Bible stories, Fairy stories, songs and games.

YOUNG PEOPLE'S MEETING—Howard Pine will lead the Young People's meeting to-night. Subject: "How much time should a Christian give?" Be on time, 6.30 sharp.

GYM CLASSES—Tuesday night 4-5, Junior boys: 7-8, High School boys; 8-10, young men; Thursday night, girls' schedule the same as the boys on Tuesday night. Games will be played on Saturday nights. See Mr. Ashburn.

TRIANGLE—Dr. Morton, head of the department of Religious Education, Iliff School of Theology, will give the second of his series of lectures on the Bible during the first period. Dr. Morgan will tell us about Scientific Eating during the second period. Wednesday evening, 7.30 sharp.

WEEK-DAY SCHOOL OF RELIGION for Primary and Junior children Monday evening, 4-5.

MOVIE—"Down to the Sea in Ships." Friday night, 7.30; 10 and 15 cents.

LABOR COLLEGE—Prof. C. E. Warne will speak at the Forum Monday night. Mrs. Cockerell, a member of the faculty of the State University at Boulder, will speak on "Primitive Methods of Work in the South Sea Islands."

NEW MEMBERS will be received next Sunday morning and evening. We want every member to aid us in calling this week. Teams will leave the church every evening at 7.00 o'clock, except Wednesday and Saturday. Let every member seek to win a member. Folks having church letters should see the pastor to-day.

GRACE PLAY SCHOOL is now running. Children taken from 3 to 7 years. Hours 8.00 A.M. to 5 P.M. Children fed, instructed by experts. Terms $3.00 per week. Tell any mothers whom this may help.

MEN'S CLASS next Sunday morning will be addressed by Prof. C. E. Warne of Economics Department, Denver University. Time 9.30 A.M.

WOMEN'S BIBLE CLASS taught by Miss Kirk is an educational opportunity. 9.30 A.M. Sunday mornings.

THE DWELLING PLACE OF GOD will be Dr. Lackland's theme next Sunday morning.

THE MOTHER'S HEALTH CLASS will meet in Evans Chapel next Friday afternoon at 2.30 o'clock. Dr. Morgan will lecture through the winter on Diet, Hygiene, and Sex Problems. Admission free.

THE LABOR COLLEGE

The Denver Labor College has quarters in Grace Church. Concretely defined, it consists of eleven courses of instruction given on Monday and Thursday nights, followed by forum sessions. The topics covered are: Public Speaking, Debate and Parliamentary Law, English, Dramatic Art, Wells' Outline of World History. A fee of $2.00 is charged for a course of nine lessons, or $3.00 for a double course. Enrollment is about 250.

Gains and Losses

The notable increase of church-membership, in connection with other institutional aspects of growth, has already been noted. Forty-seven per cent. of the 117 most recently added members were received by transfer from other churches, and 53 per cent. on confession of faith. Of those received by letter, about two-thirds were former Methodists and one-third from other denominations. In 75 per cent. of the cases studied, the new member had come to Denver within a year. This obviously reflects the natural pull on incoming population of so colorful a church as this, which maintains extensive publicity. Only 17 per cent. of the accessions studied were persons who had been previously related to the church in some systematic way for more than a year. In other words, Grace Church gets most of its new members without any extensive assimilating process. Only a small fraction of the total of new members came primarily through the influence of the Sunday school or subsidiary organizations. Attendance upon public services was the main point of contact.

The new membership is drawn from all parts of Denver. Of the 117 members whose cases were examined, 31 per cent. lived in the vicinity, 25 per cent. came from an average distance, and 44 per cent. from the more remote parts of the city. This showing harmonizes with data already presented as to the slight effect of distance on the closeness of relationship between this church and its constituency.

To attract large numbers of newcomers from all parts of the city without much previous assimilation is obviously to invite somewhat proportionate losses. In the year preceding the study, ninety-six names disappeared from the church roll, three by death, fifty-three by letter, and forty by the clearance of the roll of members of whom all trace had been lost. Of those dismissed by letter, somewhat more than two-thirds went to other Methodist churches, while two-fifths went to other churches in Denver. This apparently shows that the suburban shift is continuing and that the church is losing to the outlying sections at the same time that it is making a successful city-wide appeal.

Relations with Denomination and Community

The unique emphasis of the church, and the machinery necessary to carry out its exceptional program, has resulted in somewhat submerging the traditional machinery of the Methodist system in its local expression. Again, in trying to demonstrate its character as a community enterprise, the denominational aspects of the church have been somewhat minimized. Its chief stress has not been upon the official denominational objectives.

Nevertheless, in very large degree, the present development of the church is definitely due to the enterprising and adventurous spirit of Methodist urban development. The community-church idea has had official sanction, and the enlargement of plant that made the new program possible was generously financed by Methodist Centenary funds.

Furthermore, the denominational university and the school of theology in the city have stood in close relations with Grace Church's experiments, and have been continuously drawn upon for volunteer talent and paid workers in the carrying out of the enlarged program. The Denver Methodist situation as a whole shows, to a remarkable degree, the large and statesmanlike conceptions that are cherished by local Methodism as a body. Indeed the existence of this background largely explains the far-reaching and perhaps prophetic character of the Grace Church experiment.

On the other hand, such an experiment would not have been possible without exceptional coöperation from people and movements identified with a similar type of social idealism. Naturally the church has drawn to it a large number of social workers, including persons identified with what are sometimes regarded as extreme movements, like the Birth Control League. An exceptional number of prominent citizens, typified by Judge Ben Lindsey, have invested personal interest and support in the enterprise. The church claims that 200 of its members are identified with organized labor, including fifty in various official positions in labor bodies.

Summary

Rigid comparison of so unusual a case, even with a group of rather exceptionally developed city churches, is manifestly inappropriate. Whatever one thinks of the wisdom of the adventure, one can scarcely fail to be stirred by its sincerity and originality, and by a certain gallantry with which it has been carried out. In the definiteness and continuousness with which the pulpit, the church's forum and its publications have devoted themselves to the application of religious ideals to concrete problems of present civilization, and in its underlying philosophy and its direct alliance with organized labor, Grace Church has adventured where Protestantism has rarely gone. In so doing, it has confronted a whole new set of difficulties to top all of the ancient ones to which religious enterprise is heir.

The experiment has been striking and dynamic. It does not need to be immortal in its present phase to be significant.

The conservative aspect of the case is not to be forgotten. The presence of older elements of the constituency, both in the neighborhood and throughout the city, has been demonstrated. In very considerable measure the new program has held the older following of the church as its homes have become dispersed throughout the city.

Nevertheless, the deliberate plans and the high purpose of the church have not been stronger than the basic social forces operating in the city-community. The church which has thus been animated and strengthened is not the old one, in spite of a strong and loyal effort at the localization of ministries in the old neighborhood parish. Sitting on the same spot does not keep a church the same. The former institution really remains only in the external geographical sense, and with only a fraction of its human materials or its practical program.

What Grace Church is doing in the neighborhood is essentially a piece of missionary work, including a ministry to a residue of old families, but mainly for the sake of the children of the near-by transient population. This work is the smaller end of the total program of the church and its values cannot be regarded as primary.

The idea of popularizing the liberal Protestant outlook and of relating it to other idealistic movements through strong working alliances, is the keynote of the church's present enterprise. In this it has a right to feel that it has meaning for the entire city of Denver, the state and the nation.

But beyond all particular forms of organization under its own auspices, and beyond even its working alliances, the method of propagating ideas through multiplied occasions of public discussion is a unique and significant contribution to the current phenomena of the church. Grace Church brings to its wide public the testimony of many voices. Its elaborate publicity has made the entire state its forum. That the honest expression of common basic ideals from many angles would not be found in conflict with the gospel, but would rather receive unification and clarification from it, has been held as a faith and courageously believed. Preaching has consequently attempted to interpret the striking and sometimes strident conflict of viewpoints expressed in the Forum, as experimental aspects of the spiritual life.

The dramatic union of the movement for workers' education and the cultural ministries of the church has properly received great attention. It would seem to be in a high degree appropriate that an organization so richly endowed with the fruits of culture and education as the church is, should be of service in the organization and direction of the effort for cultural equality on the part of wage-workers. Grace Church has undertaken this as one of the legitimate functions of the church, in a candid spirit of partnership rather than of superiority and patronage.

The inclusion in the church enterprise, as affiliated members, of men and women of good will who value it for its current social significance, apart from its ecclesiastical tradition, is another unique and courageous phase of the Grace Church experiment. Viewed in itself, and apart from the inhibitions of tradition, this would seem to be merely the veriest common sense, unless one is willing to surrender the totality of his ethical and spiritual life into the exclusive proprietorship of some sectarian organization.

Many of the down-town churches of great cities cannot be expected to maintain themselves unless reënforced from such non-ecclesiastical sources, as well as by members of other

churches who will be willing to undertake dual allegiance and
the burdens of dual support in order to make religious adventure and experimentation possible.

The financial methods of the church, in the phases described,
have undoubtedly been institutionally speculative. It may be
presumed that one of the things that money is most obviously
for, is for taking risks in a good cause. Not too much of it,
probably, has been invested in the realm of religious novelty.
If there is a question about the finances of the church, it is
not whether it could be supported by exactly the methods used,
but how to support it under its peculiar circumstances. What
has been demonstrated is that proportionately large support can
be drawn from the unpledged giving of transient audiences
and from the gifts of properly qualified people who are willing
to take financial stock in an exceptional adventure. It also
appears that agencies outside the immediate community but
interested in things that such a church is attempting to do,
may be expected to give it assistance.

As compared with Grace Church as an institution before it
began its present experiment, the present church has far more
money, a greatly enlarged and improved plant, an increased
staff, and a greatly increased strength of relationships apart
from the specific services rendered through its broad and many-
sided program, either as directly regarded or through its working alliances. There are exceedingly remarkable by-products
of a notable adventure of faith and courage.

In form, Grace Church may well be inimitable. No evidence
ought to be sought in any single case that many, or even any
other church—let alone all other churches—should attempt to
be like this one. Yet the major significance of the case is
almost sure to be found in its challenge to the church at large.
In contrast with merely conventional, repetitious, unadapted
and unadventurous versions of ecclesiastical Christianity, the
existence of even a single case constitutes an implicit, reiterated query: Why the old way rather than this? And some at
least of Grace Church's experiments scarcely fail to reveal
realms of possibility, perhaps even of actual method, for other
cities and situations.

TRINITY CENTER, PRESBYTERIAN, SAN FRANCISCO, CALIF.

To show the contrasting fortunes of churches of the same metropolitan community, Trinity Center, San Francisco, was introduced in the study of the First Baptist Church, Oakland, which was presented as a church under relatively slight pressure from a typical urban situation, that of moderate deterioration of environment in connection with the growth of the city, and as successfully avoiding the consequences of the situation by good management, and particularly by the shrewd and effective use of publicity devices appealing to the city at large.

Trinity Center, on the contrary, shows a happy instance of a rather complete adjustment to a very radically changed social situation. After long rejecting the rôle of a carefully adapted community institution, the church ultimately chose it. As Trinity was circumstanced, no other option was really open to it. Its location was residential, not central, and the alternative solution, so apt in the case of the First Baptist Church, was not available for it. The characteristics of its present ministry were thus forced upon it. In the outcome, however, the church has become a striking example of the second major group which these case studies illustrate: namely, churches that have accepted rather than avoided the consequences of changes in their immediate environments, and that have remodeled themselves upon the new situation.

But while Trinity has become profoundly changed in spirit and outlook, it has been prevented by its limited resources (also perhaps by the brevity of its experiment) from undertaking many expensive additions to its program, and from making such substitutions of new methods for old as would greatly shift the balance of emphasis away from the traditional religious functions. Instead, it has made its successful new approach to the community chiefly through religious services; services made appealing through their large use of visual methods. It has not, however, been equally successful with all elements of the community. Its most obvious opportunity has been that presented by the children of the Mission District, and in less degree, by its adolescents; and it is to the meeting of their needs that the church primarily has set itself. While its spirit of adaptation has been great, the church, by making a selective response to the comparatively simple demands of a limited age-group, has still been able to avoid the necessity of any extremely novel changes in the strength of its organization, or in the fields of its functioning.

History

Trinity Presbyterian Church, San Francisco, was founded in 1868. This was at California's period of most rapid development following the Civil War and just previous to the completion of the first transcontinental railway. San Francisco's population then was less than 150,000.

The original location of the church was near the present site, close to the center of the Mission district. This historic and distinctive section of San Francisco had developed out of the original settlement of the Franciscan mission and was becoming the city's most desirable area of general residence, a considerable part of its population enjoying wealth and high social prestige. In this fortunate area of the city the church became relatively prosperous and influential and so continued for nearly forty years. Then it was shaken out of its comfort and complacency by the great earthquake of 1906.

Trinity Church stood just outside the area of total destruction by earthquake and fire. It suffered, however, even more vital disaster in the radical change in the character of the Mission district which followed. About half of the district was burned; the remainder was crowded with refugees from poorer down-town sections. The better-to-do population then removed almost *en masse* to suburban areas, the church losing sixty families at once to communities on the Oakland side of the Bay. In general, the earthquake and fire greatly stimulated the growth of Oakland, while retarding that of San

Francisco; and as the reconstruction of the latter city proceeded, the status and function of the Mission district were found to have suffered complete transformation. Railways had secured additional gateways through it, and industry had come to dominate part of its previously residential area. It was rebuilt chiefly in tenements for industrial populations. This process was followed by the gradual reconstruction of its older types of houses for multi-family occupancy. What had been a distinct residential section of the upper middle class thus become one of San Francisco's largest and most characteristic areas of wage-earners' homes and institutions.

The conservative tradition of Trinity Church ill prepared it to meet this change. As a result the church was destined to undergo nearly ten years of adversity and decline. By 1915 a financial deficit was reported for every month of the year. Membership was down to 182, and the local budget to less than $4,000. Attendance at morning services had dwindled to forty; officers were declining to accept their elections. Institutionally the church was on its back. In these straits it was forced, in 1916, to pocket its pride and appeal to its denominational extension agencies for help in "adequately financing the church and the securing of a pastor with the necessary qualifications." After about two and a half years of negotiations, the church, while retaining its ecclesiastical entity, had definitely come under the "direction and control" of national and local denominational agencies from which its chief support was coming. The conception of the church's ministry had been redefined as follows: To maintain "a center of evangelism and community service where the gospel would be interpreted in terms of our social, civic and industrial relationships—an enterprise which in a peculiar way would represent the interests and purpose of our entire Presbyterian constituency in the Bay region." [1] In token of this enlarged idea, the name "Trinity Center" was adopted.[2]

---

[1] Memorandum of June 27, 1919, adopted by representatives of the Church Extension Board of the Presbytery of San Francisco and the Presbyterian Board of National Missions.

[2] In 1920 Bethany Congregational Church, a neighboring institution which had suffered the same adversities almost to the point of extinction, was federated with Trinity Center, and representatives of the regional bodies of the Congregational denomination were given place on an advisory board established to represent the work in its community aspects.

This ushered in the new era. The statistical history of the church for the decade preceding the study, as recorded in denominational publications, shows conclusively the reversal of the downward trend after the adoption of the new order of things, and a continuous though moderate growth thereafter.

The present study of Trinity Center was made in the summer of 1925, after five years of history had been made under the new plan and under the continual pastoral leadership of the Rev. H. K. Pitnam.

I. MAJOR ASPECTS OF THE CHURCH

Members and Constituents

The constituency of Trinity Center consists chiefly of detached individuals whose families are not definitely connected with the church. It includes a disproportionate number of young people and children. It is not a highly integrated constituency. Most of its members belong to departments and activities and not to the church; or if to the church, they have no stated connection with other activities. In contrast with this general tendency, there is a small group of much-connected adherents consisting—not of adults, as in most churches—but largely of adolescents and children of the Sunday school.

FAMILY AND INDIVIDUAL CONSTITUENTS

Of 1,067 definitely connected constituents,[3] only 452 belong to constituent families, one or more adult members of which are included in the enrolled constituency, while 615 are detached individuals. This ratio reveals a very wide departure from the family type of church to which Trinity formerly belonged. Only four of the twenty-six churches have a smaller proportion of families.

Nearly 40 per cent. of the constituents are males, and 60 per cent. females.

Adults constitute only 47 per cent. of the total, whereas they are 78 per cent. of the population of San Francisco. Re-

---

3 For definition of a constituent, see p. 447.

ports as to minors fail to specify whether the majority were adolescents or children. It is clear, however, that Trinity has an overwhelming young people's constituency and that children predominate.

The adult adherents from family groups are about equal in number to those not from constituent families. It is thus chiefly minors who so largely come from non-church homes.

MANNER AND DEGREE OF ADHERENCE

The 1,067 constituents represent many varieties and degrees of adherence. Sixty-four per cent. of the constituency belong to the church only, the Sunday school only, or subsidiaries only, while the remainder—relatively a small proportion—represent different varieties of overlapping memberships. Only about 40 per cent. of the total are full members of the church. Only seventy-six, or about 8 per cent., belong at the same time to church, Sunday school and subsidiaries. Relative to the other churches studied, this core of intimately connected adherents is below average.

NUMBER OF CONNECTIONS

Over half of the constituency is connected in only one way.[4] Two connections are less than half as frequent as one, and three less than half as frequent as two; but about 6 per cent. of adherents have four or more connections. This is a more accurate way of measuring the size of the intimately connected core of the church; and it is interesting to note that the core as thus defined is made up in about equal proportions of detached individuals and persons from constituent families.

A special count was made of the 117 constituents who had the most extensive and varied relations to the church: namely, members who attended regularly, belonged to the Sunday school, and had a total of at least three other definite connections. These were found to be largely adult women or else young girls.

---

[4] Making a pledged contribution is constituted as a connection according to this reckoning.

Environment

The Mission district's loss of standing and quality following the San Francisco earthquake was so obvious as to be universally recognized. It is almost certain, however, that the stupendous and dramatic quality of the physical catastrophe has distorted local history and obscured the fact that the social quality of the district had already been slipping as newer and finer areas of the city were developing to the northwest. The great disaster simply effected overnight a deterioration that was already under way through the slow attrition of social change. The unique aspect of the situation was that neither foreigners nor Negroes particularly figured as factors in the downward process. Where the process finally left the church the following paragraphs attempt to show in some detail.

The church is located about one and a half miles south of the city hall and Civic Center. The central business district stretches for two miles beyond this Center to the ferries that connect with Oakland and the East Bay cities. What the church recognizes as the Mission district proper, and as its parish for intensive cultivation, is an area roughly comprehended within a half-mile circle drawn around the church. In three directions the area thus defined is bounded by hills so steep as to be only partly occupied by population. And even within the area the topography to the southwest is so broken that there are many blind streets.

Of the area districted for larger parish purposes, except for the relatively small district around the affiliated Holly Park Church, nine-tenths falls within a mile radius of the church. A mile circle thus drawn touches the tidal basin to the southeast, passes close to the deep valley of Islais Creek on the south, and reaches, in the northwest, to where Market Street, the main artery of the city, ends abruptly at the foot of the famous Twin Peaks—mountains almost at the very center of a great city. Within this circle the city thrusts and crowds in and out among the hills and valleys of its uniquely rugged physical site, except where it has artificially smoothed out its business section and extended the water-front and industrial area on "made land."

The main land connections of the city with the world are to the south; and beyond the church the city stretches southward along these major arteries of rail and highways for three miles to the county line.

This serves to describe the more general features of the area within which the church operates.

While the Mission district proper is restricted to residential use for the most part by the existing municipal zoning ordinance, it is gridironed by major thoroughfares devoted to retail business. The main area of heavy industry projects inward from the water-front and penetrates in a broad wedge to within about one-fourth of a mile of the church. About an equal distance to the northwest lies a small area of more desirable homes, including some new apartment-houses, especially on the high land adjoining Mission Park. In this part of the area are found many of the city's more pretentious Roman Catholic institutions. The undeveloped area on the higher hills may ultimately be brought into use for residences of a still higher quality. Otherwise the general character of the area is relatively homogeneous.

CHARACTER AND COMPOSITION OF POPULATION

In the neighborhood of Trinity Church a smaller proportion of the people are foreigners than in the city of San Francisco as a whole. The chief foreign elements in the neighborhood are from Northern Europe. The presence of large numbers from Ireland tends to explain the numerical preponderance of Roman Catholic population; while Swedes and Germans, particularly the latter, account for the concentration in the northern part of the district of a number of Lutheran churches.

The assembly district, which covers an area slightly smaller than the Mission district as previously defined, had a population of 33,387 in 1920. It is surrounded by districts less densely populated because of their topography; yet the population within a mile of the church may be conservatively estimated at about 60,000. The density of the immediate district is about that of the city as a whole; but fewer homes are owned by their occupants.

The Trinity Parish

The church is located at the corner of Capp and Twenty-fifth streets, about one block from the major business street and from the heart of the Mission business district which constitutes one of the most important secondary centers of the city.

Of all the cases studied, only the small churches of the City Parish of Los Angeles have parishes as compact as Trinity's. The parish is also relatively symmetrical, inequalities in the distribution of adherents appearing to be based upon topography rather than upon an unequally effective appeal to the community.

Out of the estimated population of 60,000 living within a mile of it, the church is able to locate a definitely connected constituency of only 948, in addition to 400 or 500 whose "prospect" cards are in its files, and perhaps from 1,000 to 2,000 other persons in occasional attendance. At best, the total is relatively small, considering the population.

DISTANCE

The 743 located constituents living within one mile of the church are 77 per cent. of the total, and of these, 343 live within one-half mile. This distribution identifies the church very closely with the Mission district which it accepts as its intensive parish. Proportionately more adherents belonging to adherent families live immediately about the church, but beyond one mile the proportions from adherent families and detached individuals are about the same.[5]

---

[5] The 119 names of constituents for which the church could not give a location, constitute an unfortunately large proportion of the total. It is not known how many of these live out of the city and with how many the church has actually lost contact. If these persons could have been located, the above distribution figures might have been somewhat different.

DIRECTION

Fifty-eight per cent. of adherents come from west of the church. This is partly because population to the east is cut off by the Bay, and partly because, here as in other cities, people in going to church generally go toward the major center of the community along lines of habitual travel.

The relative failure of the church to draw from the southeast is probably due to three factors: topography, character of population and lack of transit facilities. As already noted, unoccupied hills break the development of the city within a mile in this direction. Then also the main Italian colony of the area (naturally not a fruitful field for the church) is here, and lacks direct street car communication.

The slightly greater affinity of the church for the northwest sector may be due to the fact that this is the direction of the best residential development. At the same time, the percentage of constituents drawn from the northeast, where industry and slum conditions go hand in hand, is very little behind that drawn from the northwest. In other words, within the relatively assimilated and homogeneous population of the Mission district, the appeal of the church is socially inclusive to a marked degree. The distortions of the parish primarily reflect the rugged topography and unequal transportation facilities of San Francisco.

CLASSES OF ADHERENTS RELATIVE TO DISTANCE AND DIRECTION

Relatively more members than non-members come from beyond a mile; and detached members, on the whole, come farther than adherents from constituent families. In the blocks immediately surrounding the church, however, detached adherents are very numerous. That is to say, the church draws entire families from average distances and detached individuals from near and from very far. The directional distribution of members varies little from that of the total constituency.

Church officers, on the contrary, are drawn in disproportionate numbers from the northwest, and a higher per cent.
of them come from long distances than adherents generally do.
In short, the church seems to look for its leadership to families that have moved out of the Mission district into areas of
greater prestige and prosperity.

Pledged contributors are distributed as to distance about as
the total constituency is.

DISTANCE BY AGE-GROUPS

Adult adherents are more scattered, and children less scattered than the average of the total constituency, the per cent.
coming from within a mile being as follows:

	Per Cent.
Total constituency	77
Adults	74
Adolescents	80
Children	87

This is in general harmony with experience, which shows
that children often are not drawn from as great distances as
adults are.[6]

NUMBER OF CONNECTIONS AS RELATED TO DISTANCE

For the total constituency, and for every age-group, the
number of connections is strongly correlated with distance of
residence from the church. Near-by adherents tend to numerous connections. Remoteness cuts down the number of
connections and thus the availability of the church to give full
value in service to adherents who live at more than average
distance.

To summarize: relative to the total bulk of the community,
Trinity Center is a comparatively small affair, bringing few
adherents farther than a mile and those into few continuous
relations. On the other hand, its appeal is little limited by
differences in social level or by other distinctions within the

---

[6] The reverse is true in certain cases.

adjacent population, except that children and adolescents are the age-groups chiefly attracted.

II. AGENCIES, RESOURCES AND METHODS

Organizations and Stated Activities

The total attendance at Trinity Center for 1924 was locally reported as 115,514. A large proportion of this was so purely occasional that it cannot be dealt with systematically. Another important part consisted of coöperative activities held in the church but not exclusively under its auspices. These are considered in the section on community relationships.

A careful estimate of attendance on all organized and regular activities of the church itself for the year prior to the study reduces the total to 84,982. The Sunday attendance was 59 per cent. of the total, that of week days 41 per cent. This ratio very definitely identifies Trinity Center as a seven-day-per-week enterprise. Only three of the twenty-six churches have a proportionately larger week-day program.

The estimated attendance is divided as shown in Table LXXI.

TABLE LXXI—ESTIMATED ANNUAL ATTENDANCE ON SPECIFIED OCCASIONS AT TRINITY CENTER AND AT 26 CHURCHES

	ATTENDANCE			
	TRINITY CENTER CHURCH		26 CHURCHES	
OCCASION			Approx. Median Per Cent.	Range of Variation Per Cent.
	Number	Per Cent.		
Total *	84,982	100		
Formal religious services (Sunday and week day)..........	47,580	56	51	15–75
Sunday school	7,592	9	24	9–38
All other stated activities	29,810 †	35	22	9–51

* Sunday, 59 per cent.; week day, 41 per cent.
† Includes meetings of church officers and committees.

Although week-day activities are so outstanding, the per cent. of time given to formal church services is appreciably

greater than the average, primarily on account of the great
audiences at "movie" services. The proportion of total attendance represented by the Sunday school is very much below
the average, while that given to subsidiary organizations is
decidedly more than the average, being higher in only four
other cases.

Attendance on all other stated activities is divided among
the organized age- and sex-groups as shown in Table LXXII.

TABLE LXXII—ESTIMATED ANNUAL ATTENDANCE ON SUB-SIDIARY ORGANIZATIONS AND STATED ACTIVITIES

No.	ORGANIZATIONS Type	ATTENDANCE Number	Per Cent.
	Total	29,722	
14	Classified by Age and Sex.................	26,654	100
0	Mixed adults	0	0
1	Adult men ,...........................	300	1
1	Adult women	2,808	11
3	Mixed young people *..................	5,658	21
2	Young men	3,276	12
2	Young women ,.......................	1,300	5
1	Mixed boys and girls...................	7,176	27
1	Boys	728	3
3	Girls	5,408	20
0	Mixed children	0	0
	Classified by Function...................	3,068	

* Between 15 and 23 years of age.

About 36 per cent. of the subsidiary attendance is accounted
for by meetings of women and girls, 16 per cent. by meetings
of men and boys, 48 per cent. by meetings of the two sexes
at the same time. Trinity Center does not segregate the sexes
in subsidiary activities to such an extent as many of the
churches studied do.

The subsidiary program is carried on by fourteen organizations in addition to the choir and orchestra. The most
largely attended are those of young people (which include
groups for study of current events, dramatics and music, combining in a social and dance on Friday nights, and a Sunday
meeting of the Christian Endeavor Society); a group of athletic and social organizations for young men based on organized Sunday-school classes and rather closely graded as to age;

and the Wednesday night song and story hour for children preceding the mid-week moving-picture service which they share with adults.

Staff

The staff conducting the religious work of Trinity Center consists of four full-time workers whose education, experience, tenure and salaries are included in Table LXXIII.

TABLE LXXIII—ANALYSIS OF PAID STAFF

	Pastor	Associate Pastor	Associate Pastor	Secretary and Director of Girls' Work
Sex	Male	Male	Male	Female
Degree of education				
Academic	College	College	College	College
Professional or special...	Theological seminary	Theological seminary	Part seminary Postgraduate	School of Expression
Years of employment				
Prior to this position				
Secular work..........	...	...	...	3
Religious work........	21	2	20	...
In this position..........	6	1	1	3
Present salary				
Cash	$4,000	$2,250	$2,400	$1,500
Perquisites				
Nature	...	...	...	...
Value	...	...	...	...
Entitled to ecclesiastical pension	Yes	Yes	No	No
Length of vacation.........	1 month	1 month	...	...

Relative to the magnitude of the Center's operations, this is a staff of average size. In addition to the enumerated workers, it also benefits by the half-time services of the girls' worker attached to the office of the Church Extension Society of the Presbytery; also of an average of one and a half days per week from nine students of the San Francisco Theological Seminary who are largely engaged in house-to-house visitation.

ADMINISTRATIVE RELATIONS

The workers are technically employed by the Board of National Missions of the Presbyterian Church, and are under the supervision of its general officers and those of the Presbytery. The pastor is the executive director of the enterprise and nomi-

nates his associates. Stated reports are made to denominational agencies through the director. Otherwise administrative contacts are immediate and informal. There is a weekly
conference of the staff. The church secretary does work for
all the pastors. Though the forms of ecclesiastical government, both of the Trinity Church and of the federated Bethany
Congregational, are carefully maintained, in practice the ac-
tions of the session of the church are subordinated to the
decisions of officials. The advisory committee, composed of
influential citizens of different denominations, in addition to
denominational representatives, meets occasionally upon call
and acts upon matters of general policy, especially as concerns
larger questions of finance and community relations. A general church council consisting of representatives of all major
subsidiaries and activities, in addition to church officials, functions as a cabinet for internal administration.

The work of the staff for a week following the period of
field study was measured and classified.[7]

The combined work of the staff for this period covered 264
hours (that of the part-time workers being omitted on account
of vacations). Twenty-seven per cent. of the total was spent
in administration, and 25 per cent. in pastoral work. These
proportions closely correspond to the average of the churches
studied.[8] The association with Trinity of the Holly Park
branch church, maintaining separate services, brings the time
spent in homiletical preparation to above the average, and puts
the time spent in the strictly ministerial offices of preaching
and conducting marriage and funeral services at a higher ratio
than in any other church. This emphasis on ministerial offices
probably also reflects the fact that the church gets its large
program rather from audiences at formal services than from
a wide variety of activities. The time given to secretarial
work is much below average, reflecting the fact that there is
only a part-time worker in this field.

---

[7] It is not assumed that the week is strictly typical, but it probably illustrates
fairly the range and distribution of functions as indicative of the relations of the
workers.

[8] Pastoral visitation by theological seminary students was not going on at the
time of the study; otherwise this function might have stood at a considerably
higher percentage.

Considering the pastor alone, much more than average time is given to ministerial functions, average time to pastoral work, and less than average to administration, probably because one of the associate pastors largely takes charge of the details of the majority of the church's functions, leaving the pastor free for the more fundamental relationships.

Out of an aggregate of twenty-seven days of work by members of the staff within the week studied, eleven lasted more than ten hours each. All the workers report a long average work-day, and a single holiday taken during the week is rather apologized for.

The fact that three out of the four workers are ordained ministers reflects the relatively conservative program of the church, one in which public services are a very major factor.

On account, probably, of the lack of an adequate supply of lay volunteers in a church so deficient on the adult side, the relation of the paid staff to the subsidiary organizations of the church is not normal. The associate pastor and girls' worker have personally to be the group leaders of a considerable number of organizations. Other members of the pastor's family are heavily leaned on for service.[9]

Plant

The building occupies a corner lot. Its basement is at the street level. It has recently been put in excellent repair, and the pulpit platform and organ have been modernized. The auditorium, seating 900, is spacious, with ample galleries, the whole giving a moderately churchly impression. It has to be used for all sorts of audiences, including the main Sunday assembly. A basement room has a small stage, and combines the functions of gymnasium, dining-room, departmental Sunday-school room, general social room and place for the Daily Vacation Bible School and the children's mid-week services. There is a fairly suitable room for the primary department. Lately ill-lighted toilets and showers have been constructed in

---

[9] The problem of developing local leaders and of keeping the supply of imported student workers to tasks that local leaders cannot perform constitutes a real problem of administration.

a narrow way between the church and adjoining buildings. The kitchen is cramped and inadequately equipped. The storage space is limited. The first floor lobby, however, is spacious, and the general and Sunday-school offices are light and fairly adequate. There are also a suitably isolated pastor's study and a small choir-room. Counting both large and small rooms, the church has a total of thirteen.

Of the twenty-five churches studied, the plant of Trinity Church ranks next to the poorest. Though valued at about $90,000, it scores only 468 on the thousand-point score-card developed by the Interchurch World Movement.[10] Its rank, with respect to site, general structure and rooms devoted to church and Sunday-school purposes, corresponds exactly or closely with its total rank. On service systems (lighting, heating and ventilation, etc.) its score is slightly better, thanks to recent improvements, as are also its community service facilities. A summarized score of the church is presented in Table LXXIV.

TABLE LXXIV—SUMMARY OF SCORE OF PLANT

ITEM	STANDARD SCORE	POINTS SCORED		RANK IN 25 CASES
		Number	Per Cent.	
Total	1,000	468	47	24
Site	130	78	60	24
Building or buildings.........	150	96	64	23
Service syste.ns	160	76	48	19
Church rooms	170	105	62	24
Religious school rooms........	200	62	31	24
Community service rooms.....	190	51	27	22

The explanation of the striking deficiencies of the plant is simple. A building of ample size and substantial for its time and place, comfortable in appointment, possessing the simple dignity of well-proportioned mass and not unpleasant in detail, but erected for a conservative family church more than four decades ago, could not possibly be up to date and could be only slightly suited to a church confronted by radically changed circumstances and with a considerably modified program.

---

10 For explanation of the Interchurch scale and its application to a group of churches, see Athearn, *The Malden Survey* (Interchurch World Movement, 1920).

Of special equipment, the excellent moving-picture apparatus is most notable.

The fact that the building and equipment of Trinity Center score so low in the scale, while the church ranks so high in the total number of people who attend its activities, indicates the very grave handicaps under which its work is carried on. The plant unquestionably limits future development to an acute degree.

Finances

From the standpoint of church support, the more outstanding features are: (1) the large subsidy from the Presbyterian denomination; (2) the relatively large income from loose collections which constitute the largest single local item of income; (3) the solicitation of special funds from business firms and industrial concerns in the community at large on the score of the general importance of the work; (4) the resourcefulness of the church in securing a moderate income from the use of its plant and facilities by others.

Receipts for 1924-25 amounted approximately to $21,000, of which less than 10 per cent. was for benevolences. Of approximately $19,250 secured for current expenses, $7,500 was a grant from the Presbyterian Board of National Missions, in addition to which $525 came from the local Presbytery on account of student workers. This left about $11,000 to be raised locally for current expenses. Of this amount, only 28 per cent. came from stated pledges (made separately by members of Trinity and Bethany churches), 35 per cent. from loose collections, and 27 per cent. from special gifts (solicited particularly for building repairs and the expenses of the Daily Vacation Bible School), while 7 per cent. came from commercial transactions (including rents of the church, entertainment of sailors on account of the Young Men's Christian Association, and use of the moving-picture equipment), and 3 per cent. from miscellaneous sources.

Benevolent income includes pledges for the missionary work of the two coöperating denominations to which the women's organization contributes about one-third.

Current expenditures slightly exceed receipts, using up the small balance from the previous year. They are classified by chief items in Table LXXV.

TABLE LXXV—FINANCIAL EXPENDITURES OF THE CHURCH

Item	Amount	Per Cent.
Grand Total	$19,528	
Total Current Account	17,831	100
Salaries	8,220	46
General administrative expenses	243	1
Music	1,707	10
General operation and upkeep of property	3,601	20
Expenses of departments specially budgeted	2,939	17
Publicity	1,121	6
Investment Account		
Permanent improvement	1,697	

The special feature of expenditures is a large proportion assigned to the expenses of departments separately accounted for. These include the Sunday school, the Daily Vacation Bible School and subsidiaries, and also about $1,600 as the rental cost of moving pictures. This amount is considerably more than offset by the increased loose collections already alluded to.

The carefully departmentalized accounting is a significant feature of the Trinity Church financial records.

About 80 per cent. of the benevolence expenditures are for denominational work, divided between the Presbyterian and Congregational Boards. Ten per cent. goes to the Deacon's Fund for local charity, and the balance to the San Francisco Church Federation and the Anti-Saloon League.

Public Services and Worship

Measured by attendance, the general Sunday and mid-week services of the church constitute 60 per cent. of its total activities. The average Sunday morning attendance approximates 150. Seventy-five per cent. of the congregation on a typical Sunday was composed of adults, and 55 per cent. of women. The service convened with friendly informality. It was simple and unornate in character, like that of other less pretentious

Presbyterian churches. There was a competent chorus choir of volunteers. The service was slightly less than one hour long and the congregation dispersed after a period of leisurely sociability.

The pastor's sermon topics, as announced over a period of a year, suggest plain and non-sensational pulpit work. The associate pastor preaches frequently, and professors from the San Francisco Theological Seminary occupied the pulpit for about three months during the year of the study. This is part of a deliberate attempt to vary the pulpit ministry.

The evening service is very different. Its average attendance approaches 600. The special feature is a sermon based upon, or suggested by, a moving-picture film. At a typical Sunday evening service there was an extended prelude of organ music, at the end of which the auditorium lights were turned down and the cross above the chancel was suddenly illuminated. A series of illustrated hymns were then thrown on the screen, verse by verse, and sung by the congregation led by the organ, chorus and precentor. The responsive reading was also from the screen. A prayer-hymn followed, accompanying a colored reproduction of Holman Hunt's "Light of the World" upon which the pastor commented briefly. The hushed singing following was dominated by children's shrill voices. Then came an informal pastoral prayer, followed by more hymns upon the screen. The lights were then turned on for an anthem by the choir, which the audience applauded by clapping. Announcements followed; next an offertory prayer which included a more than indirect appeal for funds. The offering was then received by four youthful collectors, and the choir took seats in the body of the church. The film "Held to Answer" was then shown. In spite of a melodramatic plot, it was pertinent as being the work of a San Francisco newspaper man, himself formerly a minister, and as having a minister for its hero. According to the film, this minister tries to make his church "the house of the open door" for all sorts and conditions of men. In the brief talk preceding the film, the pastor explains that this is what Trinity is trying to do. He enumerates the church's ideals and methods in a sort of friendly recapitulation of its purposes and program. After a closing prayer, the showing of the film proceeds in the usual movie-house fashion, the organ suiting its music to the action with professional skill.

The service lasted about two and a half hours. The religious section of it was entirely unhurried, and never passed out of an essentially traditional atmosphere. Some of the audience left after this part of the service, but scarcely any one came in for the film alone. There was a strikingly larger proportion of family groups in attendance—father, mother and children together—than at the morning service.

In Trinity Center, this type of evening service continues throughout the year, and has now been going on for several years. The church attempts to fit sermons to films chosen from those in ordinary commercial use. The special religious film of the Pilgrim's Progress type, while occasionally employed, is not greatly relied upon. What degree of aptness the association of sermon and film may have is suggested by the following list of titles and topics:

Film Title	Sermon Topic
Who Are My Parents?	Your Neighbor's Children
Divorce	The Church in the Home
Disraeli	Jesus the Jew
Beyond	Do the Dead Rise?
Her Reputation	Good and Evil
The Mailman	Loyal Lives
Deliverance (Helen Keller)	Out of the Dark
David Copperfield	Tuning in on Happiness

In a dozen or so other cases during the year the film title was directly adopted as the sermon topic.

Obviously preaching directly upon a film is not different in theory from reviewing a book or otherwise using a literary production homiletically, as is frequently done in ordinary conservative pulpits. The observer may wonder whether the supply of movies worthy of sermonizing is as inexhaustible as the Mission audience's desire for pictures. But the seriousness of the attempt and its large measure of success challenge the sincerest respect and interest.

The mid-week service similarly occupies a whole evening. It consists of a moving picture following a largely attended and distinctly old-fashioned prayer meeting, except that it is held in the auditorium and embellished by music by the pipe-organ led by a precentor.   There is no particular connection between the theme of the service and the picture to be exhibited afterward.   The adult congregation averages 187, and from 125 to 150 children come for the picture period after a separate religious song- and story-hour of their own.   The combined attendance on the two religious services, however, exceeds that at the moving picture.

Religious Education

Sunday-school attendance constitutes only about 10 per cent. of the total annual attendance at Trinity Center.   The Sunday school is predominantly a children's institution.   Here too moving pictures constitute a habitual vehicle of education. The teachers are primarily regarded as personal leaders of boys' or girls' groups.

The school enrolls 468 pupils, which is considerably more than the membership of the church; and with its officers and teachers totals nearly 500.   The average attendance is only about 175.   Forty-five per cent. of the pupils are male, and 55 per cent. female.   The age-distribution is, children 67 per cent., adolescents 22 per cent., adults 11 per cent.

The school is departmentalized only to the extent of dividing the primary from the main school.   The main school meets in the church auditorium, and, for the most part, uses the Presbyterian version of the International Sunday-School Lessons.   Classes of adult women and older girls, and a mixed young people's class, have chosen separate lessons; the latter being conducted as a discussion group.   Five intermediate classes meet in the gymnasium for the instruction period, where they are divided by movable screens.   Others occupy stair landings to the balcony or meet in inadequately lighted basement rooms.   These facts illustrate the shortcomings of the plant as already discovered.

The Sunday-school session precedes the church services and lasts one and one-quarter hours.   An educational or scenic film is usually part of the opening exercises.   Class instruction lasts thirty-five minutes.

The associate pastor has immediate charge both of the Sunday school and of club activities. This results in a fairly integral relation between the relatively meager Sunday school and the elaborately organized group life of the church. Without a definitely worked-out theory, the tendency is to regard the total life of youth from the standpoint of a set of interrelated character-building processes.

Theoretically it is held that the Sunday school should have a lay superintendent "when one of the right caliber is available." On the other hand, the advantages of unified administrative responsibility are felt. Unquestionably such a Sunday school is right in regarding itself as primarily a set of organized personal relationships rather than as a pedagogical machine. With better facilities, however, technical improvements could be made in organization, grading and educational standards.

Methods of Growth and Conservation

A study of the sources from which accessions were drawn for the last church-year shows that Trinity Center secured nearly one-fourth of its new members from areas beyond those occupied by the great bulk of the parish; that, unlike more centrally located and popular city churches, it got more new members by confession of faith than by transfer from other churches; and that of those received by transfer, more than one-fifth were from denominations other than Presbyterian and Congregational; also that one-fourth of the total were newcomers in the community. They show that the church attracts about half of its Presbyterian recruits from long distances. This is strong testimony to the vitality and challenge of its program. In somewhat less than half of the cases, recruits who are not new in the community had been connected with the church through some subsidiary relation. In other words, in the main, the church does not dip its new adherents out of a previously created reservoir, but secures them directly from the community. This fact presumably reflects the effective appeal of its public ministries and the influence of its pastoral follow-up.

Current Life

In the rhythm of the year, the summer months show the largest attendance at Trinity Center, primarily on account of the neighborhood Daily Vacation Bible School held in coöperation with other churches.   There is no let-down in public services; and one or other of the pastors remains throughout the year.   Most of the clubs of adolescents, however, discontinue temporarily.

The major summer activities end with an exhibit and outing of the Daily Vacation Bible School.   About October first, the full round of regular activities is again under way.   The series of special features at the public services and celebration of the religious holidays introduce the chief accents into the work of the year.   Throughout the year, the church frequently participates in denominational and civic interests of the city and region.   The dramatic and musical sections of the young people's organizations give entertainments and numerous other clubs present public programs.   There are interchurch athletic meets.   No great stress is put on the observance of Lent; but the choir gives an Easter oratorio.

A typical week shows the following events and attendance:

Day		Attendance
Sunday	Two services; Sunday school; two young people's meetings; sailors' dinner....................	1,505
Monday	Staff conference; lecture to seminary students; meetings of three group organizations; meeting of elders and trustees; rehearsal of pageant....	151
Tuesday	Meetings of women's federation; Camp Fire Girls; circle of employed young women........	85
Wednesday	Meetings of two group organizations; children's story hour; mid-week devotional service and community motion pictures...................	835
Thursday	Meetings of four group organizations; men's club dinner	88
Friday	Choir practice; interdenominational young people's group meeting; young people's discussion group; social program	98
Saturday	Meetings of three group organizations of boys, including athletics...........................	64
	Total	2,826

Community Relationships

That the Mission district is a distinct community within San Francisco, is recognized by nearly all movements that base their operations on a districting of the city; and many of them have found it a natural sub-center in which to locate branches.

The immediate neighborhood of the church includes the district's business center. Here are found a cluster of banks and trust companies and a "White Way" of ten or a dozen theaters and amusement houses. The excellent building of the branch public library, the Horace Mann junior high school and branch buildings of the Y. M. C. A. and the Y. W. C. A. are also near. St. Luke's Hospital lies within half a mile, and the vast City Hospital is only a little farther away. Four of the notable boys' clubs of San Francisco have branches within the district. The Salvation Army has its city headquarters and aërial training school just on the border. There is a full quota of charitable and correctional institutions, many of them under Roman Catholic auspices. The building trades and several other branches of organized labor have headquarters within the district.

The twenty churches of the district classify roughly as follows:

```
Protestant
    Regular denominations...........................   14
        Of American origins.........................   10
        Of foreign origins..........................    4
    Irregular denominations.........................    3

Roman Catholic......................................    3
```

The foreign-speaking Protestant churches reflect the older foreign elements of the district, but also function as city-wide centers for widely scattered racial constituencies. Irregular denominations are of the familiar emotional and ultra-evangelical varieties which flourish in working-class districts.

The immediate cluster of churches constituting the nearer neighbors of Trinity consist of Grace Methodist Episcopal and the Tabernacle Baptist. These coöperate in Daily Vacation Bible School under the general auspices of the Church Federation and with the assistance of the local branches of the Young Men's and Young Women's Christian Associations. The Young Men's Christian Association also helps the church in normal training and in its program of boys' work. The most spectacular partnership with the Young Men's Christian Association, however, is for holding a series of sailors' parties for men of the United States Navy who are served meals at the church and sometimes attend the services.

Of general religious agencies, the church is especially related to the San Francisco Federation of Churches, of which the pastor has been a strong leader. The church has also actively backed the campaigns of the San Francisco Community Chest and furnished team leaders. It maintains institutional membership in the Mission Merchants' Association. Some of its women members are influential in the San Francisco Housewives League and the Corona Club, a women's organization of standing. The church is in active coöperation with respect to cases of need with the Juvenile Court, St. Luke's and the City Hospitals, and the American Red Cross. The latter organization conducts courses in first aid in some of the church clubs. A group of children from the Orthopedic Clinics are sent to the Daily Vacation Bible School. The church is represented in the associated boys' work council. Its young people sing in several hospitals and institutions. These various community interests are given active commendation in the pulpit and publications of the church.

In spite of these varied contacts, one finds no organized and systematic coöperation of community agencies through a council or federation of social work for the Mission district.

Relationship to the Denomination

The essential denominational initiative and control of the Trinity Center enterprise is written across the whole record. Ultimate authority and leadership, active planning and executive policies, and vital financial support, lie outside the local church. Arrangements not fully consummated at the date of the study are placing the Presbyterian Neighborhood House on Potrero Hill (about one mile east of the church) within

the religious responsibility of the Center, and are greatly enlarging the systematic use of the field and work of the church
by the San Francisco Theological Seminary in the training of
young ministers. The basis of the work in a federation of the
local Presbyterian and Congregational churches is recognized
in good faith, and the membership and finances of the two are
kept technically distinct. These relationships are valued as
precedents for the possible inclusion in the future of still other
of the neighboring churches.

Adaptations

In what sense, and in what ways, are the phenomena exhibited in the contemporary study of Trinity Center to be
interpreted as adaptations of a church to its urban environment, either generic or specific? The following paragraphs
undertake to summarize the main points at which such adaptation seems to be evidenced.

Trinity Center has adapted itself to the Mission district.
Here was an area that had rapidly and radically changed for
the worse. In a community of run-down and dying churches,
one church chose to identify itself all the more closely with
the neighborhood and to model its life upon the neighborhood's
need. The church began to feel itself more and more an integral part of the Mission district, to join the district's enterprises and make contact with its movements. Its women's
organizations, for example, exchanged a narrow, parochial
outlook for a distinct civic consciousness. Relatively large
numbers of people of the district are listed and more or less
known, while the area in which they live is systematically
worked as a parish.

Trinity Center has adapted itself to the changed characteristics of population. The precise change that has come to the
district is that it is no longer a desirable place of residence for
well-to-do people. The church has consequently popularized
its appeal. It offers moving pictures, with typical musical
accessories, three times a week in connection with religious
services. These services have been simplified and made informal. They are not without adequate intellectual appeal.

During the week of the study, an address of one of the pastors was an exposition of John Muir's account of the successive geological processes whereby the Sierra Nevada Mountains came to their present state, while another pastor handled the theory of miracles after the modern fashion. But a more characteristic aspect is the marked congregational participation in hymns and responsive readings, or such an occasion as the mid-week devotional meeting at which individuals from a miscellaneous audience, representing more than a dozen different denominations, repeat long series of scripture verses and volunteer short prayers from the pew.

Trinity Center has attempted to meet the growing urbanization of its district, increased congestion, inadequacy of the home, the growth of its center of commercialized recreation, the habit of crowded existence, and gang life. It has made the detached individual its unit of adherence. But it serves him more by drawing crowds into miscellaneous gatherings than by small groups organized by age and sex. To these crowds it offers long evening services, on the theory that when people living in cramped urban houses go to church at night they want to make an evening of it. (These gatherings are actually attended by many family groups.) But the church also serves the urban masses by group organizations. It has loosened up its traditional methods and widened its activities; it employs athletics and social dancing, offers an open door to street children and to transient populations such as sailors.

The church has had to adapt itself to meet the lack of adequate internal resources and the failure of traditional sources of support. It has secured denominational help from the city, the region and the nation, and has drawn money in increasing amounts from the community and especially from casual participations in its activities.

Again, the church has had to meet the lack of adequate resident ability and leadership. It has therefore fallen back upon the coöperative resources of the church at large and has adopted characteristic urban ecclesiastical methods, both denominational and federated. Specifically, it has utilized the will and resources of its denomination to make experiments.

The period of history under review is essentially such an experiment. The maintenance of a suitable staff, the alliance with the San Francisco Theological Seminary, the general character of the program, represent a focusing upon the Mission district of nation-wide experience, ability and resources.

The church has appealed to the newly developed urban community spirit and consciousness. In its advisory council, it has drawn upon the services and sympathies of citizens of large responsibility and understanding (including the present Secretary of the Navy). It is increasingly commending itself as a responsible civic force and a constructive social agency of the city.

These adaptations have enabled it to touch vastly more people, and that in many more ways. They involve at least five times the working force, and six or seven times the expenditure of the church previous to the new era. They have secured relatively slight improvements of the plant, but considerable addition to working facilities. They have brought the church into a wider and much more numerous set of relationships. These outstanding successes have had as a by-product an increasing ability to hold remoter adherents who were previously dwindling away in number, and to draw new adherents from long distances.

These conspicuous successes do not include in any due proportion the adults of the church's immediate vicinity. The church has not yet contrived to reëstablish itself as a cross section of the community. Nor has it become a strongly integrated social group. Here are worlds still to be conquered; here elements of population for whom appropriate and effective forms of service are still to be found.

Problems

As the church's new program was originally projected, it was broadly conceived as a "center of evangelism and community service." It was supposed that this implied, for example, working contacts with organized labor. In earlier phases of the experiment, health and legal clinics were actually in operation, though later abandoned.   The present program, in other words, is not so broad as that first contemplated.

Should the church still seek to carry out these original projects, or were they beside the main point?   Is it better to keep to demonstrated successes, especially as related to limited resources?   What are the limits of local resources?   How much should Presbyterian national agencies continue to do by way of financial subsidy?   Is a new appraisal of community need necessary for the answering of either question?   Some broadening of program is probably imperative simply because the church is a successful and growing institution.   Whatever is undertaken will doubtless involve enlarged plant, some increase of staff, and ultimately a clearer definition of the total enterprise both positively and negatively.

Cases XIII and XIV

PILGRIM CONGREGATIONAL AND BROADWAY METHODIST EPISCOPAL CHURCHES, CLEVELAND, OHIO

The lowering level of the waters of Lake Erie decided in advance what should be the basic structure of the future city of Cleveland. It compelled the meandering streams of the bordering plains to cut deep to reach the lake. The terrain was thus dissected into deep, dry "runs" representing discarded river beds. To utilize one of the few natural harbors on the southern shore of the lake, the developing city had to submit itself to a civic pattern predetermined by topography. It was accordingly erected upon narrow lobes of high land—almost peninsulas—between these "runs" and the bluffs that defined the deep and winding bed of the river. The railroads and growing industries, early occupying the river bottom, radiated in all directions by way of the transverse valleys; and rendered the physical subdivision of the city into small topographical areas still more permanent. In the attempt to overcome this, its naturally divisive structure, the builders of the city threw bridge after bridge across the valleys, thus creating one of the outstanding external characteristics of the present Cleveland.

As the decade of the Civil War closed, Cleveland still could boast less than 100,000 population. But during these years an infant industry, later to be known as the Standard Oil Company, had located at the river bottom just at the edge of the city. On the narrow promontory to the north, a group of Bohemian coopers which the Company had imported to make the barrels in which its product was shipped, were just founding a little colony. The promontory on the other side of the river, first used for farm lands by New Englanders migrating to the Western Reserve, had been for a decade the site of a somewhat ambitious attempt to found a model suburban educational community. This was also of Yankee origins.

With the passing of time, the increase and concentration of industry in the river valley inevitably determined the character of the adjacent populations. This tended to equalize the fortunes of two areas that had been settled under such strikingly diverse auspices. Each promontory was ultimately connected by viaduct with the central area of the city and traversed by one of its axial thoroughfares. The Bohemian settlement built up solidly with small one-story homes, largely owned by their occupants. On the other promontory, the Yankee element was at first strongly reënforced by New England elements from Connecticut, and established a polite residential neighborhood with its "College" and "Professor" streets. Gradually, however, the area was overrun, first by German and Bohemian industrial elements, and later by mixed populations from many European sources—Polish, Slovak, Ukrainian, Russian and Greek—until it had become one of the most strongly polyglot areas of the city, "College" and "Professor" streets being transferred into synonyms for great congestion of population and excessive juvenile delinquency and infant mortality.

History of the Churches

The two churches here studied together were respectively the religious expressions of the two communities described, whose religious characteristics and fortunes they exactly mirror. In the Bohemian community, Broadway Methodist Episcopal Church developed as a missionary enterprise under denominational direction, but with very strong resident backing from American manufacturing and business interests. Its story is that of the forward march under such auspices of a homogeneous, thrifty and progressive foreign population.

Pilgrim Congregational Church, on the contrary, reflects the well-conducted retreat of the Yankee stock which, in spite of reënforcements gathering to its support large elements of wealth and culture, and the establishment of a desirable residential area, had had increasingly to share its area with marginal foreign populations. These populations finally became dominant. But before the submergence of the original stock had actually taken place, the second generation of German and Slavic population had been happily assimilated by the church until it was able to take up the tradition and impress of the earlier Pilgrim group, and to help to extend them to those who came still later.

Both churches, consequently, have come to be dominated by Americans whose parents were foreigners. But the neighborhoods continue to be very different. The Bohemian community is strongly unified through a growing business center about which essentially homogeneous population has been solidly massed. The population surrounding Pilgrim Church, on the contrary, has continued to be diffused, without the dominance of a unifying center, and, on account of the racial diversity of elements, socially incoherent.

Statistical evidence for the last decade shows both churches making distinct institutional progress. The numerical growth of the membership of Pilgrim Church has been continuous since its foundation. It has averaged slightly more during the last five years than during the previous five.. Its current local expenditures have increased by 50 per cent., and benevolences have registered an advance. It has erected an excellent new community house.

The new $230,000 building of the Broadway Methodist Church was first in use during the year 1920. Its site is nearer the business center of the community, and its erection marked the transition from the earlier to the later years of the decade. The church averaged considerably larger in membership in the period subsequent to removal, though the Sunday school was slightly decreased. Ministerial support was a third higher, and benevolences, which advanced strikingly during the Centenary Movement, remained at their higher level.

This completes the parallel histories of the two churches, and the study now turns to examine them as contemporary institutions.

I. MAJOR ASPECTS OF THE CHURCHES

Pilgrim Congregational and Broadway Methodist Churches both represent a high degree of development of service-programs, with strong and definite provision for community work, Pilgrim ranking fourth and Broadway sixth in the twenty-six cases studied from the standpoint of the number of comparable items which the programs include.

Constituencies

The sizes of the constituencies that constitute the human material of the two churches are as follows:

	Adherents	Full Members
Pilgrim	1,923	1,169
Broadway	1,360	752

As already noted, both are churches of the second-generation foreigner in America. Broadway is a church of children and adolescents. Pilgrim also has proportionately numerous adolescents, but is deficient in children, with a correspondingly high per cent. of adults.

Both are women's churches. In the twenty-six cases studied, Pilgrim has next to the fewest men relative to women, while Broadway ranks just above Pilgrim.

Pilgrim ranks as next to the lowest case in number of constituents coming from adherent families, relative to the total; while Broadway occupies a medium position in this respect.

In both churches the surplus of women is located largely in the adult group of detached individuals. So far as minors are concerned, the proportion of the sexes is not far from equal, but when either church gets beyond its family groups, it contrives to win adult women but not men.

MANNER OF ADHERENCE

In the twenty-six churches studied, the most frequent percentage of overlapping membership (that is to say, of adherents who belong to church and Sunday school, church and subsidiaries, Sunday school and subsidiaries, or all three) is between 35 and 40 per cent. of the total. In Pilgrim it is 33 per cent., and in Broadway 36 per cent.; but these closely corresponding results are secured in very different ways, as is shown by the following comparison.

	Per Cent.	
	Pilgrim	*Broadway*
Member of church only...........................	34	27
Member of Sunday school only....................	13	33
Member of subsidiaries only.......................	20	4
Member of church and Sunday school..............	4	17
Member of church and subsidiaries.................	20	3
Member of Sunday school and subsidiaries..........	5	5
Member of church, Sunday school and subsidiaries..	4	11

The above showing includes some similarities and some striking variations. Broadway includes very large Sunday-school elements not otherwise assimilated to the church. In half of its enrollment its school is a separate institution. Pilgrim has a smaller, but still considerable, following belonging to the Sunday school only; but it shows a large group belonging to subsidiaries only. Pilgrim's overlapping membership in church and subsidiaries is also very high; but its nucleus of triple adherence, through church, Sunday school and subsidiaries, all three, is very small. Contrasting with this, Broadway has few members of church and subsidiaries, but a relatively large nucleus belonging to both and the Sunday school as well.

The greater hold of Broadway upon its family groups runs consistently throughout all the phases of adherence, so far as measured. This appears in the following comparison.

Adherence Through Families	Per Cent.	
	Pilgrim	*Broadway*
Total	39	51
Members	52	68
Sunday school	34	43
Subsidiaries	39	51
Triple adherence.................................	63	72

Both churches get a high per cent. of full church-members from family groups, but fewer Sunday-school children; while the per cent. of subsidiary members from this group just equals the showing of the constituency as a whole on this point. Finally, both get a very high per cent. of triple adherence from families. The adherent family is thus especially the backbone of both churches and the special source of the most closely related members of both constituencies.

On the whole, in view of its lack of children, the large membership in its subsidiaries only, and smaller total overlapping membership, Pilgrim Church appears not to be doing so well as Broadway in the integration of its constituency. Pilgrim also has a much smaller central nucleus, as well as fewer adherents from family groups. Its unity appears to be a result of active administration connecting a group of otherwise rather loosely related enterprises.

Parish

Pilgrim Church is located at the corner of Fourteenth and Starkweather streets, about a mile and a half south of Cleveland Square; Broadway Church at the juncture of Broadway and Magnet Avenue, nearly three miles southeast of the Square. The churches are about two miles apart, with the river valley and its heavy industries intervening.

DISTANCE AND DIRECTION OF CONSTITUENCIES

Forty-two per cent. of the constituents of Pilgrim Church and 50 per cent. of those of Broadway live within a mile of the respective churches; while 31 per cent. of Pilgrim's and 26 per cent. of Broadway's following come from more than three miles. Pilgrim's is thus appreciably the more scattered parish, while in comparison with the other cases the dispersal of the Broadway constituency classifies as medium.

On account of the topography of the district, the distribution of the Pilgrim parish largely falls into the sector form. Over half of all its adherents come from a single direction, the southwest. There are, however, other striking concentrations of adherents at beyond five miles distance, in the newer and highgrade residential suburbs, but to the northeast and the northwest. In these directions, more adherents live beyond five miles than in any intervening mile-zone. Individual constituents, as well as adherent families, are drawn from these distant areas. In general, however, individual adherents live a little nearer.

Broadway is located a mile farther from the center of the city than Pilgrim. Its field is more narrowly limited by topography. But it is able to draw constituents from all three directions open to it. Constituents are most numerous, however, in directions away from the center of the city. A second concentration of its adherents occurs in the two-to-three-mile zone to the southwest. So many of the more progressive younger families of the church are living here that a proposal for a branch church is under consideration. As with Pilgrim, a slightly higher per cent. of detached individuals than of family-group adherents lives near to the church.

SOCIAL QUALITY OF NEIGHBORHOODS

While both parishes are thus far-flung, and include areas widely varying in social quality, the ideal of localized service which both churches proclaim, the character of both programs in many aspects, and the fact that as many as 42 per cent. of all adherents in one case and 50 per cent. in the other actually live within a mile of the church building, indicate that the character of the respective neighborhoods may be expected to be reflected in the work of the churches.

Broadway Church has the more homogeneous neighborhood. It averages lower than Pilgrim's in the economic scale, consisting mainly of territory where rents average less than $25 per month, though with a considerable area west of the church where the average is from $25 to $50. Pilgrim Church, on the other hand, is located near the center of a considerable area, having Fourteenth Street as its axis, where monthly rents range from $25 to $50. There are many smaller surrounding areas, however, especially those bordering on the river and railroads, where rents average less than $25. As already indicated, the district includes an exceedingly varied and polyglot population, and, in certain localities, the problems of poverty and delinquency are exceptionally acute.

A Negro element (entirely lacking in the Pilgrim field) has appeared at the tip of the Broadway parish where it is connected with the central city by a bridge. A colored congregation bought the former Broadway church building and the fear of a Negro influx has been a considerable factor in the removal of the older constituency. The Broadway axis is, however, not a main line of Negro expansion, and the real menace to Broadway's present location is rather the expansion of business and industry and the rising standard of prosperity which can more easily be satisfied in outlying sections of the city.

The immediate neighborhood of Pilgrim Church, on the contrary, is now registering considerable improvement in process of becoming the site of many of the central institutions of the polyglot community. The recent erection of numerous great churches of somewhat modern architecture, and the development of other social and civic institutions of foreign populations, are helping to turn the tide of physical deterioration and to give the community at length a somewhat stabilized character.

Such are the general environmental conditions under which the two churches are identified by location and by from 40 to 50 per cent. of their adherents.

II. AGENCIES, RESOURCES AND METHODS

Organizations and Activities

With a total constituency of about a half smaller than that of Pilgrim Church, Broadway has virtually twice as large an annual attendance upon stated organizations and activities. This rather amazing difference is due to the fact that Pilgrim Church has no evening services for most of the year, that its Sunday school is much smaller, and that its let-down of activities during the summer is unusually prolonged and complete. During the months when Pilgrim's program is in full force, the difference is much less. There is a further far-reaching difference in policy: namely, that Pilgrim Church systematically lends its recreational facilities to other organizations whose attendance it does not claim as its own.

The churches are much alike in the small percentage of the program represented by attendance on formal religious services. But Broadway's attendance still falls upon Sunday to the extent of 73 per cent., in contrast with only 55 per cent. falling on Sunday at Pilgrim. As the proportions of the program work out, Broadway stands high in emphasis both on Sunday school and on subsidiaries, while, relative to the average of the churches studied, Pilgrim stresses the subsidiaries but not the Sunday school. Only three churches exceed it in the proportion of attendance falling in the subsidiary phase of its work.

These contrasts are shown in Table LXXVI.

TABLE LXXVI—ESTIMATED ANNUAL ATTENDANCE ON SPECIFIED OCCASIONS AT PILGRIM AND BROADWAY CHURCHES AND AT 26 CHURCHES

	ATTENDANCE					
	PILGRIM CHURCH		BROADWAY CHURCH		26 CHURCHES	
					Per Cent.	Per Cent.
OCCASION	Number	Per Cent.	Number	Per Cent.	Approx. Median	Range of Variation
Total	41,533	100	80,546	100		
Sunday	....	55	....	73		
Week day	....	45	....	27		
Formal religious services (Sunday and week day)	12,080	29	24,740	31	51	15–75
Sunday school	8,954	22	29,120	36	24	9–38
All other stated activities..	20,499 *	49	26,686 *	33	22	9-51

* Includes meetings of church officers and committees.

SUBSIDIARY PROGRAMS

A comparison of subsidiary programs shows other extreme contrasts between the two churches. This is shown in Table LXXVII.

TABLE LXXVII—ESTIMATED ANNUAL ATTENDANCE ON SUBSIDIARY ORGANIZATIONS AND STATED ACTIVITIES

		PILGRIM CHURCH ATTENDANCE		BROADWAY CHURCH ATTENDANCE	
ORGANIZATIONS					
No.	Type	Number	Per Cent.	Number	Per Cent.
	Total	19,880	..	26,182	
33	Classified by Age and Sex......	13,620	100	24,144	100
1	Mixed adults	0	0	780	3
0	Adult men	200	1	0	0
3	Adult women	4,460	33	840	3
1	Mixed young people *	700	5	2,176	9
6	Young men	216	2	3,088	13
4	Young women	520	4	1,921	8
3	Mixed boys and girls.........	0	0	7,808	32
8	Boys	3,464	25	4,267	18
7	Girls	1,500	11	3,264	14
0	Mixed children	2,560	19	0	0
	Classified by Function †	6,260		2,038	

* Between 15 and 23 years of age.
† In Pilgrim Church this item is composed largely of bowling alley attendance; in Broadway Church, of the choir.

Only three churches of the twenty-six studied put proportionately greater stress on women's work than does Pilgrim Church; Broadway's women's work is relatively small. On the other hand, the Broadway children's program is strong and dominating. Pilgrim is deficient in group organizations for young children, though its endowed kindergarten makes exceptional provision in that particular direction.

Nearly a third of the total subsidiary program of Pilgrim Church consists of functions not organized by age and sex. Of the attendance at these functions the chorus choir and the bowling alley furnish the major portion. Broadway also has a chorus choir which accounts for 8 per cent. of its subsidiary program.

The departmentalized women's work at Pilgrim Church, combining the usual activities of missionary and parish aid societies, is secondary in numerical strength to a more localized mothers' club which largely reflects the immediate community, and which has had a very strong cultural influence through many years. The traditional form of young people's society work has been abandoned in favor of weekly social gatherings, while expressional interests are centered in the Sunday school. The varied work for boys and girls separately organized consists of groups operated according to the standard programs of Boy Scouts, Camp Fire Girls and the Young Men's Christian Association.

The extensive work for children in Broadway Church includes a junior congregation, with a full organization and set of officers paralleling those of the senior church; week-day work in 'religious education; and a summer Daily Vacation Bible School. Clubs for boys and girls and young men and women, each with a distinctive athletic, social or religious program, are very numerous. Those for boys include a lunch-club to which members come from the neighboring public schools; also scouting groups and various athletic teams. The largest single organization for girls is the Girl Scouts.

Among the churches studied, Broadway stands high in its relative emphasis on organized work for boys and girls and, in general, in the careful grouping of activities according to age and sex. The leadership is exceptional, especially in its ability to utilize group impulse in favor of discipline and constructive interests.

Broadway Church also maintains a small amount of instruction in English for foreign-speaking constituents.

Staff

In both churches the staff is relatively large on account of the breadth and variety of the program. Only two of the twenty-six cases stand higher, ranked according to ratio of hours of paid work to total attendance.

The number and organization of the two staffs are shown comparatively in the following tabulation.

Pilgrim	*Broadway*
Pastor	Pastor
Associate pastor	Assistant pastor (Bohemian congregation)
Director of girls' work and church visitor	Deaconess
Secretary	Secretary
Kindergartner and social worker	Director of boys' work
Kindergarten assistant	Director of girls' work
	Director of social activities (part-time)

In addition to an ordained pastor and his colleague, each church has an inside clerical worker, a pastoral visitor for outside calling, and each has two technical specialists. Broadway goes beyond Pilgrim in having a part-time director of social activities whose work is chiefly that of organizing and coaching dramatic events and pageantry. (Pilgrim Church also makes large use of these methods in the Sunday school and under voluntary leadership.) Both churches have organists and choirmasters giving an unusual proportion of time to the church. In the case of Pilgrim, a studio is provided and private music-lessons offered. Pilgrim also houses a district office of the Visiting Nurse's Association and coöperates closely with the nurses' work, which, however, is no longer under immediate church direction.[1]

The pastor of Pilgrim Church was one of the oldest in point of service in his present position of the pastors of the churches studied, and is backed by an accumulation of influence, both in church and in community, while the pastor of the Broadway Church was new in his position and was just engaged in taking the first tentative steps.

The ordained associates were both ministers of experience, the assistant at Broadway being a native Bohemian with long experience as a teacher of the Slavonic languages.

The majority of the clerical and pastoral workers in subordinate positions were long-time members of the respective communities, with established relations with church life. The specialized workers, on the contrary, were, in the main, technically trained persons from outside of the community.

WORK-TIME AND WORK-CONTENT

The two churches stand in absolute contrast in that, with respect to the total time spent by the staff in pastoral work, Broadway ranks next to the highest in the twenty-six cases, and Pilgrim next to the lowest. The former illustrates the

---

[1] At this point, and in the use of the gymnasium by organizations outside of the church, Pilgrim Church shows the same policy that is much more fully developed in St. John's Protestant Episcopal Church, Detroit: namely, that of expanding its influence through alliances with other constructive forces.

method of house-to-house promotion of religious enterprise, while the latter is a business largely conducted from an office and promoted through printed publicity matter, office conferences and correspondence.

In its total staff work, only one church has a stronger administrative emphasis than Pilgrim. Emphasis on professional work in religious education is also high; clerical work falls slightly below the average; while the relative time spent in the preparation of sermons and the conduct of public worship is small, apparently reflecting the relatively slight stress on public services in the total enterprise.

Although the pastoral emphasis in Broadway is so large, the administrative emphasis is about average. The most underemphasized phase of work here is the clerical.

Both pastors reported a typical work-week much longer than the average. Thus, the pastor at Broadway, with eighty hours to his credit during the sample week, worked more than ten hours for six days out of the seven. The Pilgrim pastor, who worked sixty-six hours, is strongly of the executive type, nearly half of his time being given to administration. The Broadway pastor classifies technically as an executive-pastor, giving something near a third of his time to each of these types of service.

The two ordained associate pastors show even more strongly marked differences. Pilgrim has the most definitely developed example of the executive assistant, about three-fourths of whose time was given to administrative work during the sample week for which records were kept. In addition to responsibility for the Sunday school, he is occupied with publicity and finances, besides generally supervising the week-day program of the church and the conduct of the plant. The Bohemian pastor at Broadway, on the other hand (working more hours per week than any other reported), is engaged almost exclusively in pastoral work, administration in this case being mainly reserved to the general pastor.

Both pastors receive relatively low salaries, but the associate pastor at Pilgrim has one of the highest salaries of the associates' group, reflecting his exceptional administrative responsibility. As already noted in connection with the estimate of annual attendance, Pilgrim's activities are greatly reduced during the summer, and vacations are exceptionally long.

The directors of boys' and girls' work at Broadway work long hours but regularly take a half holiday. They are chiefly concerned with the administration and personal leadership of group activities and athletics.

Even apart from such technical positions as nursing, kindergarten work and the direction of boys' and girls' groups, the paid staff, both at Pilgrim and at Broadway, is charged with a good many kinds of service usually carried by volunteers in more ordinary circumstances. Financial promotion rests very heavily upon the office of Pilgrim, and the Sunday school and the subsidiary activities have an exceptional degree of staff direction in both churches.

Plant

The Pilgrim church building, erected in 1894, is a substantial and stately stone structure of Romanesque architecture cornering on Lincoln Park. It sets well back from the street within grounds pleasantly landscaped. A secondary structure with separate entrance is placed at right angles to the main structure and contains a thoroughly modern gymnasium and bowling alleys. It was erected in 1919.

Broadway Church is also a stone structure erected in 1918 at a cost of about $230,000. It has the simple and churchly lines of modernized ecclesiastical Gothic. The site, though ample, is without distinction.

Pilgrim plant ranks fifth in the twenty-five cases systematically compared on the Interchurch thousand-point score card, scoring 724; Broadway plant ranks eleventh and scores 604. The comparison by major items is shown in Table LXXVIII, on page 362.

As already indicated, Pilgrim excels in the quality of its site. In their structural aspects, the two churches are about equal in rank. Broadway has considerably the more modern service systems. Pilgrim, on the other hand, greatly excels in its church and Sunday-school rooms and community service

TABLE LXXVIII—SUMMARY OF SCORE OF PLANTS

	STANDARD SCORE	PILGRIM			BROADWAY		
		POINTS SCORED	%	RANK IN 25 CASES	POINTS SCORED	%	RANK IN 25 CASES
		No.			No.		
Total	1,000	724	72	5	604	60	11
Site	130	91	70	14	79	61	23
Building or buildings	150	121	81	10	124	83	9
Service systems	160	96	60	9	102	64	7
Church rooms	170	148	87	4	117	69	18
Religious school rooms......	200	149	75	4	123	62	11
Community service rooms...	190	119	63	5	59	31	18

facilities, ranking fourth, among the twenty-five cases studied, on the first two and fifth on the last of these points. Its plant is exceedingly ample for the size of the work. In addition to its spaciousness, the excellence of its detailed provision for a broad social program is high testimony, after thirty-five years, to the unusually far-sighted and skillful planning of those who built it. Broadway Church, on the contrary, though new, is crowded. The structural skimping of space at certain points is very detrimental from the esthetic standpoint. Its auditorium, though small, shows good architectural style and is pleasingly churchly. The Sunday-school facilities are well arranged for a mass Sunday school and afford many small rooms for individual classes, but the departmental rooms characteristic of the plant of a modernly organized Sunday school are lacking. Office space is scanty, and semi-isolated rooms suitable for the work of clubs and groups are not adequately provided.

Finances

The total current budget of Pilgrim Church is about $43,000, with $7,000 additional for benevolences; of Broadway Church about $30,000, with $3,000 additional for benevolences.

Pilgrim Church enjoys an income of nearly $10,000 from

interest on endowments. Broadway is still receiving install-
ments on the purchase price of its old building; so that the net
income of the two from strictly current sources is not far from
equal. Comparing particular sources, Broadway Church gets
49 per cent. of its current support from individual pledges, to
Pilgrim's 37 per cent. The two churches get proportionately
the same from loose collections, the amount being inconsider-
able in both cases. Both get about 15 per cent. of their support from special gifts. Broadway has long enjoyed the advantage of continuous special benefactions from one of the
chief originators of the enterprise, a great manufacturer of
Cleveland. Pilgrim, on the contrary, has had to create a wide
supporting constituency in the community at large, particularly
for the maintenance of its social work. Seventeen per cent. of
Broadway's income comes by way of subsidies from the Methodist denomination. Pilgrim, on the other hand, collects 6 per
cent. of its total resources from fees and dues, and the extraordinary amount of 27 per cent. as the separate income of subsidiary organizations which thus largely find the means for
financing their own programs.

The expenditures of the two churches are summarized in
Table LXXIX, on page 364.

Public Services

In both churches, public services are a relatively small factor
of the program, numerically measured. The average attendance is as follows:

Service	Pilgrim	Broadway
Sunday morning	240 (30 weeks) 90 (16 weeks)	300 (English) 55 (Bohemian)
Sunday evening	200 (10 weeks)	75 (English) 50 (Bohemian)
Prayer meeting	None	None

Instead of the traditional mid-week devotional services,
Pilgrim maintains through the active church season a series of
Wednesday night business, missionary and group gatherings,
preceded by suppers. Different organizations sponsor these
occasions, and the programs are both educational and social.
At Broadway, the Bohemian group maintains a mid-week

TABLE LXXIX—FINANCIAL EXPENDITURES OF THE CHURCHES

ITEM	PILGRIM CHURCH		BROADWAY CHURCH	
	Amount	*Per Cent.*	*Amount*	*Per Cent.*
Grand Total	$41,253	..	$28,451	
Total Current Account	39,358	100	23,101	100
Salaries	10,344	26	9,269	40
General administrative expenses	1,038	3	705	3
Music	3,219	8	3,534	15
General operation and upkeep of property..	13,237	34	5,792	25
Expenses of departments specially budgeted	7,250	18	2,777	12
Publicity	1,228	3	367	2
Ecclesiastical connections	0	0	657	3
Miscellaneous	3,042 *	8	0	0
Investment Account				
On indebtedness or permanent improvement	1,895	..	5,350	

* Including 1924 deficit paid.

devotional meeting and there is Bible study by boys' and girls' groups. Broadway also maintains a junior congregation, holding services Sunday mornings.

The services at Pilgrim Church radiate a cordial atmosphere and are carried on with moderate formality, without particular niceties of detail. A vested choir enrolling 117, with an average attendance of forty-five, embellishes the service with a processional and recessional. The average attendance reported appears to be unusually affected by the size of audiences on special occasions. An attendance of 172 on the day of the field study consisted almost entirely of adults, with twice as many women as men. The characteristic preaching is progressive, bright and even witty, with a strong intellectual and philosophical flavor, coupled with devoutness and a genius for practical application. While distinctly attractive, it does not regularly draw the widely scattered membership in large numbers.

The evening service is maintained only for the ten weeks preceding Lent. It consists of a series of special features, of which a sacred concert by the Oberlin College Glee Club, a religious drama, a moving-picture exhibition, and addresses by imported speakers, are illustrative.

Turning to Broadway Church, one also finds a vested choir and strong emphasis upon music, reflecting the racial tradition of the Bohemian people. The attendance at morning service on the day of the field study was about one hundred, the preponderance of women paralleling that at Pilgrim Church. On the other hand, one-fourth of the congregation consisted of children and adolescents, while almost none attended the Pilgrim service. The preaching revealed the somewhat strongly marked individuality of the preacher. It was vigorous and unconventional, and sometimes a bit slangy in the effort to become colorful. The architectural focus of the Broadway Church is a great panel above the chancel reproducing Da Vinci's "Last Supper" in full size. At the close of each service the auditorium lights are dimmed and this picture is especially illuminated. This brings an effective and unique emotional climax to a service that perhaps impresses the critical observer as somewhat lacking in coherence and unity.

Religious Education

The adult department at Broadway Church is much larger than at Pilgrim. This leaves Pilgrim with relatively stronger emphasis on the children's and adolescents' departments, the high-school group being particularly strong and well taught. The Pilgrim Sunday school is conducted as a thoroughly graded and departmentalized institution for thirty-six weeks of the year, but continues merely on a skeleton basis during the summer. The week-day activities of the young people's social groups and boys' and girls' clubs are theoretically conceived as the expressional aspects of religious education, and are developed under the same leadership. The discussion-group method is in evidence with the older high-school classes, one of which, for example, uses Elliot's *How Jesus Met Life's Problems*.

A large proportion of teachers are drawn from the public schools or are active boys' and girls' workers in other than the religious field. The adult classes have strong separate organizations.

As supplementing the religious education program, and in addition to the character-building values of all the boys' and girls' clubs, the specific religious features of the Christian Citizenship program for boys are specially valued. Pilgrim is also the leading factor in a community Daily Vacation Bible School operating for four weeks in the summer. During the last season this school had seven paid workers and a daily average of 128 pupils, two-fifths of whom were from Catholic homes.

Two-thirds of the members of the Pilgrim Sunday school come from families not otherwise identified with the church, and more than half bear names that are distinctly foreign in origin.

In addition to the junior church, Broadway has a week-day school of religious education for children of seven to fourteen years of age operating under the church staff, with an average weekly attendance of seventy. Its Wednesday-night boys' club consists of a group specially selected for training in responsible religious leadership. While formally departmentalized, the Sunday school itself, as actually operated, is distinguished by its very long general exercises. Music is especially featured. There is a paid orchestra in addition to the church organ which can be played in the assembly-room as well as in the auditorium by means of a second console. Extended talks are frequently made by the superintendent and imported speakers. The general tone of the Sunday school is thus that of a mass gathering enjoying an attractive and stirring program that is characterized by informal instruction from the rostrum.

A summary of enrollment and attendance of the two schools follows:

	Pilgrim	Broadway
Grand total	795	1,003
Pupils (attending departments)	581	826
Officers	7	17
Teachers	37	45
Per cent. of average attendance to enrollment of attending departments	43	69

Current Church Life

The outstanding trait of both churches is their numerous events and activities involving the participation of large numbers of adherents, generally in rather small groups. Pilgrim, for example, reports sixty-seven weddings, fifty-nine funerals, and 963 calls made by the staff in a recent year. The week-day activities organized under the Pilgrim Institute include, in addition to the various clubs and classes, the maintenance of a game and billiard room and a bowling-alley, besides the gymnasium. These facilities are assigned to various church groups on specified days, but, for about two-thirds of the time, the gymnasium is rented to outside clubs. This is done partly on grounds of financial economy, but partly to give it wider community usefulness than has been found possible through exclusive operation under the church's own auspices. Under the present policy, a large element in patronage of the bowling-alley has come to consist of groups from a Catholic social center located on the opposite side of the Park.

The meetings of the Pilgrim Women, the conventional women's organization representing the tradition of the older constituency, are chiefly held by neighborhood groups in widely separated districts of the city. From three to six such meetings per week are announced during the active church season.

The Institute provides an annual series of community entertainments which consist chiefly of musical and dramatic events. The church auditorium is very generally used for community purposes, being the largest gathering-place available. The commencements of the adjoining public schools are regularly held here.

The kindergarten, with an average attendance of fifty children from fourteen nationalities, goes on during the school-year, and the nurse, who has offices in the church but does not work under formal church direction, makes about 300 calls monthly on an average of eighty to one hundred patients. Pilgrim Church has not developed separate facilities for the conduct of summer camps, preferring to send its young people on summer outings directed by other social agencies, or to the leadership training courses conducted in the state summer assembly of its denomination.

The recurrent life of Broadway Church is equally characterized by numerous events, but with somewhat greater stress upon seasonal celebrations, apparently reflecting a continental religious tradition. Seven dramatic events and six operettas or concerts were staged in the year preceding the study. The services of a member of the staff who is a part-time worker, in addition to the services of the choirmaster, were available for the leadership of these interests. Among group organizations, a junior choir and a young women's musical club are included. The Daily Vacation Bible School is notable in that the boys' classes are conducted by boys of the leadership training group. Extensive facilities for boys' and girls' summer camps are also maintained. All this means that in both churches the social life of many groups centers in the church and is given all-around expression through physical and cultural avenues, as well as in formally religious ones.

Gains and Losses

The two churches show quite similar phenomena as a result of their efforts to win and conserve church-membership. Sources of accessions for the year preceding the study are shown comparatively in the following tabulation:

Accessions	Pilgrim	Broadway
Total	112	119
By letter	24	9
From same denomination	5	5
From other denominations	19	4
On confession of faith	88	110
Previously associated with the church more than 1 year	78	98
Previously associated with the church less than 1 year	10	12

In the case of Pilgrim Church, only four of the members received during the year, two of whom were members of the paid staff, were newcomers in the community; and, in the case of Broadway Church, only fifteen out of 119. Harmonizing with this showing is the relatively small proportion that either church receives by transfers from other churches. Neither community is receiving much new population immediately available to either church, and the throng of newcomers with church letters that so largely accounts for the growth of central churches is almost entirely lacking. This requires both churches to create an adherent body from which it may receive members. Seventy-eight out of eighty-eight, in the case of Pilgrim Church, and ninety-eight out of 119, in the case of Broadway, had had previous relations to the church for more than a year, in both cases chiefly through the Sunday school. Of new members not thus previously attached, a few came by marriage and a few came with their children when the latter were old enough to be united with the church. There was also an occasional non-Protestant who came as the result of an intellectual revolt against his previous faith.

In connection with the limited sample of those coming by letter, it is noteworthy that Pilgrim Church receives many more from other denominations than from its own, and Broadway Church almost as many. Also, in dismissing members by letters, both churches find a considerable proportion not going to the same denomination. Nearly half of those dismissed by Pilgrim Church within the year preceding the study, and all of those dismissed from Broadway Church, took transfers to other churches in Cleveland or immediate suburbs. Pilgrim's losses were chiefly to the newer and wealthier suburbs, and Broadway's to the more desirable middle-class neighborhood lying two or three miles southeast of the church. These rather pronounced shiftings of church allegiance within the city constitute a challenge to the churches' future in both cases.

Relations to Denomination and Social Agencies

Broadway Church was for a long time a mission of the Methodist denomination, and is now subsidized by the Methodist national extension boards in important parts of its social work. Pilgrim Church, on the contrary, was, and continues to be, a numerically strong independent church which has been a center of denominational influence and a source of leadership and original experimentation in social work in Cleveland. The one church represents the evolution into greater responsibility of an immigrant group; the other the original cultural advantage and prestige of the New England stock which first dominated the ideals and institutions of the Western Reserve.

Pilgrim Church therefore naturally shows far more influential and extensive relationship with the constructive forces of the community. It is represented on the executive boards and staffs of religious and social agencies by a total of forty-nine members, including sixteen in denominational organizations, thirteen in civic movements, seven in social welfare institutions, nine in health agencies and hospitals, and one in a corrective agency. It also includes as members the surprising number of sixty-three educators, most of them teachers in public schools.

Broadway Church has three official delegates to Methodist denominational organizations of the community, a representative in the Church Federation, and six members identified with various social welfare movements and agencies.

Summary and Conclusions

Pilgrim Congregational and Broadway Methodist Episcopal Churches evolved as geographical neighbors within well-marked geographical districts of Cleveland, showing interesting contrasts of history.

Both have come to be churches of the second generation of foreigners in the United States; churches with unusually broad programs in which directed group-activity—social, athletic, dramatic and musical—has been developed to reflect the all-around interests of all ages and sexes. In addition, Pilgrim Church maintains an endowed kindergarten, and houses and fosters the work of a visiting nurse.

In both churches, the leadership of the work devolves, to an unusual degree, upon a paid staff whose technical functions go far beyond the traditional ones of the religious ministry.

Both churches have to be supported through special resources, Pilgrim by endowment and the specialization of the machinery of financial appeal to remote supporters; Broadway by denominational subsidies and the large gifts of a local individual benefactor.

Both churches have shown considerable institutional growth

in recent years under their present types of program and policy.

Both churches are characterized by a high proportion of adolescents in the adherent body. Beyond this their age-tendencies contrast, Pilgrim having proportionately many adults, and Broadway many children.

Both churches show that their enterprise is not fully indigenous to the community, in that they get most of their adherents out of family groups not otherwise connected with them. Sixty per cent. of the entire following of Pilgrim Church, and about half that of Broadway, consist of detached individuals not coming from adherent families.

Both churches show a strong excess of women adherents in the adult groups. Women also dominate the public services.

Both churches still have their parishes to a considerable extent localized; but both are rapidly becoming scattered, Pilgrim showing secondary aggregations of members living in the newer suburbs more than five miles away, and Broadway a similar aggregation of members in a middle-class neighborhood two or three miles southeast of the church.

Corresponding to the age-composition of the constituency, the subsidiary program of Pilgrim Church is strongest with adult women, while that of Broadway notably emphasizes work for boys and girls. Broadway has many more subsidiary organizations, but Pilgrim greatly increases its community influence by extending the use of its facilities to outside groups. The two churches show striking contrasts in the types of work emphasized by the paid staffs. Broadway greatly excels in the amount of pastoral work, while Pilgrim Church runs to administration, the efficient control of the enterprise through a central office, and the effective investment of effort in publicity.

Broadway's Sunday school represents a wider age-range than that of Pilgrim. Both have strong adolescent Sunday-school groups. Pilgrim's Sunday school is a technically modern organization, while that of Broadway is largely conducted as a mass assembly. Both supplement religious education with Daily Vacation Bible Schools and with group-work stressing character-building and leadership training programs.

Neither church maintains the old-fashioned prayer meeting. Both churches strongly stress music and dramatics as cultural activities and as means of expressing Christian truth and feeling.

Both churches have to educate the material for their own new membership, since there are few newcomers to the community, and they not of the sort that brings church letters. Both churches register a considerable leakage of membership to churches in other parts of the city in connection with the shifting of population.

Pilgrim Church represents and maintains a very influential civic and social tradition, and has a large place of leadership in social and civic movements of the community. Broadway Church is a church of a former immigrant group just emerging into local civic responsibility and only beginning to have a place in the general counsels of the religious and social forces. On the other hand, its community, because it is more homogeneous, is more basically related to it by instinctive feeling and sympathy. Pilgrim Church stands a little outside of the conflicting inner forces of the polyglot community with which it is physically associated.

Both churches will have to look to their future policies. Pilgrim may see the gradual relaxing of the rather tenuous ties that bind its remoter adherents to it. Broadway faces the prospect of the farther removal of many of its most properous constituents and a further change in the character of the neighborhood. It has yet to prove whether it can continue to function as more than a local church and effectively hold and serve its dispersing constituency.

Pilgrim Church, with its longer history, more conscious and theoretical formulation of the duty of social adaptation, its wider experience, and as yet larger resources, bids fair to be able to meet any circumstance that its future may bring forth and to continue to serve effectively, even if not in the same ways as in the past, or as at present. The challenge before Broadway Church is whether an institution, the surprising achievement of an immigrant group, now essentially Americanized, can maintain sufficient plasticity to adjust itself to shifting conditions, and can itself serve new situations and people as effectively as it served others in the past.

Case XV

THE CITY PARISH, METHODIST EPISCOPAL, LOS ANGELES, CALIF.

(Church of All Nations; Grace; East 38th Street; Elysian Gardens; Epworth; Brooklyn Heights)

The twenty-six case studies of significant city churches, in which the six churches associated in the City Parish are treated as one case, illustrate as a group the upper range of city-church development measured by scope and variety of program.

This is not true of the several churches composing the City Parish. Judged individually, they include the smallest cases studied.[1] But with reference to a list of sixty current organizations, activities and practices of city churches, the total program of the combined enterprise ranks third from largest among the twenty-six cases studied. In total annual attendance upon all regular organizations and continuous activities, it also ranks third from largest.

The City Parish is a result of rather prolonged experience in the conscious and deliberate adjustment of church programs and administration to urban situations. It is essentially a modern adaptation of the primitive Methodist circuit system to the religious strategy of a modern city. Five of the six churches associated in it are those of white Americans whose fortunes have suffered radically as the result of successive tidal movements of foreign population. The attempt of the City Parish has been, first, to conserve these endangered churches institutionally; and, second, to make them more serviceable in spite of their adversities, primarily by means of common administrative leadership and partially common staff and system of finance. This experiment is unquestionably unique from the standpoint of urban adaptation.

---

[1] There are far more city churches of this sort than there are of the sort which the case studies as a group represent.

Administratively, the City Parish illustrates the better possibilities of a strong ecclesiastical system in coping with urban change. The plan of putting first-class leadership behind the group of problem churches was inaugurated in 1924. The executive pastorate was assigned to Rev. G. Bromley Oxnam, secretary of the Los Angeles Missionary and Church Extension Society, who had been pastor of the Church of All Nations as well for seven years. No one assumes that the experiment has necessarily reached its final form. It contains all the interest and significance of a real adventure.

History

The development of Los Angeles as a whole is so recent that no long history lies behind any of the six churches. The present Church of All Nations is a successor of a series of missionary enterprises in a district that had become occupied by a middle-class or poorer population even before its transformation into Los Angeles' chief polyglot center. Grace Church, on the other hand, up to within fifteen years ago, was one of the stronger and more influential Methodist churches of the city, having over 800 members. The other churches were never strong—a fact which, of course, made it all the more inevitable that radically adverse conditions should pull their prospects down almost to the vanishing point. The exception is the Elysian Gardens Church, which was established so recently as 1917, and which has enjoyed the advantage of rapid growth in an isolated section where it has an exclusive field.[2]

The study carefully traced the recent course of the six churches as measured by membership and Sunday-school statistics.

Their general downward trend for a decade on a statistical showing marks the group as a whole as justifying the designation "problem churches." They are bound together (except Elysian Gardens), first, by relative propinquity within the deteriorating central area of the city, and, second, by being subject to the same adverse forces. There are no other Metho-

---

[2] Since the study was made, the Elysian Gardens Church has been detached from the City Parish. It manifestly represents a different type of urban situation.

dist churches for white Americans within the area which these six occupy. The unity of the field is, however, administrative rather than strictly geographical; and the six churches have not been associated long enough to have evolved any marked unity of sentiment.

In the following study, therefore, the churches of the City Parish are treated as separate entities where their distinct characteristics are determinative; they are treated as a unit in matters in which their unified functioning is most significant.

I. MAJOR ASPECTS OF THE CHURCH

Members and Constituents

From the standpoint of the church as a social group, it is clearly necessary to study the churches of the City Parish individually, since, although under common administration, they have distinct constituencies.

FAMILY AND NON-FAMILY CONSTITUENTS

The churches differ greatly in the proportion of their adherents belonging to constituent families (a constituent family being one that has one or more adults included in the enrolled constituency), in contrast with those detached constituents from families not otherwise related to the church. The number who adhere in each of these ways is shown below for each of the five reporting churches.

Type of Adherence	Grace	Brooklyn Heights	East 38th Street	Epworth	Elysian Gardens
Family Group	554	40	98	53	287
Individual	163	78	87	158	157

As between these two classes, Grace Church shows something like the ratio of a traditional family church. Elysian Gardens, located in the new residential area, also has a strong preponderance of constituent families, though with a larger minority of detached individuals. With East 38th Street, the proportions of the two groups are not far from equal, while Brooklyn Heights has a strong preponderance, and Epworth a very strong preponderance, of detached individuals in its constituency. The same thing is known to be true of the Church of All Nations.[3] These variations show how far from conformity a group of related churches may be in fundamental group structure.

SEX

The ratio of male to female in the constituencies of the churches also reveals extraordinary variation which is worthy of note in detail. The percentage of all constituents who are male is as follows: Epworth, 62; Grace, 47; Elysian Gardens, 47; Brooklyn Heights, 46; East 38th Street, 37. The median per cent. of males in the cases of twenty-nine churches separately studied is about 43, so that four out of the five reporting churches of the City Parish show decidedly more than the average masculine tendency. No church of the entire group studied has so many males relative to females as Epworth; but, on the contrary, no church has so few as East 38th Street.

AGE

The churches of the City Parish show more agreement as to age-distribution. Among the twenty-nine cases studied on this point, they furnish the four having the smallest percentage of adults and the highest percentage of children in their constituency. These are:

CHURCH	PER CENT.	
	Adults	*Children*
Epworth	24	65
Brooklyn Heights	33	57
Elysian Gardens	35	55
East 38th Street	45	45

Grace Church also has more than an average proportion of children.

On the same basis of calculation, the population of the city of

---

[3] The absence of the Church of All Nations from these comparisons detracts seriously from the statistical completeness of the study. This church was not able to furnish membership and constituency data comparable with that secured from the other five, for the reason that its religious work was at a very low ebb pending the completion of its new plant. See pp. 402, 405 and 412.

Los Angeles is 79 per cent. adult, and 14 per cent. children. This shows how far the constituencies of the churches are from being cross sections of the population.[4]

Bringing together the factors of family relationship, age and sex in the distribution of constituents, the characteristics of the five churches relative to the twenty-nine cases are as follows:

Church	Per Cent. of Constituents Belonging to Family Groups	Per Cent. Male	Per Cent. Children
Grace	Above average	Above average	Above average
Epworth	Smallest	Largest	Largest
Brooklyn Heights ...	Next to smallest	Above average	Next to largest
East 38th Street.....	Median	Smallest	Large
Elysian Gardens	Large	Above average	Third from largest

The most influential factor explaining the tendency of all of these churches to have an excess of children, and of four of them to show an excess of males, is the fact that the City Parish has put on a strong program for children, particularly for boys. The ability of a single aspect of the work to produce such an extreme distortion in the fundamental balance of age and sex proportions shows how weak and unstable these churches are to start with.[5]

MANNER AND DEGREE OF ADHERENCE

How are the constituents of the City Parish related to their respective churches?

The results of data on this point are summarized by per cent. distribution of constituents according to ways of adherence in Table LXXX.

Every one is familiar with that large group of church people who belong to the church and presumably attend worship but who are attached to no other of the church's organizations or activities. In the case of Grace Church, this group constitutes 36 per cent. of the total constituency, which is very

---

[4] In making the above calculation, a large number of minors of unspecified age reported by Elysian Gardens were distributed in the ratio of adolescents to children among minors whose age was known.

[5] Though the statistical data are lacking, it is clear from observation that the Church of All Nations shares the above general characteristics of the group.

TABLE LXXX—ENROLLED CONSTITUENTS RELATED TO
THE CHURCHES IN SPECIFIED WAYS

MEMBER OF	CHURCHES				
	Grace	Brooklyn Heights	East 38th Street	Elysian Gardens	Epworth
	Per Cent.	Per Cent.	Per Cent.	Per Cent.	Per Cent.
Church only	36	15	7	5	5
Church and Sunday school	9	3	7	4	1
Church, Sunday school and subsidiaries	11	9	17	10	15
Church and subsidiaries	10	6	2	2	2
Sunday school only	29	20	53	55	11
Subsidiaries only	3	17	3	18	49
Sunday school and subsidiaries	2	30	11	6	17

close to the median of all cases. The other churches of the City
Parish have few adherents who are church-members only, and
generally very few.[6] Two of them, however (East 38th Street
and Elysian Gardens), have more than half of their total constituencies in the Sunday school only. No other church studied
has anything like this extreme situation. Epworth Church, on
the contrary, has nearly half of its constituents in subsidiaries
(boys' and girls' clubs) only. Only one other church at all
parallels this showing. In spite of the large group of adherents
with only a single connection, all five churches have more, and
two of the five have many more, than the median per cent. of
highly connected adherents; that is, those belonging to church,
Sunday school and subsidiaries, all three. This condition reflects the high degree of organized activity which the City
Parish has brought into its relatively small churches.[7]

---

[6] Other studies have shown that it is characteristic of the very small church
to tie its central membership to it in numerous ways. It has to do this to find
enough people to operate any semblance of a typical church. Churches no larger
than most of those in the City Parish would be likely to show few "members
only," irrespective of the special programs which they have put on under City
Parish incentive. See Douglass, *The Springfield Church Survey*, p. 223.

[7] It should be noted that the proportion of adherents who belong to subsidiaries
only would be still more increased if the separately organized clubs and playground activities at Hallenbeck Center (attached to Grace Church), and the clinic,
library and similar activities at the Church of All Nations, were included in the
data. But because these functions are separately financed by the Community
Chest, and their participants but loosely related to church life, it seemed more
reasonable not to include them statistically in discussion of the churches as social
groups.

SUMMARY

There are striking departures from the average in the relation of adherents to the churches of the City Parish. If the average of the total group studied is taken provisionally as a sort of norm, most of the churches of the City Parish are highly erratic. As a matter of fact, their constituencies consist largely of children who are not members of church families. Except in the case of Grace Church, the membership of the Sunday school is much larger than that of the church, and the subsidiary membership equals or exceeds that of the church. The core of a traditional church enterprise, on the contrary, is an adult group bound together first of all in a religious fellowship. In the City Parish, this core is unusually small. Being so small, many of its members have to be exceptionally active and assume many-sided responsibilities. Again, the churches have, in considerable measure, brought detached members of non-church families into more than usual intimacy of relation, as indicated by a high proportion of overlapping memberships.

The Present Environment

Sharply rising mountains and deep valleys force even the most enterprising and ingenuous of modern cities to submit to a pattern essentially determined by nature. These topographical features have been especially important in the distribution of the population of Los Angeles.

The original settlement of the city was on the edge of the shallow valley of the Los Angeles River surrounding the old Spanish Plaza. From this focus successive waves of settlement have spread out in all directions. The neighborhood of the Plaza has been the area of original settlement for each newly migrating race that has pressed in to swell the population. From this point, group after group of foreigners in turn has been pushed outward by the processes of city growth, seeping through passes between the hills and along paths originally determined by topography, until the entire central area of the city has been remade.

The churches associated in the City Parish, with one exception, have been located in the way of such foreign migrations starting from this focal center.

If one stands on the steps of the old Catholic Church facing the Plaza, and describes in the simplest environmental terms the surrounding area, one will have to record something like the following: A virtually level area stretches for about half a mile to the valley of the Los Angeles River. The course of the river is generally north and south. The major portion of the city lies on the west bank. Both banks are occupied by railroads.

The first mile to the west of the Plaza is solidly occupied by the central business section of the city, together with the older apartment-house district which occupies the higher ground. Beyond, in the second and third miles, lies the older area of desirable residences.

In the northern sector, topographical factors govern. The heart of this sector is unimproved mountain land largely included in a park reservation. Around this elevation, middle-class and better residences have swept to the northwest, while industry and railroad-yards occupy the river valley to the northeast. This leaves a sector nearly a mile deep directly north of the Plaza, which is occupied by foreign populations.

To the south, within a mile of the Plaza, lives the main conglomerate population of Los Angeles, including most of the Orientals. This population is dispersed through the area cut in two by the river valley and primarily given to wholesaling, light industry, and railroad-yards.

In the second and third mile zones to the east is an old residential area of American residents, once the second most desirable of the city. It has now been penetrated along the major axes by foreign populations that have finally diffused widely toward the eastern edge of the city.

Directly south of the Plaza, along the river, lies the largest single industrial area of Los Angeles, which broadens as it gets farther from the center. Southward and parallel to this area, another main stream of foreign expansion has gone, and associated with it the chief Negro movement of the city.

Turning now to the specific environments of the churches, the Church of All Nations is found near the heart of the polyglot area whose people occupy the nooks and crannies of a wholesale, railway and industrial section, with crowded homes and tributary business streets. Grace and Brooklyn Heights churches are in the direct path of the main Jewish movement. East 38th Street Church is directly in line with, and still somewhat beyond, the southward thrust of the Negro and Jewish development, while Epworth Church is between the second main-line of Jewish expansion toward the west and of Italian expansion toward the northwest. The foreign community most immediately in the neighborhood of this church is, however, Jugo-Slavic. Of the six churches, only Elysian Gardens, located more than three miles to the north, occupies an exclusively American district, which is rapidly building up with the homes of an industrial population now that the flood-control of the river has been assured.

The vicinity of Epworth Church includes the most congested area of those compared, because it includes the apartment-house district. This, however, does not greatly affect the constituency of the church. Los Angeles is characteristically a bungalow city, the single-family home being generally available even to the very poor. The proportion of rented homes relative to those owned by the occupants is highest in the vicinity of the Church of All Nations and Epworth Church, while in the vicinity of Grace and Epworth Churches nearly half of the population lives in occupant-owned homes.

Such is the variety of circumstances that have conspired to diminish the prospects of American churches of the area, and to drive the group under discussion into the administrative unity of the City Parish.

SUMMARY OF ENVIRONMENTAL DATA

Summarizing the relevant environmental data, the following points are outstanding: (1) The foreign populations of Los Angeles nearly all made their original settlements at a common core; and their later paths of radial expansion were determined by the topography of the city. (2) The absolute proportion of the foreign-born in the total population is not high compared with that found in other American cities of the same size as Los Angeles. (3) The foreign-born (and Negro) populations do not live, in the main, under conditions of excessive congestion. (4) They are, however, mostly associated with industrial areas. (5) The foreign-born of Los Angeles, however, represent more, and more widely sundered, cultures and racial conditions than those of most cities, so that the difficulty of uniting the population in normal community life is unusually great. (6) Such abnormal conditions as excessive tuberculosis mortality and juvenile delinquency are known to be closely related to the alien populations affecting the churches of the City Parish. (7) Taken together, these phenomena are extensive and acute enough seriously to threaten the life of these relatively weak churches of white Americans.

Looking to the future, it nevertheless appears likely, on the whole, that white population of the sort open to Protestant work, will remain a slender majority, or at least a considerable minority in nearly all of the areas with which the churches are closely associated; and that this population will not be permanently displaced. It will be reënforced by young people of foreign antecedents to whom the churches may increasingly minister. Prospective environmental changes do not therefore put any fatal limitations upon the future of the City Parish, but rather demand continued special provision for white Protestant minorities parallel with Protestant provision for foreign-born people and Negroes in special churches of their own.

The Parish

Within the environmental setting thus revealed, how far do the several churches draw adherents, and do they draw equally from all directions?

GRACE CHURCH PARISH

Disregarding twenty-six persons whose addresses were not recorded, 60 per cent. of all constituents of Grace Church are found to be living within half a mile of it and 39 per cent. more within a mile, while only 1 per cent. live beyond a mile. This constitutes an extraordinarily compact parish, reflecting a church very closely identified with what has been historically a distinct section of the city. The distribution of constituents shows that they exhibit little tendency to move back into the central part of the city. They tend rather to diffuse into the southeastern suburbs—following still farther out the original movement of population away from the center.

The distribution of constituents from constituent families and of detached individuals is rather different. Many more detached individuals are drawn from the first half-mile, and relatively more families from the second half-mile. In other words, adherent families are less localized than detached adherents.

The constituency lives 28 per cent. to the north and 72 per cent. to the south. It is most numerous toward the southeast in the direction of the arterial streets and major population movement. The most heavily occupied half-mile-zone is, however, to the southwest. Constituents in this direction are almost absent in the second half-mile. Individual adherents are distributed somewhat more evenly about the church than constituent families.

This distribution of constituents in the parish corresponds with the utmost precision to what has been discovered about its physical structure and social character. The parish is cut off on the north by the main line of Jewish migration from the original center of the city along the Brooklyn Street axis. It is strongest in the first half-mile to the southwest, because of the higher-grade population around Hallenbeck Park—the finest residential area within reach of the church. But it almost entirely fades out in this direction in the second half-mile because of the river bed, the industries, and the solidly Mexican and Russian colonies that occupy the valley. The area next in

importance for the number of constituents is that of the second
half-mile to the southeast, including the Euclid Heights district
—which is next to the best in economic rank.   Constituent
families show extreme avoidance of districts of foreign occupancy and extreme affinity for the more desirable residential
areas.   Detached individuals are drawn more freely from all
quarters.

BROOKLYN HEIGHTS PARISH

Brooklyn Heights Church is located slightly more than half
a mile east of Grace Church, so that the parishes overlap.   The
entire constituency of this church lives within a mile, and 81
per cent. within half a mile.   To the northwest, the deep valley
occupied by the Interurban lines limits the parish on that side
to less than a half-mile; and the continuation of the valley, as
well as the broken and undeveloped condition of the district,
keeps the parish from extending any greater distance to the
northeast.   Within the second mile to the southwest, is Grace
Church, which is so strong that the Brooklyn Church gets no
adherents from this quarter.   This leaves the only real opening
to the southeast in the direction of the major eastward growth
of the city.   In this direction 42 per cent. of its constituents are
located, fourteen living in the second half-mile.   With this
exception, the great majority of the adherents of this little
church are bunched closely about it.

EPWORTH CHURCH PARISH

Sixty-five per cent. of all adherents of this church live within
a half-mile of it, and 80 per cent. within a mile.   This area is
exceedingly complex structurally.   The lines of dispersal of
the more scattered membership are toward the northwest in the
direction of the major tendency of city growth and along the
arterial streets.   Fifty per cent. of the constituency live in this
direction, in which the development is the most desirable and
there are the fewest obstructions.   To the northeast, within a
half-mile, the parish is abruptly ended by a deep ravine un-
crossed by streets.   To the southeast, the industrial and central

business districts are increasingly surrounded by high-grade apartment-houses. But these do not yield a population of the sort available to a feeble Protestant church. To the southwest, the topography is broken, and the arterial streets converging in the business center run at right angles to the paths of churchgoing. They thus constitute additional barriers to be crossed, as well as a strong invitation to go in other directions than toward the church. There is also the Jewish colony along Temple Street in this direction. All this results in a parish that is strictly limited to the east by topography and by the occupancy of the area by industry and business; that is obstructed to the southwest, but that is open to the northwest and consequently showing marked elongation in this direction.

The detached individuals, who constitute three-fourths of the constituency, are more widely scattered than the constituent families, and show even greater tendency to live to the northwest.

EAST 38TH STREET CHURCH PARISH

Seventy-nine per cent. of all adherents live within a half-mile of the church, and 89 per cent. within one mile. To the northwest, the parish is held within the limits of a half-mile by heavy Negro and foreign populations; and railroads and a vast industrial district with a less desirable type of housing fix a half-mile limit on the east also. This leaves only the southwest as the direction of easy expansion. Accordingly, 55 per cent. of the constituency is found in this direction, where it is elongated to the extent of having 10 per cent. of the constituency in the third half-mile and 4 per cent. in the second mile. Family constituents are more widely scattered than individuals.

ELYSIAN GARDENS PARISH

The bend of the Los Angeles River, in which the Elysian Gardens community is located, and the sharp elevation to the south and west (occupied by a wealthier type of population) limit the parish of this church to a semicircular area. All but 3 per cent. of the constituents live within one-half-mile, and only

11 per cent. live south and west of the church. The church has the field to itself, but is narrowly limited by topography and social differences within the adjacent area.

CHURCH OF ALL NATIONS PARISH

A surprising aspect of this parish situation is that 60 per cent. of the church members proper live over two miles from the church, entirely beyond the zone of foreign colonization or acute pressure from foreign migration, and that 13 per cent. live in the suburbs. This represents a virtual eviction from the neighborhood of the church of the very type of people for whom the church has been able to do most. Just in proportion as its adherents have acquired progressive ideals and got a start in life, they have moved out of the congested center. The migration has been in all directions, but chiefly into the great middle-class district occupying the southwest section of the city. This movement has left only 24 per cent. of the members living within a half-mile of the church.

The social work of the church, on the contrary, is very strongly localized. The addresses of 151 members of boys' and girls' clubs fall almost entirely within a half-mile of the church, the great majority living in a small area between Fifth and Ninth Streets, particularly south of the church. This is the area intensively served by the playground, library and milk distribution. The service area of the clinic is doubtless larger, but no distribution was made of the 8,000 names on this record.

Non-geographical considerations enter into the work of the Hallenbeck Community Center attached to Grace Church. The clubs organized by this center were, however, not reported as part of the Grace Church constituency. While in considerable measure localized, they include clubs of industrial workers living in all parts of the city who make regular use of the facilities but are not otherwise related to the locality.

SUMMARY OF PARISH DATA

With the exception of the Church of All Nations, the churches of the City Parish have very compact parishes. Constituent families tend to be more widely dispersed than individual adherents are.

But none of the parishes is symmetrical. The general drift of distribution of constituents is away from the center of the city and beyond the churches in the direction that the city is growing in any particular sector. Besides this general drift, the locations of the constituents of Grace, East 38th Street, and Epworth churches, reflect social discrimination also, as well as the effects of physical barriers, natural or artificial. This discrimination is instinctive rather than deliberate; but it is clear that these churches are identified disproportionately with the better residential areas within their reach, and that they instinctively avoid near-by foreign populations. Whether their adherents originally lived in the better neighborhoods where they are now found, or whether they moved there subsequent to becoming connected with the church, is not known.

The difficult topography of Los Angeles makes it hard for most churches to find locations where their parishes will not be constricted by physical barriers. In the case of the churches of the City Parish, this, added to the social complexity of the areas occupied, makes any considerable future enlargement of service areas doubtful. Where topography does not figure, permanent barriers, like solid sections of business or industry, impose rather narrow limitations. The population within the parishes will generally grow denser everywhere, except perhaps around the Church of All Nations.

II. AGENCIES, RESOURCES AND METHODS

Organizations and Stated Activities

A careful estimate of attendance on all organized or regular activities in the six churches of the City Parish gives a total of 167,629 for the year. Thus measured, their collective work is one of the largest church enterprises included in the case studies. And it is proper, in this aspect, to treat the total work as a unit, since it is under a unified program and is administered by a staff many of whose members function in all six churches.

About 42 per cent. of this total attendance occurs on Sunday, and 58 per cent. on week days. This ratio marks the wide departure of the City Parish from the average, and establishes its character as a "seven-day-per-week" enterprise. Only one case excels the City Parish on this point.

The estimated attendance is divided as shown in Table LXXXI.

TABLE LXXXI—ESTIMATED ANNUAL ATTENDANCE ON SPECIFIED OCCASIONS AT CITY PARISH AND AT 26 CHURCHES

	ATTENDANCE			
	CITY PARISH		26 CHURCHES	
			Approx. Median	Range of Variation
OCCASION	Number	Per Cent.	Per Cent.	Per Cent.
Total *	167,629	100		
Formal religious services (Sunday and week day)	40,920	24	51	15–75
Sunday school	32,344	19	24	9–38
All other stated activities	94,365 †	57	22	9–51

* Sunday, 42 per cent.; week day, 58 per cent.
† Includes meetings of church officers and committees.

Formal religious services constitute less than half as large a fraction of the total program as with the average church studied. Sunday-school attendance is appreciably below the average. But the City Parish exceeds all but one of the churches studied in relative attendance upon subsidiary activities and organizations.

Attendance on these "all other stated activities" is divided among the groups organized by age and sex as shown in Table LXXXII, page 389.

Among activities classified by function rather than by age and sex of members, the clinic at the Church of All Nations handled over 8,000 calls during the year previous to the report, and the relief department had 150 cases. The library circulated 109 books per month, and the milk station supplied seventy-eight families per month.

Subtracting the activities classified by function, an estimated annual attendance of 75,104 on age- and sex-organizations is large, with a per cent. distribution as follows:

	Per Cent.
Men and boys	35
Women and girls	17
Mixed sex organizations	48

The largest single block of work is that for boys, consisting primarily of Boy Scout organizations and boys' clubs in all the churches. Under mixed activities for boys and girls, which

TABLE LXXXII—ESTIMATED ANNUAL ATTENDANCE ON SUBSIDIARY ORGANIZATIONS AND STATED ACTIVITIES

No.	ORGANIZATIONS Type	ATTENDANCE Number	Per Cent.
	Total	92,949	
19	Classified by Age and Sex...............	75,104	100
1	Mixed adults	3,120	4
1	Adult men	900	1
4	Adult women	2,328	3
1	Mixed young people *	2,236	3
1	Young men	6,000	8
1	Young women	720	1
3	Mixed boys and girls	17,784	24
3	Boys	19,812	26
2	Girls	9,620	13
2	Mixed children	12,584	17
	Classified by Function	17,845	

* Between 15 and 23 years of age.

rank second in attendance, are classified the playgrounds at the Church of All Nations and Hallenbeck Social Center, although in general they are used by the two sexes at different times. Children's playgrounds and handcraft work at the Church of All Nations in connection with religious instruction provide the activities for children in mixed groups. There are organizations for girls in all the churches, Camp Fire Girls and Blue Birds being preferred. This type of work accounts for 13 per cent. of the subsidiary age- and sex-program.

Organizations for young men furnish but 8 per cent. of the total attendance on subsidiary activities. Only at the Church of All Nations and Hallenbeck Social Center are there such organizations; and these places also are the only ones that have fully organized work for young women. Mixed organizations for young people take the place of separate organizations with three of the smaller churches. There are, however, Epworth Leagues without a fully developed week-day program.

Organizations for adult women, which constitute but 3 per cent. of the total subsidiary program, follow the conventional church pattern, but occur in but four of the six churches: namely, Grace, East 38th Street, Epworth and Elysian Gardens. These variations tend to show that, in spite of the common leadership and largely interchangeable staff, the elements of the community service program are not equally distributed among the associated churches, partly because facilities are very unequal. Compared with the ordinary city church of the size of these included in the City Parish, however, the weaker ones have an infinitely broader program than would otherwise be possible.

The organization for adult men, constituting but 1 per cent. of the subsidiary program, is a joint brotherhood of ninety-seven members representing all six churches. This organization has been largely relied upon to create a community spirit which should reënforce the administrative unity into which the churches have been brought.

Staff

The composition, characteristics, and parish distribution of the churches of the City Parish were reported separately. Their programs, on the contrary, were presented as a unit. The study now turns to the staff, which is the agency that actually brings the churches into such unity as they possess.

This agency is itself partly general and partly local. That is to say, some of its members represent the unity of the work, others rather the separate interests and activities of the several churches or of localized departments.

During the year of the survey, the staff consisted of twenty-three workers, eight of whom gave part-time services, while one was seasonally employed. They were a pastor, assisted by five general assistants working interchangeably with all the churches, and four assistant pastors attached primarily to separate churches.[8]   Each of these pastors was also assigned certain general or technical functions in behalf of the entire City Parish.   Thirteen other departmental or technical workers (other than janitorial) attached to single churches completed the staff.   The sex and distribution of the twenty-three workers by position, major functions, and churches in which these functions were exercised, are shown in Table LXXXIII.

This arrangement of staff relative to fields gives the four smaller churches a share in the general supervision, financial direction and leadership of boys' and girls' activities provided for the City Parish as a whole.   In addition to the major services of their own assistant pastors, a total of six workers function in behalf of each.   Grace Church, with its attached community work, has in addition a director of religious education, a secretary and three part-time club, gymnasium and playground workers; a total of ten.   The Church of All Nations has also a playground director and in addition three deaconesses specializing in children's work, two workers in the clinic, and a librarian conducting a branch city library; a total of twelve. The pastor's central office, which carries on the denominational work of City Extension as a whole, in connection with that of the City Parish, employs a secretary functioning for the work at large.   There is a camp director similarly employed seasonally.

PREPARATION, EXPERIENCE AND TENURE

Information on these points was secured for sixteen workers. (Those omitted were workers who had given up their positions just previous to the close of the year, and certain part-time workers employed for only a few hours a week.)

All members of the staff are below middle-age or young, the median age being about twenty-six.

Of the sixteen from whom reports were secured, seven were

---

[8] The staff members serving the parish at large did not give services to each church exactly proportionate to the size of its constituency, partly on account of unequal facilities and partly, apparently, for administrative reasons.   The study made no attempt to trace the exact distribution of time among churches, but this is undoubtedly an important point for local consideration.

TABLE LXXXIII—ANALYSIS OF PAID STAFF

No.	Sex	Position and Major Functions	All Nations	Grace (Hallenbeck Community Center)	Epworth	East 38th Street	Brooklyn Heights	Elysian Gardens
1	m.	Pastor						
		General supervision	x	x	x	x	x	x
		Preaching (Grace)		x (A.M.)				
2	m.	Associate Pastor						
		Finances	x	x	x	x	x	x
		Preaching (Grace)		x (P.M.)				
3	m.	Assistant Pastor (Epworth)			x			
4	m.	Assistant Pastor (E. 38th)				x		
5	m.	Assistant Pastor (Brooklyn)					x	
6	m.	Assistant Pastor (Elysian)						x
7	m.	Boys' Work Director	x	x	x	x	x	x
8	f.	Girls' Work Director	x	x	x	x	x	x
9	f.	Girls' Work Assistant *	x	x	x	x	x	x
		Boys' Workers						
10	m.	Gymnasium and playground *		x				
11	m.	Clubs *		x				
12	m.	Scout Master *		x				
13	m.	Playground *	x					
		Children's Workers						
14	f.	Superintendent Children's Department (deaconess)	x					
15	f.	Assistant Children's Department (deaconess)	x					
16	f.	Sunday-school Worker (")	x					
17	m.	Director Religious Education		x				
		Clinic						
18	f.	Superintendent (nurse)	x					
19	f.	Assistant * (records)	x					
20	f.	Librarian *	x					
		Secretaries						
21	f.	Local		x				
22	f.	Central office	(Work of Parish as a whole)					
23	m.	Camp Director (seasonal)	(Camp for all churches)					
23		Total	12	10	6	6	6	6

* Part time.

college graduates, while three part-time workers were still in college in Los Angeles. There were also four graduates of deaconess or missionary training schools, one of a nursing school, and one of a business college.

Of the six pastors, four were theological graduates and two still in the seminary. The pastor had had post graduate university work.

Previous to nine years in the ministry, the pastor had two years' experience in industry. He was also a local survey director of the Interchurch World Movement, had been three times to Europe, and once around the world in company with Sherwood Eddy in the study of social conditions. One of the graduate assistant pastors had been in the ministry four years, one five years, and the other twenty. Eight other workers had apprenticeships in the social work of the Church of All Nations, or in specialized work for boys and girls, or in athletics in the Y. M. C. A. and Y. W. C. A. One was a teacher, one a rancher, and another in the army, before taking up work in religious education. A very important element in the staff consists of those who were young people in the Church of All Nations. The church developed them, sent them to college, gave them apprentice training as paid workers, and advanced them into staff positions. Still others in the staff are in the midst of this process. No other church studied has so largely initiated and directed the preparation of its own supply of workers.

ANALYSIS OF WORK RECORDS

Fifteen members of the staff kept accurate records of their work for a week during the study. The total work of the fifteen workers averaged over one hundred hours per day for each day of the seven recorded. It is not known whether the week was fully representative; but the records bring out certain facts likely to represent permanent tendencies.

There is a great difference in the actual length of work between those workers whose hours are indeterminate and those whose hours are fixed. The former habitually work longer than the usual office worker's day and very frequently over ten hours per day. The pastors, directors and department heads tend to fall into the long-hour class, in contrast with the assistants and technical workers, even when the latter are supposed to be doing full-time work. The long days of the former group necessarily imply much evening work. Sunday is naturally the short day for those whose major work does not go on then. Otherwise Saturday is most likely to be the short day. But there is no uniformity about this nor about which day is the longest.

Of the aggregate hours of week's work, amounting for the entire group to about 702 hours, 30 per cent. is spent in administration; 13 per cent. in teaching, of which the Children's Day classes at the Church of All Nations provide the most important item; 12 per cent. in the "operation of necessary facilities," chiefly keeping the playgrounds open when no systematic group work is in progress; 11 per cent. each to the conduct of group work in clubs or on playgrounds, and the clerical work; 7 per cent. to pastoral work; and 2 per cent. each to the preparation and conduct of religious services.

This showing necessarily corresponds in general to the division of activities previously discussed; but it shows in particular how much more time-consuming are some of the social service features of the week-day program than are the traditional religious services of Sunday.[9]

EMPLOYMENT AND REMUNERATION

The ordained ministers and deaconesses in the employ of the City Parish are appointed by ecclesiastical authority under the Methodist Episcopal system. As secretary of the Los Angeles City Mission Society, the pastor functions concurrently with the District Superintendent in naming the associate and assistant pastors whose appointments he virtually controls. The pastor, as chief manager of the enterprise, employs other workers with the concurrence of the various bodies that pay salaries, among which, for example, are the official boards of the churches and the City Missions Society.

In the cases of persons ecclesiastically appointed, the formal

---

[9] A similar classification of the work-records of thirty-five city pastors who have no assistants shows that they give on the average 18 per cent. of their time to homiletical preparation, 20 per cent. to pastoral work, 7 per cent. to cultural pursuits, and only 20 per cent. to administration. The difference in distribution of time between these workers and the pastors of the City Parish is significant.

terms of employment are supplemented by detailed memoranda
of assigned duties within the City Parish. The salary agreement is specific in all cases, and the hours of labor are definitely
specified in the agreement in the case of part-time workers and
others performing duties that cover fixed hours. Vacations of
two weeks per year are assumed if not stipulated. The range
of salary payments is summarized in Table LXXXIV.

TABLE LXXXIV—SALARIES OF CHURCH STAFF

Position	Cash Salary	Perquisites	Total Value
Pastor	$3,300	Parsonage $300	$3,900
Assistant pastors in charge of churches	1,200–1,500	....	1,200–1,500
Deaconesses (regular denominational scale)	360	Board & room 480	840
Boys' work director	1,500	Board & room 240	1,740
Girls' work director	1,200	....	1,200
Clinic superintendent	1,200	....	1,200
Secretary	1,080	....	1,080
Part-time assistant	600–720	....	600–720

The ordained workers (pastors and deaconesses) are entitled to the retiring pension of their denominations without
direct contributory payment on their part.[10]

ADMINISTRATIVE RELATIONS AND METHODS

While the official boards of the respective churches maintain
their theoretical authority, their gearing in with the City Parish
actually leaves only minor business for them to do. In matters
that remain in the hands of these groups, the assistant pastors
function with respect to them as though they were pastors in
complete charge. The executive pastor has not made a practice
of meeting with the several official boards, though it is part
of his purpose to do so in the future.

Besides the relation of the pastor to the staff as the agent
of employment, virtually if not theoretically, and his incidental

---

[10] As previously indicated, the staff largely consists of young people who are
in process of development. Many of them have had promotion or enjoy the prospects of further promotion in local denominational work if not in the City Parish
itself. This fact is presumably reflected in the salary scale.

supervision, the current administrative contacts of the pastor and the various members of the staff differ. There is a weekly staff-meeting. Otherwise opportunities for conferences with the pastor are somewhat irregular, though it is presumed he is accessible daily by phone during certain hours. The assistant workers among boys and girls report directly to the directors of these departments; and the assistant deaconesses report to the deaconess in charge of general work, as well as to the denominational Women's Home Missionary Society which pays their salaries. The superintendent of the clinic is supposed to be under some technical oversight by a board of physicians coöperating with it. The work of the community workers, ultimately supported by the Community Chest, is reported to that body in detail.

All workers render formal reports weekly to the central office of the City Parish upon form blanks. The reports of the assistant pastors cover attendance at services; gains or losses of membership; sermon topics, number of hours of study; pastoral work and organized activities; also names and addresses of persons called upon, with notes as to the results of the call. The community activities of the Church of All Nations and Hallenbeck Community Center are reported by their directors in detailed summaries. All part-time workers report the program of each session of their club, while other departmental and individual workers have appropriate forms of special reports.[11]

The so-called directors of various boys' and girls' groups are actually occupied most of the time as group leaders. Out of the twenty-four boys' clubs meeting in June, 1925, only six were led by volunteers, the balance by paid workers. Little progress has as yet been made in developing unpaid leadership. The fact that the workers assume to be in general departmental charge and are so largely functioning directly in the handling of groups within the parishes of the several assistant pastors, has raised certain questions of authority and adjustment.

---

11 Examination of considerable batches of these reports reveals that they are not made out with much care. This laxity constitutes a serious limitation upon their satisfactory use as data, and raises the question of their adequacy as the basis for supervision.

These questions would not arise if the general workers promoted ideals and methods, coördinated work, trained local leaders and conducted certain joint functions like camping, while leaving more of the actual operation of the work to the several churches.

SUMMARY OF STAFF DATA

The City Parish has a staff of young people recruited and educated chiefly under church initiative, and developed through an apprentice period. Department heads, however, are generally thoroughly experienced. The average of general education is high. The salary scale is very moderate. Higher pay generally comes with very much longer hours of work. According to the time-distribution of functions performed, administrative activities are emphasized and perhaps exaggerated. Little time is given to study, and not much to pastoral work with families and individuals. As between workers with general responsibility for departments, and local workers with responsibility limited to single churches, the organization of the staff is in general logical, well-balanced and fairly well carried out through conferences and reports. The adult constituency of the smaller churches is limited. This obviously makes it hard to find resident leadership. But the attempt of non-resident specialists to do work in such a variety of places and under such a variety of auspices raises a good many administrative problems and should perhaps not be regarded as the last word of the experiment.

Plant

Of the plants of the six churches of the City Parish, that of Grace Church alone was of such size and value at the time of the survey as to warrant its formal ranking and comparison in a series of case studies.

The Church of All Nations was occupying two very dilapidated dwelling houses, which, after slight remodeling, were housing all its activities. It was, however, just on the eve of beginning the erection of a new plant to cost $75,000 (in addition to land), and an additional gift of $60,000 was in hand for the boys' club unit of the structure.[12]   In view of this prospect, it was not regarded as pertinent to make a minute study of the temporary plant.

The buildings of the four smaller churches are merely flimsy wooden bungalows, generally ample in size for the limited religious work carried out in them, and not too fine nor expensive for rough adaptation to group activities.   They so largely lack, however, those structural, esthetic and technical excellencies contemplated by the "standard" as to render their detailed study of little significance.   The values of these properties as reported in the Conference Minutes of 1924 are: Brooklyn Heights, $20,000; East 38th Street, $8,000; Elysian Gardens, $5,000; Epworth, $25,000.   The value of the Epworth Church largely lies in its site, which includes that of the parsonage and is located "close in" on Sunset Boulevard.

GRACE CHURCH PLANT

This leaves for consideration only the plant of Grace Church.

Among the twenty-five plants studied, it ranks seventeenth on the Interchurch thousand-point scale, scoring a total of 570 points.   The median of the twenty-five churches is about 600 points.

The church occupies a convenient location on St. Louis Street at the head of Pennsylvania Avenue, one block from the First Street car line and adjacent to the civic and business center of the Boyle Heights district.   It is a rather low structure, somewhat nondescript in design, but possessing reasonably churchly lines.   Its lot is 220 x 225 feet in dimension.   The original Sunday-school rooms were at the rear of the auditorium connected by a sliding door.   A subsequent addition for Sunday-school purposes, providing spacious departmental quarters, was attached to the northeast corner of the structure.

---

12 At the date of this writing, these buildings are complete and occupied.   There is immediate promise, too, of a $25,000 chapel, funds for which are already subscribed.

Later the Hallenbeck gymnasium, a fairly substantial wooden structure 45 x 96 feet in dimension, was built beside the church and partly in front of the Sunday-school addition. Beyond the gymnasium stands the parsonage, and at the rear of the parsonage and gymnasium lies the playground, about 75 x 110 feet in size. On account of the impermanent character of building materials, this entire property is valued at only about $94,000. Like most California churches it is built of wood. It constitutes, however, a very ample, varied and useful plant, ranking higher than many churches of many times more value, measured by dollars. The strong and weak points of the plant are systematically shown in the summarized score-card in Table LXXXV.

TABLE LXXXV—SUMMARY OF SCORE OF PLANT

ITEM	STANDARD SCORE	POINTS SCORED		RANK IN 25 CASES
		Number	Per Cent.	
Total	1,000	570	57	17
Site	130	87	67	17
Building or buildings..........	150	100	67	21
Service systems	160	77	48	18
Church rooms	170	112	66	20
Religious school rooms........	200	116	58	17
Community service rooms.....	190	78	41	11

In general, one should note that, with respect to structure, the church ranks below its general ranking by reason of its characterless and poorly related buildings (item 2); near its general rank with respect to site and to church and Sunday-school rooms; but well above its general rank with respect to community service facilities, which consist of a gymnasium, a playground, excellent bowling-alleys, locker and shower rooms, a small office, and boys' and girls' clubrooms.

Finances

At the time of the field study of the City Parish, the institution was carrying on active negotiations with the Los Angeles Community Chest which resulted in a considerably increased support of its social work by that agency of the community, and in a more careful financial departmentalization. Since the experiment was definitely working toward this now established phase, it seems most reasonable and instructive to present a year's finances under the new plan and relationships subsequent to the survey.

SOURCES OF INCOME

On a total budget of above $53,000 for the combined religious and social work, the distribution of income was: for the churches, 46 per cent.; for the social institutions, consisting of the All Nations Community House (boys' club, girls' club, library, day nursery, summer camp, playground, children's department), the All Nations Clinic and the Hallenbeck Heights Social Center (associated with Grace Church), 54 per cent. The sources from which this income is derived are shown in Table LXXXVI.

TABLE LXXXVI—DISTRIBUTION OF SOURCES OF RECEIPTS

	Total Per Cent.	Churches Per Cent.	Social Institutions* Per Cent.
Total	100	100	100
Pledges and collections	21	46	0
Special gifts	10	13	8
Special gifts (for deficit)	7	14	0
Subsidies			
Community Chest	39	0	72
Denominational agencies	15	22	9
Fees	6	0	11
Rents	2	5	0

* All Nations Community House; All Nations Clinic; Hallenbeck Social Center.

Twenty-two per cent. of the cost of the religious work came as subsidies from the Methodist denomination, as did also 9 per cent. of the cost of the social institutions. Less than half of the support of the churches came from the stated pledges of constituents or loose collections; the latter furnishing an exceedingly small proportion. Considerable amounts had to be raised in special gifts, including enough to cover a deficit.

Nearly three-fourths of the support of the social institutions came from the Community Chest, with 11 per cent. derived from fees, largely those of the summer camp.

Of the more than $24,000 which constituted the church budget proper, 26 per cent. was expended for benevolences. The per cent. distribution of the remaining nearly $18,000 was as follows:

	Per Cent.
Total	100
Salaries	36
General administration	4
Music	11
Operation and upkeep of property	26
Departments specially budgeted (Sunday schools and Daily Vacation Bible School)	9
Publicity	4
Ecclesiastical connections	6
Miscellaneous	4

This distribution is fairly typical, except that upkeep is relatively high, probably on account of the many different plants occupied by the City Parish.

Table LXXXVII shows the distribution of the proposed 1926 budget of the social institutions as approved by the Community Chest.

TABLE LXXXVII—DISTRIBUTION OF PROPOSED EXPENDITURES OF SOCIAL INSTITUTIONS OF LOS ANGELES CITY PARISH, 1926

ITEM	PER CENT.			
	Total	Community House	Clinic	Hallenbeck Social Center
Total	100	100	100	100
Administrative	17	21	10	11
Communication and transportation	2	2	1	2
Fixed and special charges	7	7	6	11
Repairs and renewals	4	4	4	6
Institutional supplies and events	16	20	12	9
Institutional expense	5	6	3	5
Service expense	49	40	64	56
Per cent. of total devoted to salaries	64	61	73	61

Public Services and Worship

As already noted, the per cent. of attendance on public worship is only one-fourth of the attendance on the total program of the City Parish, or very much less than with the average city church.

The average attendance on the stated services was found as follows:

Church	Sunday A.M. Services	Sunday P.M. Services	Mid-week Services
All Nations	30	0	0
Grace	232	92	70
East 38th Street	54	48	17
Epworth	30	26	11
Elysian Gardens	45	59	12
Brooklyn Heights	32	0	2

Pending the erection of its new building, no great stress was being laid on public services at the Church of All Nations. Judged by the situation at the moment of the study, and relative to the standard church practices of the denomination, one would have to say that this field had virtually ceased to be a church, and had become rather a Christian social center. The only expression of formal public worship on Sunday was found in the children's congregation of about thirty, conducted by a deaconess.

The services of the four smaller churches, with congregations of from twenty-five to sixty, were naturally characterized by informality. They were held in unpretentious buildings rather lacking in ecclesiastical character, without paid musicians or impressive equipment, and sometimes under rather inexperienced men. The services in these churches in the evening were as large as in the morning, if not larger, and included a relatively high proportion of very young children. The evening services at Epworth Church, though the majority of attendants were adults, were called a children's service and turned out to be a rather original combination of a Junior League program under child-leadership and a neighborhood song-service with excellent volunteer leaders.

The social friendliness of the smaller churches, and the interest in them of their volunteer workers, was distinctly in evidence in the atmosphere of the services.

Grace Church enjoys the Sunday-morning ministries of the pastor of the City Parish. Its attendance is considerably larger than that of the other five churches combined. On the Sunday morning of the study, about one-fourth of the audience appeared to be composed of men.   About 50 per cent. of those present were adults, 30 per cent. adolescents, and 20 per cent. children.   The children's group is definitely organized for worship in connection with the morning service, and a special children's sermon is preached.

While the congregation was assembling, an atmosphere of moderate social cordiality prevailed.   The ushering was dignified and courteous.   The service occupied one and one-quarter hours.   It was only slightly liturgical in character, lacking the Apostles' Creed, but including the Gloria following the responsive reading.   There was one anthem rendered by a vested choir of twelve members, and a soprano solo.   The minister was not gowned.   The sermon was direct, vigorous and effective, and included the delivery of a long poem written by a Los Angeles literary woman in appreciation of the social impulse and message of the Church of All Nations.   About ten minutes of active visiting among the congregation took place at the close of the service.

The second service at Grace Church is usually conducted by the associate pastor.   It is briefer, but of the same character as the morning service.

This arrangement leaves the chief pastor free to share in the ministries of the smaller churches.   The study covered a typical evening service at which he preached, at Elysian Gardens.   The service was preceded by a period of vigorous song led by a young people's choir of sixteen voices.   About two-fifths of the congregation of some sixty persons were of the male sex, and three-fifths were young people and children. The service included the installation of the officers of the Epworth League and the reception of members.   The sermon was a popularization of a carefully prepared study of the Unanswered Prayers of Jesus.   It was delivered with charming simplicity and intimacy of manner.

The extension to the smaller churches of a commanding pulpit ministry and the personal contacts of the pastor are distinctive features of the City Parish plan.

Religious Education

Measured by attendance on the Sunday school, the City Parish puts considerably less than average emphasis on religious education.

All the Sunday-school sessions are held on Sunday morning and last one hour. The scheme of departmentalization, the enrollment of pupils and teachers, and the average attendance are shown in Tables LXXXVIII and LXXXIX.

TABLE LXXXVIII—ENROLLMENT OF SUNDAY SCHOOLS

			CHURCHES			
DEPARTMENT	All Nations	Grace	Epworth	East 38th Street	Elysian Gardens	Brooklyn Heights
Total	110	276	100	160	229	97
Beginners	..	34	..	..	..	..
Primary	..	50	..	..	..	..
Beginners and Primary ..	35	..	15	50	90	..
Junior	35	46	30	10	90 *	..
Intermediate	..	37	..	37	10 *	..
Intermediate and Senior..	..	..	30	..	..	..
High School	25	..	..	..	..	..
Senior	..	23	..	12	5 *	..
Young People	..	..	15	..	..	..
Adult	..	56	..	24	10 *	..
Officers and Teachers	15	30	10	27	24	..

* Included in the "Main School."

TABLE LXXXIX—AVERAGE ATTENDANCE OF SUNDAY SCHOOLS

CHURCHES	AVERAGE ATTENDANCE		PER CENT. OF ENROLLED PUPILS UNDER 14 YEARS OF AGE
	Total	Per Cent. of Enrollment	
All Nations	61	54	74
Grace	203	74	47
Epworth	55	55	45
East 38th Street.............	98	61	37
Elysian Gardens	145	63	82
Brooklyn Heights	60	62	(Not known)

The variations among the churches with respect to the per cent. of children in the total enrollment are somewhat striking. The Elysian Gardens Sunday school is little more than a children's group. All Nations has the largest number and per cent. of adolescents. Grace, Epworth and East 38th Street churches have a fair proportion of adults.

The varying degrees of departmentalization shown in Table LXXXVIII reflect in part the size of the schools, and in part the adequacy of their facilities. Grace Church alone has adequate departmental rooms and numerous individual classrooms for the more advanced departments, together with a Sunday-school office and its equipment. Many of the classrooms, however, are small and dark, while the stairs connecting the gallery classrooms with the main floor are exceedingly awkward and appear to constitute a serious fire risk. Grace Church alone enjoys the services of a technically trained director of religious education, with consequent refinements of educational methods.

Religious education in the Sunday school is strongly supplemented in the Church of All Nations by the worship and instruction of the daily classes of the Children's Department; and more or less definitely by clubs in the other smaller churches. It was found that there was considerable discussion among staff members as to the religious elements and values to be found respectively in the junior program of the Young Men's Christian Association, which was in use in certain churches, and the character-building program of the Boy Scouts and Camp Fire Girls which was preferred in others. The City Parish can hardly be said to have thought out the problem of how its total program of activities for youth is related to religious education and how the two approaches to the task of developing character can be best organized and adjusted.

Relation to Community Agencies

Direct work for the more unprivileged groups in the community is evidenced by the numerous clubs and the character-building, recreational and health programs, especially at the

Church of All Nations and Hallenbeck Community Center. The smaller churches are essentially those of humbler people, and their maintenance is itself a definite contribution to elements of population that are frequently poorly served by religious agencies.

The significance of the work to the community is recognized by the large support which the Church of All Nations and Hallenbeck Community Center receive from the Los Angeles Community Chest.

Beyond their own organized work, the churches as a group are not strong enough to have marked community influence in their respective neighborhoods.

They are, however, in important city-wide relationships with such agencies as the Boy Scouts and the Camp Fire Girls, and in still more important localized relationships. The Church of All Nations is active in the district council of social agencies and works in close coöperation with the social agencies' registry office, the district nurses' and the city teachers' associations, and the juvenile courts, clinics and hospitals. It is in particularly close touch with departments of social instruction in the University of Southern California, from which it gets many of its workers and club leaders. Epworth and Elysian Gardens churches have particularly significant contacts with the public schools in their vicinities and the local Parent-Teacher Associations.[13]

On the whole, one may be a little disappointed at the slenderness of the organized coöperative relations between churches with such excellent ideals and the actually resident forces of their respective neighborhoods. There may be a danger that the drawing together of the group of churches into the City Parish, and the management (to a considerable degree) of their work by non-resident specialists, will serve to lessen still

---

[13] Much of the more far-reaching community work of the Church of All Nations had been discontinued at the time of the field work, owing to the delay in securing funds for the new building and in order to allow the pastor to give his energies to the development of the City Parish as a whole. It is now being reestablished in the new plant. Many of the proposed local relationships of the Hallenbeck Community Center, including the organization of a local advisory council representative of all community interests, the development of health in connection with the White Memorial Hospital, and the extension of community recreational activities, have never yet been carried out.

more their sense of local setting and responsibility. The various foreign and industrial groups in the midst of which the churches exist have their own leaders, their own organizations, and their own programs and purposes. One would like to see more definite contacts with these spontaneous movements, and more working with local populations in addition to so much working for them.

Conservation and Growth

Information as to the number and sources of accessions to church-membership for a period of a year was secured from Grace, Epworth, East 38th Street and Elysian Gardens churches. For the period indicated, these churches received accessions at the ratio of seventy on confession of faith to thirty by letter; forty-one adults to fifty-nine minors; and forty-two males to fifty-eight females. Most of the city churches studied get the majority of their new members by letter. It goes without saying, however, that a group of problem churches with failing prospects will not find people rushing to bring letters to them.

The ratio of children relative to adult accessions is in agreement with the fact that the constituency chiefly consists of children; while the favorable ratio of males to females tends to perpetuate the unusually strong masculine element in the churches as a group.

With almost no exception, save in cases of pastors' families and occasionally of denominational officials, the churches draw recruits exclusively from their immediate neighborhoods. This is in keeping with their highly compact parishes.

Of the small element that comes by letter, about half is composed of people new to the neighborhoods, while the other half is made up of adherents who have already been brought into some subsidiary relationship with the church and thus gradually into full membership. Three-fourths of those bringing letters were already Methodist, while one-fourth came from other denominations.

Of those who came into the church on confession, five-sixths had been residents in the neighborhood for some time, and fifty-two out of fifty-eight had been brought into sub-sidiary relations with the church before being received into full membership. It is not clear what per cent. of these were secured primarily by the Sunday school and what primarily by boys' and girls' clubs. Apparently the Hallenbeck Community Center does not tend to build up the membership of Grace Church very directly. On the contrary, where Sunday school and clubs are closely related, new members usually belong to both in advance, and pastors frequently feel that the influence of the clubs is the dominant one.

In general, the churches get their recruits from the con-stituencies with which their program is strong; namely, from their neighborhoods, out of a body of adherents created by their own previous efforts, and consisting primarily of children and youth with the male element unusually large. This gen-eralization probably applies also to the churches for which information is lacking.

Adaptations

For many years the churches of the City Parish have faced a succession of adverse changes in the character of their im-mediate environments. These might well have caused them to make radical departures from the average behavior of the church in the city. As a matter of fact, it turns out that the study has presented an extremely clear-cut case of urban adaptation under environmental pressure.

The following section attempts to summarize the major findings from this viewpoint.

TYPICAL URBAN ADAPTATIONS OF THE CITY PARISH

These churches have passed, particularly in the last decade, through a series of adverse changes essentially typical of the changes many churches have had to meet in every large American city of rapid growth that has received a large num-ber of foreign immigrants.

The reactions to these changes, exhibited by the churches of the City Parish, are also in many respects highly typical of what many churches have done in similar situations. They are unusual chiefly in having been directed by strong ecclesiastical machinery for the group as a whole, rather than by churches singly. These churches are more typical, however, in what they have become, than in what they have deliberately gone about to do. That is to say, the changes under which they have been relatively passive are perhaps more significant than those to which they have reacted.

First, as already noted, the results of their unconscious evolution are extreme; in no study of a single church has so small a group of closely connected adult adherents been found at the center as in these churches. This has tended to make the conscious action of these churches somewhat erratic. The feebleness of the local units, and the abnormal blend of their constituencies, has necessarily made their programs of service unusual in balance and emphasis.

Again, the constituencies of the several churches have largely evolved away from their former family basis, so that one now finds them containing a much higher proportion of detached individuals than formerly. Finally, they all agree in occupying their parish areas selectively rather than cross-sectionally. They omit certain elements of population, while drawing others. To put the matter bluntly, the data on parish distribution show that, their social ministries notwithstanding, the churches succeed much better in winning constituents in the "better" territory that is available within reasonable distance of their buildings. This fact stands out in spite of their professed and extensively organized community effort. It illustrates the dominance of deeper instincts over the more superficial sphere of deliberate planning.

Of policies deliberately adopted, obviously the most distinctive are the combination of the six churches under one administration, the pooling of and the supplementing of their financial resources by the denomination, the creation of a staff of general workers complementary to the local ministers, and the undertaking of a varied program of community work. The elements of this program have been exhibited. On the whole, they show adaptations in service to the needs of the most available types of people found in the immediate vicinities. That is to say, the simplest and easiest methods of service have been adopted rather than the best and most significant method of attacking fundamental community problems.

The chief institutional changes have been:

(1) The enlargement of the week-day program.

(2) Important additions to church plant (in the community center and gymnasium building attached to Grace Church, and the inexpensive but significant addition of clubroom facilities at Epworth and East 38th Street, as well as the permanent new plant of the Church of All Nations).

(3) The employment of numerous directors of activities and assistant specialists.

(4) The considerable increases of financial budget to support these new features.

(5) So far as the pastor himself is concerned, one must add a content of preaching and type of pulpit message underlying and interpreting the whole practical endeavor of the City Parish. It is not so clear that the public messages of the other pulpits have been significantly distinctive.

MODIFICATIONS OF OBJECTIVES

Changes in the thinking of the churches have probably been less definite than those in their programs and institutional life. The weaker churches included in the City Parish presumably accepted the new order primarily because it was authoritatively promulgated. There has not always been the most thorough-going understanding of what the leadership was headed for. A good many intimations cropped out in the course of the study that minority elements in several of the churches were not fully satisfied with the situation. The general status is one of partial evolution. Yet the experiment is unquestionably in process of educating those who have been subjected to it. Some enlargement of the concept of the churches' mission has accompanied the enlargement of program. The issues involved have simply been faced concretely and one at a time rather than theoretically. It is the impression of the present commentator that this is probably the best way anyhow to think toward a new position. What the situation seems to amount to at present is that a few strong men in the local churches are theoretically convinced of the necessity of the new program and are willing to give it a trial. The rank and file have faith in their leaders and may be expected to be ultimately convinced in about the proportion that the experiment turns out to be institutionally successful.

The pastor's vision of what he wants to accomplish is clear-cut. His denominational backing is authoritative and intelligent. What is left to do is simply to justify the several elements of the program piecemeal until a deeper meaning is read into the formula "the church meeting community needs." This will require a longer period of experiments of still wider range.

SUMMARY OF SUCCESSES

The City Parish is not old enough to have established a long record of successes or failure. It has not proved that it can transform the associated churches into strong and normal organizations from the traditional standpoint; nor that the work can continue without large financial support from the denomination permanently; nor even that all the churches can be saved from institutional extinction. This is merely to say that the successes of the plan are essentially conditioned by the will of the denomination. They must lie in the strength of the ecclesiastical group making common cause with a group of disadvantaged and imperiled churches at the heart of the city, in behalf both of their dwindling and discouraged older constituencies and of the new alien elements of population that have moved in among them.

From this standpoint, definite successes may be regarded. As the present observer views them, the outstanding ones appear to be four:

(1) The Church of All Nations has a sufficiently long history to have brought a considerable group of children out of under-privileged environments, through its Sunday school and clubs, into church and university privileges, and through ap-

prenticeship into permanent responsibility or paid leadership. There is no reason to suppose that, with equal time, the other churches may not show similar shining results.

(2) Those churches that have definitely attempted it have succeeded in making very extensive contacts with the alien groups in their neighborhoods. In spite of evidence previously adduced as to their deep-seated affinities for the better class of populations in their immediate neighborhoods, the clubs of the majority of churches very fairly reflect the composition of the surrounding populations. Thus the dominant elements of this constituency at the Church of All Nations is Mexican and Spanish-speaking. Americans come second. Orientals, Italians and Jews constitute strong minorities. This makes the membership of the clubs an essentially accurate cross section of the community. Three clubs at Hallenbeck Center are exclusively Jewish, and Italians constitute the second largest element in the Epworth Boy Scouts and Camp Fire Girls. This goes to show that these churches are serving different racial populations in something like the proportion in which these different racial elements are present in the community. On the other hand, the rather meager club work at East 38th Street does not appear to reach the more adverse foreign elements in that vicinity. Elysian Gardens has few foreigners to deal with. On the whole, therefore, the idea of community inclusiveness is made good in service for childhood. One has to note, however, that the percentage of foreign constituents who continue in connection with the work when they become adolescents and young people considerably decreases.

(3) Such results as appear up to the present have been accomplished under heavy handicaps as to facilities and support. The chief technical shortcomings of the work at the Church of All Nations will be remedied by its new plant; and much more of its projected, but never-yet-realized, program can now go into effect. The cost of the work per attendance unit is smaller than for any other church studied. This means that it is too small for fully normal results. Very much has been done in the past with very little; and all that is needed will not put severe additional strain on Methodist resources.

(4) All the churches in the City Parish have had a much broader range of services than they could otherwise have had at the hands of well-trained experts; and the smaller ones have enjoyed somewhat intimate leadership of a caliber that would never have been available to them under other circumstances, together with possibilities of careful supervision which is in the way to produce exceptionally technical results. These are solid successes in spite of the yet experimental character of the City Parish plan, and of the fact that its fusion of old and new elements and objectives is still imperfect.

Case XVI

OLIVET INSTITUTE, PRESBYTERIAN, CHICAGO, ILL.

Most of the case studies that make up this volume have been concerned with the brave second thoughts of churches that are making the best of bad situations. The pattern of circumstance and behavior that has been met over and over again is somewhat as follows: a desirable urban neighborhood goes bad; the church either flees, or gallantly sticks to its post, and by hook or crook manages to survive; in so doing it sometimes adapts itself to the particular needs of the locality in some part of the area of its service.

Olivet Institute, on the contrary, from its very early beginnings, deliberately entered into a hard situation. What it is now doing is just what it undertook to do from the first. Its story is not that of evolution into a broad ministry of seven-day-a-week Christianity, but rather that of such a ministry adopted at the outset. The enterprise is, moreover, unusual in that it has had, for thirty years, the continuous leadership of a notable personality, Dr. Norman B. Barr. In no other case studied was the institution so definitely the lengthened shadow of a man, or the story so essentially that of long-time, untiring persistence in the pursuit of a distinctive idea.

What a church will do when it is caught by the adverse tide and must do something to avoid going on the rocks, is one story. How a church sometimes deliberately sets out to build enduring foundations where the breakers roar is quite a different one.

The name Olivet Institute indicates an institution that is not merely a church. In no other case studied, save that of Trinity Center, San Francisco, have the church's departures from traditional ecclesiastical programs been violent enough, or its adaptation to the changing city complete enough, to suggest the abandonment or submergence of the customary name. A

414

transitional example is afforded by Grace Church, Denver, which now formally designates itself as Grace "Community" Church.

The week-day program of Olivet, however, is 69 per cent. of the total; while the proportion of the budget going for work directly labeled as religious is less than one-fourth. The historic core of the enterprise is indeed a church now organized as two congregations, one English-speaking and the other Italian, with houses of worship about half a mile apart. But in the internal structure of the organization, four major departments are recognized: administrative, educational, relief, and religious. Legally the Institute is a distinct corporation composed of the members of the Session of Olivet Institute Church (Presbyterian), and representatives of the organized groups behind the departments of activity. Its active administration is by a board of directors elected by the members of the Institute; so that the management of the enterprise as a whole is no longer strictly ecclesiastical.

At the time of the study, the Institute was occupying a string of about fifteen buildings. The work has since been largely unified through the completion of the main part of a great central plant. Beneath the separation of the work into the English-speaking and the Italian divisions is the fact of the polyglot community, the English-speaking group itself being a mosaic, the resultant of a succession of racial occupancies of the neighborhood.

The total enterprise thus constitutes a sort of superchurch, particularly in the aspect of its exceptionally broad and basic social ministries. It represents the largest constituency of any of the cases studied and by far the broadest program, including fifty out of the sixty items of church organization and practice by means of which the entire group was ranked.[1]

History

The institutional chronology of Olivet Institute is easily summarized in five major epochs.[2] The first, from 1888 to

---

[1] See p. 445.
[2] See p. 446.

1894, was that of missionary beginnings in what was historically one of the poorest and most demoralized areas of Chicago—that bordering on the Chicago River opposite Goose Island. The impulse and personnel of the movement in its earlier day came largely from McCormick Theological Seminary. The methods were the more usual ones of religious propaganda. The most responsive population was found to be German; there was a German Sunday school and a German-speaking assistant pastor. The enterprise in this stage was actively fostered by the local home-missionary committee of the Presbyterian denomination.

The period from 1894 to 1902 marked the beginnings of organized social work and early experimentation. A residence for workers was opened and social work recognized as a definite department.

From 1902 to 1913, institutional development went on rapidly, resulting in the establishment of most of the outstanding features of the present day. The settlement-house association, the library, the dispensary, camp, playgrounds, sickness and death benefit association, home for the aged, and numerous other features came as gradual additions from year to year. The publicity methods of the institution had corresponding development; and the period of institutional formation culminated in 1910 with the incorporation of the Institute and the organization of the board of directors that now controls it. In 1912 the institution became associated with the group of major Chicago social agencies which were undertaking a measure of financial planning in common. The year 1913 marked the Institute's twenty-fifth anniversary.

There followed an acute period of removal and readjustment. Even an institution wholly committed to localized community service may have to remove when the expansion of industry comes to occupy much of the space formerly held by its constituent population, and when the shifting of racial elements is too extreme. During the preceding twenty-five years, a large Swedish element had been superimposed upon original Irish and German populations of the district and easily assimilated into the Olivet situation. From 1903 onward, however, came a very rapid influx of Italians, which turned the Goose Island neighborhood into a "Little Sicily" ultimately harboring some 20,000 inhabitants of that nationality. This change was followed by a noticeable infiltration of Negroes. The older elements, in the main, were pushed farther north. Meanwhile a strong and progressive Hungarian colony had established itself three-quarters of a mile northwest of the church, beyond North Avenue.

The Institute consequently moved to a site about half a mile northeast of the original one, immediately contiguous to the present property. The former church building was devoted to the Italian congregation, while the building of a former Congregational church that merged with the Olivet enterprise became the new center of religious operations. The institution was thus enabled to keep in touch with its major local constituencies (which had been more than half German during the first twenty-five years, with the Swedish the second largest element) and to reëstablish itself nearer the center of clearly marked areas of polyglot industrial populations.

Ten years' delay now intervened before the culmination of the removal project in the erection of a new and adequate plant. The primary causes of the delay were the distraction and prohibitive prices of the World War period. By 1926, however, large resources had been mobilized; and, at the date of the study, the Institute was well along with the erection of a building that was to cost $750,000.

STATISTICAL TRENDS

Attendance and financial records carefully kept by departments, though not always in absolutely identical form, show the following trends as between the first and the second five-year periods of the last decade. The second five years saw a somewhat smaller total attendance, on account of the general slowing up of the program resulting from a lack of new facilities. Athletic activities were particularly diminished, partly because the Institute had no gymnasium, and partly because there was better provision for such activities in a Young Men's

Christian Association building erected in the near vicinity. The music-school averaged much larger; the "manual and mental" division, including two kindergartens and extensive craft and domestic training, was maintained on about the same level; relief (especially in the "advice and aid" section) had involved many more persons; medical work had more than doubled; outing activities had fluctuated and shown no definite trend; religious extension work had been somewhat smaller, and, numerically measured, the church activities, both at the Sedgwick and at the Vedder Street centers, had been considerably smaller. Finances, however, had improved.

These fluctuations of the work which on the whole were minor ones, are not to be wondered at, in view of the long delay in providing adequate facilities in the new location. Olivet thus presents, in the immediate past, a vast and firmly established work which has been greatly increased in various of its more technical aspects, though not as measured by gross numbers. The completion of the new building may be confidently expected to stimulate quantity as well as quality in its future growth.

This study, then, concerns Olivet Institute just as it is passing over from the prolonged period of delay into the new era of culmination and of anticipated progress on distinctly higher levels of opportunity.

I. MAJOR ASPECTS OF THE CHURCH

Constituency

In point of size, Olivet Institute, with 5,904 constituents, has a half more than the next largest church studied. Its two churches have a combined membership of only 1,097.

Over half of the total number of names listed by the church are, however, not now in any form of determinate connection.[3] They are rather previous and prospective beneficiaries, people largely representing charity or clinical cases, for whom the church feels a responsibility. The fact that half of the total social group defined under the name Olivet Institute does not

---

3 See p. 447.

belong to it in the sense that 97 per cent. of the constituents of the great majority of churches belong to them: namely, by having present membership in some phase of church activity, is a striking point of differentiation.

Of determinate adherents, 47 per cent. belong neither to church nor to Sunday school, but only to some subsidiary organization. Here again, Olivet's story presents a striking variation, though one easily explained by the fact that 97 per cent. of the contiguous population is non-Protestant. In only one other case is a church so largely composed of adherents through the subsidiary program only.

Finally, the central core of the Olivet constituency, as identified by those who belong to church, Sunday school and subsidiaries at the same time, is exceedingly small compared with other churches.

AGE AND SEX

Olivet Institute is proportionately more a young people's and children's enterprise than an institution of adults. The variation of its constituency in age-distribution from that of the general population of Chicago is, however, not extreme, as shown in the following tabulation.

	PER CENT.		
	Adults (21 & Over)	Adolescents (15-20)	Children (5-14)
Constituencies of:			
Olivet Institute	66	11	23
26 churches	73	8	19
Population of Chicago	70	10	20

Olivet very strongly tends to be a family church, detached individuals not belonging to adherent families constituting only 28 per cent. of the total constituency. It is also a man's church. Fifty-three per cent. of the total constituency is male, compared with only 43 per cent. as the average of the twenty-six churches studied. Only one other church has relatively more male constituents.

In the entire minor age-group and among adults belonging to adherent families, the proportion of the sexes is approximately equal; a condition also much beyond the average. The chief preponderance of the male element, on the contrary, is located in the adult group of detached individuals, which turns out to be largely Italian. This evidence of Olivet's success in reaching the detached male foreigner is of signal interest.

MANNER OF ADHERENCE

Besides the very extraordinary excess of constituents belonging to subsidiaries only, there is a very large overlap of Sunday-school and subsidiary membership. About one-third of the constituents consist of church-members only, which is slightly less than falls in this class on the average, leaving rather a high ratio of overlap of church-members, though not an excessive one in any single direction. The overlap of church and Sunday school is one of the smallest, while, as already noted, the triple overlap of church, Sunday school and subsidiaries is smallest of all. In brief, the total enterprise is very inadequately nucleated relative to its size as a social group. No element of the constituency functions as a strongly cohesive and determining center for most aspects of the total program. The church-membership itself is relatively small; the group of adherents through a subsidiary program only— divided among some sixty organizations and many more classes —is nearly half of the total; while the relatively small Sunday school duplicates the subsidiary membership, but overlaps that of the church only to a very slight extent.[4]

Considering these various manners of adherence from the standpoint of the relation of the constituents' families to the church, it is found that, while family groups furnish 72 per cent. of the constituency, they furnish nearly 86 per cent. of the church-membership, about three-fourths of the Sunday school, and 100 per cent. of the scant nucleus of triply overlapping memberships. On the other hand, they furnish less than 40 per cent. of the membership of the subsidiaries. It is thus left to the detached individual to dominate the subsidiaries and to constitute much the greater part of the membership of subsidiaries only.

---

[4] See Chart IV, p. 71.

All told, the Olivet constituency is strikingly different from that of any other case studied. In the first place, less than half belongs to the enterprise at all in the sense that nearly all the constituents of the other churches belong. While the inclusion of a church of 1,000 members strongly differentiates Olivet Institute from social settlements that do not have a church at the center, or from that erratic combination of church and settlement work in which the traditional church functions tend to be minimized or to fall away, the church is nevertheless numerically the little end of the situation. As the later study of organizations and activities will still more fully show, the subsidiary elements of the program are the predominant ones, and in these the detached individual constitutes the much larger part of the constituency.

Parish

The new plant of Olivet Institute is located at the corner of Blackhawk and Cleveland streets, about a mile and three-quarters slightly west of north from the Chicago city hall, and about a half-mile northeast of the north branch of the Chicago River. It thus occupies a geographically central position in that narrow lobe of Chicago locally called the Lower North Side, which lies between the lake and the river and connects with the expanded central business district on the south. The river constitutes the great industrial artery of the city and its valley is the nearest-in industrial section with reference to the center.

Passing from east to west, the Lower North Side consists of narrow zones strongly marked from the standpoint of social quality and character. First comes the "Gold Coast," a concentration of wealthy population in palatial housing along the lake front; next a zone of deteriorated residential territory in which many formerly desirable streets have found themselves given over to the uses of transient rooming-house and boarding-house populations, as retail business and major traffic arteries have plowed more and more social furrows through the district. Finally, west of the elevated railway, between the railway and river valley (the latter solidly occupied by industries) lies the foreign polyglot section with which Olivet Institute is primarily identified.

DISTANCE AND DIRECTION

Fifty-nine per cent. of the adherents of Olivet Institute, as shown by Chart IX, live within half a mile of the new central building, and 11 per cent. more within a second half-mile.[5] This massing of 70 per cent. of all adherents within the immediate community—in spite of the division of the Institute's operations between two sites—reveals a parish of median dispersal, strongly tending toward compactness.   On the other hand, the parish reflects the migration from center to suburbs, 11 per cent. of adherents living between four and five miles from the church.

Eighty-six per cent. of the population of Ward 22 (48,046 in 1920), in which the Institute is located, is of foreign antecedents.   The dominant nationalities in order of strength are: Italian, German, Hungarian, Austrian, Swedish, Polish. Slightly more than 1 per cent. of the population is Negro. Males exceed females by about 2,000.   Nine per cent. of the population ten years of age and over is illiterate.   Much of the housing of the district represents the survival after half a century of buildings originally constructed in the haste and jumble following the Chicago Fire.   Small wooden structures with basement rooms below the street level are typical of it. The excess of families over dwellings is, however, only 39 per cent. as compared with 46 per cent. for Chicago as a whole. Although the average congestion of the area is thus below the general average, the doubling up of families in the older single-family houses, and in brick tenements of four or five stories, has created exceptionally bad conditions.   All told, the district is one of the poorest in Chicago, its population consisting of the remnants of many races.   Somewhat better conditions exist adjoining to and beyond North Avenue, the main local busi-

---

[5] See p. 448.

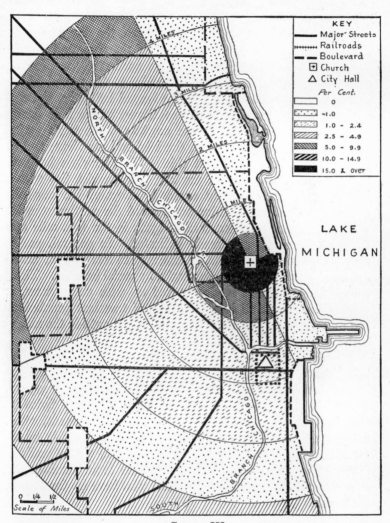

KEY
Major Streets
Railroads
Boulevard
⊞ Church
△ City Hall
Per Cent.
0
–1.0
1.0 – 2.4
2.5 – 4.9
5.0 – 9.9
10.0 – 14.9
15.0 & over

LAKE

MICHIGAN

0 1/4 1/2
Scale of Miles

CHART IX
Parish of Olivet Institute, Chicago

ness artery, which shows considerable signs of prosperity and improvement.[6]

Within the first half-mile of the church, the distribution of adherents is heaviest in the direction of the river and the old location of the Institute; while to the northeast, the effect of the elevated railway as a physical barrier to the spread of the parish is very pronounced. In the second half-mile, the distribution is still heaviest to the southwest where it is finally limited by the river, and to the northwest, the city's major direction of expansion between the lake and the river; and in general toward the northwest side. The high-class business and residential area toward the lake front, which lies within this zone, is conspicuously avoided. Beyond the one-mile radius, the constituency thins out toward the northwest, with a slight tendency to concentration again in the four-mile and the five-mile zones, as already indicated. In general, parish distribution reveals a dominant tendency to localization, modified by physical and, no less strongly, by social barriers. Thus, while Olivet Institute is closely tied up with many races, it reaches scarcely at all into the areas of transient populations and migrant labor that lie within a mile, but outside the neighborhood as socially determined.

A striking difference is discovered between the distribution, by residence, of adherents belonging to adherent family groups and of detached individuals. The former are more numerous within the first half-mile, and the latter relatively twice as numerous in the second half-mile. In other words, what Olivet gets immediately around its central building is whole families, while a little farther away (but still within walking distance) it draws adherents one by one from families not otherwise related, or wins individuals who have no families in the parish.

II. AGENCIES, RESOURCES AND METHODS

Organizations and Activities

Olivet Institute has an annual attendance of about 140,000 upon stated organizations and activities comparable with those

---

[6] See p. 448. For a more elaborate analysis of the Lower North Side, see Case Study VII, p. 207.

of other churches.[7] Special and exceptional occasions and short-term activities, including the Daily Vacation Bible School and summer outings, together with the patronage of facilities like the library and clinic, increase the attendance by about 35,000 more. In five cases of the twenty-six cases studied a larger regular attendance on stated activities was reported. These included four having very large Sunday audiences and one that yokes six churches into one administrative enterprise. In well-nigh total contrast with the method of collecting people into great gatherings for formal religious worship, the essential method of Olivet is that of ministering to rather small groups; a total of sixty separate organizations being carried on with an average of over 200 meetings or definite activities per week.

The distribution of annual attendance on organizations and stated activities is shown in Table XC.

TABLE XC—ESTIMATED ANNUAL ATTENDANCE ON SPECI-
FIED OCCASIONS AT OLIVET INSTITUTE AND AT 26
CHURCHES

	ATTENDANCE			
	OLIVET INSTITUTE		26 CHURCHES	
OCCASION			*Approx. Median Per Cent.*	*Range of Variation Per Cent.*
	Number	*Per Cent.*		
Total *	139,997	100		
Formal religious services (Sunday and week day).........	20,629	15	51	15–75
Sunday school	23,884	17	24	9–38
All other stated activities.....	95,484 †	68	22	9–51

* Sunday, 31 per cent.; week day, 69 per cent.
† Includes meetings of church officers and committees.

In no other case is the proportion of total program occurring on Sunday so small. The per cent. represented by formal religious services also is the smallest, while that represented by the activity of subsidiary organizations is the largest; so much so that Sunday-school attendance is relatively also very much below average.

Over half of the subsidiary program consists of children's

---

[7] See p. 449.

activities. This runs parallel with the fact already discovered that Olivet tends to be a young people's and children's church. Over one-fourth of the total attendance is upon the classes and organizations of the music school. The program affords a complete differentiation by age and sex, conceived as the means of all-around ministry to all elements of the population; but, numerically speaking, it is very unequally carried out. Much the largest number of people are handled in mixed, not seg-regated, sex-groups; and the ratio of the total program devoted particularly to men is very low, especially considering their preponderance in the total constituency.

TABLE XCI—ESTIMATED ANNUAL ATTENDANCE ON SUB-
SIDIARY ORGANIZATIONS AND STATED ACTIVITIES

	ORGANIZATIONS	ATTENDANCE	
No.	Type	Number	Per Cent.
	Total	93,049	
60	Classified by Age and Sex...............	72,048	100
3	Mixed adults	8,361	12
3	Adult men	1,122	2
11	Adult women	6,718	9
3	Mixed young people *	1,305	2
2	Young men	2,690	4
1	Young women	163	0
8	Mixed boys and girls	17,504	24
5	Boys	2,052	3
15	Girls	12,422	17
9	Mixed children	19,711	27
	Classified by Function		
	Music school	21,001	

* Between 15 and 23 years of age.

The particular organizations through which Olivet's vast program is carried out are too numerous for mention. The program for boys and girls includes two mixed-sex organiza-tions of the Christian Endeavor type, two junior church groups and two junior choruses. A separate program for girls is carried on through fifteen organizations, including eight for the domestic arts and crafts, and such others as dramatic and scouting groups. The largest items in the children's program are the kindergartens and day nursery.

Over 200 pupils taking private lessons in the music-school, with the choirs, bands and orchestra, make up the total aggregate attendance of 21,000.   Nearly 10,000 patronize the clinic or are visited in their homes by physicians or nurses.   Twelve thousand are reached through the various functions of the Advice and Aid section.   Combining all recorded services, and adding such items as calls, cases of advice and assistance and technical services to the count of aggregate attendance, the somewhat incoherent total of about 200,000 is reached, representing specific benefits annually afforded by the Olivet work.   This clearly justifies the institution's claim to be a "remarkable human service station."

Staff

Apart from janitors and caretakers, the paid staff of Olivet Institute numbers thirty-seven, which is larger than that of any other case studied.   The size of the staff does not reflect the magnitude of the work so much as it does the nature of the program which, as has already been noted, consists of activities of rather small groups that largely have to be served through special ministries of a technical character, in contrast with ministries to vast audiences characteristic of other notable churches.   In the number of hours of paid service per hundred attendance on stated organizations, only one case exceeds Olivet.   The obvious explanation is that the constituency is of the sort that has to be worked for to a more than usual degree.

ORGANIZATION

Olivet Institute is thoroughly and logically organized administratively through four major departments and sixteen sections.   The executive head is termed "superintendent" with respect to the total enterprise; he is also the long-time pastor of Olivet Institute Presbyterian Church.

The treasurer, and those who handle the permanent funds and major finances, are Chicago men of large affairs who are only remotely identified with the localized work.   The present treasurer, Rufus C. Dawes, is a brother of Vice-President Dawes.

In the administration of the actual work, the superintendent actively heads the administrative and religious departments, while his wife is primarily responsible for the educational and relief departments.

The administrative department has five formally distinct sections: namely, the office; promotion; the Olivet Press; the Olivet "Item" (weekly periodical) ; and the workers' residence, of which the superintendent's wife is matron. The office force consists of a head bookkeeper, acting as manager, with five assistants. An ordained minister, as promotional assistant, specializes in the solicitation of funds. The Press has its own working superintendent and helpers.

The educational department is sectionalized under the groupings: (1) athletic, (2) "manual and mental" (3) instrumental and vocal. Six workers, two for girls and four for boys (all the latter being part-time employees), carry on the program of athletics and group activities. The kindergarten, crafts and domestic work included in the "manual and mental" section involves two kindergartners and two crafts instructors. The music-school has its own director and ten instructors, mainly employed for part-time.

In the relief department, the Advice and Aid section is directly managed by the superintendent's wife. The day nursery, adjoining the Italian church, has a manager and assistant, and the clinic a nurse-supervisor and nine doctors and a dentist, each giving considerable time, besides numerous other medical advisors.

The religious department, centering in the church of which the superintendent is pastor, has three sections: namely, the extension work, including street and shop meetings; the regular services of the English-speaking congregation, using the Sedgwick Street church; and the Italian congregation, using the Vedder Street church. There are two associate pastors, one of whom is primarily related to each of the two congregations, and also a woman missionary operating particularly in the Italian parish.

PREPARATION AND EXPERIENCE

The ordained ministers of the staff represent the usual full preparation of Presbyterian clergymen and have had ample experience in pastoral and promotion work. Most of the clerical force are drawn from previous business or commercial positions and have had usual office experience. The technical social workers are largely people of limited experience from the various religious and social training schools of the city, and from Chicago University. The instructors in music represent particularly the musical tradition of the German and Swedish populations. Otherwise the working force is, in only a small degree, drawn from the immediate community. This is in striking contrast with the situation in the Methodist City Parish of Los Angeles which affords the most nearly comparable case.

WORK-TIME AND WORK-CONTENT

When the kinds of work performed by the combined staffs of the twenty-six churches are classified, most of the time is found to be occupied by the preparation for sermons, preaching and the conduct of public worship, pastoral and administrative routine and clerical work, with attendance upon services as a secondary item but one nearly always occurring. At least a quarter of all of the work-time of the Olivet staff is devoted to the performance of technical duties that in most of the cases are entirely absent or occupy only a negligible time. This obviously reflects the unusual elements in the program. Again, the time required by clerical work, particularly in the keeping of records and the production of publicity, is exceptionally great.[8]

As executive head of such an enterprise, the superintendent is primarily an administrator. Executive duties took a larger per cent. of time in only one of the cases studied. During his sample work-week, he was on duty seventy-three hours, or about ten hours more than the average. Pastoral work constituted a strong secondary element in his week; but no other

---

[8] See p. 449.

class of duties reached anything like the average. The assistant pastor for extension and English-speaking work also showed an exaggerated amount of executive work, together with a very long work-week. The Italian pastor, on the contrary, was primarily engaged in pastoral duties, administration being largely absorbed by the central office. In general, all types of workers tend to show considerably longer hours than the average of their groups. Those observing the regular office-day with a Saturday half-holiday, showed a long average week, as did the outside workers combining pastoral and minor executive functions. The technical social workers in the fields of education and the crafts were on duty somewhat more than ordinary school hours. The work-time of the entire staff is prolonged because of the requirement that every one do some "voluntary" religious work weekly, in addition to that for which he is specifically engaged.

The majority of the social and clerical workers live together in the workers' home and receive living expenses as part of their remuneration.

The tendency of the salary scale is low. Although Olivet is one of the largest of the twenty-six cases studied, the superintendent has one of the smallest salaries. Clerical workers represent the lower ranges of pay on the commercial scale; and the missionary character of the work is rather strongly stressed in connection with the entire matter of remuneration. There appears to be a very heavy annual turnover in the working force, a condition partly caused by the employment of a considerable proportion of student assistants.

Plant

At the time of the study, Olivet Institute was occupying two mission-church buildings. All the rest of its work was housed in buildings designed for other purposes, five or six of them being of the sort constructed in haste and poverty after the Chicago Fire and typical of the worst housing conditions of the district. One had been a corner saloon. Of the total of fifteen buildings in use, the majority were grouped within four or five adjoining blocks surrounding the site of the new church.

The Vedder Street church, occupied by the Italian congregation and erected in 1894, is a fairly substantial two-story brick structure with basement. The workers' residence consists of a comfortable, double, brick structure of three stories. The building at the camp on Lake Geneva is specially designed for its purposes and in excellent condition.

Apart from these three structures, no building was fit for the use to which it was being put. In the midst of this motley array of structures, the new building, occupying half of the block frontage on Blackhawk Street between Cleveland and Hudson streets, was under erection. It is a beautiful three-story structure, well proportioned, completely modern in construction and appointments, and designed as three units though built simultaneously. At the corner comes the church proper, including an adequate and thoroughly dignified auditorium. The middle section will house educational and musical activities, while the third section includes a large gymnasium and recreational room with facilities for general social and group activities. The total new plant, including land not yet improved, will represent a value of close to $750,000. It will house all the activities of the Institute except the Italian church, the workers' residence, the dispensary, advice and aid department, the guest home for aged and infirm, and the printing plant. These will be located in the more permanent of the older buildings.

In brief, a plant, one of the most unsuitable and handicapped that it would be possible to imagine, was just at the point of giving way to one of the best, combining satisfactory esthetic qualities, modern structural design and modern service facilities with carefully thought-out provision for the great program that has been described.

It was manifestly unfair to attempt to appraise either the old plant or the incomplete new one by the process of scoring applied to the other churches. Undoubtedly, however, with its new facilities, Olivet would rank high.

Finances

The financial situation, as complicated by the long-continued effort to build, also presents aspects that make detailed comparison with other cases invalid. Furthermore, at the time of the study, a special effort was being made to raise endowment. A total of about $167,000 on these two accounts had been secured during the preceding year, including a $50,000 legacy.

A total of about $75,000 of financial support was received for strictly current work. The cost, $52 per hundred attendance on stated organizations and activities, is just about median for the twenty-six cases studied; and, in the light of the very large additional program, indicates a very modest scale of operations.

Considering sources of income, two-thirds was found to come in special gifts from benevolent supporters outside of the local constituency, and only 12 per cent. from the pledges of church-members. An additional 9 per cent. was received from sundry commercial transactions (primarily the job press), and 8 per cent. from the fees and dues of those using facilities and belonging to organizations. The loose collections at the church services amounted to less than 1 per cent. of the total. The condition revealed by the above analysis is doubtless permanent. It is expected that the church may increase its self-support; but Olivet Institute as a whole is, and is to be, supported as one of the established philanthropies of Chicago. It is widely recognized as a social asset of the city; it has built up a fairly dependable public to which it may directly appeal in addition to the more general backing it gets as part of the recognized group of constructive agencies. The church itself pays only for its religious services in the narrower definition of them, and it does not even pay entirely for these services if the cost of facilities and overhead administration is considered; while beneficiaries through the various phases of social work contribute only a negligible fraction of its cost through their fees and dues.

All told, the peculiarities of the case render the financial categories devised for more standardized churches largely inapplicable. For, obviously, when one visualizes a church with its traditional expenditures as the center of the enterprise, relatively small supplemental amounts going to special departments, one is not thinking about Olivet Institute. Certain comparisons as to distribution of expenditures may nevertheless be made.

Sixty per cent. of the total expenditures goes to the payment of the salaries of the staff. This proportion is exceeded in only one other case. This means that the primary investment of Olivet Institute is in experts, most of whom are carrying on specialized functions or leading small groups of people in activities regarded as morally and culturally constructive. The music-school pays 45 per cent. of its expenses from fees, and music for the church is secured without direct cost as a by-product. Publicity costs are low because the Institute has its own press which is partially income-producing. The upkeep and operation of a scattered and run-down plant has been relatively high.

The per cent. distribution of expenditures on current account is shown in Table XCII.

TABLE XCII—FINANCIAL EXPENDITURES OF THE CHURCH

Item	Amount	Per Cent.
Total Current Account	$72,310	100
Salaries	43,615	61
General administrative expenses	3,026	4
Music	0	0
General operation and upkeep of property	24,575	34
Expenses of departments specially budgeted	0	0
Publicity	196 *	0
Miscellaneous	898	1

* Total expenditures for Olivet Press equaled $7,712.32, distributed between salaries and supplies.

Public Services

The average attendance at public services of the English-speaking congregation worshiping in the Sedgwick Street church is as follows:

Sunday morning	132
Sunday evening	95
Mid-week service	50
Children's church	180

On the Sunday morning of the field study, three-fourths of the 121 persons present were adults, and two-thirds were female. The service was relatively informal, its atmosphere being hearty rather than ecclesiastically refined or restrained. Participation of the congregation in responsive services was exceptionally vigorous. There was spirited music by a chorus of twenty, and extended verbal announcements of the week's events by church officers. Rather simple religious and ethical themes, aptly but not strikingly expressed, appear to characterize the habitual type of preaching; though occasional topics of the day appear, as in·a sermon on the Dayton evolution trial. The assistant pastor preaches at this service on about half the Sundays.

The attendance of the Italian congregation at Vedder Street is small. The Sunday-morning attendance averages only twenty, the Sunday-evening attendance, sixty, with twenty-five at the mid-week service. However, 140 children are reported, on the average, in the children's church.

The Italian congregation appoints its own elders and deacons, subject to the approval of the Session of the Olivet Church of which it is ecclesiastically a part. The standard forms of church life are observed; but the main success of the Italian work lies in other fields than that of public religious services.

All told, the place of religious services in the total Olivet enterprise is numerically uncommanding and the ecclesiastical aspects are secondary. The church, as an ecclesiastical body, has divided its immediate functions between two congregations; it has delegated its more general responsibilities for the Institute, as a whole, to the board of directors. As already noted, the total Olivet constituency has a relatively weak central core. Many of the more active leaders of the church are no longer closely identified by residence within the immediate vicinity. They appear to include a rather strong preponderance of the German and Scandinavian elements. Expressions of religious experience seem to show a rather traditional coloring.

Religious Education

Each of the congregations maintains a Sunday school with two sessions, one in the morning and one in the afternoon. The combined average attendance is nearly 50 per cent. larger than that on the four preaching services just discussed. Both

Sunday schools are preponderatingly children's enterprises, though the Sedgwick Street school has a fair proportion of adolescents in its morning session. The double session plan has grown up out of experience, simply because "some can come at one time and not at the other," and because "many do not like to get up on Sunday morning."

The organization and enrollment of the schools are shown in Table XCIII.

TABLE XCIII—SUMMARY OF SUNDAY-SCHOOL STATISTICS

| | MORNING | | | | AFTERNOON | | | |
| | PUPILS | TEACHERS | | | PUPILS | TEACHERS | | |
DEPARTMENT	*Age*	*Enrollment*	*Male*	*Female*	*Age*	*Enrollment*	*Male*	*Female*
			SEDGWICK STREET BRANCH					
Total	...	162*	4	7	...	101	5	8
Primary	6–8	28	0	1	6–8	54	..	..
Junior	9–11	60	0	2	9–11	16	..	..
Intermediate ...	12–14	11	1	2	12–14	11	..	..
Senior	15–18	31	0	1	15–18	14	..	..
Young people ..	19–20	16	1	1	19–20	..	..	..
Adults	21 & over	16	2	0	21 & over	6	..	..
			VEDDER STREET (ITALIAN) BRANCH					
Total	...	130	1	11	...	118	2	5
Primary	2–7	45	0	4	2–7	35	0	1
Junior	8–11	40	0	5	8–11	50	1	2
Intermediate ...	12–15	45	1	2	12–15	33	1	2

* Plus 28 in confirmation class with one teacher.

In the Sedgwick Street Branch the addition of three officers to the 162 pupils and eleven teachers gives a total of 176 for the morning session, at which time the attendance averages 80 per cent. of the enrollment.

The approximate age-distribution is as follows:

| | MORNING | | AFTERNOON | |
	Number	*Per Cent.*	*Number*	*Per Cent.*
Children	99	61	81	80
Adolescents	47	29	14	14
Adults	16	10	6	6

In the Vedder Street Branch there are two officers at the morning session, making a total enrollment of 144. Attendance averages 88 per cent. of the enrollment. At the afternoon session there are also two officers, which brings the total enrollment up to 127. The attendance at this time averages 81 per cent. of the enrollment.

The paid staff furnishes a high proportion of the teachers in the religious education enterprise as a whole. The Italian congregation, in particular, furnishes no teachers from its own ranks. Instructors in the Vedder Street school come from the Institute staff, and from the various religious training schools of Chicago which deputize students in connection with their apprenticeship in Christian work.

A home department for Bible study, enrolling 175, is maintained by the Institute but regarded as separate from any of the four schools. A confirmation class is systematically conducted every winter; and several groups for instruction meet following the mid-week devotional service.

The most unusual feature of the program of religious education is, however, the week-day children's church held for twenty minutes, just before the beginning of the daily school session, for the children of the public schools adjoining the two churches. This voluntary service has been carried on for many years, and is a striking example of how the religious element may be helpfully associated with publicly supported education.

Current Church Life

Any generalized account of the total activity of Olivet Institute is exceedingly difficult because it lacks so much of constituting a unity. The two religious congregations are distinct, and the numerous small groups and classes, largely kept up by the personality of the leaders, are not closely integrated with one another. The technical functions provided by the Institute go on and benefit multitudes of people not otherwise connected with the enterprise. Of over 200 listed meetings and stated occasions which occur weekly, a single day's sample will serve to suggest the remarkable scope and variety, as well as the many different places in which the work has had to be carried on.

THURSDAY

Activities	Leader	Place	Hour
Nursery	Mrs. E. Matts	663 Vedder	7.30–5.30
Nurse Calls	Miss L. Dennis	District	8.00–11.00
Office Hours	A. G. Brown	444 Blackhawk	8.00–6.00
Children's Church	Mrs. B. I. Brown	665 Vedder	8.30–8.55
Children's Church	Mrs. N. B. Barr	1444 Hudson	8.30–8.55
Advice and Aid	Mrs. N. B. Barr	1502 Hudson	9.00–12.00
Kindergarten	Mae Post	1452 Hudson	9.30–11.30
Kindergarten	Elnora Bollinger	665 Vedder	9.30–11.30
Eye, Ear, Nose, Throat	Dr. Von Colditz	1500 Cleveland	10.00–10.30
Band and Orchestra	E. Callerman	1500 Cleveland	1.30–9.30
Dispensary	Miss L. Dennis	1500 Cleveland	11.00–12.00
Piano Instruction	F. V. Burrell	510 Blackhawk	11.00–12.00
Kindergarten	Grace Hamilton	665 Vedder	12.00–5.00
Nurse Calls	Miss L. Dennis	District	1.30–3.00
Piano and Vocal Lessons	J. O. Rydstrom	1500 Cleveland	1.30–6.00
Dispensary	Miss L. Dennis	1500 Cleveland	3.00–5.00
Cooking	Elnora Bollinger	665 Vedder	3.15–4.45
Sewing	Mrs. B. I. Brown	665 Vedder	3.15–4.45
Manual Training	Lloyd Coveney	1444 Hudson	3.15–4.45
Craft Club	Grace Hamilton	1452 Hudson	3.15–4.45
Sewing	M. Lindesmith	1452 Hudson	3.30–4.45
Cooking	Gladys Slater	1452 Hudson	3.30–4.45
Violin Instruction	C. F. Criswell	1500 Cleveland	3.30–5.30
Dental Cases	Dr. A. P. Baur	1500 Cleveland	3.30–5.30
Piano Instruction	Miss E. Bloom	1500 Cleveland	3.30–6.00
Harmony	J. O. Rydstrom	1500 Cleveland	3.30–6.00
Dramatic Art	Rita Smith	1500 Cleveland	4.00–6.00
Intermediate Basket Ball	Otto Bach	Seward Park	5.30–7.00
Plucked Instruments	Rita Smith	1500 Cleveland	6.00–9.00
Supper Club	Miss Schutz	1452 Hudson	7.00–8.30
Piano Instruction	F. V. Burrell	1500 Cleveland	7.00–9.00
Dressmaking	M. Lindesmith	1452 Hudson	7.00–9.00
Women's Citizenship Class	A. M. Martignetti	665 Vedder	7.00–9.00
Dispensary	Dr. M. H. Barker	1500 Cleveland	7.00–9.00
Office Hours	Clara Schappel	444 Blackhawk	7.00–9.00
Young Men's Basket Ball	Otto Bach	Seward Park	7.00–9.00
Mothers' Club (1st)	Elnora Bollinger	665 Vedder	7.30–9.00
Sunday Eve. Choir	Miss Seidschlag	Homes	8.00–9.30
Olivet Band	F. Bilotta	Armory	8.00–10.00
Emergency Calls	Dr. M. H. Barker	District	Night

Gains and Losses

Of ninety-four persons recently added to the English-speaking congregation of Olivet Church, only nine were by letter.

All of these were Presbyterians, and only five (in most cases paid workers) were new in the community. This reveals the fairly obvious fact that the community is not growing in material easily assimilable by the church, and particularly that Presbyterians with church letters are not moving into the Olivet district.

Sixty-five of the eighty-five established residents in the community had been definitely enlisted in some of the enterprises of the Institute before uniting with the church. These were about equally divided between attendants at public services and pupils of the Sunday school. Eleven recent accessions were non-Protestant.

Of the ninety-four cases studied, seven-tenths were those of residents of the immediate community, the others were those of persons coming from long distances. These included a considerable proportion of paid workers; but it is significant that so generally localized a church nevertheless exercises a certain wide appeal, sometimes to persons desiring opportunity to render personal service, but also to friends and relatives of constituents who have moved out of the immediate neighborhood.

Of sixty-eight church-members lost during a corresponding period, sixty were dropped; four died; and four were granted letters, only one of which was to a Presbyterian church. Long non-attendance, generally accompanying removal from the neighborhood, was almost the only reason for the dropping of names. Members lost in this way had generally had long connection with the church. This, in connection with the very small number of transfers by letter, is perhaps significant. It may be that Olivet is too unusual an enterprise to make it easy for its departing members to fit into other and more ordinary churches.

Relations to Denomination

Up to 1910, Olivet was a missionary enterprise of the Presbyterian denomination, upon the ecclesiastical machinery of which it depended for care and assistance. With the establishment of the Institute corporation, however, the enterprise became financially independent. Its legitimate demands were proportionately too large to be dealt with as a part of a merely denominational enterprise, and it was becoming securely established among the social agencies of Chicago. The largest single givers at crucial times, however, have been members of Presbyterian families that had sentimental regard for the enterprise in the light of its origin, and valued it also for its current work. It is a legal requirement that a majority of the directors be Presbyterians. The major stress of the enterprise, however, is non-sectarian. No denominational requirement is made as to members of the employed staff.

Relations to Social Agencies

Besides numbering on its boards of directors and trustees, and among its supporters, some of the large figures of Chicago's civic enterprise, the Institute has unusually close and massive relationships with the notable movement of the socially constructive forces of the city. First, it is related to numerous other churches as a beneficiary. The superintendent appears in their pulpits appealing for funds, and they respond by financial assistance.

Again, according to its means, Olivet Institute itself is a supporter of constructive social agencies. Its congregation contributes directly to three Presbyterian philanthropies, the Chicago Church Federation, and one correctional agency. Its superintendent has an honored place in Presbyterian and inter-denominational affairs, and is especially identified with the peace movement and the Chicago Forum Council. Through him the Institute gets personal representation in important social movements, while it is officially related to seven agencies through delegated representatives. It has habitual and recurrent exchange of services with no fewer than twenty-eight agencies covering all realms of social effort. In the more acute cases and situations, it takes all of these resources to supplement the Institute's own wide ministry, with the still more highly technical processes required. The Institute is in close relation with the training schools from which it secures workers, and shares in the systematic conferences of groups of social agencies concerned with the conduct and technique of social work. The total is an impressive demonstration of the inter-relationship of social forces and movements, both on the side of preventive effort, and on that of alleviation and control of the community's ills.

Summary

Institutionally defined, Olivet Institute is obviously more than a church. Much of its time, and most of its energies and money, is devoted to things the average church does not do at all, and that even go far beyond the programs of most of the highly developed churches studied. Aside from the church, the Institute is essentially a group of social agencies for specific purposes, performing technical functions or providing constructive activities for small groups, the whole being unified by administration.

Again, and consequently, the constituency of Olivet Institute is much broader than the actively adherent group ordinarily identified by membership in the church or some of its organized subsidiary activities. In more than half of its extent, it is a benefited group and not a continuously participating one. The Institute, as the dominant social agency of its locality, extends services to a large population which more or less habitually depends upon it but does not become in any sense responsible for supporting it.

The fact that the Institute maintains a church of over 1,000 members which it regards as its moral and motivating center, is highly significant, though perhaps less unusual and actually less controlling than is claimed or imagined. As the only English-speaking Protestant organization in an area largely abandoned by other churches, its responsibility is conspicuous and definite. The history of the enterprise from the beginning is conclusive proof that the Protestant church fulfills a profound social necessity in the lives of the second-generation foreigner who, quite apart from any formal Protestant propaganda, has outgrown his traditional religion.

The creation of the Italian church-membership within a relatively brief period is a signal achievement; but, relative to the total services of the Institute, the Italian church is an exceedingly small item.

With respect to both congregations, numerical growth without reënforcements coming by letter, though slow, is distinctly notable. While the great central churches have a wealth of numbers cast up at their doors by the tide of population growth and movement, Olivet from the first has had to create almost the whole of its constituency against all previous antecedents. It has done this through patient assimilative processes, its only advantage being that the younger foreigner has Americanized faster than the parent group.

The inclusive constituency of the Institute, as identified by the field of its ministries, is essentially a normally distributed cross section of the population, with the masculine element more fairly represented than in most cases. On the other hand, the group that definitely belongs to stated organizations and activities tends strongly to be juvenile and adolescent, and includes a very disproportionate number of detached individuals.

There is little cohesion in the constituency as a whole. The several elements have little in common. The many groups and classes, in large measure, constitute separate entities. The nucleus of the enterprise is very small.

The identification of the Institute with a clearly defined geographical neighborhood is very strong. The people living within this area, however, are massed together between physical barriers rather than voluntarily and consciously associated through common interests. The locality does not constitute an integrated community, and there are no recognized central agencies of the population as a whole with which to make alliance. The Institute has had large influence for civic improvement at both ends of the district, and has strong and happy associations with other constructive agencies maintained by forces originating outside of the area. But neither it nor all such forces have been able to create any strongly tangible community spirit. Within the sphere of the Institute's own work, the unity appears to be administrative rather than psychological.

Removal of location was good practical strategy, and the present site will doubtless remain permanently more central. Nevertheless, removal revealed the limitations of the Institute's relations to the community. It is able to deal with the Italian group in adjunct institutions without losing its older constituency; but the situation has not developed, and perhaps shows no signs of soon developing, into the complete assimilation of the more diverse racial elements.

In those aspects of the Institute's work that are programized, that is to say, organized for regular attendance and the carrying on of group functions, the children's interests are by far the most developed. This is perhaps both cause and consequence of the localization of the bulk of the constituency within a short distance of the work, and of the definite appeal which the program makes to pupils of the neighborhood public school.

The outstanding mark of the Olivet method is that it sets up many small organizations.

Most of the individual activities are not highly original nor carried out with commanding distinction. The aggregate is what impresses—the 200 occasions and more per week on which people come together to meet the staff leader in some worth-while activity, or to receive benefits from a technically proficient professional worker.

Nor are the religious services or Sunday school particularly unusual. On the other hand, the great music school, operated by musicians representing the culture of the older racial elements, and the week-day "children's church," providing a brief chapel exercise for public-school children before the opening of the school session, are worth a second notice as highly original features.

With noble and notable continuous leadership, the general influence of which has broadened through the years, the staff, as a whole, reveals a large but rather transient group whose members are little related to the neighborhood except at the points where their technical services lie.

After a long period of hope deferred, the Institute is just entering upon the possession of a new central plant and notable equipment that should insure better work.   Such a radical change of fortunes constitutes a challenge to an enterprise which, in the past, has been so largely a thing of the spirit that its inner graces shall still be kept in advance of its outer facilities.

The financing of the institution requires untiring energy; but the energy is not spent in vain.   It rests back upon a well-established community habit of support, with able and dependable traditional sources at its center.   The institution is a permanent philanthropy.   Under no conceivable circumstances could the resident forces of the community carry the major portion of the financial burden.   The chief objective of the current expenditure is the support of numerous workers.   The upkeep and use of the poor and scattered facilities of the past have been a disproportionate financial burden, and the ratio may well be reduced in the new quarters.

While strongly maintaining the sense of its historic origins and relationships, the Institute has evolved beyond the Presbyterian denomination and become a social enterprise of the community and city.

It is no longer merely the creation of social impulse arising elsewhere and the beneficiary of benevolent effort, but has itself become a center from which broad lessons of successful experience radiate in social work.   It is intimately related with the network of the social agencies of the city of which it is an important unit.

Olivet Institute stands on the eve of a new era that is sure to be one of technical improvement, and probably one of great increase of activities and constituency, numerically measured. One would like to prophesy that it will also be an era of a more comprehensive grappling with underlying community problems. Might not one of its distinguishing marks be the control of policy by scientifically devised and exactly recorded experimentation, while, at the same time, the spirit of the undertaking is no less human and devoted?

APPENDIX

METHODOLOGICAL NOTES

I. DETERMINATION OF CHARACTER OF CHURCH PROGRAMS

Comparative statements relative to the scope and degree of development of church programs are based upon a list of sixty organizations, activities and practices sometimes carried on by city churches. The program of each church was checked against this list to indicate which and how many of the sixty items were included in it. The median case covered about half of the total number. From this standpoint, a simple and narrow program is that consisting of few activities and they only usual and habitual ones; a complex, varied and highly developed program is one consisting of many items combining exceptional with usual ones; or an extreme, all cases consisting chiefly of exceptional activities.

The sixty items, arranged in the order of the frequency of their occurrence in the twenty-six churches, follow.

Item	Number of Churches Maintaining
Outside bulletin board with weekly notices	26
Young People's Society, League, Union or equivalent	25
Church office open daily	25
Sunday school completely graded (class for every 3 years)	24
Annual every-member financial canvass	24
Calendar or bulletin issued weekly	24
Organized athletic teams or contests	24
Boy Scouts or equivalent	23
Confirmation class or Catechetical instruction	23
Organized Welcome (by ushers or others definitely delegated)	22
Regular paid newspaper advertising	22
Church choir (8 voices or more)	21
Formal coöperation with organized churches	21
Religious education formally organized as separate department (with special board)	20
Young Women's Clubs (Service League, Girls' Friendly, etc.)	19
Gymnasium instruction	19
Girl Scouts, Camp Fire Girls or equivalent	18
Children's congregation meeting separately for services	18
Women's Guild—Ladies' Aid Society, etc.	17
Men's Club, Brotherhood, or equivalent	17
Daily Vacation Bible School (2 weeks or more annually)	17
Sunday school financed by church as part of regular budget	17
Women's Missionary Society (Home, Foreign or both)	16
Girls' Clubs (other than Scout type)	16

	Number of Churches
Item	*Maintaining*
Sunday evening social gatherings or teas	16
Dramatic organization	15
Regular use of motion pictures	15
Concerts (periodic or frequent)	14
Boys' Club (other than Scout type)	13
Church receptions or dinners (4 times per year or oftener)	13
Library (general or reference) in regular use	13
Mission Study Classes (separately organized)	13
Lectures (periodic or frequent)	12
Unified women's organization (combining missions and parish aid)	11
Mothers' or parents' organization	11
Church open daily for private devotions	11
Vacation farm or country property used for outings	11
Employment Agency	11
Music-classes	10
Dramatics (as phase of social service interest)	9
Local church paper (issued monthly or oftener)	8
Week-day religious school (2 days per week, 3 months or more)	8
Sewing or millinery classes	8
Orchestra or band	7
Domestic Science or home-making instruction	7
English classes for foreigners	7
Forum (public discussion by general audience or large group)	6
Health classes	6
Children's sermons regularly	5
Kindergarten	5
Systematic vocational advice	5
Dormitory or boarding facilities for constituents	4
Civics or economics classes	4
Services in more than one language	3
Visiting nurse	3
Dispensary or clinic	3
Branch church (served in whole or part by church staff)	2
Day Nursery	2
Special services for industrial or other employees	2
Outdoor or street preaching (periodic or frequent)	2

II. HISTORICAL SOURCES

At the beginning of each case study, an inventory of all available literary and historical data bearing upon it was made. Comparable historical materials covering most of the aspects of the study did not exist. Nearly all of the churches, however, possessed historical materials published in brief form, largely in connection with the celebration of anniversaries, while a few had histories of worthy literary quality and social insight. These sources, together with more general local histories, furnished the basis for historical statements. Statistical data, more precise in character, were found in the annual yearbooks or general minutes that all well-established denominations issue (some nationally, others by smaller territorial districts) covering such conventional items as church-membership, Sunday-school enrollment and financial expenditures. In most cases these records were tabulated and compared for the decade preceding the field study.

III. METHOD OF INVESTIGATING MEMBERS AND CONSTITUENTS

It was assumed that a church, sociologically speaking, consists of the entire social group that is related to it in any adherent or constituent capacity. To determine the composition of such a group, the study stipulated that each church investigated should make out schedule cards for all adherents, showing age, sex, family relationship and all particular relationships with the church. As a result, 48,195 adherents were reported in twenty-nine churches (data on this point in the other two being incomplete in form).

(1) By *constituent family* was meant one in which one or more adults functioning as family heads are adherents of the church, along with one or more other adults or children. The application of this definition discovered a primary group exhibiting a religious unity that was being carried over into the church in whole or in part. All adherents outside of such family groups were denominated "detached individuals." Even two or more Sunday-school pupils from a single family were put in this category unless one of the heads of the family was also an adherent.

(2) By a *determinate adherent* was meant one who had formal membership in, or regularly attended or contributed to, either the church, the Sunday school or some subsidiary organization of the church. Eighty-nine per cent. of the total reported constituency of the twenty-nine churches was found to be of this sort; but 11 per cent. of names appearing upon current parish lists were those of persons who did not belong to the churches in any determinate present relation. These were accepted as constituting a legitimate marginal group properly included in the constituency on psychological or theoretical grounds. Some were persons for whom the church felt morally responsible, or whom it had recently served without winning their adherence in any concrete fashion. In other cases, churches habitually carried names on the grounds of some type of remote formal adherence, for example, because the persons named had been baptized or confirmed. The study counted as adherents whomever the church listed, and simply sought to know how many there were of each sort.

(3) Determinate adherents were classified as standing in either *exclusive* or *overlapping relationships*. Assuming that a church commonly expresses itself in three fields of activity: namely, its worship and public services, its Sunday school and its subsidiary organizations, the study proceeded to measure the manner and

degree of the constituent's adherence in terms of his relationship to these divisions of church life.

All statements relative to constituencies were based upon a careful statistical count of the constituents' cards as furnished by the churches and thrown according to these categories.

IV. Sources of Social and Environmental Data

The more important special sources of information on these topics are cited above in appropriate footnotes to the several case studies. The United States Census is the most authoritative general source. It includes important social data by wards for cities of 100,000 population and over. The more intimate sources, being largely local in origins, naturally vary from city to city, so that the environmental section of the study could not be standardized as to contents.[1]

In the field work of the present studies, the results of a limited examination of the more relevant sources discovered were mapped whenever possible and the data invariably supplemented by first-hand study. The points systematically observed were: political boundaries—municipal and ward; topography; census precincts if precinct data were available; present use of areas—by industry, business or residential occupancy on different social levels; zoning; transit facilities and system of major traffic streets; business centers—primary, secondary and tertiary; locations of foreign and Negro populations, foreign centers, etc.; natural neighborhoods—defined by physical barriers or by common tradition and the use of common facilities; elementary school districts (where school district data were available); natural communities—the larger areas and populations possessing strongly marked social unity; institutional locations—schools, churches, other social agencies (parks, playgrounds, social centers, philanthropic, health and corrective agencies); areas of acute social change; probable structure of the city and the neighborhood of the church in the future. Large numbers of manuscript maps embodying field observations on these points were rapidly made without attempt at complete accuracy.

V. Method of Summarizing Parish Data

In each case study, the distance and direction from the church of the residences of all constituents and of several different classes of constituents, were counted by mile zones and directional sec-

---

1 For an important summary of sources and kinds of data commonly existing and useful in investigating the social background of church work, see Carpenter, "The Research Resources of a Typical American City as Exemplified by the City of Buffalo," *Proceedings of the Twentieth Annual Meeting* (1925) *of the American Sociological Society* (University of Chicago, 1926),

tors and summarized on maps similar to those shown on pages 51 and 157. These maps were then compared with the series of social data described in the last section, and the probable reasons for the correspondence or contrast of phenomena were considered. Generally the story of social attractions and aversions was plainly revealed by the facts.

VI. Method of Studying Organizations and Stated Activities

Under this head it was meant to include everything that a church regularly does as frequently as once a month throughout the active church season (whether or not the activity is organized around determinate memberships, but provided that there are regular officers or leaders and that the activity is recognized by the church); also whatever the church habitually does seasonally through several consecutive days or weeks, such as the operation of summer camps and Daily Vacation Bible School. But it was meant to exclude all special and occasional activities or single events, even though occurring annually.

In reaching an estimate of attendance on organizations and stated activities, the particular local names of each service and stated activity and of each major and subsidiary organization were entered upon a schedule, which classified them as to the age or sex of the persons for whom the service was performed, or by function if age and sex were not the basis of membership. Weekly and yearly attendance was then calculated by totals for week day and Sunday, for church services, Sunday school and subsidiaries separately, and by types of subsidiary organization as illustrated in the previous studies.

The results do not purport to give total attendance, but rather comparable attendance on the stated activities which definitely characterize the church and operate during significant periods of time. They thus constitute a uniform basis of comparison among churches, though not pretending to be complete for any.

VII. Method of Securing Data Concerning the Church Staff at Work

Every full-time or part-time paid worker of the church (excluding sextons and musicians, except where the latter had continuous religious or administrative duties in addition to musical ones) was asked to fill out a daily work-schedule for seven consecutive days, accounting for all working hours, or, in the case of part-time workers, for the time during which they were on duty for the church.

The data secured covered: (1) a description of the particular duties in the performance of which each worker was engaged throughout every period of the day for a week; (2) the number of minutes devoted to the performance of each duty-item; (3) a designating term indicating under what category or classification the worker thought the particular duty-item belonged, as, for example, pastoral, homiletical, janitorial, secretarial; (4) notes were also invited throwing light on the larger situations of which the particular duty recorded was a part, as suggested by such questions as: Who aided you? Who else was there? Where were you? What travel, if any, was involved? What was your particular objective? What problems were you trying to solve? [2]

These data were then tabulated so as to compare staff with staff, and worker with worker within the same kinds of positions.

It was not assumed, however, that the record of a single week was sufficient basis for the permanent characterization of any individual; and the time-measure of work was not regarded as a measure of either value or efficiency.

VIII. Method of Studying Church Finances

The churches were presumed to have accurate financial records. Frequently, however, their records were not complete in that they did not cover the finances of the subordinate divisions of the church; and no grounds existed for expecting them to be kept in comparable form.

The study of financial data was therefore devoted: (1) to bringing together the finances of all organizations and activities of each church investigated into a single statement.

(2) To ruling out duplicatory items resulting from the transfer of funds between the treasuries of the church and its subsidiaries without properly balancing all accounts involved.

(3) To distinguishing, both in receipts and in expenditures, between current finances (in the sense of money both secured and expended during a given year) and money derived from accumulated sources or invested in permanent improvements or endowments.

(4) To reporting the results in terms of a few rather inclusive items indicating the church's main sources of support and the comparable major objects of expenditure.

Absolutely scientific accountancy cannot be derived from, nor applied to, existing data. It will be possible only when accounts are kept according to uniform and standard forms over a period of time.

The results derived from the methods used are, in any particular church, generally congruous with the other information

---

[2] The unusual detail in which data as to the paid workers' duties were secured was explained by the fact that it was intended to be utilized in connection with another project of the Institute.

secured concerning it and constitute important collateral evidence as to its organizational trends and methods of work.

IX. METHOD OF STUDYING THE CHURCH PLANT

The study of plant and equipment was made by means of the Interchurch 1000-point score-card for rating city churches developed by the Interchurch World Movement and used in the well-known Malden Survey.[3]

The Interchurch score-card contains 121 items grouped under major and secondary headings. Each item and group of items was assigned a numerical value, the total adding to the perfect score 1,000.

In the actual field study, the church plant was carefully inspected and independently scored, item by item, against the standard score by two competent judges who had previously scored many churches. They subsequently compared their judgments and agreed upon the final figure. A more valid method would be to have three judges score the church independently, the final figure being the average of the three scores.

X. METHOD OF RECORDING IMPRESSIONS OF PUBLIC SERVICES

No attempt was made in the field studies to reduce observations on the character and conduct of public services to a precise schedule. An outline of a systematic method of observations was, however, followed and supplemented by a collection of church calendars and other descriptive data. The field worker attended one or two of each of the major services. The approximate age- and sex-distribution of the congregation was carefully estimated where exact count was lacking. The prevailing tone of the period before the actual opening of service was studied, together with the order and content of the broad items of the service, the degree to which the ritual elements were present or emphasized, the place and character of the music, and the tone of the preaching. In further investigation of pulpit work, a digest of a year's sermon announcements was made, the frequency of special services and the character of the habitual topics being noted. With these data in hand, the pastor was interviewed as to his own conception of the character and significance of his preaching, and the resulting statement was submitted for the church's criticism.

XI. METHOD OF STUDYING RELIGIOUS EDUCATION

Religious education was studied by means of a carefully prepared schedule summarizing major aspects of current Sunday-

---

[3] *Standards for City Church Plants* (New York; Interchurch World Movement, 1920). Athearn, *Malden Survey;* Athearn, *The Indiana Survey of Religious Education* (New York; Doran, 1924), Vol. I, Pt. II; Vol. II, Chapter V.

school records. This was supplemented by data concerning other
organizations of the church regarded as included in or allied to
the religious educational program. The general policy of conducting religious education and its place in the church were systematically noted; but the study did not attempt any extensive and
technical appraisal of organization, courses of instruction, or
particular methods employed.

XII. How Gains and Losses in Membership Were Studied

The data presented in the preceding studies were secured by an
examination of church records covering members received and
dismissed for the church year previous to the study (or over a
longer period in churches where the number concerned was
small). In addition to the usual classification by sources of accessions (transfer from other churches, confession of faith, etc.)
and causes of loss, the following points were noted: (1) the previous adherent-relation of the new member to the church (as
through regular attendance, Sunday-school membership or belonging to a subsidiary); (2) the length of his residence in the
community; (3) the distance of his home from the church. In
this it is sought to ascertain what process of assimilation preceded
the actual admission of the member to the church, the relation of
church growth to movements of population, and the size and directions of geographical areas over which a church shows capacity to
attract new recruits.

XIII. Sources of Data Concerning Current Church Life

Besides living with a church almost continuously for ten days
or two weeks, the investigator made a digest of a year's bulletins
and publicity matter, so as to get the sense of on-going life spread
over a period of time.

XIV. Methods of Studying Formal Community Relations

In each case, all institutions and interests of the community
with which the church might properly have coöperative relationships were listed and classified. Five questions were then asked
with respect to each: (1) Has the church contributed money to
this organization within a year? (2) Has it had members on the
paid staff or board of directors? (3) Has it appointed official
representatives in the organization? (4) Has it had practical
coöperative relations, and if so, how? (5) Has it advocated the
work of the agency in its pulpit or publicity? The summarization
of these data was supplemented by observations as to the degree
of activity and influence which the church seemed to exert in the
community.

XV. Categories for the Study of Denominational Relationships

Denominational relationships were informally studied from the following point of view: (1) the relative influence of the churches in denominational enterprise and counsels was noted. (2) Formal relationships of the churches as beneficiaries of their denomination were classified as temporary or permanent. With respect to temporary relationships, it was asked whether the church had received special denominational assistance in time of crisis or whether it was the object of special denominational experimentation or backing in the effort to solve some particular problem of the urban church or to develop advanced types of service. With respect to permanent relations, it was asked whether the church belonged to the dependent-rich type permanently sharing in the affluence of great endowments; or whether, on account of its relative poverty, it found itself in more or less extreme dependence upon denominational support, so as to be classified as a missionary enterprise.

XVI. Basis of Summary of Adaptations and Suggestions

On the basis of the entire factual data of the study and the observations of the field worker, a summary of each case study, with certain interpretative conclusions and suggestions, was reached. This was distinctly intended to afford opportunity for the observer to record his personal reactions freely and originally, but with as explicit and systematic reference to the data as possible. The degree to which specific suggestions were ventured upon was determined by the attitude or request of the individual churches. When asked to do so, the investigator attempted to formulate expert opinion, but advice in detail was not forced upon the churches, and, in the main, has been excluded from the case studies as here presented. Those making the studies have by no means told all they think they know, but have rather attempted to describe the more comparable phases of each case dispassionately, and then to summarize what seem to them its more outstanding and illuminating aspects from the general viewpoint of the total study.

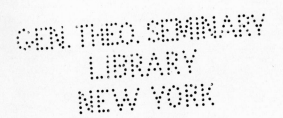

DATE DUE

GAYLORD			PRINTED IN U.S.A.